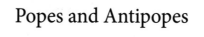

Popes and Antipopes

# Studies in the History of Christian Traditions

*General Editor*

## Robert J. Bast
Knoxville, Tennessee

*In cooperation with*

**Henry Chadwick,** Cambridge
**Paul C.H. Lim,** Nashville, Tennessee
**Eric Saak,** Liverpool
**Brian Tierney,** Ithaca, New York
**Arjo Vanderjagt,** Groningen
**John Van Engen,** Notre Dame, Indiana

*Founding Editor*

## Heiko A. Oberman†

VOLUME 159

*The titles published in this series are listed at brill.nl/shct*

# Popes and Antipopes

## The Politics of Eleventh Century Church Reform

*By*

Mary Stroll

BRILL

LEIDEN • BOSTON
2012

*Cover illustration:* Sketch of a fresco in the *camerarius pro secretis consiliis* in the Lateran Palace by Calixtus II (1119-1124) of Alexander II using Cadalus as a footstool. Barb. Lat. 2738, fol. 105v, Biblioteca Apostolica Vaticana.

This book is printed on acid-free paper.

Library of Congress Cataloging-in-Publication Data

Stroll, Mary.
  Popes and antipopes : the politics of eleventh century church reform / by Mary Stroll.
    p. cm. -- (Studies in the history of Christian traditions, ISSN 1573-5664 ; v. 159)
  Includes bibliographical references (p.  ) and index.
  ISBN 978-90-04-21701-0 (hardback : alk. paper) 1. Church history--11th century. 2. Popes.
3. Antipopes. 4. Papacy--History. I. Title.
  BX1187.S85 2012
  282.09'021--dc23

                                                         2011039354

ISSN 1573-5664
ISBN 978 90 04 21701 0

Copyright 2012 by Koninklijke Brill NV, Leiden, The Netherlands.
Koninklijke Brill NV incorporates the imprints Brill, Global Oriental, Hotei Publishing,
IDC Publishers, Martinus Nijhoff Publishers and VSP.

MIX
Paper from
responsible sources
FSC
www.fsc.org   FSC® C008919

PRINTED BY AD DRUK BV - ZEIST, THE NETHERLANDS

*To Avrum*

# CONTENTS

Acknowledgments ............................................................. xi
Preface .......................................................................... xiii
Abbreviations ................................................................ xv

Introduction ..................................................................... 1

1. Imperial Authority over Papal Elections .......................... 9
   The Patricius Romanorum ........................................... 10
   Bonizo ....................................................................... 12
   Petrus Damiani ........................................................... 15
   Benzo ......................................................................... 17
   The Response of the Reformers .................................... 19

2. Henry III's Popes ........................................................ 21
   Henry's Authority ....................................................... 21
   The Three Iniquitous Popes ........................................ 22
   Clement II ................................................................. 24
   Damasus II ................................................................ 30

3. Leo IX (1049–1054): The Normans and
   the Byzantines .......................................................... 33
   The Election of Bishop Bruno of Toul ......................... 33
   The Normans .............................................................. 35
   The Byzantine Empire ................................................. 39
   The First Wedge Between Eastern and
      Western Churches ................................................... 40
   Leo's Legacy .............................................................. 46
   Summary and Conclusion ........................................... 48

4. Victor II and Stephen IX ............................................. 51
   Part 1: Victor II (1055–1057) ..................................... 51
   Conflicting Sources .................................................... 51
   The House of Lotharingia/Canossa .............................. 54
   The Normans .............................................................. 57
   After Henry III's Death .............................................. 57

Part 2: Stephen IX (1057–1058) ............................................... 61
The Lotharingia/Canossa Alliance ....................................... 61
Stephen IX's Reign ............................................................... 63
The Significance of Stephen IX's Reign ............................. 65

5. Benedict X, Antipope: Romans Versus Reformers.................... 69
The Elections of Benedict X and Nicholas II ..................... 69
Benedict's Tragic Reign......................................................... 71
The Pierleoni ........................................................................ 74
Petrus Damiani..................................................................... 75
Leo of Ostia ......................................................................... 77
Liber Pontificalis .................................................................. 77
German Sources .................................................................... 78
Bonizo.................................................................................... 79
Panvinius............................................................................... 80
Conclusion ............................................................................ 82

6. Nicholas II (1059–1061).............................................................. 83
Background and Election...................................................... 84
Coronation ............................................................................ 86
The Collection of 74 Titles .................................................. 89

7. Nicholas II: Papal Electoral Decree and
Break with the Regency................................................................ 95
The Papal Electoral Decree of 1059 .................................... 95
Two Versions of the Papal Electoral Decree ....................... 96
Signatures ............................................................................. 98
Panvinius ............................................................................... 101
Cardinal Bishops and the King............................................ 104
Questions Continue .............................................................. 106

8. Nicholas II: The Normans and the Collapse of
Imperial Goodwill......................................................................... 109
The New Norman Policy ...................................................... 109
The North .............................................................................. 111
A Critical Reign..................................................................... 116

9. The Election of Alexander II (1061–1073) ................................ 119
Anselm as Bishop ................................................................. 119
Patarines ................................................................................ 121

Anselm, Nicholas II and the Regency.......................................... 123
The Role of Hildebrand ............................................................. 124
How the Election was Carried Out ........................................... 126
Conclusion ................................................................................. 130

10. The Election of Cadalus, Honorius II.......................................... 133
Cadalus as Bishop....................................................................... 134
After the Death of Nicholas II ................................................... 135
The Council of Basel .................................................................. 137
Hugo Candidus............................................................................ 140
Empress Agnes............................................................................. 141
Petrus Damiani............................................................................ 143
Papal Authority and the Lombards............................................ 149

11. Conflict in Rome and the Abduction of Henry IV..................... 151
Benzo in Rome ........................................................................... 152
The Arrival of Cadalus............................................................... 156
Only an Electus........................................................................... 160
Kaiserswerth................................................................................ 162
The Kidnapping .......................................................................... 165

12. From Kaiserswerth to Mantua ..................................................... 169
The Effects of the Abduction on the Schism........................... 169
The Council of Augsburg ........................................................... 171
Dissension Within the German Church .................................... 174
The Easter Council of 1063 and the Renewal
    of Violence .............................................................................. 178
Cadalus Returns to Rome .......................................................... 179
War................................................................................................ 183
Change of Fortunes and the Appeal to the King...................... 184
Conclusion .................................................................................. 188

13. The Council of Mantua ................................................................. 191
Petrus Damiani Calls for a Council ........................................... 192
The Council of Mantua (May 31-June 3, 1064)....................... 196
Benzo's Purported Exposé........................................................... 199
Analysis of Mantua ..................................................................... 203

14. Instability Following Mantua ....................................................... 205
Adalbert of Bremen and Anno ................................................... 205

Quedlinburg.................................................................. 206
Ceremony of Henry's Coming of Age ...................... 209
Anno's Letters.............................................................. 211
Letter of Petrus Damiani to Henry ......................... 214

15.  Ambivalence and Self Interest.................................... 219
Expedition of Godfrey to Rome................................ 219
Expedition of Anno, Henry of Trent, and
    Otto of Bavaria to Italy....................................... 222
Petrus Mezzabarba..................................................... 224
Beatrice and Godfrey Chastised................................ 229
Hugo Candidus............................................................ 230
Cencius Stephani......................................................... 236
Frayed Loyalties and the Deaths of Cadalus
    and Alexander II ................................................... 239

Conclusion   The State of the Papacy at the
                End of the Schism ......................................... 243

Bibliography ....................................................................... 249
Index of Subjects............................................................... 261

# ACKNOWLEDGEMENTS

I express my appreciation to the many people and institutions that have contributed to the creation of this book. The Vatican Library has always been my chief resource, and my research began there. When it closed for renovations I mainly worked at the Deutsches Historisches Institut in Rome. The directors and staff there were more than courteous and helpful. The libraries of the University of California provided their services while I was writing in La Jolla, and the department of history at UCSD supported me in every way. The Medieval Academy of America provided a grant so that I could present a paper on my research at the Leeds International Congress. And I am eternally grateful to The American Academy in Rome for granting me and my husband the use of its facilities and the pleasure and stimulation of interacting with its residents and staff. Throughout the years our good friend, Pina Pasquantonio, the assistant director, has facilitated our every need and brightened our lives with conversations on any subject.

Charles Radding and John Wei read early versions of my manuscript and offered valuable suggestions. Marianne McDonald and James Diggle expertly translated the epitaph for Cadalus/Honorius II. The editors of Brill, Ivo Romein and Professor Robert J. Bast, have been invariably helpful and responsive, and the anonymous reviewer far exceeded the requirements for assessing my manuscript. He was thoughtful, insightful, and knowledgeable about the subject, and meticulous with the specifications for footnotes and bibliography. Dan Connolly skillfully compiled the index, and my son, Ted, solved many of my computer problems. My entire family has been steadfastly supportive, and my husband, Avrum, has graciously read every version of my manuscript, making substantive as well as editorial suggestions. It is to him that I dedicate this book.

PREFACE

I have always worked in the twelfth century, assuming that the origin
of the issues I analyzed was the movement in the eleventh century for
ecclesiastical reform within the church and its release from secular
bondage. I saw the leaders of this movement as idealistic clerics, who
strived to free the papacy from the control of Roman aristocratic families, and to create a universal papacy as the head of all of Christendom.
In this book I investigate these beginnings myself, concentrating not
just on ecclesiastical reform, but also on all of the other events that
were taking place such as the incipient split between the Greek and the
Latin Churches, and the influx of Normans into Southern Italy. I pay
special attention to the antipopes to see what they represented, and
delve into the character and motivations of all of the important
personae.

I am not the first to see this period as far more complex than
ecclesiastical reform, and the attempt to free the church from secular
interference or even tutelage. Perhaps I carry my investigations a bit
further by delving into contradictions and dissonance, and I do not see
a relatively smooth line of progress. I perceive the outcome of what
began in the middle of the eleventh century with the deposition of
three popes and the appointment of another by a powerful emperor as
a reversal of power between a weak papacy and a strong empire. By the
end of the thirteenth century the papacy had become the theocracy
that Hildebrand, its chief protagonist in the eleventh century, had envisioned, but at the sacrifice of the spirituality that he and other reformers had exemplified and engendered.

La Jolla, July 2011

# ABBREVIATIONS

| | |
|---|---|
| Amatus. *Storia* | *Storia de'Normanni* |
| Amatus, *History* | tr. *History of the Normans* |
| *Annales Altahenses* | MGH SRG 4 |
| Arnulf, *Gesta* | *Gesta Archiepiscoporum Mediolanensium* |
| Baronius | *Annales ecclesiastici* |
| Beno, *contra Gregorium* | *Benonis…contra Gregorium VII* |
| Benzo, *Ad Heinricum,* | *Ad Heinricum*, MGH SRG 65 |
| Bernold, *Chronicon* | Ed. Robinson |
| Berthold, *Chronicon* | Ed. Robinson |
| Bonizo, *Ad Amicum* | *Liber ad Amicum*, MGH LdL 1:568–620 |
| Chron. Mont. | *Chronicon Montecassino* |
| Clm 147–152 | Munich, Bavarian Staatsbibliothek |
| Falco, *Chronicon* | *Chronicon Beneventanum* |
| Hüls, *Kardinäle* | Hüls, *Kardinäle, Klerus und Kirchen Roms* |
| IP | *Italia Pontificia* |
| Jaffé, *Biblioteca* | *Biblioteca Rerum Germanicarum* |
| JL | Jaffé, *Regesta Pontificum Romanorum*, vol. 1 |
| Lampert, *Annales* | MGH SRG 38:3–304 |
| Lib. Pont. | *Liber Pontificalis* |
| Mabillon | *Annales ordinis S. Benedicti* |
| MGH | Monumenta Germaniae Historica |
|   DD | Diplomata regum et imperatorum Germaniae |
|   LdL | Libelli de lite imperatorum et pontificum saeculis XI et XII conscripti |
|   SRG | Scriptores in usum scholarum |
|   SS | Scriptores |
| Mansi | *Sacrorum Conciliorum…Collectio*, vol. 19 |
| Panvinius, *De varia creatione* | Bavarian Staatsbibliotek, Clm 147–152 |

| Petrus Damiani, *Briefe* | *Die Briefe des Petrus Damiani*, ed. Reindel |
| PL | *Patrologiae cursus completus, series Latina*, ed. J.P. Migne |
| RIS | Rerum Italicarum Scriptores |
| Watterich | *Pontificum Romanorum Vitae* |

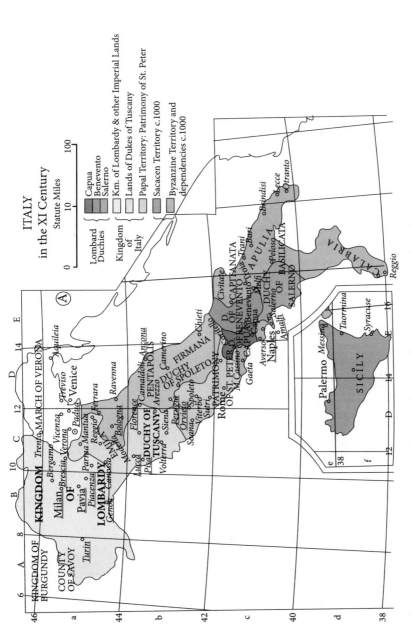

ITALY
in the XI Century

Statute Miles

0    10    100

Lombard
Duchies

{ Capua
  Benevento
  Salerno

Kingdom
of
Italy

Km. of Lombardy & other Imperial Lands

Lands of Dukes of Tuscany

Papal Territory: Patrimony of St. Peter

Sacacen Territory c.1000

Byzanzine Territory and
dependencies c.1000

KINGDOM OF
BURGUNDY

COUNTY
OF SAVOY

Turin

KINGDOM    MARCH OF VERONA
OF
LOMBARDY

Trento    Aquileia

Bergamo  Vicenza    Treviso
Milan  Brescia  Verona    Padua  Venice
Pavia  Mantua
Piacenza  Parma  Reggio  Ferrara
Genoa  Canossa  Modena  Ravenna
Bologna

Lucca    Camaldoli  Ancona
Pisa  Florence    PENTAPOLIS
DUCHY OF  Arezzo  Camerino
Volterra  TUSCANY  Perugia  FIRMANA
Siena  Orvieto  Spoleto  DUCHY  Chieti
Soana  Viterbo  OF SPOLETO
Sutri  PATRIMONY
Rome  OF ST. PETER  D. OF CAPITANATA
M. Cassino  Civitate
Gaeta  CAPUA  D. OF  Troia
Aversa  Capua  BENEVENTO  Bari  Trani
Naples  Benevento  APULIA  Melfi
Amalfi  Salerno  Peloso
DUCHY OF BASILICATA
SALERNO  Brindisi
Lecce
Otranto

CALABRIA

Reggio

Palermo  Messina
Taormina
SICILY
Syracuse

Politics of Eleventh Century Church Reform

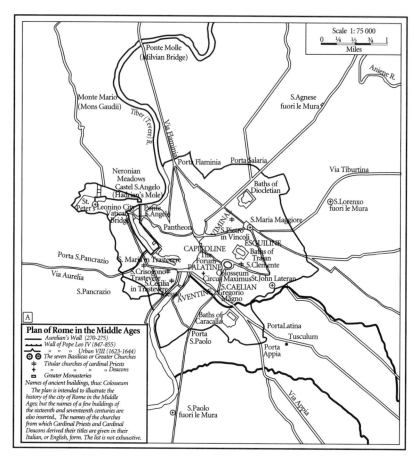

**Plan of Rome in the Middle Ages**

Aurelian's Wall (270-275)
Wall of Pope Leo IV (847-855)
  ,,   ,,   ,,   Urban VIII (1623-1644)
The seven Basilicas or Greater Churches
Titular churches of cardinal priests
  ,,      ,,      ,,      ,, Deacons
Greater Monasteries

*Names of ancient buildings, thus: Colosseum*
*The plan is intended to illustrate the*
*history of the city of Rome in the Middle*
*Ages; but the names of a few buildings of*
*the sixteenth and seventeenth centuries are*
*also inserted., The names of the churches*
*from which Cardinal Priests and Cardinal*
*Deacons derived their titles are given in their*
*Italian, or English, form. The list is not exhaustive.*

Politics of Eleventh Century Church Reform

# INTRODUCTION

A revolution shook the Christian world in the second half of the eleventh century. Many eminent historians, most prominently Louis Duchesne and Augustin Fliche, point to Gregory VII (1073–1085) as the prime mover of this revolution that aspired to free the church from secular entanglements and to return it to its state of paleochristian purity.[1] Following the lead of these historians, scholars frequently hail this movement as the Gregorian Reform. They differentiate Gregory from other reformers as the pope who encapsulated the various strands of partially fulfilled reforms, and who forcefully challenged the abuses that threatened the Western Church. By his own personal piety he set the example.

What was the state of the church in the middle of the eleventh century? One of the two main schools of thought was represented by Sigibert of Gembloux (1030–1112), master of the abbey of St. Vincent of Metz, and later monk of Gembloux.[2] As the most influential intellectual of Lower Lotharingia he championed church reform against simony, and promoted clerical chastity and the enforcement of monastic discipline. His exemplar was Bishop Theodoric of Metz, who represented cooperation, and he looked back to what he perceived to be the halcyon days of emperor, Otto I. "I call the times of Otto [I] happy and rightly so; for the commonwealth was reformed, the peace of the churches restored, and the integrity of religion renewed by famous bishops and wise men."[3]

Sigibert saw prelates allied to the king as workers for good. They were excellent soldiers and comrades-in-arms in the camp of the Lord

---

[1] *Lib. Pont.*, 2:xxi, 21; Augustin Fliche, *La Réforme grégorienne et la reconquêst chrétienne (1057–1125)*, vol. 8 of *Histoire de l'Église* (Paris, 1940); for other examples see John Gilchrist, "Was There a Gregorian Reform Movement in the Eleventh Century?," *The Canadian Catholic Historical Association, Study Sessions* 37 (1970), 1–10 at pp. 1–3.

[2] Sigibert of Gembloux, *Chronicon*, MGH SS 6:300–374; *Catalogus Sigiberti Gemblacensis monachi de viris illustribus*, ed. R. Witte, Lateinische Sprache und Literatur des Mittelalters 1 (Frankfurt, Berne, 1974); Ian Robinson, "Reform and the Church," pp. 268–334 of *The New Cambridge Medieval History* 4.1; c. 1024–1198, ed., David E. Luscombe and Jonathan Riley-Smith, pp. 276–277.

[3] *Vita Deoderici episcope Mettensis*, PL 160:700, c. 7: "Iure felicia dixerim Ottonis tempora, cum claris praesulibus et sapientibus viris respublica sit reformata, pax aecclesiarum restaurata, honestas religionis redintegrata;"

of the Sabbath, and they were fellow soldiers in the affairs of the king, be they at war or at leisure.[4] He praised the Ottonian bishop, Adalbero of Metz, who labored to restore monastic discipline on the apostolic model.[5] In sum, he saw the monarchy and the church as partners in the quest for restoring the purity of the church.

Humbert, a monk of Moyenmoutier, and cardinal bishop of Silva Candida by February, 1051, was Sigibert's antithesis. Rather than perceiving the emperor as a collaborator in effecting ecclesiastical reform, Humbert saw him as an impediment.[6] Along with a number of other supporters and advisors, including Hildebrand, he traveled to Rome with Leo IX (1049–1054), the former imperial bishop of Toul, after Leo was selected as pope by Henry III. This core group of reformers conceived of the reform in two senses: moral reform, and the transformation of the papacy into a monarchy.[7]

While Sigibert saw the reign of the Ottonians as the golden age, Humbert saw it as a time of rampant buying and selling of ecclesiastical offices throughout Germany, Gaul, and all of Italy.[8] To him it was a period in which kings and princes devoted all of their power, ingenuity, and the infliction of terror to attacking and claiming for themselves the ecclesiastical property that they were duly bound to protect.[9] More than any of their predecessors, Humbert viewed the Ottonians as usurpers of the priestly office. For this he concluded that God punished them by extinguishing their line after three generations. Following them, Henry II had no male heirs at all.[10]

The competition between the empire and the church in the eleventh century was always waged under the rubric of ecclesiastical reform, but there were many other factors that contributed to such a contest. One was the acceleration of economic growth produced by a rise in population, territorial expansion, an agrarian revolution, the extension of commercial activity, and the rise of a money economy.[11] Ecclesiastical

---

[4] Ibid., 701.

[5] *Vita Wicberti* MGH SS 8:511.

[6] Hüls, *Kardinäle*, pp. 131–134.

[7] Werner Goez, *Kirchenreform und Investiturstreit 910—1122* (Stuttgart, 2000), pp. 95–96.

[8] Humbert. *Libri III Adversus Simoniacos* MGH LdL 1:95–253, at 206.

[9] Ibid., 204.

[10] Ibid., 217.

[11] Ian Robinson, *The papal reform of the eleventh century: Lives of Pope Leo IX and Pope Gregory VII* (Manchester, 2004), Introduction, p. 1 & n. 1.

property grew more valuable, and as the church became wealthier, the struggle between it and secular powers for its assets became more intense. It is therefore not surprising that the emphasis on moral reform evolved into a struggle to control of these assets in what is widely called "the investiture contest."

If there was a beginning to the shift in the balance of authority, it probably occurred during the reign of Henry III when he appointed four German popes, all thought to be worthy, and a fifth was elected after his death. This intensive intervention of the emperor with the papacy coincided with the appearance of Hildebrand, most probably born between 1020–1025, and who styled himself a monk.[12] Born in the remote town of Soana or Sovana in South Tuscany near Lake Bolsena, Hildebrand seemed like an unlikely candidate to exercise power far beyond that of his appointments as subdeacon and then as archdeacon. But both before and after he became pope as Gregory VII he stood out as the dominant figure of this period.

The focus of ecclesiastical reform was clerical celibacy and the rejection of simony, in its most simple sense, the buying and selling of ecclesiastical offices. At first simony meant the purchase of an ordination. Later the concept was expanded to mean the acquisition of an ecclesiastical office from a secular person, and there was concern that the practice would lead to the propensity to gain these offices through money and favors. If no money was exchanged, the transaction was not technically simony, but the attainment of offices in this way was still forbidden. The abolition of this extended concept of simony entailed the prohibition of lay investiture of bishops and abbots with their benefices and ecclesiastical offices.

When Hildebrand became the *éminence grise* behind the papacy at mid century, the popes were weak, and the emperor strong. With seemingly naïve audacity, he sought to reverse this equation, arguing by the time that he became pope in 1073 that secular authority must be subject to spiritual authority. He sought nothing less than the transformation of the whole relationship between *regnum* and *sacerdotium*, loosely translated as state and church since there were no nation states, but only kingdoms and the Empire.

---

[12] Uta-Renate Blumenthal, *Gregor VII. Papst zwischen Canossa und Kirchenreform* (Darmstadt, 2001), pp. 29–30; Herbert Edward John Cowdrey, *Pope Gregory VII, 1073–1085* (Oxford, 1998), pp. 27–37.

But unlike his eponymous predecessor, Gregory I (590–604), Gregory VII was not always perceived as being "great." He was criticized for his excessive resort to military force, and he alienated cardinals, bishops, and other prelates as well as powers within the secular realm by his radical valuation of papal authority. The distinguished medievalist Henry Charles Lea said that when he passed away he left to his successors "the legacy of inextinguishable hate and unattained ambition."[13] A less learned and more partial protestant theologian in the nineteenth century thundered: "It may with no less propriety be called the period of Gregory VII, for he was the great master builder who combined the forgeries and frauds of all preceding ages, augmented by some of his own, into the model of that gigantic ecclesiastical despotism that during four centuries reigned sole monarch of Christendom."[14]

But his defenders were and are equally passionate. As early as the sixteenth century Caesare Baronius stated: "Through Gregory investitures of churches were clearly emancipated from the hands of rulers, free election by resumption of rights of the Roman pontiffs was restored, church discipline that had so completely collapsed was made good, and numerous other benefits brought about."[15] With some reservations, two of our most distinguished historians today see him as a seminal force, who strove to keep the secular world out of ecclesiastical affairs, and who challenged the power and the authority of the emperor to control the papacy.[16]

The underlying assumption of Christian society was that God had divided the government of the church between his spiritual and temporal vicars.[17] But the division was not clear cut, and was inherently unstable because the bishops exercised temporal authority and the king was anointed with holy oil. The Salian emperors in this period, Henry III (1039–1056) and Henry IV (1056–1106), believed

---

[13] Henry Charles Lea, *A History of Sacerdotal Celibacy* (3$^{rd}$ ed. revised, London, 1907), p. 287.

[14] Rev. Edward Beecher, *Papal Conspiracy Exposed, and Protestantism Defended in the Light of Reason, History and Scripture* (New York, 1855), pp. 331–364; 331.

[15] Baronius, *Annales Ecclesiastici,* 17:531; cited by Gilchrist, "Was There a Gregorian Reform Movement in the Eleventh Century?," pp. 1–2.

[16] Cowdrey, *Gregory VII,* p. vii; Blumenthal, *Gregor VII.,* p. 1.

[17] *Imperial Lives & Letters of the Eleventh Century,* tr. Theodor E. Mommsen & Karl F. Morrison, with an historical introduction by Karl F. Morrison (New York, 2000), p. 3.

that their office was both temporal and spiritual in nature, and that through the imperial church they had the right to intervene in ecclesiastical matters unless they were sacramental. Many bishops accepted their position, but others on the basis of their spiritual authority, temporal wealth, and administrative rights claimed superiority over secular powers.

Commonly, the emperor intervened in the church under the aegis of his duty to protect the papacy. It was generally agreed that Henry III carried out this responsibility conscientiously, dismissing popes deemed to be unworthy, and appointing others who appeared to represent the highest ideals of Christianity. Hildebrand cooperated with the emperor in this intervention, but by the time he became pope he saw it as an infringement on the independence of the church, and Henry III's son, Henry IV, as a moral reprobate unfit to exercise this traditional role.

Armed with a fiery personality, Hildebrand/Gregory VII challenged the Salian dominance of the church. Under his inspiration the popes acknowledged that secular authority was divinely disposed, but maintained that it was delegated through priestly authority. Consequently, all Christian government was subject to ecclesiastical prelates, who were under the absolute authority of the pope. As pope, Gregory VII pushed claims for papal authority beyond the assertions of any of his predecessors. His lodestar was reform centralized under absolute papal authority.[18] The church hierarchy must be totally subordinate to the papacy, and secular rulers must conform to its dictates. He conceded that his opponents had custom on their side, but stressed that the Lord did not say "I am the custom," but "I am the truth."

Not all of his contemporaries agreed that he did have truth on his side, and saw him as an unscrupulous tyrant who was systematically breaking down all cohesion in Christian society. They supported the antipopes, who promoted internal ecclesiastical reform, but were more or less content to live with the traditional intertwining of *regnum* and *sacerdotium*. Even though historians have generally seen the reform from Gregory's perspective, John Gilchrist, a prominent historian of canon law, questions whether there was such a thing as a

---

[18] Alison Sarah Welsby, "Pope, Bishops and Canon Law: A Study of Gregory VII's Relationship with the Episcopate and the Consequences for Canon Law," http://www.leeds.ac.uk/history/studentlife/e-journal/welsby.pdf.

Gregorian reform.[19] He notes that there were other reformers and reforms, and asks whether Gregory's aggressive, papal-oriented initiatives were more successful and substantively different from the others. He argues that they were not.

Gilchrist also notes that historians single out the Gregorian period for its stress upon the recovery of law and the beginnings of the science of canon law, but suggests that they molded their analyses to conform to the conventional world picture.[20] From his own examination of collections of canon law he concludes that one could find a program in the eleventh century as powerful as that attributed to Gregory without any reference to him at all.[21] Despite the feverish energy devoted to Roman law during the last quarter of the eleventh century, Gregory seems to have had little contact with it.[22] Nevertheless, his advocacy of unprecedented papal imperial authority may have been inspired by the widespread renewal of interest in Justinian's *Corpus Iuris Civilis*.

Recently studies of areas such as Salerno, the Abruzzi and Verona recognize the contributions of local elements, especially the roles of monasteries and bishoprics.[23] They did not always agree with the papal ideals of reform, and they were loath to relinquish their customary practices. In Salerno, for example, even though there was not outright opposition to the papacy, priests continued their tradition of clerical marriage. In Lombardy the episcopal hierarchy generally supported ecclesiastical reform, but not total papal authority over their sees and provinces, and not the dissolution of imperial authority over bishoprics and abbeys. They also did not agree that the pope should have the authority to depose emperors and to release their subjects from their oaths of fidelity.

---

[19] Gilchrist, "Was There a Gregorian Reform Movement in the Eleventh Century?," *passim*; see also Ovidio Capitani, "Esiste un 'Età Gregoriana'? Considerazioni sulle tendenze di una storiografica medievistica," *Rivista di Storica e Litteratura Religiosa* 1 (1965), 454–481.

[20] Ibid., 4.

[21] Ibid., 5.

[22] Charles M. Radding, & Antonio Ciarali, *The* Corpus Iuris Civilis *in the Middle Ages* (Leiden, Boston, 2007), pp. 104, 212.

[23] Valerie Ramseyer, *The Transformation of a Religious Landscape: Medieval Southern Italy 850–1150* (Ithaca & London, 2007), pp. 112–115; John Howe, *Church Reform and Social Change in Eleventh-Century Italy: Dominic of Sora and His Patrons* (Philadelphia, 1997), pp. 19–96; Maureen Miller, *The Formation of a Medieval Church: Ecclesiastical Change in Verona, 950–1150* (Ithaca, 1993), pp. 53–54.

While insisting that the laity relinquish any authority over the church, the reformers did not require that prelates do likewise in the secular realm, and totally devote themselves to spiritual and ecclesiastical pursuits. They still welcomed grants of privileges, land, and economic and political prerogatives from secular powers. The one pope who acknowledged the consequences for the church of retaining these powers was Paschal II (1099–1118). In negotiations with Henry V in February 1111 he proposed that bishops and abbots give up their *regalia*, essentially their benefices and governmental perquisites, in return for the renunciation of imperial investitures. The bishops rebelled against discarding their vast powers, and Paschal was branded a *simplicitas* for his willingness to return the church to a state of early Christian purity.

I now join the many historians who have analyzed this pivotal period, in my case by concentrating on the antipopes, starting with Benedict X (1058–1059). Benedict, a local bishop from Lazio, was the candidate of the Roman and suburban nobles, who still thought that they had the right to select their own bishop. On the initiative of the Romans Cadalus, the next papal challenger, came from Parma in Lombardy. The regency chose him as Honorius II (1061–1071) in the same year as the Hildebrandine faction elected Alexander II (1061–1073). Although his candidacy had lost most of its credibility by the Council of Mantua of 1064, he never renounced his claims to be the true pope, and he had a further brief impact on papal/imperial affairs before his death in 1071 or possibly in 1072.

While not neglecting ecclesiastical reform, I emphasize the protagonists' political positions: their motivations, their actions, and how geographic factors and personal associations shaped their attitudes. I examine, for example, how the birth of Cadalus in Parma informed his consciousness. I speculate on how the kidnapping of the boy king, Henry IV, by Archbishop Anno of Cologne affected the future emperor's character, his relationship with individual bishops, and with his mother, Agnes. I take note of the German bishops that supported or opposed Henry IV, and scrutinize their rivalries. I analyze why Cardinal Hugo Candidus kept changing sides, and why different factions in Rome supported one side rather than the other.

I explore what the Normans and the papacy wanted from each other, and why the eastern and western emperors perceived the Normans as a threat. I investigate how the reformers' assertion of international papal primacy elicited the reaction from the Greek Orthodox Church that led to the inception of a schism between the two churches. I also concentrate on other massive geopolitical shifts with the emergence of the Duchy of Canossa/Lotharingia in Central Italy, and the flexing of the self consciousness of Lombardy.

What differentiates my study from others are the factors I emphasize, the questions I ask and the anomalies I observe. I see Hildebrand as a reformer, but primarily as a political figure. Benedict X represented the continuation of the papacy as the bishopric of Rome, but Cadalus was more than just a provincial Roman candidate or an imperial lackey. He represented the growing power of Lombardy and a viable alternative to the separation of *regnum* and *sacerdotium*. I place the reform not at the vortex of change, but as one factor among many that led to the diminution of imperial sacral authority, and the creation of the papal monarchy.

Given the enormous consequences of the movement to restructure Christian society, the literature and the sources are vast. Most prominently, there are letters, decrees of councils, narratives, collections of canon law, a beginning of the application of civil law, and a variety of sometimes venomous polemical tracts. Assessing the allegations of their shrewd authors, and the cogency of their arguments is a daunting task, but a task worth pursuing. At stake is the understanding of all of the developments involving the Eastern and Western Empires, the impact of the Normans on the Lombards, Greeks and Muslims of Southern Italy, and the disparate conceptions of the papacy. To understand how the emperor could justify his intervention in ecclesiastical affairs I begin by discussing his authority as *patricius Romanorum*, and describe some of the major sources that deal with this and other issues during this period.

## CHAPTER ONE

IMPERIAL AUTHORITY OVER PAPAL ELECTIONS

It is important to remember that in the middle of the eleventh century there was not a sharp distinction between the secular and the religious, and that the emperor was not seen as an opponent of the church because he intervened in ecclesiastical affairs. Even after a cleft developed between many of the reformers and those who still saw the Christian world as a unity, we shall see that some of the most pure of the reformers still conceived of the emperor as anointed with sacral authority.

The Ottonians and Salians took on attributes of *rex et sacerdos*, priestly kingship. Their special and direct relationship with God was depicted in occasionally bizarre iconography, and was stressed liturgically. One of the tangible benefits of these dual powers was the authority to control the papacy and Italy. Most popes at that time lacked prestige, but the papacy remained an authority generally acknowledged by the German episcopate. As *rex et sacerdos* the king had the authority to short-circuit this potentially dangerous outside influence.[1]

It was generally recognized that Henry III (1039–1056) was empowered to intervene in papal elections because as the monk, Wipo, attested, he embodied sacral as well as secular authority. In his life of Conrad II (1024–1039), the first Salian emperor, Wipo stated that you are the vicar of Christ—*vicarius es Christi*, and the lauds for his successors would have echoed the same praise.[2] It can almost be said that Henry III founded the reform movement, for he created the popes in the middle of the eleventh century that gathered around themselves a nucleus of internationalist reformers who were not tied to any Roman faction.

After its long, meandering history, Henry III revived the privilege of the *patricius Romanorum* that gave him specific authority over the selection of popes. But his untimely death in 1056 left his six year old

---

[1] Timothy Reuter, *Medieval Polities and Modern Mentalities*, ed. Janet L. Nelson (Cambridge, 2006); "Contextualising Canossa: excommunication, penance, surrender, reconciliation," pp. 147–166; "The 'imperial church system' of the Ottonian and Salian rulers: a reconsideration," pp. 325–354 at 327.

[2] *Gesta Chuonradi imperatoris*, MGH SS 11:260.

son, Henry IV (1056–1106), with the burden of trying to implement
this authority when the church was beginning to discriminate more
precisely between the ecclesiastical and the secular, and to free itself
from any secular control.[3]

## The Patricius Romanorum

As an indication of just how vague the authority of the *patricius
Romanorum* was, and in contra-distinction to the most recent scholar-
ship, the eminent nineteenth-century German historian, Lothar von
Heinemann, claimed that there were two types of *patricius*.[4] The first
was the authority to influence papal elections that the exarch of
Ravenna passed on to the Carolingians and Ottonians, and then as a
hereditary right to Henry III and Henry IV. He concludes that the
emperor as *patricius* gave his consent to the papal elect after his election, but prior to enthronement.

Von Heinemann distinguishes this authority from the patriciate of
the city of Rome, which was exercised by the nobility in the name of
the people. Henry III united both powers after his coronation in 1046,
but relinquished the city patriciate in 1055. Von Heinemann alleges
that Henry IV relied upon his inherited authority except in 1061 when
he accepted the city patriciate from an embassy of Romans, and used it
to justify his appointment of Bishop Cadalus of Parma to the papacy.
He surmises that the papal electoral decree of 1059, which will be dealt
with during the reign of Nicholas II, implicitly left the imperial patriciate intact.

Von Heinemann's analysis reveals the ongoing ambiguities in the
concept of the *patricius Romanorum*. Why should Henry IV have
relied upon the authority of the city patriciate to nominate Cadalus as
pope in 1061 if he already had inherited the authority to nominate
popes? The sources are conflicting, but they reveal some of the strands
of thinking about the broad acceptance—even by the reformers—of
the emperor's authority to intervene in papal elections.

---

[3] Guido Martin, "Der salische Herrscher als *Patricius Romanorum*. Zur
Einflussnahme Heinrichs III. und Heinrichs IV. auf die Besetzung der *Cathedra Petri*,"
*Frühmittelalterliche Studien* 28 (1994), 257–295; Reuter, "Contextualising Canossa,"
pp. 147–166; "The 'imperial church system'," pp. 325–354.

[4] Lothar von Heinemann, "Das Papstwähldekret Nikolaus II. und die Entstehung
des Schismas vom Jahre 1061," *Historische Zeitschrift* NF 29 (1890), 44–72 at 58–59.

Guido Martin presents an excellent analysis of the power of the Salian *patricius* during the 24 years stretching from the granting of the dignity to Henry III in 1046 until Henry IV appealed to this authority to justify the elevation of Clement III to the papacy in 1080 during the reign of Gregory VII.[5] He summarizes its different interpretations, and describes how ambiguous and perplexing this crucial provision for imperial influence over the papacy continued to be.[6] He explores the controversy over the legal and political meaning of the patriciate, noting that both its legal and its political implications changed from the reign of Henry III to the reign of Henry IV when the church became stronger and more aggressive.[7] The following is his analysis.

Between 1046 and 1054 Henry III, a religious man who supported the reform, demonstrated the theocratic conception of his rule. Needing a pope worthy to crown him in Rome, Henry arranged a synod in Sutri in 1046 that nominated such a person, who would take the name of Clement II. The *acceptio*, the subsequent election by the clergy and the people that was requisite for the nominee to be recognized as pope, took place in Rome.

Martin points out that contrary to other sources, both the Chronicle of Montecassino and the *Annales Romani* report that the Romans presented Henry III with the symbols of the *patricius* after his coronation.[8] He contends that the same procedure was followed for Clement's successor, Damasus II, who was nominated by the emperor and subsequently elected in Rome. Bruno of Toul went through the same process when he was elected Leo IX in 1049, but he insisted that his election be confirmed in Rome. Although his insistence is interpreted as an attempt to emancipate the church from imperial control, in 1054 Victor II was elected following an equivalent process as his three predecessors.

The German sources during the reign of Henry III are pretty much silent on the emperor as *patricius*, probably because as a reform-oriented

---

[5] Martin, "Der salische Herrscher als *Patricius Romanorum*," pp. 257–295.

[6] Ibid., 257–258 & ns. 1, 2.

[7] Ibid., 258–263.

[8] *Chron. Mont.*, p. 322: "Tunc temporis eidem Heinrico patriciatus honorem Romani contribuunt, eumque preter imperialem coronam aureo circulo uti decernunt." *Annales Romani, Lib. Pont.* 2:332: "Itaque serenissimus princebs (sic), cernens Romanorum omnium voluntatem, circulum quod ab antiquitus Romani coronabant patricios, cum omnium voluntatem sicut imperatori decreverant, in capite posuit suo. Et ordinationem pontificum ei concesserunt...."

protector of the Roman church it was unnecessary for him to appeal to his authority as *patricius*. Even before being granted the title during the consecration of Clement II in 1046, Henry deposed three alleged popes, and designated another. Everything changed when he died and his six-year old child, guided by a weak regency, had urgent need for this authority. Theoretically it could only be exercised by an emperor, but clearly the reformers felt that even before he became emperor, Henry IV held vital power over papal elections, since they sent delegations to him and the regency to confirm Stephen IX in 1057 and to reject Benedict X in 1058.

### Bonizo

Bonizo is almost always referred to as Bonizo of Sutri, where he became bishop at the latest by 1078. Sutri is a small town north of Rome on the Via Cassia, and was an important stopping point for dignitaries coming from the North. Hildebrand and Nicholas stopped there on their way from Siena to Rome, and held a council. But Bonizo's identification was actually with Lombardy, where, he was born into the lower classes at Cremona between 1030 and 1045.[9] He became subdeacon of Piacenza, and as a committed Patarine, drew the attention of Hildebrand/Gregory VII. Urban II wanted him to remain there, but both clerics and laymen opposed him, and he fled to Cremona in 1089. From then on he was identified as the bishop of Sutri.

As one of the most ardent supporters of the reform movement, he wrote two influential works, *Liber ad Amicum*, and *Liber de Vita Christiana*. He wrote *Liber ad Amicum* shortly after the death of Gregory VII on May 25, 1087, when everything looked bleak for the Gregorian cause. There was no immediate successor to the papacy, and his faithful supporter, Mathilda, had lost almost all of her upper Italian positions. Bonizo's friend may have felt that the situation was hopeless, and Bonizo was trying to encourage him, sometimes—either intentionally or mistakenly—by using historically inaccurate facts.

In 1089 Bonizo was attacked and mutilated. He was blinded, and his nose, ears and tongue were injured. In this condition he wrote some of his seminal works, including *Liber de Vita Christiana*. He believed that

---

[9] Bonizo, *Liber de Vita Christiana*, ed. Ernst Perels (Berlin, 1930); Walter Berschin, *Bonizo von Sutri: Leben und Werk* (Berlin, 1972), pp. 4–8.

women should be subordinate to men, and broke with Mathilda. He continued to fight against the schismatics, and was not interested in a crusade, believing that the fight should be against the enemies within the church, not without. Almost friendless, he died in 1094 in Cremona.[10]

Commenting on Bonizo's polemic against the patriciate in his English translation of Ad Amicum, To a Friend, I.S. Robinson sums up the history of the patriciate as he sees it.[11] Robinson states that prior to the mid-eighth century the Byzantine emperor entitled his representative in Rome as *patricius*. Without specifying how the popes gained control of the office, he says that they granted the same title to the Frankish kings in the second half of the eighth century to emphasize the kings' duty to defend the papacy.

Robinson states that in the early eleventh century the great Roman noble families used the title to signify their control both of the city and of the papacy. In 1046 the Romans granted the title to Henry III during his coronation, Robinson notes, and he used it to justify appointing four German popes. Robinson points out that in his proceedings against Gregory VII, Henry IV claimed to have inherited the title from his father.[12] It was, Robinson concludes, this use of the authority that provoked Bonizo's diatribe against "the empty title."

Going back to the inception of the *patricius*, Bonizo said that since the Roman emperors were prevented by the barbarians from bringing help to the Roman church, and since the Franks were alienated from the church, the captains of the city gave themselves the empty title of *patricius*, and vigorously laid waste to the Roman church.[13] Not only was the title meaningless, he asserted, but it also was never found in the registers of the Roman magistrates. He reported that the Byzantine emperors sent military men such as Narses and Belisarius to help the Romans in the sixth century, and that the simple Roman people called

---

[10]  Berschin, *Bonizo von Sutri*, pp. 8–40.

[11]  Robinson, *The papal reform of the eleventh century*, n. 21, p. 174; idem, *Henry IV of Germany, 1056–1106* (Cambridge, New York, 1999), p. 36.

[12]  *Die Briefe Heinrichs IV.*, MGH *Deutsches Mittelalter* (Leipzig, 1937), nr. 11, p. 15; Robinson, *Imperial Lives and Letters*, pp. 146–147; p. 147: "...I also give my assent, revoking from you every prerogative of the papacy which you have seemed to hold, and ordering you to descend from the throne of the city whose patriciate is due me through the bestowal of God and the sworn assent of the Romans."

[13]  Robinson, *The Papal Reform of the Eleventh Century*: "The Book of Bishop Bonizo of Sutri which is entitled 'To a Friend,'" pp. 158–261; Book III, p. 174.

them *patricii*, fathers of the city. He alleged that these *patricii*, sometimes laymen, abused the Roman church and appointed the popes, and
as a result the church became debased.[14]

At the end of the tenth century, he continues, a captain of the city
named Crescentius claimed the meaningless title of *patricius*, and
established a tyranny. Crescentius expelled the pope, who had crowned
Otto II, and although he tried to make amends, he failed. Otto killed
him and mutilated the pope whom he had imposed.[15] The papacy
became so degraded that John XIX (1024–1032? 36?) was at the same
time both pope and prefect.[16] During the reign of Henry III (1039–
1056) Bonizo reports that the captains of Rome, especially the Tusculani, laid waste the Roman church under the empty title of the patriciate,
and seemed to possess the papacy by hereditary right.

Following Henry III's coronation by Clement II in 1046, Bonizo
states that after Henry had been adorned with the imperial dignity, he
took pity on the misfortunes of the empire (*res publica*), and freed the
city from the tyranny of the *patricii*.[17] Bonizo says that Henry would
have been deserving of praise for this action had he himself not immediately thereafter seized the tyranny of the *patritiatus*. What could be
more bitter or more cruel, he lamented, than that he who had recently
punished the Tusculani for their tyranny should imitate those whom
he had condemned. The reason for this contradictory action, he con-
jectured, was that Henry believed that the dignity of the *patricius* gave
him the authority to appoint the Roman pope.

Bonizo alone claims that Hildebrand was a candidate for the papacy
in 1054, and associates him with the patriciate.[18] He said that after the
clergy and the people had expressed their wishes that he be their pope,
Hildebrand crossed the Alps with other religious men, and approached
the emperor. During frequent conversations Bonizo claims that
Hildebrand demonstrated to the emperor how great a sin he had committed in making appointments to the papacy. Agreeing with these
charges, the emperor relinquished the tyranny of the patriciate, and
granted the Roman clergy and people their ancient right of electing the

---

[14] Ibid., 175.
[15] Ibid., Book IV, 179.
[16] Ibid, Book V, 182.
[17] Ibid., 187; Bonizo, *Ad Amicum*, p. 586.
[18] Ibid., 193–194 & n. 96; Bonizo, *Ad Amicum*, p. 589.

supreme pontiff.[19] Forthwith the clergy and the people who were present brought back the bishop of Eichstätt (Gebhard), the steward of the emperor, and he was elected in St. Peter's according to ancient custom, and enthroned by the cardinals as Victor II.

Whereas Bonizo reports that Victor II was elected against the will of the emperor after having relinquished his rights as *patricius*, all other sources present the election of Victor as similar to those of his immediate predecessors. Thereafter the emperor never had a chance to verify Bonizo's contention that he had given up the tyranny of the *patricius*, for he died in 1056. When Benedict X was elected in 1057, Bonizo said that it was through the intervention of Gregory of Tusculum, who claimed the empty title of *patricius*.[20] Presumably Gregory as *patricius* claimed to be representing the Roman people.

Gregory's intervention in the election of Benedict X may have been more a matter of might than right. Henry III had been powerful enough to impose his will, but the regency headed by his wife, Agnes, acting for their young son, Henry IV (born in 1050), was weak. If Henry III had not relinquished the patriciate, as Bonizo maintained, and if the regency had been strong enough, it might have declared that Henry IV had inherited this authority, as Henry IV would assert during his conflict with Gregory VII. Since the regency did not declare this right, there was no reason for the reformers to contest it.[21] For all of its weakness, however, the regency did contribute to the deposition of Benedict X by confirming the election of Nicholas II, the choice of the reformers.

### Petrus Damiani

Petrus Damiani was one of the most idealistic, passionate, but independent exponents of the reform. Born the youngest of at least six children in Ravenna in 1007, he received a good education in the liberal arts in Faenza and Parma, and became a teacher of rhetoric in Ravenna. In 1035 he became a monk at Fonte Avellana in northeastern Italy, and

---

[19] Bonizo, *Ad Amicum*, p. 589: "Qui eius salubri acquiescens consilio tyrannidem patriciatus deposuit cleroque Romano et populo secundum antiqua privilegia electionem summi pontificis concessit."

[20] Ibid., 592; Martin, "Der salische Herrscher als *Patricius Romanorum*, p. 274.

[21] Martin, "Der salische Herrscher als *Patricius Romanorum*, p. 276.

a priest when he was about 30. A prolific writer, and in many ways a product of his time, his first extensive work was titled "A Tract against the Jews."

He encountered the papacy at the latest by 1045 during the reign of Gregory VI, whose election he welcomed, but whom Henry III deposed. At the instigation of Hildebrand, Stephen IX created him cardinal bishop of Ostia at an uncertain date, but around the winter of 1057.[22] Petrus frequently protested his frustration at having been thrust into the thick of things, and claimed that he longed for the solitude of Fonte Avellana. Nevertheless, he remained cardinal bishop until 1072, and used his position to exhort his fellow cardinal bishops to undergo a spiritual renewal. Unlike Humbert of Silva Candida and other reformers who aggressively promoted a papacy with absolute authority, Petrus believed in the sacral character of the emperor and the unity of *regnum* and *sacerdotium*, both of which he deemed to be directly established by God.[23]

In his *Liber gratissimus* focusing on simony, and written after the Lenten synod of 1051, he speaks of the authority of Henry III to fill vacancies of the apostolic see. He states that the holy Roman Church is ordered according to his (Henry's) will, and that no priest can be elected to the apostolic see without his approval.[24] To be sure, Petrus is not presenting a precise legal formulation of the dignity of the *patricius*, but rather is describing the actual situation.[25] At the least he acknowledges that the emperor has the authority to intervene in papal elections.

In the Lenten council of 1059 Nicholas II issued a decree defining the procedure for holding papal elections that placed the election in the hands of the cardinals. In 1061 Bishop Cadalus of Parma was elected in opposition to Alexander II, and at the end of October, 1062, an imperial council was held to debate the legality of each election. As preparation for that debate in April 1062 Petrus Damiani created a mock debate between a royal advocate and a defender of the Roman

---

[22] Hüls, *Kardinäle*, pp. 99–100.

[23] *Petri Damiani Liber gratissimus* MGH LdL 1:15–75 at 31: "Regnum namque et sacerdotium a Deo cognoscitur institutum."

[24] Ibid., 71: "Hoc sibi (Henry III) non ingrata divina dispensatio contulit, quod plerisque decessoribus suis eatenus non concessit, ut videlicet ad eius nutum sancta Romana aecclesia nunc ordinetur, ac preter eius auctoritatem apostolicae sedi nemo prorsus eligat sacerdotem."

[25] Martin, "Der salische Herrscher als *Patricius Romanorum*, p. 267.

church that he called the *Disceptatio synodalis*.[26] In the debate the royal advocate defends Henry III's legal rights as *patricius* in papal elections. The advocate tells the defender of the church that he cannot deny that [Henry III] was made *patricius* of the Romans, by which title he received perpetual control over the election of the pope.[27]

More recently, the advocate notes, Pope Nicholas confirmed this right in a page of a synodal decree, almost certainly the papal electoral decree. The essence of the advocate's position is that the election of the Roman pope is not valid without the assent of the king of the Romans.[28] Taking into consideration the allegation that this dignity originated with the Romans, who, in conjunction with the clergy, enjoyed the right to elect their bishop, the advocate concluded that the *patricius* was the voice of the people in papal elections.

### Benzo

Benzo of Alba was one of the most dedicated and feisty advocates for the emperor during the reform, and his Seven Books written to Henry IV are a testimony beyond the ordinary.[29] Revealing a mind of exceptional agility and wit, they are one of the most significant literary monuments of the eleventh century.[30] In many respects Benzo can be paired with Bonizo as representing the contrary point of view. His life before he accompanied Archbishop Guido of Milan and other suffragans to the Lenten Council of Nicholas II in Rome in 1059 is mainly speculative.[31] He was an acerbic critic of Hildebrand, the hated Prandellus as he called him, and he became the chief supporter and defender of Cadalus in the schism with Alexander II in 1061.

But Benzo was not just a polemicist, as many historians perceive him to be, but also a reformer opposed to simony and clerical marriage. He urged Henry to be very discriminating in creating bishops lest he

---

[26] Petrus Damiani, *Briefe*, nr. 89, 2:541–572; tr. Blum, 3:336–367; Robinson, *Henry IV of Germany*, p. 36.

[27] Ibid., 547; tr. Blum, 3:342.

[28] Ibid., 543: "...nisi Romani regis assensus accesserit, Romani pontificis electio perfecta non erit." tr. Blum, 3:338–339.

[29] Benzo, *Ad Heinricum*; Saverio Sagulo, *Ideologia imperiale e analisi politica in Benzone, vescovo d'Alba*. A cura di Glauco Maria Cantarella (Bologna, 2003).

[30] M. Oldoni, "L'immaginario e il suo contrario, la scienza," *I Normani popolo d'Europa MXXX-MCC* (Venice, 1994), p. 306.

[31] Bonizo, *Ad Amicum*, pp. 593–594.

draw disgrace upon himself from the iniquity of a new incumbent. He advised Henry to examine the morals of his intended appointments, and not to mistake a cupid for an angel, nor to elevate a Priapus to an episcopal office.[32] He lauded Otto III, who had restored the monarchy of the empire thanks to the support of the bishops. To him Otto's reign was a golden age, when reason reigned, the earth enjoyed tranquility, and the clergy showed themselves as pious as the choir of angels.[33]

Benzo profoundly disagreed with Bonizo that the *patricius* was an empty title. In his seventh book dedicated *Ad Heinricum* where he summarizes the relations between the pope and the emperor, he describes the origin and the cases that pertained to the *patricius Romanorum*, and analyzes the functions connected to this authority.[34]

He states that after his conversion to Christianity Constantine issued an edict commanding that those of high office and all other Romans should conform to his sacred faith. Constantine then established a *patricius* in Rome to defend the *res publica*, and he wanted an *apocrisarius* appointed by the pope to be in Constantinople to maintain ecclesiastical discipline.[35] The *apocrisiarius* would protect the faith, while the *patricius* would protect the Roman church. Since the election of the pope had been carried out in subterranean chambers out of fear of the pagans, Constantine directed that it be celebrated solemnly in an assembly of the people. If the emperor could be present within two months, he should preside. If not, the *patricius* would take his place and the election should be performed by the clergy, the senate and the people according to God's will. The elect must obtain imperial consent before consecration.[36]

Describing the election of Clement II in his own time, Benzo reports that in 1046 after deposing three prelates purporting to be pope, Henry III presided over a council of bishops and the whole Roman

[32] Benzo, *Ad Heinricum*, 5.3, pp. 462–464: "In episcopis creandis si es discretissimus…Sit discreta, rex o bone, manus impositio, ne fortasse labem trahas ex tyronis vicio, vita prius requiratur, mores et conditio. Ne accipias pro agno barbatum cornigerum, nec pro Iovis ave summas nocturnum aligerum, nec constituas Priapum in numero syderum." Robinson, *Reform and the Church*, pp. 279–283.
[33] Ibid., 3.6, p. 284.
[34] Ibid., 7.2, pp. 588–590; tr. Robinson, *The Papal Reform of the Eleventh Century*, pp. 368–369 & n. 34; Martin, "Der salische Herrscher als *Patricius Romanorum*, p. 264; Sagulo, *Ideologia imperiale e analisi politica in Benzone*, especially pp. 13–14; 50–55.
[35] Ibid., 582; tr, Robinson, *The Papal Reform of the Eleventh Century*, p. 366.
[36] Ibid., 584: "Consecrari denique nullatenus praesumatur, donec per se aut per suam epistolam imperialis consensus adhibeatur." tr. Robinson, *The Papal Reform of the Eleventh Century*, pp. 367–368.

nobility in St. Peter's. He told the Romans that they could continue to choose whomsoever they wished as pope, but they unanimously acknowledged that when the royal majesty was present the election was to be held according to his will rather than their own. If he was not present, he was nevertheless represented by his deputy, the *patricius*.

They conceded that their choices had been flawed, and that it was the right of the imperial power to improve the laws and morals of the republic, which would entail control of the Apostolic Church. After the approval of the synod and the commendation of the senators and Roman people, it was decreed that like Charles (Charlemagne), Henry and his successors should become the *patricius*. The king was then invested with the symbols of this office, and he was requested to elect a pope. The synod then approved his candidate, who as Clement II crowned him emperor the following day.

Other sources assert that although Charlemagne inherited the title in 774, he dropped it when it was incorporated into his imperial authority upon his coronation as emperor in 800. Still others, such as the *Annales Romani* and the Chronicle of Montecassino allege that Henry III received the title and the symbols of the patriciate after his coronation, not before.[37] The justification for receiving them after the coronation would be that Henry could not exercise this authority until he was crowned emperor. But if Henry already possessed the authority to nominate the pope before he held the authority of the *patricius*, the title and its symbols would be redundant.

It has been suggested that Benzo created his narrative to justify Henry IV's later claim to Gregory VII that he had inherited the patriciate.[38] If, however, Bonizo is right that Henry III cast aside the tyranny of the patriciate after the death of Leo IX [1054], what happened in 1046 would not have been relevant. In any case, Henry IV received the title again in 1061 when the Romans brought its symbols to Henry IV so that he could nominate Bishop Cadalus of Parma as Honorius II after the reformers had elected Alexander II.

## The Response of the Reformers

The main charge that the reformers leveled against their opponents who defended the right of the emperor to intervene in papal elections

---

[37] See n. 8 above.
[38] Martin, "Der salische Herrscher als *Patricius Romanorum*, p. 264.

and violated other principles of the reform was heresy, and the weapon
to combat it was excommunication. The mistake of the reformers was
to overuse this spiritual authority for secular purposes so that in the
course of time heresy became disobedience rather than disbelief. This
evolution is clear from Gregory VII's famous statement in his *Dictatus
Papae* that he who is not in concord with the Roman Church should
not be considered to be Catholic to Boniface VIII's equally famous
declaration in *Unam Sanctam* in 1302 that obedience to the pope is
essential for salvation.[39]

The reformers will also exploit the Donation of Constantine, the
mid eighth to the mid ninth century forgery that granted the papacy
spiritual and temporal supremacy over the whole empire.[40] Already in
1054 Leo IX referred to the Donation in a letter to Michael Kerularius,
the patriarch of Constantinople.[41] Petrus Damiani refers specifically to
the Donation in his *Disceptatio* in which the *defensor ecclesiae* asks
how the emperor can elect the pope since he does not have power over
the Roman church.[42] Gregory VII makes this query his mantra.

The defender's stance that the emperor had no power over the Roman
Church underscores the transformation that many of the reformers
had undergone since 1046 when they welcomed the emperor's intervention to rid the church of bad popes and to seat a worthy pope by
invoking his authority of *patricius Romanorum*. Let us see how Henry
III conceived his authority, and what impact its exercise in 1046 had on
this nascent stage of the reform.

[39] Alexander Patschovsky, "Heresy and Society: On the Political Function of Heresy
in the Medieval World," pp. 23–41 at p. 26 of *Texts and the Repression of Medieval
Heresy*, ed. Caterina Bruschi & Peter Biller; York Studies in Medieval Theology 4 (York,
2003); Y.M.-J. Congar, "Der Platz des Papsttums in der Kirchefrömmigkeit der
Reformer des 11. Jahrhunderts," pp. 196–217 of *Sentire ecclesiam*, ed. J. Daniélou &
H. Vorgrimler (Freiburg, Basel and Vienna, 1963).
[40] H.E.J. Cowdrey, "Eleventh-Century Reformers' Views of Constantine," nr. I
of *Popes and Church Reform in the 11th Century* (Variorum, Bury St. Edmunds, 2000),
p. 70.
[41] JL 4332.
[42] Petrus Damiani, *Briefe*, nr. 89, 2:546–547; 547: "Audisti, quia terrenus imperator
non habet in Romana aecclesia potestatem, quomodo ergo sine illius arbitrio, qui ibi
potestatem non habet non licet eligi sacerdotem? Ipse vero Constantinopolim velut
in secunda Roma perpetuo regnaturus abcessit." tr. Blum, 3:341–342; Cowdrey,
"Eleventh-Century Reformers' Views of Constantine," pp. 78–79.

CHAPTER TWO

# HENRY III'S POPES

Henry's imposition of German popes did not follow a smooth process whereby all but a faction of disgruntled Roman nobles approved of his initiatives. He was doing his best to ensure that the popes who occupied the Holy See would be of the stature to place their imprimatur on imperial coronation. He also wanted to hold on to his control of Italy, and needed to choose a pope with the requisite approval and connections. It was a complicated process, and his first two appointments were failures.

## *Henry's Authority*

Henry III (1039–1056) saw the king as the vicar of the heavenly king on earth, and rulership as the king as penitent, witnessed by a series of penitential rituals that marked his early reign.[1] The church was the body of Christ, and the king the head, the *caput ecclesiae*. As the head of a divine world order, Henry did not construct a well developed political organization. Rather, as the *vicarius Christi* he believed that he must transmit the divine order, and be the mediator between clerics and people. The sacrality of the king, he deemed, must be passed down from father to son.

Two pages of the ornate Codex Aureus present the program of the Salian sacral kingdom as it existed in 1045 under Henry III.[2] On the first page on the left are Henry's father, Conrad II, and his wife, Gisela, kneeling at the foot of the divine majesty. On the right are Henry and his wife, Agnes. In the inscription Conrad says that he is weeping in front of the majesty because of his sins. He asks the majesty, who through his goodness has made him emperor, for forgiveness. The readiness for penitence and the plea for the grace of God also characterize Henry III and his idea of peace.

---

[1] Stefan Weinfurter, *Canossa: Die Entzauberung der Welt* (Munich, 2006) pp. 30–47.
[2] Codex Aureus; Escorial, Cod. Vitinas 17, fols. 2v; 3r, preserved in the Escorial; Weinfurter, *Canossa*, pp. 32–33.

The page on the right depicts Mary enthroned as the queen of heaven before the cathedral of Speyer, dedicated to her, and the church with which the Salians identified. Henry III and Agnes kneel before her, and Henry presents her with the golden book of the evangelists. Mary places her left hand on Agnes's head in expectation that she will help Agnes to produce a male heir. The inscription implores Mary not to reject him as king, and asks her to be his benevolent helper. Henry had been gravely ill, and when he recovered he came to Speyer and presented her with the *Codex Aureus*. Symbolically, it was on the feast day for the birth of Mary in 1046 that Henry departed for his coronation in Rome, and on the same day he made several donations to the cathedral in Speyer.

Wipo, Conrad II's biographer, and Henry's teacher, frequently compared Henry with David.[3] David was seen as the pre figure, and Henry as the post figure of Christ. Guided by the principle of unity of the church and the world, Henry emphasized mercy, humility, and penitence. Churchmen revered him because of his zeal for ecclesiastical reforms, but he wielded absolute authority. Even though he had to consider the will and consensus of the bishops, no one became bishop against his will.[4]

## The Three Iniquitous Popes

But the principle that laymen could not mix themselves in the affairs of the church was beginning to germinate, and Henry was in danger of becoming a *rex iniquus* because, as Othloh of S. Emmeram charged, he never had time to listen to the poor.[5] It was under these shifting circumstances that Henry deposed two popes in a synod at Sutri in 1046, and secured the abdication, if not the deposition of a third. The genesis

---

[3] Weinfurter, *Canossa*, p. 36; *Imperial Lives and Letters of the Eleventh Century*, ed. Robinson, introduction p. 42 for description of Wipo; Wipo, *The Deeds of Conrad II*, pp. 52–100.

[4] Ibid., 83; the story of how Gebhard became bishop of Eichstatt illustrates Henry's relationship with bishops: The emperor was the absolute authority; but when no one became bishop, he must listen to the will and consensus of the bishops. Only irreproachable bishops were tolerated; Henry later named Gebhard as pope Victor II (1055–1057).

[5] Othloh of S. Emmeram, *Liber visionum*, MGH *Quellen zur Geistesgeschichte des Mittelalters* 16 (Darmstadt, 1974); Othloh, p. 86, said that since Henry never had time to respond to the complaints of the poor, he was inflicted with an early death.

of this action intended to restore integrity and legitimacy to the papacy began in Rome in 1045 when the scandalous Tusculan pope, Benedict IX (1032–1044), was driven from office, and was replaced by Bishop John of Sabina from a competing noble faction as Pope Sylvester III.[6] A mere three months later Benedict expelled Sylvester, and returned to his dissolute ways.

Shortly thereafter Benedict entered Rome, and on May 1, 1046, he abdicated in favor of his godfather, Johannes Gratianus, who seems to have passed his godchild some money, either in compensation for stepping down, or as payment to Benedict's troops.[7] Johannes Gratianus arranged some sort of election, and reigned for eighteen months as Gregory VI. In general he was well received by the reformers, especially by Petrus Damiani, but soon he was considered to have been tainted by simony.[8]

This chaotic situation led to the intervention of Henry III, who, in order to become emperor, was required to be crowned in Rome by an indisputable pope of impeccable moral stature. In Germany Henry had appointed exemplary bishops and abbots; now he could perform the same function with the papacy. In the autumn of 1046 he crossed the mountains into Italy and held councils at Pavia, where simony was forbidden, and at Piacenza, where he met Gregory VI. There, the two men concluded a pact of intercession that looked like a concordat of mutual acceptance and cooperation.[9]

But by the time that Henry reached Sutri, he had changed his mind, and judged Gregory VI to be guilty of simony. Sources report both that Gregory deposed himself, and that he was deposed at the council. Georg Gresser argues persuasively that whether legally or not,

[6] Harald Zimmermann, *Papstabsetzungen des Mittelalters* (Graz, Cologne, Vienna, 1968), pp. 119–139; Cowdrey, *Gregory VII*, pp. 21–26; Idem, *The Age of Abbot Desiderius: Montecassino, the Papacy, and the Normans in the Eleventh and Early Twelfth Centuries* (Oxford, 1983), pp. 80–81; Lino Lionello Ghiarardini, *L'antipapa Cadalo e il tempo del Bene e del Male: Grandezza e Miseria del più 'Famoso Vescovo di Parma (1045–1071)* (Centro di Studi Canossiani, 1984), pp. 10–11.
[7] Bernhard Schimmelpfennig, *The Papacy* (New York, 1992), p. 114.
[8] Petrus Damiani, *Briefe*, nr. 72, 2:363; tr. Blum: 145; Cowdrey, *Gregory VII*, p. 22 & n. 84.
[9] Hermann of Reichenau, *Chronicon*, pp. 615–707 of *Quellen des 9. und 11. Jahrhunderts zur Geschichte des Hamburgischen Kirche und des Reiches* (Darmstadt, 1961); anno 1066, pp. 680–682; Heinz Wolter, *Die Synoden im Reichsgebiet und in Reichsitalien von 916–1056* (Paderborn, 1988), pp. 378–382; Georg Gresser, *Clemens II.: Der erste deutsche Reformpapst* (Paderborn, etc., 2007), pp. 36–39.

he was deposed.[10] After being imprisoned, he was sent to Germany accompanied by Hildebrand, his chaplain and most probability his nephew, and placed in the custody of Archbishop Hermann of Cologne. Many years later in 1080 Hildebrand as Gregory VII testified that he had escorted Gregory VI [to Germany] only unwillingly, but whether he actually felt that way in 1046 is open to question.[11] In Sutri Henry also deposed Benedict IX and Silvester III.

## Clement II

The day after he arrived in Rome on December 23, 1046, Henry held a synod. The main issue was to elect a pope, but a niggling hurdle remained. Gregory VI had persuaded the Roman populace to take an oath that they would not elect another pope as long as he lived, but the oath seems to have been overlooked.[12] Besides the participants who had been present at Sutri, Roman clergy and laymen as well as Boniface, the margrave of Tuscany, attended.[13]

Who was this Margrave Boniface, whose presence was emphasized? Originally he had been the strongest ally of Conrad II in Italy, and even though his relationship with Henry III was more adversarial, he continued to be one of the most influential men of his time.[14] By taking over the Duchy of Tuscany, presumably in 1027, he became the most powerful prince between the middle Po and the northern boundary of the Roman Duchy. In 1037 he married Beatrice, the daughter of Duke Frederick II of Upper Lotharingia, and of their three children, their daughter, Matilda, survived. While Boniface was hated by his underlings for treating them so harshly, and he was reviled for defending Benedict IX, his wife and daughter would become fervent supporters of the international papacy championed by Hildebrand/Gregory VII.

---

[10] Gresser, *Clemens II.*, p. 44.

[11] *Das Register Gregors VII*, 2 vols., ed. Erich Caspar, (Berlin, 1920–1923, 3rd, ed., 1967), 2.2, p. 483: "…invitus ultra montes cum domno papa Gregorio abii."

[12] Bonizo, *Ad Amicum*, p. 586: "Sacramento enim [populum] prestrinxerat prefatus Iohannes numquam se vivente eos alium laudaturos pontificem."

[13] Benzo, *Ad Heinricum*, 7.2, p. 586: "Interfuit de universis gradibus tota nobilitas Romanorum circumstantibus ducibus diversarumque dignitatum proceribus, inter quos etiam marchio Bonefatius."

[14] Elka Goez, *Beatrix von Canossa und Tuszien. Eine Untersuchung zur Geschichte des 11. Jahrhunderts*; Vorträge und Forschungen Sonderband 41 (Sigmaringen 1995) pp. 13–20.

The council nominated the reformer, Bishop Suidiger of Bamberg, as pope. Long a member of the royal chapel he was opposed by the Romans as a foreigner. Bonizo and Desiderius, a monk at Montecassino, who became abbot in 1058, and pope as Victor III in 1087, asserted that the council designated him only because there were no suitable candidates within the Roman church.[15] The Chronicle of Montecassino stated that it was more a matter of necessity than of canonicity.[16] A modern biographer of Clement II concludes that Henry did not appoint him, but that the German influence on his election was over-whelming.[17] Named after the successor of St. Peter, Clement II presumably was enthroned immediately after his election on December 24, and consecrated the next day.

Given his dedication to Henry III, Benzo presents a detailed description of the whole process.[18] He reports that wishing to receive his consecration in Rome, Henry heard about the "three devils" that had usurped the apostolic see. On his way to Rome he deposed them in a synod at Sutri, and presided over a council at St. Peter's the next day. Those present included bishops, the whole Roman nobility in all its ranks, dukes and princes, and the powerful margrave, Boniface.

The king arose and said: "Roman lords, hitherto you have been allowed to make a wise or a foolish election, choosing whomsoever you wished in whatever way you pleased: Behold! Let your election be made in the customary manner; take whom you will from this whole assembly."[19] With a single spirit they replied: "When the royal majesty is present, the election is no longer in our jurisdiction or according to our will. And if you happen to be absent on a number of occasions, nevertheless you always participate in the elevation of a pope through

---

[15] Bonizo, *Ad Amicum*, p. 586: "Intereat cum non habuerent de propria diocese... languescente capite in tantum languida erant cetera membra, ut in tanta aecclesia vix unus posset reperiri, qui non vel illiterates vel symoniacus vel esset concubinatus—hac necessitate eligunt sibi Socherum Pabenbariensem episcopum." *Chron. Mont.*, p. 322: "Facta itaque discussione, quisnam in eadem ecclesia dignus tanto sacerdotio habere-tur, cum nullus heu pro dolor reperiri valeret—omnes enim exemplo miseri capitis preter cetera vitia tum precipue fornicationis ac symonie peste languebant..." *Annales Romani, Lib. Pont.* 2:331–350 at 331–332; Gresser, *Clemens II.*, pp. 39–47 at 47 & n. 193; Wolter, *Die Synoden im Reichsgebeit und in Reichsitalien*, pp. 386–390.

[16] *Chron. Mont.*, p. 322: "...demum electione necessaria potius quam canonica Babenbergensis episcopus papa Romanus levatur, eique Clemens nomen imponitur."

[17] Gresser, *Clemens II.*, pp. 52–55.

[18] Benzo, *Ad Heinricum*, 7.2, pp. 586–590; tr. Robinson, *The Papal Reform of the Eleventh Century*, pp. 367–368.

[19] Ibid., 586; tr. Robinson, *The Papal Reform of the Eleventh Century*, p. 368.

the office of the patrician, who is your deputy. For the patrician is not the patrician of the pope but rather the patrician of the emperor, to attend to the affairs of the *res publica*. We confess, therefore, that we have gone astray, and, less than wise, we have enthroned fools and ignorant men. It belongs to your imperial power to improve the *res publica* with laws, adorn it with morals, and control this holy apostolic church with your defending arm, so that it suffers no harm."

They then took counsel, Benzo continues, and with the approval of the holy synod and the commendation of the senators, the other Roman citizens, and the multitudes of nobles and people, it was decreed that King Henry and his successors in the imperial monarchy should become the *patricius* just as they had read had happened with Charles (Charlemagne). Immediately the clerics and laymen raised a shout to heaven praising God. The king was then clad in a bright green mantle, invested with the ring of the *patricius*, and crowned with the golden circlet of that office. Then all of the people on bended knee requested that he elect according to God's will and after careful investigation such pontiffs whose teaching would purge the pestilential sickness of the Church and recall the feeble world to salvation.

At the king's command they rose and sang the holy litany, and then the king took the bishop of Bamberg with his powerful right hand and caused him to sit on the apostolic seat. They all saluted according to custom, and the synod ended. On the day of the Lord's Nativity the pope was consecrated and King Henry was anointed by his hands with the oil of the Holy Spirit and raised to the empire (December 25, 1046). The pope was called Clement since he was good and kind, and pleasing to God and men.

Although Benzo's accounts of situations concerning the emperor and the papacy are frequently discounted because they are so tendentious, they are almost always the most detailed. Among the inferences of this account are that there was no opposition to Henry's deposition of the three popes, and that Henry had not objected to the Romans' practice of electing popes. It was not he, but the participants who interjected that when he was present, he had the authority to nominate the pope. When he was not present, they said that he could act through his *patricius*, whom he, not the pope, had appointed.

Why according to Benzo's account they named him the *patricius* is mysterious since the synod had affirmed that if he were present, he already had the authority to elect the pope without it. If he were not, there was a second person, his *patricius*, who would represent him.

If he united both titles in his person, there would be no other person to represent him if he could not be present. Probably Benzo was not thinking through the logical implications, but understood that the patriciate with its ornate symbols gave the emperor a kind of legitimacy that was demanded in contentious cases. It is noteworthy that the next time that the Romans granted him these symbols it was in another contentious case, the schism of 1061.

It was necessary that the emperor have the authority to nominate the pope before he was crowned, because there had to be a pope to perform the coronation. If Henry were crowned before he received the symbols of the patriciate, it would seem as though he were justifying after the fact acts that were seen by many as springing from gigantic arrogance.[20] By emphasizing the presence of the margrave, Boniface, Benzo shows that the most powerful figure between Rome and Lombardy was in accord with the proceedings.

Other sources describe the procedures somewhat differently. Relying on a forgery seemingly produced about 1080 at the time of the schism of Clement III and Gregory VII the *Annales Romani* report that Henry crowned himself with the circlet with which Romans since ancient times had crowned their patricians.[21] Bonizo stated that even though the canons forbid that anyone can be elected pope who has not been ordained priest or deacon of that church, Bishop Suidiger was elected because of the emergency.[22] But citing Innocent I, Bonizo said that once the emergency was over the practice should cease, and it had not. He noted that Clement II was the first in a series of popes to be consecrated elsewhere.

Bonizo complained that after Henry had been crowned, he freed the city from the tyranny of the patricians only to seize that very same tyranny. He surmised that what motivated Henry was the authority to appoint the pope, and then rebutted all of the arguments that purported to support such an authority. Between the time that Henry was granted the patriciate and the time that Bonizo was writing, the power had become contentious, and he may have been speaking more of future situations than of the circumstances of 1046.[23] A contemporary view is that as the *patricius* Henry was the first citizen of Rome and the

---

[20] Weinfurter, *Canossa*, pp. 40–41.
[21] *Annales Romani, Lib. Pont.* 2:332; see also *Chron. Mont.*, p. 322.
[22] Bonizo, *Ad Amicum*, p. 586.
[23] Ibid.

voice of the people. As such he could exercise authority over papal elections and predominant influence over the nobility, powers that had been in abeyance since 1012 under the Tusculan popes.[24]

A second synod was summoned a few days later, probably on January 4–5, 1047. The emperor and the pope shared the presidency of the council, which dealt largely with issues of the reform, especially with simony.[25] Many subsequent synods would wrestle with the same problems. It was during Clement's reign that Petrus Damiani came on the scene, and became fervently active in the reform movement.[26] Although he attended both the synod of Sutri and that of Rome, and presented a cogent argument through the royal advocate that the emperor held decisive authority over the election of popes, he was bitterly disappointed in Clement.[27]

At the end of April 1047 he wrote to Clement, informing him of the emperor's request to bring the miserable situation in the Marche to his attention. In the course of his letter he expresses his disillusionment that his hopes that Clement would bring about reform had been dashed:[28] "…and the bishop of Osimo also involved in so many and such unprecedented crimes, and others deserving of condemnation for similar guilt, now returning from your court with such gloating arrogance, my joyous hope is forcibly changed to grief. I indeed had hoped that you were about to set Israel free."[29]

After the synod Clement left Rome with Henry for Salerno and points south, and never returned. After they split up, Henry returned to Germany, and Clement wended his way north. At the latest on September 24, 1047, he became violently ill at the abbey of San Tommaso in Foglia near Pesaro on the Adriatic coast.[30] On his deathbed he uttered a message to Henry, granting him his ring to wear on his right hand in memory of him.[31] The ring was a symbol of the marriage of the

---

[24] Cowdrey, *Gregory VII*, p. 23.

[25] Gresser, *Clemens II.*, pp. 58–64.

[26] Ibid., 95–98.

[27] Petrus Damiani, *Briefe*, nr. 89, 2:547: "…in electione semper ordinandi pontificis principatum." tr. Blum, 3:342.

[28] Ibid., nr. 26, 1:239–242; tr. Blum, 1:244–246.

[29] Blum 1:246.

[30] Gresser, *Clemens II.*, pp. 103–108.

[31] Ibid., 190–191, Anhang A + 18: "Clemens episcopus, servus servorum Dei, dilectissimo prius domino, inde filio, nunc vero nec filio iam nec domino H(einrico), invictissimo imperatori prepotentissimo augusto novissimam apostolice bendictionis salutem. Anulum digiti mei digito tuo devovi, ut quotiens illum videris, Clementis

bishop to the Church, but since the reign of Henry it was also the insignia which the king gave to the bishop along with the pastoral staff during investitures, and which raised a fire storm among the reformers. Clement's intention probably was only to give the emperor something to remember him by, not to authorize the king to use spiritual symbols in investitures.

By October 9, 1047, the blond-headed pope from the North was dead from acute lead poisoning, most likely administered by one of his opponents.[32] Boniface IX, who tried to make a comeback, could well have been the villain. Clement II's biographer, Georg Gresser, considers him to be the first reform pope, the papal historian, Lino Ghiardini, considers him to be little more than an imperial chaplain, and the supporters of Benedict IX perceived him as an antipope.[33] A foot note in the *Annuario Pontificio* written in the third administration of Benedict IX attests that the depositions of Benedict were not legitimate, and that both Gregory VI and Clement II were antipopes.[34] There was virtually no canon law to decide the issue, and the fact that the Church recognized Clement II as pope may have been the deciding factor. At least an argument could be made from Henry III's authority as *patricius*.

At this point, the papacy fell apart. Henry III consulted Wazo of Liège, who replied that while another pope still lived—Wazo may have had in mind Gregory VI or Benedict IX—the emperor had no authority to fill an alleged vacancy. The pope, he asserted, could be judged by no man, but by God alone, a principle that Gregory VII will tenaciously uphold.[35] More stridently, the putatively French author of the tract, *De ordinando pontifice*, written between December 1047 and January 1048, branded Henry III as an emperor *nequissimus*, who acted against canonical authority by designating popes. The election of popes, the author asserted, should be transacted by the clergy supported by the people. According to the author, Benedict IX, Gregory VI and Clement II, the shadow pope created to sanction Henry's incestuous marriage,

---

recorderis. Illius enim mens sollicitudinis pregravata ab eius non cadet memoria, cuius anulum fers in dextra."

[32] Ibid., 108–114; Gresser, who has exhaustively examined the literary and chemical evidence of poisoning, points to the examination of his corpse buried in Bamberg that indicated that he died from massive lead poisoning.

[33] Ghiarardini, *L'antipapa Cadalo*, pp. 18–20.

[34] Gresser, *Clemens II.*, p. 154 & n. 374.

[35] Anselm of Liège, *Gesta episcoporum Leodiensium*, MGH SS 7:189–234 at 228.

were all illegal.[36] Besides denying Henry III's authority to choose
the pope, he also drew attention to the international character of the
papacy, and implicitly challenged the Romans' unfettered right to elect
their bishop.[37]

## Damasus II

Be that as it may, after the death of Clement II the Tusculani reasserted
their power in Rome, and with the secret support of Margrave Boniface
of Canossa and Tuscany, they reinstated Boniface IX.[38] Not all Romans
supported this tenacious relic, and on Christmas Day of 1047 a delegation of Romans arrived in Saxony to meet the emperor to request that
he create a successor to Clement II. Henry received them in his palace
with great honor, and then called a council of the most distinguished
religious and secular leaders. The Roman delegation wanted Archbishop
Halinard of Lyons, who spoke Italian and was popular in Rome, but in
January 1048 the council, together with God, and "according to the
decrees of the holy fathers," elected a Bavarian, Bishop Poppo of Brixen
(Bressanone), as Damasus II. For Henry, who faced competition for
control of Northern Italy from Margrave Boniface, a pope from the
Tyrol may have been strategic.

When Damasus encountered Margrave Boniface on his way to
Rome, he requested that Boniface accompany him, but Boniface
declined, stating that the Romans had reinstated Benedict IX, and also
that he was too old for such a trip. Damasus returned to Henry III to
relate these excuses, and perceiving Boniface's support of Benedict IX
as a challenge to his own authority, Henry forced him to escort the new
pope to Rome. After Benedict IX refused to step aside, Boniface had an
associate in Rome throw him out, and on July 17, 1048, Damasus was
consecrated. Reigning only 23 days, and like Clement II, probably poisoned, on August 9 he died in Palestrina just outside of Rome. If he was
poisoned, the most likely perpetrator would have been a supporter of
Benedict IX, or someone instigated by Margrave Boniface.

Short though the reign of Damasus II may have been, his election
was ground breaking as the first election since Henry III had been

---

[36] *De ordinando pontifice*, pp. 75–83 of H.H. Anton, *Der sogenannte Traktat 'De ordinando pontifice'* (Bonn, 1982).
[37] Cowdrey, *Gregory VII*, pp. 24–25.
[38] *Annales Romani, Lib. Pont.* 2:332–333; Schmidt, *Alexander II.*, pp. 70–71.

granted the symbols of the patriciate. The election of Benedict IX was a throwback to elections carried out by the Roman nobility, but obviously the nobility was split, and one faction traveled to the emperor to request that he intervene. It is significant that in the case of Clement II it was Henry III who took the initiative. In the case of Damasus II it was the Romans.

But Henry made his own selection, and it is not surprising that Bonizo was scathing in his criticism. He charged that acting under the tyranny of the patriciate, Henry appointed a certain bishop, a man filled with *superbia*, who became Damasus II.[39] His enemies treated this man who had invaded the apostolic see in their customary way—viz., they poisoned him—and his tenure in office was brief in the extreme. Thus far Henry's efforts to reform the papacy had fallen on fallow ground.

As the power of the house of Lotharingia/Canossa exemplifies, ecclesiastical reform was far from the only focus of the reformers. They had to deal with the challenge that Margrave Boniface posed to the emperor and the papacy, and they had to adjust to the influx of other powers. While Henry III was still alive he struggled mightily to keep the Kingdom of Italy under his authority, but the weak regency that followed his early death in 1056 would be unable to mount much of a defense.

In the South the Normans, at first recruited to help local powers in their conflicts with one another, became virtual invaders. The popes had to decide whether to deal with them as ruthless savages, or as a powerful force added to the already rich brew of Lombards, Greeks, Latins and Muslims. The inroads of the Normans intensified the competition between the Roman and Byzantine Empires for authority, and their Churches for universality. Both the popes and those who claimed to be popes tried to manipulate the movements in the South and those between the emperor and the house of Lotharingia/Canossa to their advantage. The short reigns of Clement II and Damasus II did not make a dent in all of this.

---

[39] Watterich, 1:78–79; *Ex Bonizonis episcopi Sutriensis ad Amicum* Libro V: "Mortuo interea Clemente Romano pontifice, Romani ad imperatorem tendunt, rogantes, dari sibi Pontificem. Qui et consensit. Nam patritiali tyrannide dedit eis ex latere suo quemdam episcopum, virum omni superiba plenum, mandans inclyto duci Bonifacio, ut eum Romam duceret et ex parte sua inthronizaret. tr. Robinson, *The Papal Reform of the Eleventh Century*, p. 189; Walter Berschin, *Bonizo von Sutri: Leben und Werk* (Berlin, 1972).

CHAPTER THREE

# LEO IX (1049–1054), THE NORMANS AND THE BYZANTINES

It is generally agreed that papal reform really began with Leo IX. Like his two predecessors he was chosen by the emperor, but no insipient opponents cut off his reign, and he survived for five very eventful years. He never relinquished his fidelity to the emperor, but he also acted aggressively as pope. Since his reign overlapped with the influx of the Normans in Southern Italy and the concomitant threat to the Greek settlements still attached to the Byzantine Empire, he became involved in politics and military action at the highest level. His great asset was the ability to offer spiritual rewards in return for services rendered. Although not always successful, under his leadership the papacy became a dynamic, if morally ambiguous force.

## *The Election of Bishop Bruno of Toul*

Following the untimely death of Damasus II an embassy of Romans made its way to the emperor to select a successor, but given the fate of Clement II and Damasus II, no German bishop wanted to take a chance on assuming the hazards of the papacy. After several months and much consternation, the emperor looked to Lotharingia and to his cousin, Bishop Bruno of Toul. In November 1048 he gathered together a council of religious men along with the Roman delegation at Worms to implore Bruno to accept their nomination as pope.

The anonymous author of the *Vita Leonis IX* depicts Bruno as a very pious man, who frequently wept and was anything but worldly.[1] Amatus of Montecassino, who wrote a *History of the Normans* after 1078 that ended in the middle of the reign of Gregory VII, provides color and detail in his account. Amatus says that he was very handsome with red hair and a lordly stature. He was a master of letters, and was beloved by the emperor as well as by the whole Roman Church.

---

[1] Watterich, 1:127–170; tr. Robinson, *The Papal Reform of the Eleventh Century*, pp. 97–157; intro., pp. 17–26 for the author.

He came to Rome as a pilgrim, and following his consecration as pope, he waged war against the perversity of Simon, that is, against simony.[2]

Bruno of Segni, a cardinal bishop from the 1080s, and abbot of Montecassino from 1107 to 1111, contrasted Bruno of Toul's virtues with the corrupt world and the church, including the papacy.[3] He said that Bruno reluctantly agreed to accept the nomination only on the condition that he be elected by the Roman clergy and people.[4] It is open to question whether the candidate insisted on an election in Rome to comply with canonical requirements or whether he was simply shrewd enough to curry favor with the Romans so that he too would not die a mysterious death after a very brief reign. Although he never questioned the emperor's right in papal elections, he might not have wanted to be branded exclusively as the imperial candidate. Bruno of Segni's opinion is significant because he speaks for the position of the reformers on papal elections, perhaps not in 1049, but at the time that he was writing.

After his election in Worms Bruno set the tone by traveling to Rome in humble clothing without an imperial guard, but accompanied by a new wave of what were to become influential reformers. They included Hildebrand, who had accompanied Gregory VI to Germany, Udo of Toul, Azolin of Compiegne, Humbert of Moyenmoutier, Frederick of Lotharingia, Archbishop Halinard of Lyons, and Hugo Candidus of Remiremont.[5] Frederick was the closest member of his inner circle, and in 1057 he will succeed Victor II as Stephen IX. Hugo Candidus was the least constant of Leo's attendants, and will change his allegiance more than once during the schisms of Alexander II/Honorius II and Gregory VII/Clement III.

The Romans were captivated by the papal elect when he asked them to accept him as pope, and said that he would return to Germany if they did not. They organized a grand procession at the Porta Leonina, and on February 21, 1049, he was ordained as Leo IX.[6] When he took

---

[2] Amatus of Montecassino, *The History of the Normans*, tr. Prescott N. Dunbar; revised with introduction and notes by Graham A. Loud (Woodbridge, Eng. & Rochester NY, 2004), III, 15, p. 91.

[3] Brunonis episcopi Signiensis vita sancti Leonis PP. IX., Watterich, 1:96.

[4] Ibid.: "Ego, inquit, Romam vado, ibique si clerus et populus sua sponte me sibi in Pontificem elegerit, faciam quod rogatis; aliter electionem nullam suscipio."

[5] *Lib. Pont.* 2:275; ibid., *Annales Romani,* 2:333; Goez, *Kirchenreform und Investiturstreit*, p. 96.

[6] Ghiararardini, *L'antipapa Cadalo*, p. 20.

over the papacy its finances were in a desperate state.[7] There were no revenues or sustenance until he became world renowned, and gifts started pouring in.

He initiated many reforms, and summoned councils which forbade simony and nicholaitism—priestly marriage—and decreed that only the clergy and the people can elect bishops. Amatus said that he had common sense, and that "like the good gardener who straightens the newly planted flower when it falls to keep it from perishing, [Leo] bore upon his shoulders the weight of the sinners and shared the burden so that it might not break the back of the person who carried it."[8]

Leo promoted Hildebrand to subdeacon, and deposed bishops, abbots and cardinals who did not rise to the mark, replacing them with those who did.[9] In 1051 he appointed Frederick of Lotharingia bibliotecarius and chancellor, and from then on, Frederick was at his side if he was not on an assignment. Setting a trend, Leo spent little time in Rome, and much time in the North and in the South. Amatus said that Leo went to Melfi to oppose the acts of the most mighty Normans, and begged them to abandon their cruelty and injuries to the poor.[10] Thereafter he returned to Rome.

### The Normans

After attending to affairs there, Leo set out for Apulia to restore the Christian religion, which seemed to him almost to have perished in that land, and to establish harmony between the native inhabitants and the Norman invaders. Southern Italy straddled the borders of the Latin-Christian West, the Greek-Christian Byzantine East, and the Arab-Islamic North Africa and Spain.[11] In the eleventh century Calabria and Apulia were controlled by the Byzantine Empire, the Lombard principalities of Salerno, Capua and Benevento were virtually independent, and Sicily was divided among Muslim potentates. Originally the

---

[7] *The Life of Pope Leo IX*, II, 8, tr. Robinson, *The Papal Reform of the Eleventh Century*, p. 134.
[8] Amatus, *History of the Normans*, III, 15, p. 91.
[9] Bonizo, *Ad Amicum*, p. 588; Watterich, 1:103–104; Robinson, *The Papal Reform of the Eleventh Century*, pp. 190–192.
[10] Amatus, *History of the Normans*, III, 16, p. 91.
[11] Hiroshi Takayama, "Law and Monarchy in the South," pp. 58–81 of *Italy in the Central Middle Ages*, ed. David Abulafia (Oxford, 2004) at p. 59.

Normans worked as mercenaries for the Lombards and Byzantines, but by the middle of the eleventh century they were a force in their own right.

Leo acknowledged that they had originally been welcomed to fight against foreign peoples [Saracens], but who, according to his biographer and others, had become savage tyrants and ravagers of their homeland.[12] Even Amatus, whose heroes were Prince Richard of Capua and Duke Robert Guiscard of Apulia, acknowledged that they were brutally cruel. Of Robert Guiscard during his early times in Southern Italy he said:

> Finally Robert returned to his brother and told him of his poverty, and what he said with his mouth was shown by his face, for he was very thin. But Drogo [his brother] turned his face away as did everyone in his house. Robert returned to his fortress, passing through those areas where he hoped to find bread. Wherever it pleased him, he kept plundering the land. Now he did openly what before he had done in secret. He took the plough ox, the mare which gave good colts, ˙˙˙ ten fat pigs, and thirty sheep. And for all these things he received only thirty bezants. Moreover, Robert began to seize men whom he ransomed for bread and wine, and still he was not satisfied.[13]

On his way to Apulia, Leo stopped at Benevento on July 5, 1051, and remained there until August 8. In the early 1050s the Beneventans expelled the Lombard prince [Pandulf III] after Leo had visited the city, and chose the pope as their sovereign.[14] Based upon broadly interpreted interpretations of the donations of Charlemagne, Louis the Pious, Otto I, and Henry II, Leo accepted the invitation, and asked Henry III to confirm his authority. Since Leo represented the emperor, from 1051–1054 Benevento effectively functioned as a papal/imperial protectorate.[15] The occupation put him on a collision course with the Normans of Melfi, who were trying to create a principality at the expense of the Lombards and the Byzantine Empire.[16]

---

[12] *The Life of Pope Leo IX*, II, 14, tr. Robinson, *The Papal Reform of the Eleventh Century*, p. 141; Hermann of Reichenau, *Chronicon*, 1053, MGH SS 5:132.

[13] Amatus, *History of the Normans*, III, 9, p. 89.

[14] Ibid., III, 17, n. 24, p. 92; Robinson gives the dates as May-June, 1053; *The Life of Pope Leo IX*, 20, p. 149, n. 309.

[15] *The Life of Pope Leo IX*, II, 14, tr. Robinson, *The Papal Reform of the Eleventh Century*, p. 141; Loud, "The Papacy and the Rulers of Southern Italy, 1058–1198," p. 155.

[16] *Lib. Pont.* 2:275, n. 4 by Louis Duchesne.

Prince Guaimar of Salerno was an ally of Leo and of Drogo, the brother of Robert Guiscard. Drogo, who had put himself and his troops at Guaimar's disposal, had been summoned at Leo's request to defend the city, and he promised to do so in return for remission from his sins. But when Drogo left Benevento followed by Leo and Prince Guaimar, the Normans attacked. When word of Drogo's broken promise reached Leo, he vowed to find a way to defend the city and to break the pride of the Normans.[17] Guaimar swore an oath defending Drogo as an honorable man, but soon thereafter Drogo was killed by his enemies. Both Guaimar and Leo mourned him, and in a combination of his spiritual authority and his political interests, Leo absolved him of his sins. Guaimar met with the Normans and made Drogo's brother, Humphrey, count.

Once Leo had departed from Benevento, Amatus said that he became eager for the ruin and dispersal of the Normans.[18] He sought the aid of Henry III, the king of France and others, promising them absolution from their sins and great gifts. Shades of the crusades: if you fight in my cause, I will grant you spiritual rewards. Frederick, Leo's chancellor, was the only one to respond. No admirer of Frederick, Amatus said that although Frederick did nothing about the others who lived there, he took steps against the malice of the Normans. The chancellor said that "Even if I had a hundred effeminate knights, I would fight against all the Norman knights." Men from Gaeta, Valva, the Marche, Marsia and other counties rallied to the cause, but like gentle sheep, Amatus said, they were sent against the mighty wolf.[19]

Unlike Frederick, Prince Guaimar of Salerno refused to consent to the destruction of the Normans, since he had hired them at great time and expense. To those who would go against the Normans he said: "You will find what you seek, O wretches, you will be meat for these devouring lions, for when they let you feel their claws, you will know what force and power are in them...." [20] Losing heart, the pope's army abandoned him.

After an elaborate campaign of plots and intrigue a conspiracy of Guaimar's relations and household murdered him and one of his brothers. Guido, another brother escaped, and threw himself on the

---

[17] Amatus, *History of the Normans*, III, 18, p. 92.
[18] Ibid., III, 23, p. 94.
[19] Ibid., III, 24, pp. 94–95.
[20] Ibid., III, 25, p. 95.

mercy of the Normans, who had gathered to await battle with the pope's knights.[21] The Normans did not weep for Guaimar, but captured Salerno to avenge the treachery of his relatives and closest companions. Guido selected Guaimar's son, Gisulf, as Guaimar's successor, and the Normans swore fealty to him. He, in turn, invested them with their lands. The traitors were released without retribution, but Normans faithful to Guaimar cut them all down.

When Leo learned of the death of Guaimar, who, Amatus emphasizes, had been aided by the Normans, he prepared to destroy the Normans. He had spent Christmas of 1052 with Henry III at Worms, and had complained about the violence of the Normans and the injuries that they had perpetrated by holding the property of St. Peter [Benevento] by force, and by the cruelty that they had inflicted on the Christians. Bonizo said that he first struck them with the sword of excommunication, and then concluded that they must be struck down by force. Although Henry lent a sympathetic ear, and promised him the help that he needed, his chancellor, Bishop Gebhard of Eichstätt, the future pope, Victor II, succeeded in getting Henry to withdraw his promise.[22] Leo recruited three hundred Germans on his own, and with the increased the size of his army, he advanced against the Normans.[23]

On June 18, 1053, battle was joined at Civitate, a battle that would become a potent symbol, for the pope was badly defeated, and the Normans emerged as the invincible rulers of the South by the will of God. Amatus said that the Normans had first sent emissaries offering peace and harmony, but that Frederick, Leo's chancellor threatened them with death if they did not flee.[24] The animus generated between Frederick and the Normans on this and previous occasions dogged him after he became pope as Stephen IX. The battle itself was a slaughter, and Amatus reports that even the inhabitants of Civitate seized the baggage of the pope and his men as well as the treasure of his chapel.[25] The Normans treated Leo graciously in defeat, and escorted him to Benevento, furnishing him with food and necessities. Ten months after the battle he was able to return to Rome, where he died on April 19, 1054.[26]

---

[21] Ibid., III, 18, 30, p. 97.

[22] Cowdrey, *The Age of Abbot Desiderius*, pp. 109–110.

[23] Amatus, *History of the Normans*, III, 37, & n. 55, p. 99; Hermann of Reichenau, *Chronicon*, MGH SS 5:132; Bonizo, *Liber ad Amicum*, p. 589.

[24] Ibid., III, 39, p. 100.

[25] Ibid., III, 40, p. 101.

[26] Ibid., III, 41, 42, p. 101.

## The Byzantine Empire

While in Benevento in January 1054 before he returned to Rome, Leo wrote to Michael Kerularios, the patriarch of Constantinople, and also a short letter to the Byzantine emperor, Constantine IX Monomachus (1042–55), describing what had happened.[27] He spoke of how the Normans had risen up against the churches of God with unheard of fury and with an ungodliness worse than that of the pagans. They slaughtered Christians everywhere and afflicted some of them with new and horrible tortures, even unto death. They spared neither child nor old men and women, and made no distinction between the sacred and the profane. They plundered and burnt the basilicas of the saints and tore them to the ground. Leo said that he rebuked and threatened them with divine and human punishment, but that they only became worse. Given this situation, Leo said that he had no other option than to raise a defensive force to bear witness to their iniquity.

During this time Leo told Monomachus that he had decided to seek counsel of your most faithful man, the duke and commander, Argyros, (the Byzantine governor or katapan of Southern Italy). But Leo said that while he was trying to break down the obstinacy of the Normans, they launched a sudden attack against our forces (at Civitate). Rather than the Normans' rejoicing in their victory, Leo said that they were grieving, for as a result of their presumption, they could expect even greater wrath to overtake them. He promised not to relinquish his intention of liberating Christendom, and not to desist until the church was at rest. This may have been putting a generous construction on the situation, for later the Normans would state that Leo had conceded that the Normans held the southern Italian lands and those that they would capture by *haereditali feudo* from St. Peter.[28]

Leo told Monomachus that he required help, and that daily he was expecting the arrival of the emperor. He urged the restoration of the patrimony of the Roman Church, and spoke of the arrogance of Michael, the patriarch of Constantinople, while commending his own legates. Thus, on the eve of dispatching a delegation to Constantinople

---

[27] JL 4322, 4333; *Vita Sancti Leonis*, Watterich 1:163–165; *The Life of Pope Leo IX*, II, 20, tr. Robinson, *The Papal Reform of the Eleventh Century*, pp. 149–150.

[28] Gaufredus Malaterra, *De rebus gestis Rogerii Calabriae et Siciliae comities et Roberti Guiscardi ducis fratris eius*, RIS 1.14, p. 15; Cowdrey, *The Age of Desiderius*, p. 110.

to discuss issues between the eastern and western churches with the patriarch of Constantinople, Leo viewed the Byzantine Empire as an ally against the Normans.[29] How could these negotiations have led to the beginning of a split between the two churches that exists until the present? And how could they have led to overtures from the Byzantine emperor to Cadalus/Honorius II in1062/1063, when Cadalus was not recognized as pope in the schism with Alexander II?

### The First Wedge Between Eastern and Western Churches

The proximate cause of the dispute went back to 1053 when the Byzantine patriarch, Michael Kerularios (1043–58) requested that Archbishop Leo of Ochrid denounce the "priesthood of the Franks and the reverend pope" for observing Jewish rites through their celebration of the Eucharist with azymes, the same kind of unleavened bread used for Passover.[30] Leo of Ochrid complied in a letter to Archbishop John of Trani, a province coexisting with Latin and Greek traditions that had been destabilized by the invasion of the Normans.[31] The letter was passed on to Humbert of Silva Candida, who translated it into Latin, and presented it to the pope. About the same time Leo IX and Humbert learned that the patriarch had anathematized all of those observing the Latin rite in Constantinople.[32]

A flurry of letters between the pope, the patriarch, and the Byzantine emperor, Constantine IX Monomachos, did not resolve the issues, which historians still dispute whether they were political or liturgical.[33] For example, Brett Whalen emphasizes the liturgical, while Axel Bayer stresses the political. Bayer says that in a time of weakness of the

---

[29] Peter Herde, "The Papacy and the Greek Church in Southern Italy between the Eleventh and Thirteenth Century," tr. Carine van Rhijn, Inge Lyse Hansen, G.A. Loud, and A. Metcalfe in *The Society of Norman Italy*, ed. G.A. Loud & A. Metcalfe, pp. 213–251 (Leiden, 2002); n. 1, p. 213 for earlier versions. Herde, pp. 216–217, sees the breach between the eastern and western churches of 1054 as overrated by modern historians.

[30] Brett Whalen, "Rethinking the Schism of 1054: Authority, heresy, and the Latin Rite," *Traditio* 62 (2007), 1–24, at p. 1; Axel Bayer, *Spaltung der Christenheit. Das sogenannte Morgenländische Schisma von 1054.* (Beihefte zum Archiv für Kulturgeschichte 53), Cologne, 2004.

[31] Ibid., n. 1.

[32] Cornelius Will, ed. *Acta et scripta quae de controversis ecclesiae Graecae et Latinae seculo undecimo compositat extant* (Leipzig, 1861), pp. 56–64.

[33] Whalen, "Rethinking the Schism of 1054," pp. 2–3, and ns. 7–10.

Byzantine Empire—1025-1081—a strong ecclesiastical consciousness developed that led to a considerable increase of power against the state. He concludes that the Eastern schism was not in the first line ecclesiastic or religious, but rather the working out of political rivalries.[34]

Whalen, by contrast, thinks that it is not fortuitous that the disputes erupted during the beginning of the ecclesiastic reform movement in Western Europe. He notes that scholars use the label of reform as shorthand for a sweeping effort by the papacy and its supporters to separate the laity from the clergy, to purify the priesthood of perceived pollution, and firmly to establish the primacy of Rome over the offices, doctrine, and sacraments of the universal church. This veritable revolution of the world order had a critical impact on the development of Latin Christendom, envisioned as a coherent community of believers tied together by its common rite, common sacred language, and common sense of obedience to Rome.[35]

Whalen observes that by accusing Rome and its Latin followers of religious error, the Greek patriarch and his partisans stepped over the line of orthodoxy at the same moment that it was being redrawn and fortified by the advocates of a new order in Christendom. From the perspective of the papacy and its supporters, he argues, notions of papal primacy, orthodox doctrine, and the proper form of the Christian rite mutually reinforced each other. Whalen rightly comprehends that power, belief, and discipline were interwoven threads, and that if you pulled on one, the entire tapestry might unravel.[36]

He believes that the emphasis on papal primacy, a cornerstone of the program to liberate the church from lay power and pollution, generated a heightened level of institutional and juridical antagonism between Rome and Constantinople. Here, he may have been looking backwards, for it wasn't until the papal electoral decree of 1059 and the papacy of Gregory VII that there was a deliberate attempt to liberate the church from lay power. Leo IX was nominated by Henry III, and relied upon him throughout his reign. Leo's dispute was not with the Byzantine emperor, but rather with the patriarch. Certainly he would not tolerate criticism of Roman sacraments or the refusal to acknowledge papal primacy, but he wanted the cooperation of the Byzantine emperor in his opposition to the Normans. Most probably Kerularios wanted the

---

[34] Bayer, *Spaltung der Christenheit*, p. 209.
[35] Whalen, "Rethinking the Schism of 1054," p. 4 & n. 11.
[36] Ibid., 5.

church in South Italy with its Byzantine heritage to be under the aegis of the eastern patriarchal authority.[37]

A controversy over the Eucharist in the West coincided with the charges of Kerularios. The views of Berengar of Tours, who emphasized the symbolic nature of the bread and wine, were condemned in Tours in 1054. The charges of Kerularios were quite different, but Berengar may have initiated a sensitivity to the interpretation of the Eucharist in the West. Contemporary Latin accounts viewed the Greek charge against the use of azymes as central, not peripheral, to the confrontation with the Greek patriarch.[38] For example, the author of the Vita of Leo, who was hardly enmeshed in Greek theology, said: "At that time there arose the heresy of the *fermentacei*, which poured scorn on *the holy Roman see*, or *rather the whole Latin and western Church*, for offering a living sacrifice to God in unleavened bread."[39]

The anonymous author continued to describe the controversy in emotive language, contending that the charges of Kerularios attacked the very essence of the Western Church. He avowed that Michael [Kerularios] and Leo of Ochrida had "set down this *slander* in written form, *willfully breathing out pestilential vapours against the holy and apostolic* faith. He said that this slander was an affront to all of the Latins, and that after Humbert of Silva Candida had translated it into Latin, the pope composed a *Libellus* to counter their charges. When they did not accept the correction he anathematized them.[40]

Leo saw the letter of Leo of Ochrida to Archbishop John of Trani as an attack on papal primacy, and the *Libellus* that he wrote from Benevento to Kerularios and Leo of Ochrida in January 1054 forcefully asserts papal prerogatives and secular dignities.[41] The *Libellus* validates Rome's primacy by associating the see with Constantine I (306–37),

---

[37] Dieter Hägermann, *Das Papsttum am Vorabend des Investiturstreits: Stephan IX. (1057–1058), Benedikt X. (1058), und Nikolaus II. (1058–1061)*, vol. 36 of Päpste und Papsttum (Stuttgart, 2008), p. 17.

[38] Whalen, "Rethinking the Schism of 1054," p. 9.

[39] Watterich, 1:161; tr. Robinson, *The Papal Reform of the Eleventh Century*, p. 146, & n. 282.

[40] Ibid.; tr. Robinson, *The Papal Reform of the Eleventh Century*, pp. 146–147, & n. 290; we shall see that the delegation that Leo sent to Constantinople excommunicated them on July 16, 1054.

[41] JL 4332; Will, ed., *Acta et scripta*, pp. 65–85; *Pontificia commissio ad redigendum codicem iuris canonici orientalis, Fontes*, series III, 4 vols. (1043–1054); 1:780–782, nrs. 371–372 (PL 143:744–769); Whalen, "Rethinking the Schism of 1054," pp. 10–14; Cowdrey, "Eleventh-Century Reformers' Views of Constantine," pp. 75–78.

and the Donation of Constantine, the eighth or early ninth forgery confirming Rome's primacy over the other major sees of the ancient world including Constantinople.[42] Probably baring the hand of Humbert, and appropriate for the goals of those reformers marching in the steps of Hildebrand, it granted the rule of the West to the bishop of Rome. Leo's *Libellus* also defended the Roman rite through the primacy of St. Peter, the rock on which the church was built, who guaranteed Roman orthodoxy against those who would attack it.

The *Libellus* not only defended, but also attacked, accusing Constantinople of being a seedbed of heresies. Leo said that the current attack by the Greek patriarch fit into a pattern of abuse. Like a daughter, who has rejected her mother, Constantinople has exhibited a history of arrogance and rebellion against the Roman church. Leo concluded that the Greek charge against azymes or unleavened bread was part of its heresy. But while he held that the papacy and the Roman Church are without error, those who strived for unity in the Eastern Church held a parallel position for the patriarch of Constantinople and the Eastern Church. Similarly to what the reform popes in the West were trying to do, the Greek Church was striving to enforce unity and uniformity, and their conflicting views of primacy clashed.[43]

In spite of theological differences, in 1053 Leo was still interested in forming an alliance with the Byzantine Empire against the Normans. Archbishop John of Trani, Argyros and Patriarch Dominikus Marango of Grado left on a mission to Constantinople to convince Kerularios of the necessity of an anti-Norman alliance with the pope. A joint letter from Kerularios and Constantine IX proposed such a military alliance joined by Henry III, but the unwillingness of Kerularios to relinquish his position on the azyme controversy shattered any possible alliance.

In response to the two letters from Constantinople, in 1054, probably in the middle of March, Leo dispatched a legation to Constantinople consisting of his chancellor, Frederick of Lotharingia, Humbert of Silva Candida, and Archbishop Peter of Amalfi, an agile politician, who had seized power from the pro Byzantine party.[44] The legates were aptly

---

[42] H.—G. Krause, "Das Constitutum Constantini im Schisma vom 1054," *Aus Kirche und Reich: Studien zu Theologie, Politik und Recht im Mittelalter; Festschrift Kriedrich Kempf*, ed. H. Mordek (Sigmaringen, 1983), 131–158.

[43] Bayer, *Spaltung der Christenheit*, p. 65; Bayer, p. 73, says that the letter was not sent.

[44] *Chron.Mont*, 85, p. 333; Bayer, *Spaltung der Christenheit*, p. 80.

chosen, for Humbert had written a response to the attack of Michael Kerularios and Leo of Ochrida. Frederick was Leo's advisor in his confrontation with the Normans, and Archbishop Peter of Amalfi may have held views similar to other writers from Amalfi critical of the Greek position.

The legates carried Leo's letter to Constantine written in January 1054, and while they were there, additional issues of religious contention between the two parties were raised. They included their different positions on clerical marriage, and their dispute over the *filioque* according to which the Latin doctrine held that the Holy Spirit proceeds from the Father and from the Son, not just from the Father alone.[45] The dispute over the azymes remained front and center, and was scrutinized in the *Dialogi* written shortly before or during the legation to Constantinople.[46] The Romans viewed the attacks of Kerularios and Leo of Ochrida on the papacy as none worse, and perceived them as creations of the devil. The Greeks in turn did not refer to the question of Roman primacy, and left the impression that they were hardly aware of the claims of the reformers. In a further aggressive move Kerularios convinced Petros of Antioch to reject an alliance with the Latins.[47]

Kerularios rejected the Latins' demands out of hand, and refused to meet with the delegation. On July 16, 1054 the legates went to Santa Sophia and complained about his obstinacy, and when the clergy had prepared for mass, they placed a document of excommunication against Kerularios and his supporters in the name of the pope on the altar before the eyes of the clergy and the people, and immediately departed.[48] Leo's anonymous biographer reports that they then put the Latin churches in Constantinople in order, and pronounced anathema on all who thereafter received communion from the hands of a Greek who disparaged the Roman rite. On July 18 with the leave of Constantine Monomachus, from whom they had received the kiss of peace,

---

[45] Whalen, "Rethinking the Schism of 1054," p. 17.

[46] Ibid., 13; *Acta et scripta*, ed. Will, pp. 93–126; Bayer, *Spaltung der Christenheit*, p. 86.

[47] Bayer, *Spaltung der Christenheit*, p. 96.

[48] *Excommunicatio qua feriuntur Michael Caerularius*, ed. Will, *Acta et scripta*, pp. 153–154: "Quicunque fidei sanctae Romanae et apostolicae sedis ejusque sacrificio pertinaciter contradixerit, sit anathema, Maranatha, nec habeatur Christianus catholicus, sed prozymita haereticus, fiat, fiat, fiat." Bonizo, *Ad Amicum*, Watterich, 1:104; Robinson, "Bonizo to a friend," *The Papal Reform of the Eleventh Century*, p. 192; Whalen, "Rethinking the Schism of 1054," p. 17; Bayer, *Spaltung der Christenheit*, p. 96; Weinfurter, *Canossa*, pp. 85–86.

and who had given them gifts for themselves and St. Peter, they departed for the West.[49]

Leo's biographer reports that Constantine was furious with Kerularios for having refused to come to a council with the papal legates. He approved of his excommunication, deprived him and his friends of their honors, and turned them out of the palace forever.[50] But Kerularios convinced Constantine to ask the legates to return, and they did. When they saw that new negotiations would be held in a synod without the emperor, however, they decided that the situation was hopeless, and left for good on July 21.

Soon after their departure, the Greek Church imposed an interdict over the Roman Church, and Kerularios continued his campaign against Constantine, who capitulated, and gave up his policy of cooperation with Rome. The basileus also rescinded the sentence of anathema on Kerularios, and a synod anathematized all of those associated with the excommunication of Kerularios. Kerularios wanted to promote Byzantine interests in South Italy and to bring them under control of the Byzantine Empire.[51]

This goal conflicted with that of Leo IX, who wanted an alliance against the Normans, and was prepared to make concessions to the Byzantine church. He might have been satisfied if Kerularios would have recognized Roman primacy, but Kerularios emphasized religious differences and opposed an alliance between Constantinople and Rome. The Latin Church saw the refusal to recognize papal primacy over the whole church as heresy, but it was never able to side-line Kerularios.[52] As Petrus Damiani stated, "The holy canon law regards anyone as a heretic who is not in agreement with the Roman church."[53]

Like Berengar of Tours, Kerularios and his followers had challenged Rome's interpretation of the Eucharist and its interpretation of salvation history. The bishops of Rome rejected both as heretics. The azyme controversy was one component of a broader authorizing process by which the reform papacy in revolutionary terms claimed the right to determine what constituted proper behavior and belief in Christendom.

---

[49] *Vita sancti Leonis PP. IX*, Watterich, 1:162–163; Robinson, "The Life of Pope Leo IX," *The Papal Reform of the Eleventh Century*, pp. 148–149.

[50] Ibid.

[51] Bayer, *Spaltung der Christenheit*, pp. 101–103.

[52] Ibid., 105.

[53] Petrus Damiani, *Briefe*, nr. 88, 2:521; tr. Blum, 3:315.

Starting in the reign of Leo IX, in a concrete way Christendom meant a properly ordered Christian community that recognized papal leadership, followed Roman doctrine, and practiced the Roman rite. In principle, every land and every Christian people were part of Christendom.[54]

## Leo's Legacy

The delegation did not arrive back in Rome until after Leo's death in April 1054. According to Bonizo, Leo was laid out before the *confessio* in St. Peter's, and in the presence of the Roman clergy and people, he handed over the care of the church to Hildebrand, and then died.[55] He held the distinction of being the only pope in the high middle ages to be sainted immediately after his death.

During his reign he initiated the tradition of Lenten councils, modernized the administration of the chancery, and consolidated what in 1089 would be called the curia, the papal version of the *curia regis*.[56] Although he is credited with internationalizing the papacy, he was not a revolutionary. His personal sense of loyalty to the emperor and the German church acted as a counterweight to his activity on behalf of the universal authority of the papacy and of the reform church.[57]

But there was much more to his reign than ecclesiastical reform. He failed in establishing good relations with the Normans, leaving them instead of the papacy as the major arbiters of power in Southern Italy. It is questionable whether leading an army into battle and offering spiritual rewards to those who fought, as he did at Civitate, was consistent with the ideology of the reformers. Critics reproved Gregory VII for the same practices.

With the Byzantine patriarch, Leo met his match. Kerularios was just as determined as he to interpret orthodoxy in church doctrine, and since the two leaders reached an impasse, their solution was to excommunicate one another. Patriarch Dominique of Grado saw the

---

[54] Whalen, "Rethinking the Schism of 1054," pp. 23–24.
[55] Bonizo, *Ad Amicum*, p. 589; tr. Robinson, *The Papal Reform of the Eleventh Century*, p. 193.
[56] See the analysis of Kathleen C. Cushing, *Reform and the Papacy in the Eleventh Century: Spirituality and Social Change* (Manchester & New York, 2005), pp. 65–68.
[57] Goez, *Kirchenreform und Investiturstreit*, pp. 97–98.; Paul Kehr, "Vier Kapitel aus der Geschichte Kaiser Heinrichs III.," *Abhandlungen der Preussischen Akamedie der Wissenschaften, Jahrgang 1930, Philosophisch-historische Klasse*, nr. 3, p. 56.

merits of both positions, and did not believe that the two sides were justified in cutting off one another.[58] But to Leo it was a matter of Rome's primacy over the universal Church. Humbert, Frederick, and Peter enjoyed Leo's confidence, and when they excommunicated Kerularios and Leo of Ochrida, they did not intend to jeopardize Byzantine support for action against the Normans. By this time Leo was dead, and the problems with the Normans and the Byzantine Empire were left to his successor.

Pantaleo, one of the writers from Amalfi critical of the Greek position, wrote a report over the break between the Latin and Byzantine churches, emphasizing the azymes dispute, and calling Kerularios a heretic rather than a patriarch.[59] In his report Pantaleo omitted the name of Humbert as one of the delegates, according the editor of his report because he was a rich merchant and not an adherent of the reformers.[60] But it is not clear that that was the reason that Pantaleo eliminated Humbert, for he spoke very highly of Frederick, who was also considered to be a reformer, and who was elected pope as Stephen IX in 1057.[61] The editor's (Anton Michel) inference may be an example of the propensity to analyze significant actions or events in terms of the reform. Laycus, an Amalfitano cleric, also wrote a letter critical of the Greek position, but he did not delve into the events of 1054.[62]

Michel suggests that while aware of all of the documents relating to the split between the two churches, Pantaleo may have tailored his report to suit the conditions of 1062/1063. At that time as consul

---

[58] Whalen, "Rethinking the Schism of 1054," p. 21.

[59] "Der Bericht des Pantaleo von Amalfi über den kirchlichen Bruch zu Byzanz im Jahre 1054 und seine angebliche Sammlung der Aktenstücke," ed. Anton Michel, "Amalfi und Jerusalem im griechischen Kirchenstreit (1054–1090), *Orientalia Christiana Analecta* 121 (1939), Exkurs II, pp. 52–56; p. 53: "...erat quidem Michael Constantinopolitanae sedis patriarcha, actibus et intellectu stultissimus, qui prout verba eius attestantur, haeresiarcha potius quam patriarcha esse omnibus innotuit. Hic levitate sui cordis exactus sanctae Romanae sedis eucharistiam nefanditer infamabat, tractans secum, quod melius esset Graecorum sacrificium quam Latinorum, eo quod ipsi fermentatum et Romana ecclesia, ut ab apostolis acceperat, azymum sacrificat." There are two recensions, which differ markedly; Michel, pp. 54–56; Whalen, "Rethinking the Schism of 1054," p. 9 & n. 31.

[60] Ibid., 55.

[61] Ibid., 53: "Interea, dum praefatus patriarcha, ut libelli sui apices asserverant, sacrificium Latinorum arguere conaretur, hoc sanctissimus Leo papa IX. audiens, more solito ad nefandam altercationem exstirpandam, dominum Stephanum [Frederick's name as pope] cancellarium religiosissimum virum, qui tertius post eum papa Romanae sedis exstitit, et honestae sedis pontificem..."

[62] Ibid., 35–47; Whalen, "Rethinking the Schism of 1054," pp. 18–19.

Pantaleo approached Cadalus (Honorius II) in the interests of establishing an alliance between the papacy and the Byzantine Empire.
Pantaleo almost certainly calculated that Cadalus would be more sympathetic to his cause than Alexander II who was generally considered
to be pope. Alexander's predecessor, Nicholas II, had established an
alliance with the Normans, while Cadalus was elected under the auspices of the regency, and presumably would have been more sympathetic to imperial interests.

According to Leo's biographer, after his capture Leo was reconciled
with the Normans, who carried him on a litter from Benevento back to
Rome. He spent a short time at the Lateran palace, and then, after a
vision, had himself conducted to the oratory of St. Peter's. From there
he was brought to the episcopal residence where, after prayers and
demonstrations of respect and sadness from the throng around him,
he died in 1054 at the age of 50. His biographer said that the whole
population of Rome thronged to his funeral, and that he was buried
next to Gregory I in St. Peter's.[63]


*Summary and Conclusion*


Leo has been seen as "the real founder of the papal monarchy over the
church" because he brought the leaders of the reform movement in the
North with him to Rome.[64] These strangers from Lotharingia brought
to Rome new ideas of the pope's function and dignity, but to a lesser
extent the same could also be said of Clement II. The Italian popes had
been preoccupied with the maintenance of their position among the
Roman and suburban factions, and seldom ventured outside of Italy.
They had little concept of the papacy as a universal power as the leader
of Christendom, a concept that Leo lived and promoted while still
being devoted to the emperor.

Unlike his two predecessors, he avoided a quick demise, but during
his five year papacy he spent barely more than six months in Rome.
Three times he crossed over the Alps to France and Germany, where
he held synods, issued decrees against simony, nicholaitism, violence,

---

[63] *Leonis IX Vita*, Watterich 1:167–170; "The Life of Pope Leo IX," tr. Robinson, *The
Papal Reform of the Eleventh Century*, pp. 154–157;
[64] See the always insightful analysis of Geoffrey Barraclough, *The Medieval Papacy*
(New York, 1968, repr. 1970), pp. 74–76.

and moral laxity, and settled countless disputes. In all, he held twelve synods, six of them in Rome. No longer perceived as an object of shame and scandal, the papacy won the support of the reform movement spearheaded by monastic leaders of Cluny and Lotharingia. An eminent medievalist concluded that when the spirit of the reform penetrated Rome, and came into contact with an Italian and Mediterranean environment, it was imperceptibly altered. The first consideration for the Romans who joined the reformers was not moral regeneration, but the reinforcement of papal authority.[65]

If the growth of papal power and the expansion of its sphere of influence is considered to be an integral constituent of papal reform, then Leo IX can lay claim to being more than just a conveyer of moral reform. His determination to subdue the Normans and to establish papal authority, and his insistence on papal supremacy in his negotiations with the orthodox patriarch makes that conclusion indisputable.

---

[65] Ibid., 75.

CHAPTER FOUR

VICTOR II AND STEPHEN IX

*Part I:  Victor II (1055–1057)*

The sainted Leo IX was succeeded by another German pope, but accounts of how Victor II was elected vary. Some sources suggest that Henry III nominated his own candidate, and that the election resembled the elections of Victor's immediate predecessors. Others emphasize the influence of a delegation from Rome, and some of these specifically mention Hildebrand, Humbert of Silva Candida, and Boniface of Albano. Contemporary historians draw attention to Hildebrand's good relations with Henry III and the German court at this time, and conjecture that he clarified the papal situation in Rome and courted the emperor's participation.

The end result of whatever precisely happened was that Henry III's powerful chancellor, Gebhard of Eichstätt, a reformer, was selected pope at a huge council in Mainz in November 1054.[1] After first refusing to accept the honor, Gebhard finally bowed to the will of the delegates at a Council held in Ratisbon in March 1055, a long lapse under such challenging circumstances. Almost always a presence during these papal transitions, Hildebrand accompanied him to Rome, where on April 13, 1055, he was enthroned as Victor II. Like Leo IX he succeeded in surviving his first months in office, and served out an eventful two-year reign.

*Conflicting Sources*

An analysis of the relevant sources will help to clarify the evolving points of view of the competing factions. The *Annales Romani* imply that it was a broader group than just Hildebrand and other leaders of the reform who traveled to Germany. They report that the Roman people gathered together and sent legates to the emperor with the request that he appoint a pious pastor of the Roman Church. A multitude of

---

[1] Cowdrey, *Gregory VII*, pp. 33–34; Blumenthal, *Gregor VII.*, pp. 79–80.

clerics and laymen met [in Mainz], and elected a candidate pleasing to God, and sent him with Roman legates to Rome. To the jubilation of the Roman people he was consecrated and took the name of Victor.[2]

The anonymous *Vita of Victor II* also reports the dispatch of a legation of Roman primates to Mainz that requested that the emperor designate a pope. After long deliberations they selected Gebhard [of Eichstätt], who invented all kinds of ways to avoid accepting the burden, but when these failed, he accepted the position at a council in Ratisbon. He informed Henry that following his orders, he was giving his body and soul to Saint Peter, with the stipulation that Henry also return to St. Peter whatever were his rights. Armed with the emperor's promise, he jubilantly arrived in Rome where he was received with deep devotion, and consecrated as Victor II.[3] The question that stands out was what Victor and Henry meant by the rights of St. Peter that Henry promised to return.

Leo of Ostia, writing in The Chronicle of Montecassino, and Bonizo both emphasize Hildebrand's role in Victor's election. Leo reports that after Leo IX's death Hildebrand, then subdeacon, was sent by the Romans to the emperor, who would act in place of the Roman clerics and people to elect a pope, because there was no suitable candidate in those parts [Rome]. Hildebrand and the Romans selected Gebhard of Eichstätt, known to be the most powerful man in the kingdom after the emperor. The choice made the emperor very sad because he held Gebhard to be very dear. Even though both Henry and Gebhard were reluctant, because Henry could not convince Hildebrand to accept any other candidate, he allowed Hildebrand to lead Gebhard to Rome. There he was given the name Victor, and received the assent of all.[4]

Bonizo is the only source to report that Hildebrand himself was nominated, adding that even though the Roman clergy and people agreed to his candidacy, Hildebrand convinced them to follow his counsel in electing a successor to Leo.[5] After persuading them to seek out the opinion of the emperor, he and other religious men crossed the mountains to discuss the issue with Henry. In the course of frequent

---

[2] *Annales Romani, Lib. Pont.* 2:333–334.

[3] *Victoris II vita ex Anonymi Haserensis libro de episcopis Eichstetensibus,* MGH SS 7:263–266; Watterich, 1:177–183 at 179–180.

[4] *Chron. Mont.,* 2.86, p. 336; Watterich, 1:183; Cowdrey, *Gregory VII,* pp. 33–34; Blumenthal, *Gregor VII.,* pp. 79–80.

[5] Bonizo, *Ad Amicum,* pp. 589–590; Watterich, 1:184–185; tr. Robinson, *The Papal Reform of the Eleventh Century,* pp. 193–195.

conversations Hildebrand developed such a close relationship with the emperor that he persuaded him that he had committed a grave sin in making appointments to the papacy. Following Hildebrand's advice Henry relinquished the tyranny of the patriciate, and reinstated the right to elect the pope to the Roman clergy and people according to ancient custom.

Bonizo says that the choice fell on Gebhard [of Eichstätt], Henry's *oeconomus*, whom Henry held to be very close. Because Henry was opposed to the selection, and because Gebhard was reluctant to assume the burden of the papacy, it was against the will of both of them that Hildebrand and the Roman legation conducted Gebhard to Rome forthwith. There, according to ancient custom the clergy elected him, the people acclaimed him, and the cardinals enthroned him in St. Peter's as Victor. Bonizo's assertion that Henry relinquished the power of the *patricius* seems improbable, for it is difficult to imagine what would have motivated the emperor to relinquish such critical authority. Yet, it is suggestive that the anonymous author of the life of Victor II also mentions that Henry returned certain rights to St. Peter.

We shall see that when Nicholas II died in 1061, a legation from Rome presented Henry IV with the symbols of the patriciate to participate in the selection of Nicholas II's successor. No one mentioned that Henry's father had relinquished such authority, but the fact that the Romans delivered the symbols to Henry IV after they had been granted to Henry III implies that Henry IV did not automatically inherit them. A possible hypothesis is that writing as a supporter of Gregory VII in late 1085 or 1086, Bonizo may have been providing spurious evidence to demonstrate that the vague authority granted to the emperor in the papal electoral decree of 1059 did not encompass the broad authority of the *patricius* to influence papal elections.

As always, Benzo presents the most tendentious and conspiratorial account.[6] He spoke of the three monks—Hildebrand, Humbert and Boniface (presumably cardinal bishop of Albano)—who came, ostensibly from Rome, but in fact from other places. He said that Archbishop Herman of Cologne told them that since they were monks, the affair did not concern them, and he chided them for not abiding by the Rule of St. Benedict. He advised the emperor that he would keep them

---

[6] Benzo, *Ad Heinricum*, 7.2, pp. 590–592; tr. Robinson, *The Papal Reform of the Eleventh Century*, pp. 370–371; Tilmann Schmidt, "Zu Hildebrands Eid vor Kaiser Heinrich III.," *Archivum Historiae Pontificiae* 11 (1973), 378–386.

under guard until the Romans arrived, which they did [for the council of Mainz]. Benzo volunteered that the Romans were amazed at the deceits of the monks, and that it was the will of the bishops that the emperor bind them with an oath according to which they would swear that they would never become popes nor intervene in any elections of popes. And this was done.

Benzo's assertion that a delegation of Romans arrived after Hildebrand and his colleagues may be accurate.[7] He implies that the delegation of the Romans accompanied the papal elect to Rome, and that the acephalous monks (those without an abbot) followed. Although he contends that these monks were not received into the pope's secret councils, Uta Renate Blumenthal argues that Hildebrand acted as a virtual chancellor, and that he was used as a legate.[8] Benzo compliments Hildebrand for being more cunning than the others, forming links with bankers, even though he was excluded from the fullness of grace. In this way, he could still be influential with the pope through financial necessities whether the pope liked it or not. In subsequent accounts of papal elections Benzo emphasized the critical help of Leo, the son of Benedict (né Baruch), who had converted from Judaism in the mid eleventh century, and founded the family that will be called the Pierleoni.

## The House of Lotharingia/Canossa

Victor II was not just a continuation of his predecessor. Many of his objectives such as the strengthening of the papacy, the use of legates, the holding of reform synods, the promotion of monasteries, especially Cluny and Vallombrosa, and opposition to simony and clerical marriage remained the same as Leo's. He continued to value Humbert as a close advisor, but not Frederick, for in addition to Frederick's anti-Norman policy, his brother, Duke Godfrey the Bearded of Upper Lotharingia, was in conflict with Henry III, and the Salians saw Frederick as a natural partisan of their opponents.[9] Henry III demanded Frederick's capture, but after 1053 the former papal chancellor and bibliotecarius fled to the security of Montecassino,

---

[7] Blumenthal, *Gregor VII.*, pp. 79–80.
[8] Ibid.
[9] Egon Boshof, *Die Salier* (Stuttgart, Berlin, Cologne, 1995), p. 146; Hägermann, *Das Papsttum am Vorabend des Investiturstreits*, p. 9; Elke Goez, *Beatrix von Canossa*, pp. 20–29.

where he first became a monk at its daughter house of Santa Maria in Tremiti.[10]

The main concern of the empire was not the Normans, but the security of middle Italy against the combined houses of Lotharingia and Canossa. Of the duchies Lotharingia was the most serious danger.[11] Unlike the others it was not a tribal territory, but a collection of lordships under Duke Gozelo until his death in 1044. His son, Godfrey the Bearded, co-duke of Upper Lotharingia, wanted to be invested with his father's territory, but Henry III would not tolerate his assertion to a claim by hereditary right, and they clashed.

Deafeated, Godfrey departed for Italy, where the emperor's situation became precarious in April 1054 when Godfrey secretly married Beatrice of Canossa, herself a Lotharingian, and the widow of Margrave Boniface, who had been murdered in 1052 by a poisoned arrow shot by one of his *milites*.[12] Godfrey did not request the emperor's consent to his marriage as required by feudal law, a legal and moral transgression that was viewed as tantamount to treason.

The pair held Henry III in a pincer grip. Enormously wealthy, Beatrice owned large allodial lands in Lotharingia, controlled the property of the house of Canossa, and possessed the margavate of Tuscany. Lampert of Hersfeld even reported that Godfrey intended to split off Upper Italy from the Empire or to form an alliance with the Normans.[13]

Henry was not about to tolerate the creation of a power block in Northern Italy by a repeatedly rebellious subject, and rumors that Godfrey was about to seize imperial land prompted Henry's second trip to Italy (March-November, 1055).[14] He forced Godfrey to flee, and seeing no other way to survive, Beatrice took Matilda to Florence where Henry and Victor II were holding a council.[15] Compounding the dynastic links, Matilda was probably already betrothed to Godfrey the Humpbacked, the son of Godfrey the Bearded by a previous

---

[10] *Chron. Mont.* 2.86, pp. 335–336.
[11] Horst Fuhrmann, *Germany in the High Middle Ages c. 1050–1200*, tr. Timothy Reuter, (Cambridge, etc., 1986), p. 41.
[12] Elke Goez, *Beatrix von Canossa*, pp. 20–22.
[13] Lampert, *Annales*, p. 64.
[14] Ian Robinson, *King Henry IV of Germany, 1056–1105* (Cambridge, 1999, paperback 2003), pp. 24–28.
[15] MGH DD H III: 341–343; Gresser, *Konziliengeschichte*, pp. 30–31; Elke Goez, *Beatrix von Canossa*, p. 24.

marriage. Henry appears to have chosen a location in the heart of Godfrey's domain to demonstrate his power. Most of the approximately 120 bishops who attended were Italian, but they included Archbishop Adalbert of Bremen, and the bishops of Naumburg and Regensburg.

According to Petrus Damiani at the Council of Florence there were also proceedings against Bishop Cadalus of Parma, which had already been enacted in synods of Pavia in 1049 and Mantua in 1053. In a later letter written to Cadalus in March or April 1062 Petrus said that in many ways the Roman Church has dealt lightly with you, and often shielded you from the rigorous chastisement that you deserved. But he charged that those present at the councils of Pavia, Mantua, and Florence claimed that an unambiguous sentence of condemnation was handed down against you. In all cases, however, he said that the Church compassionately forgave you with maternal love and apostolic affection. He alleged that even though Cadalus might not have been deposed by the judgment of the bishops, at least he was by the authority of the canons.[16]

Given Petrus' extreme antagonism toward Cadalus at the time of the schism, one might exercise some caution in trusting these charges. No other source mentions any condemnations, and other records show that the relationship of Cadalus both with the emperor and the church was good.[17] What is known about the synod of Mantua that Petrus mentioned is that after Leo IX's return from Germany, he held a synod there on February 21, 1053, mainly composed of Lombard bishops. The conditions were tumultuous as the populace massively interfered with the procedures intended to deal with simonistic and unchaste bishops, but no decisions of the council have been transmitted.[18]

Even though Beatrice tried to justify herself in a speech before the emperor while in Florence, Henry took her and Matilda into captivity, and brought them back to Germany. Finally, to offset the combination of Canossa and Lotharingia he arranged the marriage of his five-year old son, Henry, with Bertha of Turin to create an alliance of Savoy and Turin. To enlist support in securing his Italian kingdom, he conferred the Duchy of Spoleto and the March of Fermo on Victor II. In addition to the Council of Florence these actions demonstrate the continuing close alliance between the emperor and the pope.

---

[16] Petrus Damiani, *Briefe*, nr. 88 2:516; tr. Blum, 3:309–310.
[17] Baix, "Cadalus," pp. 56–58; Gresser, *Konziliengeschichte*, pp. 30–31; Blum, 3:310, n. 5.
[18] Gresser, *Konziliengeschichte*, p. 28.

*The Normans*

As the former imperial chancellor responsible for the recall of most of the imperial troops sent to aid Leo against the Normans in 1052/53, Victor was not predisposed to continue Leo's anti-Norman policy.[19] After the battle of Civitate the Normans plunged ahead at full throttle, but even though both the papacy and the Byzantine Empire suffered losses, Victor II did not oppose them.[20] In fact, Amatus of Montecassino has nothing but good things to say about Victor.[21] While Henry III was in Italy, however, he had contact with the South Italian princes, and sent Bishop Otto of Novara to Constantinople to set up an alliance. There were no negotiations with Kerularios, but the diplomacy in 1055–1056 led to a pact against the Normans. Whether Victor was a partner in this pact is not known, but given his closeness to the emperor, the two leaders probably had some sort of understanding.

Victor dispatched Hildebrand to France to encourage the rejection of simony and clerical marriage, and he himself accepted the emperor's invitation to meet in Germany. They met at Goslar on September 8, 1056, where, in the face of aggressive Norman expansion, Victor reversed his policy, and asked Henry III to move against the threat.[22] Amatus does not mention any change of policy, but states that Victor went to the emperor's court to ask for the transfer of the land of Arpino (on the border between Capua and the papal Campagna south of Sora), which rightly belonged to the Church of St. Peter of Rome.[23] Henry was poised to grant the petition when he set off for his palace at Bodfeld to do some hunting. There, he suddenly fell ill, and died on October 5 at the age of thirty nine.

*After Henry III's Death*

On the emperor's deathbed numerous powerful ecclesiastical and secular dignitaries seem to have affirmed the election of his son as his successor at Tribur in 1053. Victor, into whose care Henry III had placed his son, was the leading figure; among the others were Patriarch

---

[19] *Chron. Mont.*, 2, 81:328–329.
[20] Bayer, *Spaltung der Christenheit*, pp.117–118.
[21] Amatus, *The History of the Normans*, III, 47, p. 103: "This Pope Victor was extremely courteous, generous, and a great friend of the emperor. He did not create hostile relations with the Norman knights but upon sage advice made an amicable peace with them."
[22] Bayer, *Spaltung der Christenheit*, 118.
[23] Amatus, *The History of the Normans*, III, 48, p. 103.

Gotebald of Aquileia and Bishop Gebhard of Regensburg.[24] Victor managed to work out peace between the emperor and some of his opponents, most notably Godfrey and Beatrice even though they still threatened Salian authority in Italy.[25] Apart from the empire, the reconciliation had momentous repercussions for Victor's relationship with Frederick, Godfrey's brother.

Victor choreographed his close friend's burial at Speyer, mirroring the idea of the unity of church and empire. Thereafter he managed the transfer of authority to Henry IV by requiring the magnates of the whole kingdom to swear an oath to the boy king, thus confirming his kingship.[26] Between Henry's death and December, Victor brought the six year old king to Aachen, placed him on the royal throne, and probably repeated the unction and coronation performed in Aachen in 1054.[27]

Victor's primary role in this delicate transition signified a heady fillip for the papacy, which so recently had relied upon the emperor for its mere survival. In an otherwise critical letter to Victor II Petrus Damiani emphasized that Christ had added monarchies to the pope's powers, and had given him jurisdiction over the whole of the Roman Empire while vacant.[28] Later Gregory VII and his supporters would echo these sentiments, claiming that Henry IV became king by permission of Victor.[29] From the other side, the *Annales Romani* also recognized his role.[30]

It has been suggested that Victor was acting in his capacity as the imperial bishop of Eichstätt, a position he still retained, rather than as

---

[24] *Chronicon Wirziburgense*, MGH SS 6:17–31 at 31; Lampert, *Annales*, p. 69.

[25] Weinfurter, *Canossa*, pp. 43–45 states that there was much dissension at end of Henry's short life. The plan to murder him had failed, but major nobles opposed him. Godfrey of Lotharingia married Beatrice without Henry's permission; Elke Goez, *Beatrix von Canossa*, pp. 20–22,149 & n. 41.

[26] *Chron. Mont.*, 2.91, p. 345.

[27] *Annales Altahenses*, anno 1056, p. 53.

[28] Petrus Damiani, *Briefe*, nr. 46, 2:41; tr. Blum 2:250–251.

[29] Paul of Bernried. *Vita Gregorii VII papae*, ed. Watterich, 1:474–546, p. 506: "Tertio igitur Henrico mortuo, quartus ille Henricus rex, permittente Romano Pontifice Victore, qui tunc morienti praesens erat, haereditario iure, nimirum puer successit..."

[30] *Annales Romani, Lib. Pont.* 2:334: "Qui perrexit ad inperatorem supradictum pro ea causa qua et predecessor suus, ut eicerent Agarenos, quia clamor populi illius regionis non valebat sufferere; set minime impetravit, quia imperator invenit in maxima infirmitate iacentem: ad ultimum commendavit ei Heinricum filium suum adhuc puerulum, ac eius manibus defunctus est. Tunc dictus pontifex tradidit regnum per investimentum dicto puero Heinrico, et cepit proficisci Rome, et in itinere ex hac vita subtractus est."

pope, but the sources do not refer to Victor as bishop, but as pope.[31] Moreover, since the passage of the emperorship from father to son, and the unification of the empire around the son were such critical transitions, it seems improbable that a bishop would have had the authority and the gravitas to transact them. In the deepest sense Victor was probably acting as an old, trusted friend of the emperor.

Now, with a child king under the regency of his mother, Victor may have recognized the shift of power to the alliance of Lotharingia/Canossa, and positioned the papacy accordingly. Evidence of this shift is the court held at Cologne in December 1056 in which a reconciliation was worked out with Godfrey and Beatrice, and also with the two Balduins of Flanders.[32] Victor wanted to integrate the house of Lotharingia/Canossa into the Empire, and to support it in the kingdom of Italy. The switch in policy from opposition to integration had the beneficial effect for Victor that Godfrey and Beatrice supported church reform and a solution to the Norman problem, especially militarily. In the schism with Alexander II Godfrey would become the dominant figure in opposing Cadalus.

Victor left Henry IV in the hands of his mother, Agnes, as regent, and returned to Rome in the company of Godfrey, Beatrice and Matilda in February 1057. On April 18 he presided over a Lateran council, the only council that he held in Rome.[33] Probably realizing that he had no hope of thwarting the Normans without Henry III, like other realists he made peace with the intruders.[34] The Chronicle of Montecassino reports that Henry III had harbored great mistrust of Frederick of Lotharingia because he considered his brother, Godfrey, to be a most odious enemy, but all of these policy changes entailed a change in Victor's attitude toward Frederick.

When Frederick returned from his legation to Constantinople with a great amount of money, Henry feared that he might use this money to the advantage of his brother. Henry called upon the pope [Victor II] to capture him and quickly to transmit him to himself. Learning of this threat in Rome Frederick secretly spoke to Richer, the abbot of

---

[31] Robinson, *Henry IV*, p. 27.
[32] Gresser, *Konziliengeschichte*, pp. 31–32; Elke Goez, *Beatrix von Canossa*, p. 149 & n. 42.
[33] Ibid., pp. 32–33.
[34] *Annales Augustani*, MGH SS 3:124–136 at 127; Bayer, *Spaltung der Christenheit*, p. 118.

Montecassino, and also a fellow Lotharingian, requesting that he be taken in as a monk, and Richer immediately assented.[35]

After Richer's death on December 11, 1055, Victor II wanted Frederick to be elected as abbot of Montecassino because Peter, the choice of the monks, was not very adept in secular affairs.[36] Henry's reconciliation with Godfrey before his death made Victor's task much easier. He commanded Humbert of Silva Candida to examine Peter's election, and to depose him if there were cause. Peter swore at the high altar that he had been elected against his will, and that because of his advanced age he did not wish to accept the burden of abbot. He agreed to relinquish his office in the presence of Humbert, and not missing a heartbeat, on May 23, 1057, Victor II appointed Frederick as abbot.[37]

Montecassino was no mere monastery, but a regional power in its own right. The *terra sancti Benedicti* with its 80,000 inhabitants controlled the Via Latina to the South, and functioned as a bridge between the Roman Church and the Lombard principalities of Benevento, Capua and Salerno that were in the process of becoming Norman. Apulia and Calabria were still Greek, but c. 1050 Leo IX had appointed Humbert of Silva Candida as archbishop of the Muslim ruled island of Sicily.[38] Serving as abbot of the spiritual and territorial titan of Montecassino burnished Frederick's already bright luster from having functioned as *bibliotecarius* and chancellor to Leo IX. Perhaps sensing that with the backing of his brother Frederick would some day become pope, on June 14, 1057, Victor enhanced his prestige by promoting him to cardinal priest of S. Grisogono.[39]

Victor may have had a premonition of his own impending death slightly over a month later. In order to settle a dispute between the bishops of Arezzo and Siena *in situ*, he traveled with Hildebrand to Arezzo, where the dispute was settled in favor of Arezzo in a council held on July 23, 1057.[40] According to the archives of Arezzo, besides Hildebrand, entitled provisor of the monastery of S. Paolo (S. Paolo fuori le mura), among the notable prelates present were Gerard, bishop of Florence (the future Nicholas II), and Frederick, chancellor of the

---

[35] *Chron. Mont.*, 2.85–86, p. 334.
[36] Amatus, *The History of the Normans*, III, 49, p. 103.
[37] *Chron. Mont.*, 2.89, p. 341; Hägermann, *Das Papsttum*, pp. 18–19; Meyer von Knonau, *Jahrbücher* 1: 26–27.
[38] Hägermann, *Das Papsttum*, p. 20; Cowdrey, *Abbot Desiderius*, p. 2.
[39] Hüls, *Kardinäle*, pp. 168–169, 248.
[40] Gresser, *Konziliengeschichte*, p. 33.

Roman Church, and now abbot of Montecassino.[41] Five days later, with Hildebrand in attendance, Victor died. No matter how unreliable Benzo's later assertion that Hildebrand had poisoned four of his predecessors, it gives pause to those inclined toward conspiracy theories, for Victor was not mentioned as being ill, and Hildebrand was the only one noted as remaining with him.

Victor's reign illustrates his great flexibility and his ability to adjust to changing conditions. Although he was dedicated to Henry III, he accommodated himself to the new power structure of the Lotharingia/ Canossa alliance, and to the growing strength of the Normans. He supported the reform, but his central focus was on political affairs, especially within the Empire, Southern Italy, and the Byzantine Empire, and he expected influential churchmen such as the abbot of Montecassino to function well within the secular world. He continued to work closely with Hildebrand, who did not object to his close ties with the Empire. A serious break for papal independence from the empire would come with the election of Victor's successor during the weak regency of Henry IV. It marked the beginning of a profound change in the ratio of papal to imperial power.

### Part 2: Stephen IX (1057–1058)

#### The Lotharingia/Canossa Alliance

By July 27, 1057, Frederick had returned from Arezzo to Rome, where he celebrated mass and took possession of his title church. On July 31 Cardinal Bishop Boniface of Albano entered Rome with the news of the sudden death of Victor II.[42] During the turbulent times that followed people flocked to Frederick at Santa Maria in Pallara, a monastery on the Palatine belonging to Montecassino where he was staying, possibly because he had been a member of Victor II's inner circle.

In answer to their question of whom he would recommend as a successor to Victor he reputedly suggested five people: Humbert, cardinal bishop of Silva Candida, Cardinal Bishop John of Velletri (possibly the John of Velletri who became Benedict X), Bishop Otker of Perugia, Cardinal Bishop [Peter] of Tusculum, and Hildebrand, subdeacon of

---

[41] JL 4370; Kehr, IP, nr. 21, 3:150.
[42] *Chron.Mont.*, 2.94, p. 352–353; Hägermann, *Das Papsttum*, pp. 11–13.

the Roman church. But when an assembly gathered together in Rome could not agree on any of the above, or whether they should wait for Hildebrand to return from Tuscany or Tuscia, they seized upon Frederick himself.

Without contact with the imperial court, Frederick was brought to the basilica of S. Pietro in Vincoli near the Pallara, and elected pope on August 2, 1057, the feast day of St. Stephen. With great rejoicing the Romans escorted him to the Lateran, and the following day they led him through the whole city to St. Peter's, where it was said that all of the cardinals had gathered together with the clergy and people. There, they consecrated him universal pope as Stephen IX.[43]

Frederick's selection as pope is not surprising given his illustrious career, Henry III's reconciliation with Godfrey, and Victor II's recent moves. As an escort of Leo IX on his way to Rome, he had as companions such future leaders of the reform as Hildebrand and Humbert. As *bibliotecarius* and papal chancellor under Leo IX, as a member of the delegation to Constantinople, and as abbot of Montecassino, an office that he retained until 1058, he had wide experience in diplomacy and administration. His recent appointment as cardinal priest of S. Grisogono may have been designed to make him even more *papabile*. Not a bishop, but imbued with the spiritual and secular virtues of monks embodied in Hildebrand, Victor II seems to have groomed him for the job.

Such quick action may have been intended to preempt the interference of the Tusculani and the Crescentii, who were not dormant. The election did not seem to be directed against the monarchy, but with a child king, and a weak regency, Stephen seemed to feel no urgency in informing the German court of his election. Not until December, long after the fact, did he take action. He dispatched Hildebrand and Bishop Anselm of Lucca, a close observer of the Salian court, and later Alexander II (1061–1073) as leaders of a delegation to the German court to obtain the approval of Agnes.[44] By the time that they returned on March 29, 1058, Stephen IX had already died in Florence after a

---

[43] Ibid.; *Annales Romani Lib. Pont.* 2:334; *Annales Altahenses*, p. 54; Bonizo, *Ad Amicum*, p. 590; JL 1:553; Michel Parisse, "Stephen IX," *Enciclopedia dei Papi* 2:166–167; Meyer von Knonau, *Jahrbücher*, 1:330–31; Gresser, *Konziliengeschichte*, p. 33; Hägermann, *Das Papsttum*, p. 27.

[44] *Annales Altahenses*, p. 54; Lampert, *Annales*, pp. 72–73; Weinfurter, *Canossa*, p. 87; Hägermann, *Das Papsttum*, pp. 30–31.

reign of less than eight months. He may have died from malaria, but Benzo will charge that he was poisoned by Hildebrand.[45]

## Stephen IX's Reign

Even though his reign was short, it was critical, for it marked the beginning of a shift in the balance of power between the papacy and the empire. Henry III's premature death and the weak regency tipped the scale in favor of the papacy, and transformed the character of the reform. The ecclesiastical authority of Stephen IX backed by the military power of Godfrey changed the relationship of the papacy with the young king. As the guardian of Henry IV, Victor II had held de facto authority over Italy, and although this authority ceased when he died, a grant by Henry III entitled the papacy to the Duchy of Spoleto and the March of Fermo.[46] With Godfrey's marriage to Beatrice, the Lotharingian brothers virtually controlled Central Italy.[47]

As his first documented act on March 6, 1058, Stephen cemented his reforming credentials by confirming the property and the rights of Cluny.[48] But after the more diplomatic reign of Victor II, he reverted back to the reign of Leo IX with its hostility toward the Normans, and it was even rumored that he intended to crown his brother king in order to oppose the Normans more forcefully.[49] He opened negotiations with the Byzantines, who also felt threatened by the Normans, and set up a legation consisting of Cardinal Stephen of S. Grisogono, Desiderius, then abbot-elect of Montecassino, and Mainard, the future cardinal bishop of Silva Candida to travel to Constantinople.[50] But before they could depart, he died, and they aborted their mission.

Amatus of Montecassino, had nothing positive to say about Stephen. He charged that even as abbot of Montecassino he had aroused all of the people that he could, and had used his power to destroy the

---

[45] Hägermann, *Das Papsttum*, p. 32.

[46] Meyer von Knonau, *Jahrbücher*, 1:32–33.

[47] Ibid. for the boundaries of his territory; Hägermann, *Das Papsttum*, pp. 29–30; Elke Goez, *Beatrix von Canossa*, pp. 150–154.

[48] JL 4385.

[49] *Chron. Mont.* 2.97, p. 355: "Disponebat autem fratri duci suo Gotifrido apud Tusciam in colloquium jungi eique, ut ferbatur, imperialem coronam largiri, demum vero ad Normannos Italia expellendos, qui maximo illi odio erant, unacum eo reverti."

[50] Ibid., 3.9, pp. 369–371; Hägermann, *Das Papsttum*, p. 34; Meyer von Knonau, *Jahrbücher* 1:77; Cowdrey, *Abbot Desiderius*, p. 111; idem., *Gregory VII*, pp. 33–36.

Normans. As pope he plotted to destroy them, but since his death was
close, and he lacked enough silver, he was unable to fulfill his desire.[51]
But, Amatus emphasized, he tried. Soon after Stephen's return from
Montecassino in 1058, Amatus said that still as abbot, he had the
provost of the monastery transport its whole treasure, its gold and
silver, to Rome to be used in a campaign against the Normans in which
Godfrey and other magnates were expected to participate. According
to Leo of Ostia in the Chronicle of Montecassino Stephen intended to
meet his brother in Tuscany, to grant him the crown, and then return
with him to vanquish the Normans, whom they hated.[52]

Even though Stephen had promised to return the treasure with
interest after the campaign, Amatus claimed that the monks were dis-
traught about being deprived of their livelihood. One of the young
monks had a dream on the night on which the treasure was taken that
a monk issued forth from the altar where St. Benedict and his sister,
Santa Scholastica were laid. The weeping monk said that he had been
robbed of everything, and wanted justice. Another monk followed
him, telling him not to weep, and promising that the treasure would be
returned. When the brother awakened he revealed his dream so widely
that it became public knowledge.

Amatus thought that the comforting monk was St. Benedict, and
that the treasure was returned after Stephen's death. Another source
contends that observing the distress of the monks who brought the
treasure to Rome, Stephen was driven to tears, and quickly returned
the treasure with his own embellishments.[53] But the mere fact that he
contemplated using spiritual treasure for secular purposes demonstrates
his pragmatism, and suggests that other reformers shared his values.

The *Annales Romani* present a different story. They report that when
Frederick returned from Constantinople with great treasure, he found
that Victor had died. He was elected pope, but the Romans confiscated
his treasure, and he angrily left Rome to notify his brother [Godfrey].
The terrified Romans dispatched Braczutus from Trastevere to poison
him, and he died.[54] The *Annales* confuse Leo IX with Victor II, and
they also appear to confuse the treasure that Frederick had brought

---

[51] Amatus, *The History of the Normans*, III, 50, p. 104; Meyer von Knonau,
*Jahrbücher* 1:78–80.
[52] *Chron. Mont.* 2.97, p. 355; Hägermann, *Das Papsttum*, p. 36.
[53] Amatus, *The History of the Normans*, III, 51, p. 104.
[54] *Lib. Pont.* 2:334; Hägermann, *Das Papsttum*, p. 54.

back from Constantinople, and which had been stolen at Chieti, with the treasure of Montecassino. Nevertheless, the report of poisoning coincides with the claim that Braczutus confessed to the acts when Gregory VII was accused of poisoning his four predecessors.

The Chronicle of Montecassino suggests that the *Annales Romani's* assertion that Stephen IX was poisoned could be accurate. The Chronicle reports that at the end of November, 1057, he came to Montecassino, and that he was already so ill by Christmas that he thought that he was about to die.[55] Returning to Rome, and still ill, he wanted to see his brother [Godfrey] in Florence. Before departing he announced that if he should die, there was to be no election before Hildebrand returned from his mission to the empress.[56] He departed from Rome in mid March, 1058, and died in the arms of Hugh of Cluny at the home of his brother in Florence on March 29.[57] Amatus reports that some of his brothers from Montecassino were present, and that after joyfully hearing Stephen's recommendation that Desiderius would be their best choice for abbot, they sadly witnessed his death. Following his burial, the monks returned to Montecassino bearing the treasure that had been appropriated.[58]

## *The Significance of Stephen IX's Reign*

The short papacy of Stephen IX was nevertheless noteworthy for its alliance with Godfrey and the house of Lotharingia/Canossa, and for its anti-Norman posture.[59] In Southern Italy Stephen strengthened the papal sphere of influence by controlling Montecassino and the *terra sancti Benedicti*, and also the archbishoprics of Benevento and Salerno. In Lombardy he supported the *pataria*, the secular reform movement rising from the lower classes, and centered around Milan.[60]

---

[55] *Chron. Mont.* 2.96, p. 355.

[56] Ibid., 2.98, p. 356.

[57] Meyer von Knonau, *Jahrbücher* 1:73–82; pp. 81–82 for his death & n. 57 for sources; Hägermann, *Das Papsttum*, pp. 54–55.

[58] Amatus, *The History of the Normans*, III, 52, p. 105.

[59] Parisse, "Stefano IX," *Enciclopedia dei Papi*, 2:166–167; Hägermann, *Das Papsttum*, pp. 44–55.

[60] Arnulf of Milan, *Liber gestorum recentium* iii.9–iv.3, ed. Claudia Zey, MGH SRG 67:174–220; Landulfus senior, *Historia Mediolanensis* iii.5–30, ed. Cutolo, RIS 4, pt. 2, pp. 85–123; H. Keller, "Pataria und Stadtverfassung, Stadtgemeinde und Reform: Mailand im 'Investiturstreit', pp. 321–350 of *Investiturstreit und Reichsverfassung*, ed. J. Fleckenstein, Forträge und Forschungen 17 (Sigmaringen, 1973); Alexander Patschovsky, "Heresy and Society: On the Political Function of Heresy in the Medieval

Beginning with the legation of Hildebrand and Anselm of Lucca to Germany on October 18, 1057, that stopped over in Milan, Stephen imposed the yoke of the Roman papacy on the "bullheaded" bishops opposed by the *pataria*.[61]

The two individual acts for which Stephen is most remembered are appointing Petrus Damiani as cardinal bishop of Ostia, and just before his death, stipulating that there should be no election until Hildebrand returned.[62] Stephen knew that Hildebrand would not allow the Roman nobility to control the election of his successor, and that he would give Godfrey a strong voice. Ironically, even though there was strong sentiment that Hildebrand should have been present at his own election, he allowed it to take place without his presence, probably to preempt any action by the Roman nobles. Bonizo insinuates that the same threat remained, and that Stephen wanted Hildebrand to be present because he knew that laymen would try to take over the election of his successor.[63]

Bonizo says that Pope Stephen was said to have the gift of prophesy, for a few days before he died, he called together bishops, cardinals and deacons, and said to them: "I know, brethren, that after my death there shall rise up among you men, loving themselves, who will seize this see not according to the decrees of the Holy Fathers, but through lay persons." Those attending vehemently denied that they would do such a thing, and swore with their hands within those of the pope that they would never ascend to the papal throne, nor consent to another's ascent except by the decrees of the Holy Fathers. Bonizo states that a few days later the pope arrived in Tuscany, where, feeling weak, he gave up his spirit to heaven.

With a child king and a vulnerable regency, the nobility of Rome and the suburban areas, particularly the Tusculani and the Crescentii,

---

World," pp. 23–41 of *Texts and the Repression of Medieval Heresy*, ed. Caterina Bruschi & Peter Biller; York Studies in Medieval Theology 4 (York, 2003), esp. p. 27; Sascha Ragg, *Ketzer und Recht: Die weltliche Ketzergesetzgebung des Hochmittelalters unter dem Einfluss des römischen und kanonischen Rechts*. MGH Studien und Texte, vol. 37 (Hannover, 2006).

[61] Hägermann, *Das Papsttum*, p. 52; see the translation and informative introduction to "The Pataria: Andrea da Strumi's passion of Arialdo," by Bill North; *Medieval Italy: Texts in Translation*, ed. Katherine L. Jansen, Joanna Drell, & Frances Andrews, (Philadelphia, 2009), pp. 337–350.

[62] Petrus Damiani, *Briefe*, nr. 58, 2:193–194; tr. Blum, 2:392.

[63] Bonizo, *Ad Amicum*, p. 592; Watterich, 1:201; Robinson, *The Papal Reform of the Eleventh Century*, pp. 200–201.

saw their chance, and as Stephen had foreseen, they took it. Immediately after Stephen's death they engineered the election of a pope of their choosing. Their pope lasted but a short time, but the contest would be broadened to pit the reformers against those who broadly defended tradition. The stakes will be much higher, and what had been a supportive relationship between the papacy and the empire will become competitive and combative.

Even though the intentions of the unheralded Victor II were simply to help the transition to the new monarch after the death of Henry III, to his successors he had already set the stage for papal superiority over the emperor. Both sides promoted internal ecclesiastical reform, but the reformers will demand the abolition of lay investiture. The reign of Gregory VII will be a turning point, going beyond ecclesiastical reform and the prohibition of lay investiture to establishing universal papal rule.[64]

Amatus had an astonishingly negative opinion of the popes following Stephen IX. He said: "We shall not speak further of the name and succession of the pontiffs of Rome since honour declined in Rome after the disappearance of the Germans. If I should speak further of their behaviour and elections, I would have to lie, and if I were to tell the truth, I would incur the wrath of the Romans."[65] After Stephen IX Amatus carried out his vow, discontinuing any narrative of their reigns.

---

[64] Manfred Weitlauff, "Von der Reichskirche zur 'papstkirche': Säkularisation, Kirchliche Neuorganisation und Durchsetzing der papalistischen Doktrin," *Zeitschrift für Kirchengeschichte* 113 (2002) nr. 3, 355–402.

[65] Amatus, *The History of the Normans*, III, 53, p. 108.

CHAPTER FIVE

## BENEDICT X: ROMANS VERSUS REFORMERS

Stephen IX was the last pope since Henry III restored order within the papacy to reign without challenge until the end of the century. The two men who claimed to be his successor—Benedict X and Nicholas II— begin a series of papal schisms, the nature of which will differ. Benedict X represented the Roman nobility, while Nicholas II represented the reformers, and was supported by the Normans and the house of Lotharingia/Canossa. With the exception of Philipp Jaffé, who emphasized that Benedict was elected first and therefore not an antipope, historians acknowledge Nicholas as pope.[1]

This lone voice focused on what was crucial about this otherwise mostly inconsequential schism. Benedict was swiftly elected more or less according to traditional procedures. Faced with this fait accompli, Hildebrand and the reformers had to act creatively to emplace their own candidate. They crafted procedures without precedent, and elicited the confirmation of the emperor/regency before the election. In an exercise in *Realpolitik*, they formulated a canonical decree to justify his election after their candidate had prevailed.

The backers of both contenders used military force and money. Benedict's short reign revealed the diminution of power of his local backers, and the rise of a new Roman aristocracy. The reign of Nicholas was important for many reasons, foremost among them the alliance of the papacy with the Normans, and the papal electoral decree of 1059. His critics will scorn him as a mere pawn in the hands of Hildebrand.

### The Elections of Benedict X and Nicholas II

On April 5, 1058, only days after Stephen IX's death on March 29, the Romans elected Cardinal Bishop John of Velletri as Pope Benedict X.[2]

---

[1] Lino Lionello Ghirardini, *L'antipapa Cadalo e il tempo del Bene e del Male: Grandezza e Miseria del piu'Famoso Vescovo di Parma (1045–1071)*; Centro di Studi Canossiani (1984), p. 25.

[2] Lampert, *Annales*, p. 73: "Sedem apostolicam protinus inconsulto rege et principibus, invasit Benedictus quidam Lateranensis, adiutus factione popularium, quos

Since Stephen had died in Florence, and the news of his death took time to reach Rome, the election was organized in remarkable haste. Such speed suggests two possible causes: (1) that the Romans and the most powerful counts, the *capitanei*, were not to be caught off guard by a quick election by the reformers as they had been with Stephen IX, and (2) that they anticipated Stephen's death, and were prepared to spring into action.

The election itself was hardly pro forma, for we recall that Stephen had made the Roman clergy swear that they would not allow laymen to participate in the election, and that they would wait for the return of Hildebrand before acting. The *capitanei*, who regarded Hildebrand as their enemy, persuaded the Roman clergy—including John of Velletri—to disregard their oath, and to submit to their intervention. In the middle of the night lit by torches John was elected as Benedict X. Promoted to cardinal by Leo IX, of good character, but unimpressive, John did not want the job. He probably acceded to the request because he felt that he represented the Romans in the face of German intrusions.[3] He was derisively called mincio, a simpleton, a clever play on words based on a reference in the *Regesto farfense* that he was related to a Gregorio Mincio.

Even though he was elected before Hildebrand returned and did not have the consent of Henry IV and the regency, he was considered to be pope until the five cardinal bishops, who had arrived in Florence, declared on dubious grounds that his election was illegal.[4] Not until December 6, 1058, after securing the consent of Henry IV and the regency, was Bishop Gerard of Florence elected as Nicholas II in Siena by a small group of men of international origin. There was no participation of the clergy and the people of Rome, and not even an acclamation. For those who elected him, the pope was not so much the bishop of Rome as he was the leader of Christendom and the promoter of moral/ethical reform in the West. To them, Benedict's election meant nothing.

---

pecunia corruperat." *Chron. Mont.* 2.99, p. 356; Bonizo, *Ad Amicum*, p. 592; *Annales Altahenses*, p. 54; Ovidio Capitani, "Benedetto X antipapa," *Enciclopedia dei Papi*, 2:168–171; Hägermann, *Das Papsttum*, pp. 57–64; Meyer von Knonau, *Jahrbücher* 1:85–92; Blumenthal, *Gregor VII.*, pp. 85–86 & n. 100.

   [3] Alexander Cartellieri, *Der Aufstieg des Papsttuums im Rahmen der Weltgeschichgte 1047–1095* (Munich, Berlin, 1936), p. 44.

   [4] Goez, *Kirchenreform und Investiturstreit*, pp.103–104.

The regency ordered Godfrey to accompany Nicholas and his entourage to Rome, and in January on the way they stopped at Sutri, where Benedict was deposed. Godfrey's army from Tuscia or Tuscany attacked Benedict's supporters in Rome, and on January 24, 1059, Benedict fled, first to Passarano (Tivoli), and then to Galeria. There he kept his claim to be the legally elected pope alive until May 1059, when Hildebrand and Nicholas invoked their southern strategy. Hildebrand personally traveled to Capua to solicit the support of Richard, its Norman leader, against Benedict, and in return for swearing an oath of fidelity to the Roman church, Richard received the investiture of Capua as a principate.

Richard immediately demonstrated his loyalty by sending three hundred troops under the command of three counts to assist the forces of Nicholas, who attacked Galeria in May. The first attack failed, but a second one in June raised the fear of a siege. Benedict climbed on top of the wall and cried out to the Romans that it was you who forced me to be pope even though I was unwilling. Guarantee me my life, he shouted, and I will abdicate. Three hundred Romans agreed to do so.[5] Benedict knelt before Nicholas, who permitted him to return to Rome in the summer of 1059, and to dwell in the area around Santa Maria Maggiore, where his mother still lived. Seeing that the die was cast, the towns of Palestrina, Tusculum and Nomentum (today, Mentana) submitted. From this outline, let us examine germane sources to see the differences in understanding, proclivities, and perspective.

### Benedict's Tragic Reign

The *Annales Romani*, describe Benedict's failed reign in melodramatic detail. Not uncharacteristically, they are riddled with errors, but by winnowing out the wheat from the chaff, one can still glean valuable information.[6] They erroneously report that Hildebrand secured the election of the bishop of Florence [Gerard] before the election of John of Velletri, and state that Hildebrand promised Gerard that if he would come with him to Rome, he would make him pope. Gerard agreed, and carrying a great amount of money, they began their journey with 500 horsemen.

---

[5] *Annales Romani*, *Lib. Pont.* 2:335: "Vos me invitum nolentemque elegistis pontificem, vos me securum facite, et ego rennuo vestrum esse pontificem."
[6] Ibid., 2:334–336.

Reacting in anger, those faithful to the emperor elected the bishop of Velletri from the area around Santa Maria Maggiore as Benedict. Although John was at first unwilling to accept the honor, willingly or not, he was ordained as Roman pope. The Roman people were given money to win their favor, and counts around the city, including Albericus [in fact it was his son, Gregory, brother of Benedict IX], the count of Galeria, the count of Tusculum, and the sons of the Crescentii of Monticelli supported him.

Hearing this, Hildebrand brought his procession to a halt, and sent money from Benedictus Christianus and other conspirators. The Roman people were divided, and began to fight among themselves. The Transtiberini sent legates to Hildebrand inviting him swiftly to come to Trastevere, which he did. Thereafter, he moved on to the island of Lyaconia [an island in the Tiber between Trastevere and the city]. The counts divided themselves between the two sides as daily fights and murders continued.

During this turmoil Hildebrand along with his papal elect and conspirators deposed Peter, the prefect from the region of S. Angelo [across the Tiber from Trastevere], and replaced him with John Tiniosus from Trastevere. In the end the supporters of Benedict were defeated, and he fled from the Lateran to the castle of Passarano under the control of the son of the prefect, Crescentius. Thereafter, the archdeacon (subdeacon), Hildebrand, took his papal elect to the Lateran where he was ordained Roman pope with the name of Nicholas [January 24, 1059], and money was distributed.[7]

Nicholas toured the city to gain the allegiance of the people. Some swore with their left hand, saying, "Because with the right hand we swear fidelity to our lord pope Benedict, to you, indeed, we give our left." Then, secretly in the night, Benedict slipped away from Passarano to Count Girard at Galeria. Later, having garnered the support of 300 Normans, Nicholas and his Roman army attacked. The attack failed, but fearing a siege by the Romans, Girard succumbed to a second incursion. About 300 noble Romans responded to Benedict's plea to save him, swearing an oath to protect him in every way, and to keep him secure in Rome with all of his possessions.

---

[7] Hildebrand is not known for sure to be archdeacon until Oct. 14, 1059; Cowdrey, *Gregory VII*, pp. 37–39.

Nicholas II returned to Rome with his army, and Benedict, having removed his papal vestments, also returned to the home of his mother near Santa Maria Maggiore. After thirty days [April 1060] archdeacon Hildebrand apprehended him through force, and took him into the chapel of the Savior in the Constantine basilica (the Lateran), where a hearing was held before Pope Nicholas in the third week after Easter.[8] Denuded of his priestly vestments, Benedict was led to the altar before Nicholas. A paper on which were written all of the crimes and sins that iniquitous men had committed was placed in his hands.

At first he refused to recite them, protesting that the charges did not pertain to him, but unwillingly, and with lamentations and tears, he eventually read them. Standing with loosened hair, his mother and those supporting her groaned and beat their chests. At this point Hildebrand intervened and told the Romans to hear what kind of man they had elected pope. Thereafter, he told Benedict to put on his papal garments as though he were pope, and he was deposed and expelled from the priesthood. The private hearing had been arranged during the Lenten Council that dealt with broader issues of the reform.

Benedict was then incarcerated in the church of Santa Agnese, where, deprived of the divine office, he eked out a miserable life until Suppus, the archpriest of St. Anastasius, and the spiritual advisor of Nicholas, asked the pope to be merciful. Nicholas restored some privileges, and Benedict lived until Hildebrand was elected pope as Gregory VII in 1073. Suppus informed Gregory of Benedict's death, and suggested the way in which he should be buried. In the end Benedict's old enemy conceded that he should be honorably buried in the basilica of Santa Agnese, and all of the Roman clergy attended.

Such is the account of the *Annales* that may conflate the electors of Benedict with the electors of subsequent popes, who were more identified with the emperor. Henry III had rejected the Roman candidates and appointed his own, and the regency and Henry IV approved Bishop Gerard of Florence as Nicholas II. Benedict was the choice of the Romans and the local counts, and did not seek the approval of the regency. Perhaps the confusion arises because the *Annales* are clearly hostile to Hildebrand, who in the future as pope will dispute imperial rights over papal elections, and many of the Romans will support the emperor. In this period, as the leader of the reform Hildebrand like

---

[8] *Annales Romani, Lib. Pont.* 2:335–336; Gresser, *Konziliengeschichte*, p. 51.

Henry III appropriated the election of the pope from the Romans and the local counts.

## The Pierleoni

While sharply curtailing the rights of the present-day powerful counts in papal elections, Hildebrand did not eschew accepting help from the nobility. Indeed, he relied upon it, but it was the newer nobility, especially the Frangipani and the Pierleoni, in contrast to the more established families. The *Annales* mention Benedictus Christianus, who, they say, contributed money that enabled Hildebrand and Gerard to make it to Rome. Benedictus Christianus was formerly Baruch, the head of a Jewish family of financiers, who converted to Christianity in the middle of the eleventh century. In this case it was not Baruch, but his son, Leo.

Benzo of Alba especially frequently mentions the close connection between Hildebrand and Leo. Even though Leo was born a Christian, and was baptized, he is often referred to as Leo Judeus. Leo sired a son, Petrus Leonis after whom the Pierleoni were named, and from the beginning they were staunch supporters of the reform papacy.[9] Petrus, the son of Petrus Leonis, became cardinal priest of Santa Maria in Trastevere, and was elected pope as Anaclet II a few hours after Gregory of S. Angelo was elected Innocent II in 1130. Among other propaganda used against him in his losing campaign to be recognized as the legally pope was his family's Jewish origin.

The family at first seems to have been located in Trastevere, but as they prospered they took over the island between Trastevere and the right bank, and eventually established their stronghold around the Teatro Marcello, transformed into a fortress, and the adjoining area known as the Schola Graeca. The church of S. Nicola in Carcere in this area became their virtual *Eigenkirche*. Under the influence of this new family, Trastevere reached out to Hildebrand, and provided a safe haven for him in Rome. The elections of Nicholas II and Benedict X chart the beginning of the tilt of the newer nobility toward Hildebrand and the reformers.

---

[9] Pietro Fedele, "Le Famiglie di Anacleto II e di Gelasio II," *Archivio della R. società Romana di Storia Patria* 27 (1904), 339–443; Mary Stroll, *The Jewish Pope: Ideology and Politics in the Papal Schism of 1130* (Leiden, 1987), *passim*.

## *Petrus Damiani*

Petrus Damiani was an eye witness to the events surrounding the election of Benedict, and although he was not present at the election of Nicholas II, he was active during his reign. He participated in the drafting of the ground-breaking papal electoral decree of 1059, and analyzed it in the subtle dialogue between a royal advocate and a papal defender. He was sent on a mission to Milan, where he encountered an uprising of the *patarini*, with which Gregory VII would ally himself. After calming tempers, he succeeded in getting the see of Milan, the church of St. Ambrose, to accept the primacy of Rome.

This prolific, talented communicator discharged many missions, and did not hesitate to pit his positions against those of others determined to shape the course of the reform. Although basically Hildebrand's ideological ally, he also coined the most striking moniker of the fiery leader. In a letter written between June and December 1058 to Hildebrand and to the papal elect, Bishop Gerard of Florence, Petrus calls Hildebrand his "Holy Satan." He holds him to be responsible for making himself cardinal bishop of Ostia, and begs to be relieved of his duties because of health and old age.[10] The combination of "Holy" and "Satan" adroitly expresses the dichotomy that many contemporaries felt about Hildebrand, a pious ascetic given to extremes, and according to some, to nefarious practices of necromancy and even worse. In this same letter Petrus states that people are accustomed to admiring the man who occupies the Holy See, and he bemoans the fact that it is now occupied by the despicable Mintio [Benedict X].

At the end of 1058 Petrus wrote to Henry, archbishop of Ravenna, comparing Benedict X with Nicholas II.[11] In Rome when Benedict was elected, he criticizes the candidate of the Romans as a simonist, who was unable to clear himself of this crime. He reports that in the face of the outcry, the objections, and the terrible anathemas of the cardinal bishops at Rome, and with armed mobs rushing about, Benedict was enthroned during the night. Thereafter, Petrus charges, Benedict acquired the tainted patronage of wealthy men, and even

---

[10] Petrus Damiani, *Briefe*, nr. 57, 2:167: "Sed hoc ego sancto Sathanae meo respondeo, quod filii Ruben et Gat Moysi ductori suo respondisse noscuntur:" tr. Blum, 2:369–389; Reindel says that the letter probably never was sent.

[11] Ibid., nr. 58, 190–194; tr. Blum, 2:390–393.

broke into the ancient treasury of Saint Peter, disbursing money in every alley throughout the city.

He accuses Benedict of trying to conceal his crime of simony in every way that he could, using the excuses that he had been dragged into becoming pope, and that he was forcibly compelled to act in the way that he did. Petrus admits that he does not know all of the facts, but observes that since Benedict was so obtuse and lazy, and a man of so little talent, that one could conclude that he might not have been capable of planning these events himself. But he charges that Benedict was nevertheless guilty because he willingly wallowed in the foul mess into which he had been thrown.

Realizing that he has gone on at length about Benedict, Petrus proceeds to the humiliating course of events that this bishop constrained to be pope was forced to traverse. He states that while we bishops were going our individual ways into hiding [to escape the violence in Rome], the followers of Satan seized upon a priest of Ostia, and forced him to promote [the bishop of Velletri] to the apostolic see. The priest of Ostia to whom he referred was the archpriest, whose right it was to consecrate the pope if the bishop was absent, and in this case, the bishop was Petrus himself. Petrus derides the archpriest for not even being able to read correctly, and regards his participation as uncanonical, and the election as invalid. If that was not enough, he adds that under the penalty of excommunication Pope Stephen had ordained that if he were to die before subdeacon Hildebrand returned from the court of the empress, the Apostolic See should remain vacant until he returned.

Petrus goes on to praise the papal elect (Nicholas II) as well-educated, a man of brisk intelligence, chaste above all suspicion, and generous in giving alms. But then he covers himself a bit, declining to say more so as not to appear amenable to everything that Nicholas did, and restricting himself to serving as an advocate for specific actions. As for Benedict, Petrus vowed that if the man who would be pope could say anything on his own behalf, he would no longer utter a word against him. Rather, he would take his hand, kiss his feet, and call him not merely apostolic, but an apostle. Dripping with sarcasm, he chides Benedict for being incapable of saying the most trivial thing in his own defense. He concludes by pleading that his letter be made public so that all would realize the danger that Benedict's election presented to the whole world. In sum, Petrus depicts Benedict as an ignominious pawn in the hands of local forces, and sees the Romans rather than the counts as the prime movers.

## Leo of Ostia

Leo of Ostia was greatly influenced by Petrus Damiani's account of Benedict's election and downfall, but in the *Chronicle of Montecassino* he describes it from his own perspective.[12] He reports that after the death of Stephen IX, the brothers, who had accompanied the pope to Florence, were terrified to return to Montecassino through Rome, and took a detour through the Marche. They rightly feared violence in Rome, Leo says, for Count Gregory of Tusculum had allied himself with Girard of Galeria and powerful Romans, and in the middle of the night they invaded Rome with a fury of armed men, imposing the reluctant [Bishop] John of Velletri on the throne as Pope Benedict. More than Petrus, Leo stresses the role of the counts in imposing the hapless Mincius on the papal throne.

Petrus was horrified at the way that John was forced upon the papacy, Leo notes, and his opinion carried great weight, since from boyhood he was exceptionally knowledgeable in both divine and secular letters, and went from being a hermit to the bishop of Ostia during the reign of Stephen. Leo says that when Petrus discovered what had happened, he cooperated with other cardinals in resisting in whatever way that they could, but that in the end they were forced to flee into hiding. After a scathing reference to the archpriest of Ostia, Leo mentions Humbert of Moyenmoutier, now cardinal bishop of Silva Candida. More radical than Petrus, Humbert's positions on issues concerning the reform were frequently contrasted with those of his sometimes rival, but in this context Leo simply mentions that Humbert returned to Rome from Florence with Peter, bishop of Tusculum, and seeing the turbulent situation, he moved on to Benevento.[13] When Desiderius assumed the office of abbot of Montecassino at Eastertide, 1058, Humbert was there, and participated in the ceremonies.[14]

## Liber Pontificalis

In his Hildebrand-centered account in the *Liber Pontificalis*, Peter William is nevertheless less hostile in his appraisal of John of Velletri,

---

[12] *Chron. Mont.*, 2.98–99, pp. 356–357; 3.9–12, pp. 369–373.
[13] *Annales Camaldulenses*, 2:189; The *Annales Camaldulenses* rely heavily on Petrus Damiani, and Leo of Ostia.
[14] Cowdrey, *Abbot Desiderius*, p. 117.

and he reveals the depth of Benedict's support in Rome.[15] Peter identifies John as a Roman, and says that he was expelled and deposed from
the papacy by archdeacon Hildebrand, who was outside of the city
(Rome) at the time of the election on instructions from the bishops
and the cardinals, and that it had been stipulated that no election
should take place until he returned. Without mentioning the election
of Nicholas II in Siena, he reports that hearing about the death of the
pope when he was in Florence, Hildebrand brought Gerard, bishop of
Florence, with him to Rome, and learned what had happened.

When Hildebrand questioned the bishops and cardinals about
whether they had kept their promises, Peter William says that some of
them did not defend themselves, and admitted that they should not
have done what they did. Others did defend themselves, protesting
that John of Velletri was good, wise, humble, chaste and kind, and that
they had done the right thing. The quarrel persisted for a long time,
Peter William reports, but in the end the supporters of Benedict were
unable to sway Hildebrand, and most of the clerics and laymen sided
with him. After deposing and ejecting Benedict from the papacy, they
elected Gerard, bishop of Florence as Nicholas II.

*German Sources*

Berthold of Reichenau and Bernold of Konstanz, two influential South
German writers, stress an imperial/papal perspective.[16] Berthold, a
monk, a scholar, and a writer at the imperial abbey of Reichenau, was a
student and close friend of Herman the Lame, who supported the Salian
monarchy and its close relationship with the church, and who died in
1054. Berthold wrote two versions of his chronicle, and in a previous
edition, his first account was considered to be a continuation of the
chronicle of Herman, partly because his first version was pro-imperial.

---

[15] *Lib. Pont.* 2:279.

[16] *Die Chroniken Bertholds von Reichenau und Bernolds von Konstanz, 1054–1100,*
ed. Ian S. Robinson, MGH, SRG Nova Series14; the first and second versions of
Berthold's chronicle are printed side by side through 1066 when the first version ends;
pp. 163–202; second version, pp. 163–381; Bernold's chronicle, 1054–1100, pp. 385–
540; see the excellent review by Uta Renate Blumenthal, *Speculum* 81 (2006), pp.
588–590.

See also *Bertholds und Bernolds Chroniken,* ed. Ian Stuart Robinson, German tr. by
Helga Robinson-Hammerstein and Ian Stuart Robinson, (Darmstadt, 2002); Bertholdi
Chronicon, forma prima, pp. 19–33; forma secunda, pp. 35–277; Bernoldi Chronicon,
pp. 279–433; the chronicles and German translation are printed side by side; for an
older edition of Berthold's Chronicle, MGH SS 5:264–326.

Later, greatly influenced by his colleague, Bernold, the most zealous supporter of Gregory VII in Southern Germany, Berthold became a partisan of Gregory, and a fierce opponent of Henry IV. A second chronicle that he wrote shows these proclivities, and offers an invaluable contrast between his original thinking, and what it became. In the case of Benedict, Berthold states inaccurately in both versions that Pope Stephen died at Rome, but in the first version he was more expansive. He identifies Benedict as a certain John, and reports that money was involved. Both versions state that Benedict was elected against the canons, and that in a matter of days he was expelled by Duke Godfrey [the bearded], and Nicholas II was elected.[17]

Bernold was a polemicist, who wrote on the conflict between the papacy and the empire, emphasizing obedience, the relationship between clergy and laity, and papal primacy. In his chronicle he transmitted an array of letters, conciliar decisions, and ideas, mostly of Gregory VII. As an indication of how non contentious the election of Benedict appeared in Germany, he conveys virtually the same information as Berthold I and II.[18]

The *Annales Altahenses* from the monastery of Altaic are a valuable source because they are more neutral and less polemical. They state that after Stephen died, another [Benedict X] was elected and secretly consecrated. Since this was not acceptable to the chief men (*principes*), a legate was sent to the king requesting his sanction of the bishop of Florence. The king approved the petition, and Nicholas was accepted as pope.[19] The chief men were obviously Hildebrand and the other reformers, who found it expedient to appeal to the king, but who would diminish the king's role in papal elections in the Lenten Council of 1059.

### Bonizo

In *Ad Amicum* Bonizo reports that exactly as Stephen IX had predicted, it was the *capitanei*, and especially Gregory of Tusculum, who were

---

[17] Ibid., version 1, p. 184: "Romae Stephanus papa obiit. Romani accepta pecunia quendam Ioannem contra canones elegerunt, qui sine consecratione per aliquot dies sedens, a Gotefrido duce expellitur..." version 2, p.184: "Rome post Stephanum quidam Benedictus contra canones privata quorundam gratia electus, sine consecratione mensibus VII prefuit ecclesie. Qui a Gotifrido duce expulsus..."

[18] Ibid. 389.

[19] *Annales Altahenses*. p. 54.

responsible for Benedict's election.[20] He charges that Gregory created a
tyranny, claiming for himself the worthless dignity of *patricius*. With
that authority, and contrary to the oath that John of Velletri had sworn
to Stephen IX, he set up John as pope. Like almost all other writers,
Bonizo mentions that John was derisively called Mincio. His innovation
was the allegation that Gregory of Tusculum claimed the empty title of
*patricius*. As we recall, the Romans had granted the dignity of *patricius*
to Henry III at the time of his coronation, and that Henry had used this
authority to select four German popes. Bonizo could very well be
accurate, however, for Henry III was dead, and in 1061 the Romans
will bring the emblems of the patriciate to Henry IV.

*Panvinius*

Panvinius, a sixteenth-century Augustinian canon and artist, who
described and sketched many monuments in Rome, wrote several
books, and edited a book of popes written by Platinus that briefly mentions Benedict. Although far removed from the eleventh century,
Panvinius had access to materials that have since been lost, and for this
reason his accounts generally merit some consideration. In 1563 he
referred to the elections of Benedict and Nicholas in *De varia Romani
pontificis creatione*.[21] He states that without consulting the king and the
princes, but supported by the people, who were corrupted by money,
Benedict invaded the Lateran.

In the meantime the Roman princes sent a message to the king
promising him the same fidelity that they had shown to his father
[Henry III], and requesting that he transmit the name of his choice for
pope. After consulting with his advisors, the king chose Gerard, bishop
of Florence, who was agreeable both to the Germans and to the
Romans, and designated Duke Godfrey to accompany him to Rome.
In this way, Panvinius concludes, Benedict, who had usurped the
throne without the order of the king and the princes, was rejected, and
Gerard accepted as Nicholas II.[22]

---

[20] Bonizo, p. 592; Robinson, *The Papal Reform of the Eleventh Century*, p. 201.
[21] Clm 147; Stroll, *The Medieval Abbey of Farfa*, pp. 157–158.
[22] Ibid., 148, fols. 98v–99r: "Interim Romani principes satisfactionem ad Regem
mittunt se, scilicet fidem, quam patri dedissent, filio, quoad possent, servaturos, eoque
animo vacanti Romanae sedi pontificem usque ad id tempus non subrogasse, eius magis super hoc expectore sententiam, orantque sedulo, ut quem ipse velit, transmittat.

In the book of popes by Platinus that he edited Panvinius states that "Mintio," bishop of Velletri, was originally from Capua, and attributes his election to outside forces.[23] He asserts that [Benedict] was created pope by a few nobles when Agnes (the empress) sent Guibert of Parma, a person lacking in judgment, to govern the kingdom of Italy. This is the same Guibert, who will become archbishop of Ravenna, and who will be elected [anti]pope, Clement III, in 1080/1084. At this time, however, he was acting in concert with Hildebrand.

Panvinius also mentions that Godfrey was a major force because he was married to Mathilda, the daughter of Beatrice and Boniface of Lucca, who was very powerful in Italy. Here Panvinius is way off because the Godfrey that married Mathilda was the son of the Godfrey "the bearded," who married Beatrice, and it was this Godfrey, who was much involved in papal/imperial politics at this time. Panvinius, however, was correct in emphasizing the strength of this family that controlled Lucca, Parma, Reggio, Mantua, and that part of Tuscany that in his time was called the patrimony of St. Peter.

Panvinius said that when Hildebrand returned from Germany, a great contest ensued once he discovered that Benedict had been elected, perceived as a prudent person, and approved by many. Others, he pointed out, seeing him as elected illegitimately, reproved and abased him. Finally, at the instigation of Hildebrand, and with the approval of the majority of the clergy, Panvinius says that Bishop Gerard of Florence was recognized as worthy of the papal dignity. Benedict was deposed, having held the papacy for two years and six months. A footnote states that Benedict was not the legitimate pope because, according to a letter written by Petrus Damiani, he was elected through simony.

The two versions slightly vary, but in the first he distinguishes between the people, who supported Benedict, and the princes, who supported Nicholas. Those princes must have been the descendants of Benedictus Christianus and other new nobility. Secondly, the reformers

---

Nihil eius ordinatione obstante, se quis non per legitimate electionis ostium, sed aliunde ascendisset in ovium ovile. Rex habita cum primoribus deliberatione, Gerardum Florentinum Episcopum, in quem et Romanorum et Teutonicorum studia consenserant, pontificem designate, Romamque per Gotefridum ducem transmittit. Ita Benedicto, qui iniussu regis et principum sacerdotium usurpaverat, reprobate, Gerardus, qui et Nicolaus II, pontificatum obtinuit."

[23] Onofrio Panvinio, *Le Vite de'Pontifici di Bartolomeo Plantina Cremonese* (1567), p. 227.

still maintained that it was requisite to have the imprimatur of the king, and Gerard of Florence was his choice. In the case of Stephen IX they could ignore the king because they did not need him. Now they did. It was a matter of pragmatism, not a matter of the correct relationship between *regnum* and *sacerdotium*.

## Conclusion

From these and other disparate and conflicting sources some features stand out. The old Roman nobility and the counts from the surrounding area had lost much of their power over the papacy, and new families allied with Hildebrand, most prominently the family of Benedictus Christianus, were replacing them. The Lotharingian, "Godfrey the Bearded" and his wife, Beatrice, were the most powerful rulers in Italy, and with his military force, Godfrey was becoming the arbiter of disputed papal elections. He assured the triumph of his protégé, Bishop Gerard of Florence as Nicholas II over Benedict X.

Still a subdeacon when Benedict was elected, Hildebrand performed brilliantly as a consummate politician. No more meticulous than the counts and the Romans in achieving his goals, he drew on both money and military force. With dwindling support, Benedict seemed to be relieved to relinquish the burden of the papacy, and to live quietly with his mother, but for Hildebrand this was not enough. He must be humiliated and scorned. Under his impetus, but with the titular authority of Nicholas, a hearing was held in the chapel of the Holy Savior in the Lateran palace where Benedict was mortified and deposed wearing his papal garments. Prohibiting him from carrying out his priestly functions while in captivity was a further form of degradation that would make any churchman think twice before challenging Hildebrand's candidate.

As yet, there was no cleavage between the reformers and Henry IV and the regency. On the contrary, Hildebrand sought the approval of Henry IV for the election of Gerard in order to displace Benedict. This amity will cease with the death of Nicholas and the advent of another papal schism. As a sign of significant changes, this time the candidate opposing the reformers will have the approval of both the regency and the Romans, but be a Lombard.

CHAPTER SIX

NICHOLAS II (1059–1061)

Viewed through the prism of the reform, the reign of Nicholas II looks like a crucial link in the long progression of popes starting with Leo IX. He was the choice of Hildebrand and the reformers, he drafted a decree that put the election of popes in the hands of the cardinals with scant authority allocated to the emperor, he diminished the emperor as the protector of the papacy by making the Normans in Southern Italy its chief defenders, and he was the first pope to prohibit lay investiture— that no cleric or priest shall receive a church from layman in any fashion, whether freely or at a price.[1] The record cannot be denied, but it must be put into context to see what factors other than ecclesiastical reform motivated these innovations.

Was the papal electoral decree, for example, a declaration of ecclesiastical independence directed by the reform papacy against both the emperor and the factions of Roman nobility that had manipulated papal elections in the past? Did the decree ignore the rights of the emperor that had accumulated since the time of Charlemagne, or was it also, if not primarily, a means for justifying Nicholas' own questionable election?[2] Did Nicholas look to the Normans as a means to divest the papacy from imperial control, or was he motivated primarily by the recognition that the regency acting for a child king was not capable of defending the papacy?

Long by comparison with the reigns of his recent predecessors, the reign of Nicholas produced a number of almost revolutionary developments besides those mentioned above. In addition to the Normans, Nicholas looked to Godfrey and Beatrice, and the combined power of the houses of Lotharingia and Canossa for support. During his reign the collaboration between the papacy and the *patarini*, the secular movement mainly dedicated to opposing the clerical hierarchy in

---

[1] MGH Constitutiones et Acta 1:547.
[2] Brian Tierney, *The Crisis of Church & State 1050–1300 with selected documents* (New Jersey, 1964), p. 36; e. g. Johannes Haller, *Idee und Wirklichkeit*, 5 vols. (Munich, 1950–53, repr. 1965), 2:324.

Lombardy, coalesced. And perhaps most pregnant for the future, as the first pope to be crowned he instilled a monarchical character to the papacy. All of these factors contributed to producing the subsequent papal schisms that were generated not simply from tensions between *regnum* and *sacerdotium*, but from a multiplicity of causes.

## Background and Election

Little is known of Gerard's early life. He was born in Burgundy, and became the bishop of Florence by January 9, 1045, doubtless with the approval of Boniface, Beatrice's first husband.[3] Florence had become an important city because it was the residence of her second husband, Duke Godfrey, and since the house of Lotharingia/Canossa was allied with the reform papacy, Gerard's position became even stronger. He participated in synods of Leo IX prohibiting clerical marriage and simony, and he also participated in a large synod at Florence called by Victor II in which Henry III was present.[4] He was known for his piety, and he encouraged the clergy to live as canons regular, a policy that he pursued as pope in the Patrimony of St. Peter. Petrus Damiani speaks very favorably of his intelligence and character.[5]

When Stephen IX died in Florence on March 29, 1058, after a scant eight-month reign, Gerard was poised to be his successor. As we have seen, the Romans did not keep their oath to wait for Hildebrand to return from the German court to elect a successor, but elected Bishop John of Velletri as Benedict X on April 5, 1058.[6] Unwilling to accept this swift election, Petrus Damiani and the other cardinal bishops fled to Florence.

Meanwhile, Hildebrand was enjoying excellent relations with the regency in Germany, where he and Anselm of Lucca had traveled to secure its approval for the election of Stephen IX. The two legates joined Henry and Agnes in the consecration of the bishop of

---

[3] For an excellent synopsis of his reign see Annamaria Ambrosioni, "Niccolò II," *Enciclopedia dei Papi*, 2:172–177; Hägermann, *Das Papsttum*, pp. 65–217; Cowdrey, *Gregory VII*, pp. 43–49; Elke Goez, *Beatrix von Canossa*, pp. 154–157.

[4] Gresser, *Konziliengeschichte*, pp. 30–31.

[5] Petrus Damiani, *Briefe*, nr. 58, 2:190–194; tr. Blum, 2: 390–393.

[6] Lampert, *Annales*, p. 73; Lampert was well educated at the cathedral school of Bamberg; and entered monastery of Hersfeld in 1058. He was greatly influenced by Roman historiography. To him Henry was responsible for the evil afflicting his realm;

Poleda in Thuringia, and spent the Christmas holidays with them at Merseburg.[7] Not until May 15, 1058, over two months after Stephen IX's death, did they return to Florence to oversee the election of a successor.[8]

Most probably they collaborated with Godfrey of Lotharingia, whom they saw on May 16, and Guibert of Ravenna, the German chancellor and imperial vicar representing the regency in Italy.[9] Responding to Godfrey's wishes, Hildebrand consulted with the Roman clergy and laity at Florence, and then sent a delegation to the German court at Augsburg to obtain the regency's consent to the selection of Gerard as pope. Lampert of Hersfeld reports that the regency declared that Gerard was suitable both to the Germans and the Romans—by which he obviously meant the reformers opposed to Benedict X—and granted their approval on June 9, 1058.[10]

After confirmation at a council in Augsburg on June 12, the group repaired to Siena, where, in the presence of Wibert of Ravenna, and most probably Godfrey and Beatrice, Gerard was elected as Nicholas II in December, 1058, most likely on December 6.[11] Why the long wait

---

[7] Jean Mabillon, *Annales ordinis S. Benedicti occidentalium monachorum patriarchae* (Lucca, Paris, 1739-1740), 4:536: "Eodem anno [1058] in festo sancti Johannis apostoli consecratus est Gundekarus Eitetensis episcopus in loco Turingiae dicto Poleda, cui Hildebrandus sanctae Romanae ecclesiae subdiaconus cum Heinrico imperatore & Agnete augusta interfuisse dicitur. Lambertus suffragatur, testatus, regem Merseburgi natalem Domini celebrasse, ibique adfuisse, inter alios regni principes, etiam Hildebrandum abbatem de sancto Paulo, mandata deferentem ab sede apostolica, virum & eloquentia, & sacrarum litterarum eruditione valde admirandum: quaenam fuerint illa, sedis apostolicae mandata, incertum est."

[8] Blumenthal, *Gregor VII.*, pp. 87–88 & ns. 110–112; Ambrosioni, "Niccolo II," p. 173; Stroll, *The Medieval Abbey of Farfa*, pp. 169–174.

[9] Duchesne, *L'État Pontifical*, pp. 392–393; Elke Goez, *Beatrix von Canossa*, p. 154 & n. 98.

[10] *Lampert, Annales*, p. 74: 1059, but pertains to previous year: "Rex, habita cum primoribus deliberatione, Gerhardum Florentinum episcopum, in quem et Romanorum et Teutonicorum studia consenserant, pontificem designat, Romamque per Gotefridum marchionem transmittit. Ita Benedicto, qui iniussu regis et principum sacerdotium usurpaverat, reprobato, Gerhardus, qui et Nicolaus, pontificum obtinuit."

[11] Boso, greatly influenced by Bonizo, wrote in the *Liber Pontificalis* 2:357: "Interea Ildebrandus archidiaconus cum episcopis et cardinalibus, quia in urbe Roma non poterant libere catholicam electionem facere, apud Senam pariter convenerunt, ibique convocatis circumpositis episcopis et aliis ecclesiarum prelatis, post multuam deliberationem, invocata Spiritus sancti gratia, dompnum G., Florentinum episcopum, in pastorem sibi et Romanum pontificem unanimiter elegerunt, et nomen sibi mutantes Nicolaum appellarunt." *Chron. Mont.*, 3.12, p. 373; see also JL 1:557; Jasper, *Das Papstwahldekret*, pp. 42–43 & n. 160; Goez, *Beatrix von Canossa*, p. 155.

between the confirmation and the election is not clear.[12] Thereafter, escorted by Godfrey's forces, the entourage arrived in January 1059 at Sutri, where they held a council that deposed Benedict.[13] Both Godfrey and Wibert were present as well as bishops from Tuscany (Tuscia) and Lombardy. Then, with the military support of Godfrey and the financial support of Leo, son of Benedictus Christianus, they traveled on to Rome without difficulty. Once there they encountered stiff resistance, but with Godfrey's help they prevailed.[14]

## Coronation

The *Annales Romani* report that Archdeacon Hildebrand arrived at the Lateran palace with his papal elect, who was consecrated Roman pontiff on January 24, 1059.[15] Thereafter Nicholas rode through the city to receive the fidelity of the people and the clergy, most probably on his way to St. Peter's where, according to Bonizo, he was enthroned.[16] Benzo claims that while in Rome he witnessed the subjection of his archbishop to the pope, and observed the innovation of the papal coronation ceremony.[17]

---

[12] Hägermann, *Das Papsttum*, pp. 73–84, deals with the complications of the dating.

[13] Bonizo, *Ad Amicum*, 593: "Hic [Nicholas II] idem prefatum Guibertum Italici regni cancellarium ex parte beati Petri et per veram obedientiam invitavit ad synodum et cum eo magnificum virum Gotefridum et non solum Tusciae, sed et Longobardiae episcopos, ut venientes Sutrium de periuro et invasore tractarent consilium. Quos ubi Sutrium adventantes audivit prefatus Benedictus, conscientia accusante sedem, quam invaserat, deseruit et ad propriam domum se contulit." tr. Robinson, *The Papal Reform*, pp. 201–202 & n. 37 for sources and literature; JL 4392; Gresser, *Konziliengeschichte*, p. 41.

[14] *Annales Romani, Lib. Pont.* 2:334: "Tunc cum quingentis equibus et cum magna pecunia ceperunt Romanum iter."

[15] Ibid., 335: "Tunc dictus Ildibrandus archidiaconus cum suo electo pontifice perrexerunt ad patriarchium Lateranensem et ordinaverunt eum Romanum pontificem, cui posuerunt nomen Nicolaus, et dederunt pecuniam;." n. 2 for Duchesne's date.

[16] Bonizo, *Ad Amicum*, p. 593: "Hoc postquam Sutrio nunciatum est, venerabilis Nicholaus sine aliqua congressione victor Romam intravit et ab omni clero et populo honorifice susceptus est et a cardinalibus in beati Petri intronizatus est sede." JL, p. 558; Hägermann, *Das Papsttum*, p. 84; Goez, *Beatrix von Canossa*, n. 118, p. 156; Gresser, *Konziliengeschichte*, p. 42. Uta Renate Blumenthal, "The Coronation of Pope Nicholas II," in *Life, Law and Letters*; Miscelánea histórica en honor de Antonio García y García, ed. Peter Linehan (Studia Gratiana 28, 1998), pp. 121–132 at p. 129.

[17] Blumenthal, "The Coronation," p. 129; idem, *Gregor VII.*, pp. 85–93; n. 116 for sources and literature; Nikolaus Gussone, *Thron und Inthronisation des Papstes von den Anfängen bis zum 12. Jahrhundert* (Bonn, 1978), pp. 232–234; Hägermann, *Das Papsttum*, pp. 85–86.

He states that having amassed a great deal of money, and with much lying, Hildebrand devised and carried out the ceremony to the shock of the bishops present.[18] When the bishops saw that Prandellus (Hildebrand) had crowned his idol (Nicholas II) with a royal crown, they became like dead men. Benzo alleged that the inscription on the lower circlet of the crown read: "The crown of the kingdom from the hand of God;" and on the upper: "The diadem of the empire from the hand of St. Peter." He likened the coronation to Pompey, who was rumored to have wanted to be king. But he sneered that Prandellus fed Nicholas in the Lateran like an ass in a stable, and that Nicholas did nothing that was not ordered by him.

Uta Renate Blumenthal and other scholars note that Hildebrand had just been appointed archdeacon, and that it was his position as archdeacon to officiate at the coronation.[19] Other scholars note, however, that there is no proof that Hildebrand was archdeacon until October 14, 1059.[20] Besides initiating the imperial papacy, the coronation might have been designed to counterbalance the anomaly that Nicholas had been elected outside of Rome. Again, the question is where and when was he crowned. According to some scholars, in a rare break from tradition he was crowned in the papal synod of April, 1059, but Blumenthal argues that it is more probable that he was crowned in January either during or just after his consecration at St. Peter's.[21]

Benzo's disdain may be discounted because of his boundless animus toward Hildebrand, but no source questioned his description of the crowning and the crown as part of the papal insignia that stamped the reform as the imperial papacy.[22] Citing contemporary sources Blumenthal suggests that since the time of Nicholas there was a papal crown that was distinct from the miter, and which symbolically corresponded to the imperial crown. To neutralize any disapproval,

---

[18] Benzo, *Ad Heinricum*, 7.2:596: "Corrumpens igitur Prandellus Romanos multis peccuniis multisque periuriis indixit synodum, ubi regali corona suum coronavit hydolum. Quod cernentes episcopi *facti sunt velut mortui*. Legebatur autem in inferiori circulo eiusdem serti ita: *Corona regni de manu dei*, in altero vero sic: *Diadema imperii de manu Petri.*" tr. Robinson, *The Papal Reform of the Eleventh Century*, p. 372 & ns. 74–78.

[19] Blumenthal, *Gregor VII.*, pp. 94–97.

[20] Cowdrey, *Gregory VII*, p. 37; Cowdrey says that the first date that Hildebrand can be positively identified as archdeacon is October 14, 1059.

[21] Blumenthal, "The Coronation," p. 129.

[22] Ibid., *passim*; idem, *Gregor VII.*, pp. 88–89.

Innocent III (1198–1216) will distinguish the miter as the papal crown from the tiara as the imperial.[23]

In the eleventh century clerics were very much aware of the Donation of Constantine and its assertion that [Pope] Silvester had refused to wear a crown with imperial symbols.[24] Petrus Damiani would surely have objected to such a crown, and he as well as Benzo most probably attended the coronation. In his famous letter/tract 89 to Cadalus written in 1062 he distinguished himself from Hildebrand, noting specifically that according to the Donation of Constantine, Silvester would only wear the insignia that pertained to his office, and that he rejected the crown.[25] In an earlier letter to Cadalus he had referred to the miter as the papal crown.[26]

According to Benzo, Alexander II perpetuated the coronation ritual, crowned like a king in a synod.[27] In a letter to Alexander in 1066/1067 Archbishop Siegfried of Mainz stated that the crown of the kingdom and the diadem of the Roman Empire are in your possession through the hand of Peter.[28] As Alexander's successor, Gregory VII declared in the *Dictatus papae* that he [the pope] alone can use the imperial insignia.[29] During Gregory's reign Bruno of Segni averred that the pope wore the crown and the purple cape because the emperor, Constantine, had handed over all insignia of the Roman Empire to Silvester. He said that in great processions the popes wear the insignia that at one time were worn only by Roman emperors.[30]

---

[23] Blumenthal, *Gregor VII.*, p. 91; idem, "The Coronation," pp. 123–127.

[24] Cowdrey, "Eleventh-Century Reformers' Views of Constantine," pp. 74–79.

[25] Petrus Damiani, *Briefe*, nr. 89, 2:546–547; tr. Blum, 3:341; Blumenthal, *Gregor VII.*, p. 90.

[26] Ibid., nr. 88, 2:523–524; tr. Blum, 3:317.

[27] Benzo, *Ad Heinricum*, 7.2, p. 600: "Et talis super christianum populum exaltatur et, quod auditu necdum visu horribile est, quasi rex in synodo coronatur." tr. Robinson, *The Papal Reform of the Eleventh Century*, p. 374.

[28] *Codex Udalrici*, nr. 32, ed. Jaffé, *Monumenta Bambergensia, Bibliotheca. Rerum Germanicarum* (Berlin, 1869), 5:61; Blumenthal, *Gregor VII.*, p. 91 & n. 127; idem, "The Coronation," p. 128 & n. 40.

[29] *Das Register Gregors VII*, ed. E. Caspar, MGH Epistolae selectae 2, 1–2 (Berlin, 1920/23; 1967), 2, ch. 8, 55a, p. 204.

[30] Bruno of Segni, *Tractatus de sacramentis Ecclesiae*, PL 165: 1108: "Summus autem pontifex propter haec et regnum portat (sic enim vocatur) et purpura utitur non pro significatione, ut puto, sed quia Constantinus imperator olim beato Silvestro omnia Romani imperii insignia tradidit. Unde et in magnis processionibus omnis ille apparatur pontifici exhibetur qui quondam imperatoribus fieri solebat." Blumenthal, *Gregor VII.*, pp. 89–90 & n. 121.

The problem with Bruno's appeal to the Donation of Constantine was, as Petrus Damiani stated, that Silvester had refused to accept the crown. In spite of this inconsistency, the momentum toward creating a papal crown with imperial symbolism was too strong to stop. With Hildebrand almost surely as the architect, from the time of Nicholas there was a papal crown and a coronation ceremony.

Besides the crown and the coronation ceremony Nicholas adopted other imperial imagery, most prominently his Rota on which he imprinted *Christus vincit*. This laud was part of the lauds for Frankish rulers introduced by the Carolingians in Rome on Easter 774, and which were always used for a ruler: *Christus vincit, Christus regnat, Christus imperat*. They slipped into desuetude in the tenth century, but were reintroduced in the eleventh by Nicholas, signaling his conception of the papacy as an *imitatio imperii*.[31] Thereafter the *Liber politicus*, written c. 1140 by Benedict, canon of St. Peter's, reveals that they were incorporated into the lauds used in papal coronations.[32]

### The Collection of 74 Titles

In addition to ritual and imagery, collections of canon law also convey prevailing views and the ideology of their compilers. The contrast between the state of mind at the time when Henry III nominated Clement II to the papacy in 1046 and the wide spread attitudes prevalent during the dominance of Hildebrand/Gregory VII is reflected in two collections of canon law. About 1012 Burchard of Worms compiled a *Decretum* of canon law conveying the outlook of his time. In close touch with the reformers in the North, Burchard emphasized clerical celibacy, simony, and moral questions such as the indissolubility of marriage, but he paid scant attention to the papacy.[33] He did not,

---

[31] Blumenthal, *Gregor VII.*, p. 92; Hägermann, *Das Papsttum*, pp. 85–86; Rome, Biblioteca Vittorio Emanuele, Lat. MS 2096 (Sessorianus 52).

[32] *Le Liber Censuum de l'Eglise romaine*, ed. Paul Fabre & Louis Duchesne, Bibliothèque des Écoles françaises d'Athène et de Rome (Paris, 1889–1910), nr. 4, 2:91.

[33] Greta Austin, *Shaping Church Law Around the Year 1000: The "Decretum" of Burchard of Worms* (Farnham, Surrey UK & Burlington, VT, 2009); see also the review of Edward Peters, *The Medieval Review* October 2, 2009; Austin, "Authority and the Canons in Burchard's *Decretum* and Ivo's *Decretum*, pp. 35–58 & n. 2 for sources in *Readers, Texts and Compilers in the Earlier Middle Ages: Studies in Honour of Linda Fowler-Magerl*, ed. Martin Brett & Kathleen G. Cushing (Bodmin, Cornwall, 2009).

for example, feel that the pope was absolutely essential for conferring authority on a given source, or that papal sanction was requisite for a council to have authority. His focus was more episcopal than papal, and his model of authority more corporate than top down.[34]

By contrast the *Diversorum patrum sententiae* or *The Collection of 74 Titles*, compiled by an anonymous writer, most probably between c.1050 and 1075, concentrated somewhat less on moral reform, and emphasized the legal position and the prerogatives of the pope.[35] Rather than relying upon the church fathers or synodal decrees, it drew its sources mainly from papal letters. None of them were contemporary, and many of them were taken from the spurious decretals of Pseudo Isidore extolling the papacy. Title One, entitled, "On the Primacy of the Roman See," cited ten authorities.[36] In c. 8 Pseudo-Silvester states: "No one may judge the First See. Neither the emperor, the clergy or the people shall judge." Pope Gelasius states in c. 10: "The whole church throughout the world knows that the holy Roman church has the right to judge every church."[37]

Title One was not the only title to emphasize the primacy of the Roman Church. Title Two, for example reads: "Jesus established the primacy of the Roman Church, Matthew 16:18; c. 82 of Title Ten states: "Bishops may not be deposed without the authority of the Apostolic See; c. 91 of Title Eleven states: "Bishops deposed without the authority of the Apostolic See shall be restored;" c. 178 of Title Twenty-Three states: "The decrees of the Apostolic See shall always be observed;" c. 227 of Title Forty-One: Church and State: Pope Gelasius to Emperor Anastasius, the famous *Duo Sunt*. "….Two there are, august emperor, by which this world is chiefly ruled, the sacred authority of the priesthood and the royal power. Of these the responsibility of the priests is

---

[34] Austin, "Authority and the Canons in Burchard's *Decretum* and Ivo's *Decretum*," p. 55.

[35] *Diversorum patrum sententie sive Collectio in LXXIV titulos digesta*, ed. John T. Gilchrist; Monumenta Iuris Canonici Corpus collectionum 1 (Vatican City, 1973); Christof Rolker, "The *Collection in Seventy-four Titles*: A Monastic Canon Law Collection from Eleventh-Century France," pp. 59–72 of *Readers, Texts and Compilers*.

[36] http://faculty.cua.edu/Pennington/Canon%20Law/GregorianReform/74Titles. htm.

[37] John Gilchrist, *A Collection in 74 Titles: A Canon Law Manual of the Gregorian Reform* (Medieval Sources in Translation 22) (Toronto, 1980), esp. p. 29; Kenneth Pennington, *A Short History of Canon Law from Apostolic Times to 1917*, The Eleventh Century and the Reform of the Latin Church, at http://faculty.cua.edu/Pennington/ Canon%20Law/ShortHistoryCanonLaw.htm.

more weighty in so far as they will answer for the kings of men themselves at the divine judgment."

At the end of the nineteenth century Paul Fournier interpreted the
collection as the first manual of the reform, and deduced an Italian
origin, probably a member of the curia.[38] Shortly after 1076 the zealous
Gregorian, Bernold of Constance, appended a note to his copy stating
that legates of the apostolic see had brought the collection over the
Alps *in Gallias* to use in ecclesiastical trials.[39] This statement does not
preclude the possibility that the collection existed before that time, and
although some scholars have assumed that the collection was compiled
under Gregory VII, others argue for an earlier date, possibly with
Humbert of Silva Candida as its author.

As to its intention, from the 1970s the conventional view no longer
holds that the reform had a clearly defined program or that it was
mainly inspired by the papacy.[40] Not altogether persuasively, Linda
Fowler-Magerl has even argued for an origin in the vicinity of Cologne
instead of Italy.[41] Recently she and Christof Rolker have suggested that
the goal of the collection was not specifically Gregorian but was monastic, and emphasized the goals of monastic reform.[42]

Rolker observes that the compiler modified his Pseudo-Isidorian
sources in favor of monasteries at the expense of bishoprics. While
recognizing that the opening title on Roman primacy was unusual,
he emphasizes that the fourth title on monastic liberties was unprece-
dented.[43] He notes that among others Burchard of Worms opened
his collection with canons on Roman primacy, similar, but fewer to
the ones in *The Collection of 74 Titles*. Rolker argues that the *libertas
monasteriorum* was protected by papal authority, and presents other

---

[38] Paul Fournier, "Le premier manuel canonique de la réforme du XIe siècle,"
*Melanges d'archéologie de l'École française de Rome* 14 (1894), 147–223; 285–290.

[39] Rolker, "The *Collection in Seventy-four Titles*, pp. 60–61; Johanne Autenrieth,
"Bernhold von Konstanz und die erweiterte 74-Titelsammlung," *Deutsches Archiv* 14
(1958), 375–394; Blumenthal, *Gregor VII.*, p. 214 & n. 54, 232–233.

[40] Ibid., 62; John Gilchrist, "Was there a Gregorian reform movement in the eleventh century?," *Canadian Catholic Historical Association;* English section 37 (1970),
1–10.

[41] Ibid., 64–65; Linda Fowler-Magerl, "The use of the letters of Pope Gregory I in
northeastern France and Lorraine before 1100," ed. Mario Ascheri, Friedrich Ebel et
al., *Ins Wasser geworfen und Ozeane durchquert*, Festschrift für Knut Wolfgang Nörr
(Cologne, 2003), pp. 237–260 at 238.

[42] Linda Fowler-Magerl, *Kanones. A selection of canon law collections compiled between 1000 and 1140* (Piesenkofen, 2003), p. 56;

[43] Rolker, "The *Collection in Seventy-four Titles*, pp. 66–69 & n. 35.

arguments to show how the author defends monastic privileges, especially against episcopal interference.

Rolker discerns that as exemptions became more common during the eleventh century monasteries emphasized papal preeminence as a defense against episcopal control. He concludes that although the author of the collection highly valued the prerogatives of the papacy, the stress on this primacy was not an aim in itself. The collection was mainly concerned with monastic liberties, he maintains, and should be understood principally as a very rare and distinctive case of a monastic law collection.[44]

But if it were primarily a monastic law collection, would it have been so widespread and so influential?[45] Even if much of the collection was concerned with monastic liberties, it is a quantum leap to insist that the stress on papal primacy was not an aim in itself. Moreover, the two objectives were complimentary.

In general monasteries such as Vallombrosa and Camaldoli supported the reform movement and the papacy against the bishops. In like manner, Hildebrand was known for favoring monks against their bishops, and he also took the side of the *pataria* against the bishops. In the case of a conflict between Bishop Cunibert of Turin and the monastery of S. Michele della Chiusa Hildebrand supported the monastery on the principle of monastic exemptions from episcopal authority. In his defense of its abbot, Benedict, he stood firmly upon the principle of monastic exemption and upon the rights and duties of the Roman Church.[46]

It is germane to the relationship between the papacy and monasticism that Hildebrand, Humbert, and Stephen IX were all monks, and that they were sometimes placed on the defensive for playing such an active role outside of the monastery. We have observed that Hildebrand and Humbert allegedly had to swear to Henry III that they would never allow themselves to become candidates for the papacy, and Benzo constantly criticized Hildebrand for defying the supervision required for monks, who had fled the world to devote themselves to the spiritual life. Petrus Damiani clearly was uncomfortable with his functions as cardinal bishop, and repeatedly endeavored to return to his monastery.

---

[44] Ibid., 71–72.
[45] Ibid., 59; Rolker notes that it was one of the most widespread and influential collections in the eleventh century.
[46] Cowdrey, *Gregory VII*, pp. 65–66.

Thus, it was consistent for *The Collection of 74 Titles* to be what Fournier called a handbook of the reform, and to concentrate on monastic liberties. Moreover, since Bernold of Constance stated that papal legates transmitted the collection to be used in ecclesiastical trials, the objective of the pope that sent them would have been to assure that the trials would be instituted under papal authority.

When the collection was compiled remains a matter of conjecture, but its principles were consistent with the reign of Nicholas. As one of his modern biographers has pointed out, not content with affirming the customary doctrinal authorities for papal primacy, the universality of the papacy, and the unqualified love toward the vicar of St. Peter, the chancery of Nicholas created new formulae and images underscoring the unique authority of the papacy. It was the instrument of God for illuminating the whole church, for giving stability to all ecclesiastical institutions, for correcting errors, and for uniting members with the head of the church.[47]

When Hildebrand became pope he codified these principles in the *dictatus papae*, and Anselm of Lucca's *Collectio canonum*, composed during his reign, is frequently seen as an exemplar of a "reform collection" of the "Gregorian Revolution.[48] Anselm was the nephew of the Anselm of Lucca, who became Alexander II in 1061. Starting with the Collection of 74 Titles, there was a steady progression toward an emphasis on papal authority.

---

[47] Ambrosioni, "Niccolò II," p. 177.
[48] Kathleen Cushing. *Papacy and Law in the Gregorian Revolution: The Canonistic Work of Anselm of Lucca.* (Oxford Historical Monographs.) (New York: Oxford University Press. 1998).

CHAPTER SEVEN

# NICHOLAS II: PAPAL ELECTORAL DECREE AND BREAK WITH THE REGENCY

## *The Papal Electoral Decree of 1059*

Clearly there were multiple reasons for establishing canonical procedures for papal elections. The whole process was in a state of flux after recent elections in which the emperor had played the decisive role, but could no longer do so with a child king and a weak regency. The Roman and suburban nobility still believed that they had the right to elect their bishop, and Nicholas II, having been elected after there was already a sitting pope, needed affirmation of the legality of his election.

No provisions had been stipulated since a synod called by Stephen III in 769 decreed simply that the pope be elected by the Roman clergy.[1] A constitution promulgated by Lothar, son of the Carolingian emperor, Louis the Pious, in 824 concurred that the pope should be elected by the Romans, but required that the laity as well as the clergy be included.[2] It also mandated imperial consent and an oath by the papal elect in the presence of the imperial *missi* and the people.[3] This constitution was observed far more than the decree of 769, producing a reaction from the Roman clergy and lay leaders, who elected a series of popes from the great Roman families.[4]

---

[1] *Lib. Pont.* 1:476; Duchesne transmits the decree itself, n. 52, p. 483; Stroll, *The Medieval Abbey of Farfa*, p. 151 & n. 20.

[2] PL 97:459, nr. 3: "Volumus ut in electione pontificis nullus praesumat venire neque liber neque servus, qui aliquid impedimentum faciat, illis solummodo Romanis, quibus antiquitus fuit consuetudo concessa per constitutionem sanctorum patrum eligendi pontificem. Quod is quis contra hanc iussionem nostram facere praesumperit, exilo tradatur." Richard Krautheimer, *Rome: Profile of a City, 312–1308* (Princeton, 1980), p. 117.

[3] Ibid., 460–462: "....et quod non consentiam utiliter in hac sede Romana fiat electio pontificis canonice et iuste, secundum vires et intellectum meum; et ille qui electus fuerit, me consentiente consecratus pontifex non fiat, priusquam tale sacramentum faciat in praesentia missi domini imperatoris et populi, cum iuramento, quale factum habet per scriptum."

[4] Louis Duchesne, *Les Premiers Temps de l'État Pontifical* (Paris, 1911), pp. 199–303; Stroll, *The Medieval Abbey of Farfa*, p. 152.

On April 13, 1059, 113 bishops, all of them Italian except for Archbishop Hugh of Besançon, gathered at the Easter synod in the Lateran basilica.[5] Noteworthy was the presence of bishops from South Italy—the archbishops of Amalfi, Benevento, Capua and Salerno with some of their suffragans. The council dealt with issues of the reform, especially simony and clerical marriage, and for the first time prohibited clerics from receiving churches or property from laymen. This decree seems to have articulated a general principle rather than to have been directed against the emperor, who was consecrated, and therefore more than a layman.

The decree with the greatest resonance defined the procedures for papal elections, placing primary authority in the hands of the cardinals.[6] Its immediate significance was that it harmonized with the election of Nicholas II, and assured that he would be recognized as pope in the schism with Benedict X. Besides validating Nicholas' election, the decree dramatically reduced secular input from the Roman citizens, and made the emperor's authority ambiguous. Curiously, it was more often cited by the imperial side to justify succeeding disputed elections.

### Two Versions of the Papal Electoral Decree

In the sixteenth century Onophrius Panvinius discovered that there was an original and a forged version, and recognized the momentous political implications. Since no autograph copy exists, and indeed, it may have been excised from Nicholas II's Register, scholars until recently have speculated over which version was genuine, and what the differences signified. Most scholars are now convinced by the exhaustive study of Detlev Jasper, who argues that what used to be called the papal version was the original, and the imperial version the forgery. I shall refer to them as version A and version B.[7]

---

[5] JL, pp. 558–559; Gresser, *Konziliengeschichte*, pp. 41–48; Goez, *Kirchen Reform und Investiturstreit*, p. 105; Ghirardini, *L'antipapa Cadalo*, p. 33.

[6] Jasper, *Das Papstwahldekret*; ex codex Vat. Lat. 1984, Watterich, 1:229–233; JL, pp. 558–559; Cushing, *Reform and the Papacy in the Eleventh Century*, pp. 70–72; Hägermann, *Das Papsttum*, pp. 102–119; Stroll, *The Medieval Abbey of Farfa*, pp. 169–174.

[7] Ibid., 98–119 for the texts; for the editions and literature, p. 1, ns. 1,2; MGH Const., nrs. 382–385, 1:537–549 for the decrees of the council; version A of the electoral decree, pp. 538–539; version B, pp. 541–542; Gresser, *Konziliengeschichte*,

Both versions make the point that elections in the past have been fraught with difficulties, and that it is necessary to set down statutes to preclude such evils from occurring in the future.[8] Guided by precedents and the authority of the holy fathers, version A says that the cardinal bishops should diligently discuss a successor. Soon, they should summon the cardinal clerics and then the other people to approve the election. Since popes do not have a metropolitan, the guidance of Leo I, who instructed that the cardinal bishops should take their place, should be followed.

The decree states that if the cardinal bishops cannot find a suitable candidate within the Roman see, they can select one from another, save by the honor and reverence owed to king Henry, who, it is hoped, in the future will be emperor. This honor and reverence is also owed to his successors, who personally receive this right from the pope. If adverse conditions prevent carrying out the election in Rome, even though they may be few, cardinal bishops with religious clerics and catholic laymen may hold an election in a place they judge to be suitable. If violence breaks out and he cannot be enthroned, the elect may nevertheless exercise papal authority. Those who violate the decree will be subject to a long list of punishments.

Without singling out the cardinal bishops, version B states that the cardinals should come together to confer, save by the reverence owed to Henry, now king, and who, it is hoped, in the future will be emperor. This honor has already been conceded through W[ibert], the king's mediator, the text continues, and will be granted to the king's successors, who personally obtain this right from the pope. They may give their consent to the election. To avoid violence, religious men along with our king, Henry, should move the election forward, and the others may merely follow. Leo I is not cited, but as in version A, the decree states that if the election cannot be held within the city, even a few men along with the invincible king can

---

pp. 41–48; Hans-Georg Krause, "Die Bedeutung des neuentdeckten handschriftlichtlichen Überlieferung des Papstwahlsdekret von 1059: Bemerkungen zu einen neuen Buch," *Zeitschrift der Savigny Stiftung für Rechtsgeschichte* KA 107 (1990), 89–134; Idem, *Das Papastwahldekret von 1059 und seine Rolle im Investiturstreit, Studi Gregoriani* 7 (1960); Cowdrey, *Gregory VII*, pp. 44–45; Hägermann, *Das Papsttum*, pp. 102–119; Stroll, *The Medieval Abbey of Farfa*, pp. 145–208; ns. 2, 3, p. 145 for literature; for criticisms of Jasper, pp. 166–167 & ns. 3, 4; see also the critical review of *The Medieval Abbey of Farfa* by Kenneth Pennington in *The American Historical Review* 105 (2000), 262–263.

[8] Jasper, *Das Papstwahldekret*, pp. 98–119.

find a suitable place to hold it. It adds a few maledictions to those in version A.

Version A thus restricts the king's role to the case where the cardinal bishops cannot find a suitable candidate within the Roman see, and must select one from another. Such authority would only be token, and would greatly diminish the rights that had been exercised by Henry III. Version B is far more expansive. It specifies that the king's wishes were to be honored in elections whether they were regular, whether a candidate is found outside the Roman church, or whether an election must take place outside of Rome.[9] Most historians agree that version A reflected the views of Nicholas, Hildebrand, and Humbert after April 1059, but what these critical prelates believed at the time of the council is less clear. The signatures and imperial prerogatives in each decree yield valuable clues.[10]

*Signatures*

While only the manuscript from Bergamo of version A includes signatures, those of version B routinely do.[11] Of the 81 participants who signed version A, most of them were from central Italy, and the archbishop of Besançon stood out as the only foreigner. Five were cardinal bishops, eight were cardinal priests and deacons, and some were subdeacons of the Roman church.[12] Among the signatories of version A were Anselm of Lucca (the future Alexander II); Benzo of Alba; Gregory of Vercelli; Humbert of Silva Candida; Desiderius; and Petrus Damiani. Among the non signers were Cadalus, bishop of Parma, Wibert, the imperial chancellor, and most conspicuously, Hildebrand.

There are five more signatories in version B than in version A, and they are more completely identified. With minor variations Hildebrand is listed as "Hildebrandus subdiaconus et monachus." Stressing how rare it was for Hildebrand to be entitled "monachus," and arguing that

[9] Stroll, *The Medieval Abbey of Farfa*, p. 153 & n. 28.
[10] Ibid., 166 & n. 1 for some of the literature; Gresser, *Konziliengeschichte*, n. 20, p. 42.
[11] Jasper, *Das Papstwahldekret*, pp. 25–31, 109–119; Bergamo, Biblioteca Civica Angelo Mai, MA 244, sigle B2; Krause, "Die Bedeutung," pp. 111–112, 115; Stroll, *The Medieval Abbey of Farfa*, pp. 205–207.
[12] MGH Const. nr. 384, 1:547; Hägermann, *Das Papsttum*, p. 103.

in April 1059 Hildebrand had already been promoted to archdeacon, Jasper concludes that the signature is a forgery.[13] Hans-Georg Krause begs to differ, arguing that the signature is genuine.[14] He gives examples of when "monachus," was used to describe Hildebrand, and argues that there is no proof of when he was promoted archdeacon.[15] Jasper concedes the point, and also acknowledges the evidence that a certain Mancius was the archdeacon. In both versions of the decree his signature appears as Mancius diaconus, and in some manuscripts of version B he is entitled archidiaconus.[16]

In the partisan decree of the synod of Brixen of June 25, 1080, which deposed Gregory VII, it was said that Hildebrand had snatched the office of archdeacon away from Mancius.[17] Beno, Hildebrand's fierce antagonist, implies that Hildebrand was promoted as archdeacon just before the pope's death. He charged that by money, lies and inflicting many injuries Hildebrand forced Nicholas to appropriate the title from Mancius and to grant it to himself. Beno uttered darkly that after a few days Nicholas died, suffocated by poison, as it was said.[18] The reliable Rudolph Hüls states without reservation that Mancius as archdeacon signed the papal electoral decree of 1059, and volunteers that soon after May he probably lost his office at the instigation of Hildebrand.[19]

Jasper acknowledges that the signature of Mancius as *diaconus* is uncontestable, but even though he cites Hüls, he nevertheless concludes from circumstantial evidence that neither the signature of Mancius as *archidiaconus* nor that of Hildebrand as *monachus et subdiaconus* in version B could be genuine.[20] Apart from the oddity of identifying himself as *monachus*, the reason that Hildebrand's signature

---

[13] Jasper, *Das Papstwahldekret*, p. 38; Uta Renate Blumenthal concludes that Hildebrand "wahrscheinlich" did not sign the decree; "Rom in der Kanonistik," pp. 29–30 of *Rom im Hohen Mittelalter: Studien zu den Romvorstellungen und zur Rompolitik vom 10. zum 12. Jahrhundert*, ed. Bernhard Schimmelpfennig & Ludwig Schmugge (Sigmaringen, 1992).

[14] Krause, "Die Bedeutung," p. 101 & ns. 47, 48.

[15] *Vita Iohannis Gualberti anonyma*, MGH SS 30, 2:1107; Cowdrey, *Gregory VII*, pp. 37–39.

[16] Jasper, *Das Papstwahldekret*, pp. 34, 111 & n. 60; Hüls, *Kardinäle*, p. 251.

[17] MGH Const. 1:119: "His itaque questibus pecunia cumulata, abbatiam beati Pauli invasit, supplantato abbate. Inde arripiens archidiaconatum, quendam nomine Mancium, ut sibi officium venderet, decipiendo seduxit, et Nicolao papa nolente, tumultu populari stipatus in economum se promoveri coegit."

[18] Beno, *Contra Hildebrandum* MGH LdL 2:379–380.

[19] Hüls, *Kardinäle*, p. 251.

[20] Jasper, *Das Papstwahldekret*, pp. 45–46.

could not be valid, Jasper argues, is that the evidence is overwhelming that in April 1059 Hildebrand was already archdeacon.

Jasper believes that the forgers entitled Hildebrand "subdeacon" to substantiate the charge at the council of Brixen in 1080 that he had bought the office of archdeacon. He reasons that in 1080 the oldest manuscripts of both versions of the papal electoral decree were unknown, and that starting from this period the forgers substituted *archidiaconus* for *diaconus* as the title for Mancius. Hildebrand could not have bought the office if he had already held it in April 1059, as Jasper points out. He argues that the need by Gregory VII's opponents in 1080 to identify Hildebrand as subdeacon in 1059 is strong evidence that the 1080s were the time of origin of the forgery. His final thought is that trustworthy evidence indicated that neither Mancius as archdeacon nor Hildebrand as subdeacon could have signed the decree. The manuscripts that did so were forgeries.

Historians continue to wrestle with the conflicting evidence of when Hildebrand became archdeacon. Uta Renate Blumenthal concludes that it was some time between the summer of 1058 and January 1059, while H.E.J. Cowdrey argues that there is no certainty until October 14, 1059.[21] Yet, he accepts Jasper's view that the discovery of the text of version A that contains the signatures, and which does not contain Hildebrand's, makes it virtually certain that Hildebrand did not sign the electoral decree.[22]

But Jasper's conclusion that the text of version A containing the signatures had to be the original because version B identified Hildebrand as subdeacon and he was demonstrably archdeacon flies in the face of Cowdrey's conclusion that Hildebrand could not reliably be identified as archdeacon in April 1059. Thus, Jasper's argument for the validity of version A is not convincing. Moreover, from a political perspective, it defies credulity that Hildebrand would not have been present at the council and signed the decree. Even though writing in the 1070s and 1080s, eyewitnesses testified that he did sign the decree.[23]

---

[21] Blumenthal, *Gregor VII.*, p. 94; Cowdrey, *Gregory VII*, pp. 37–39; JL 4413; see also Krause, "Die Bedeutung," pp. 103, 109.

[22] Cowdrey, *Gregory VII*, p. 44; Jasper, *Das Papstwahldekret von 1059*, pp. 34–36, p. 111 for the signature.

[23] Krause, "Die Bedeutung," p. 110 for examples; Wolfgang Stürner. "Das Papstwahldekret von 1059 und seine Verfälschung. Gedanken zu einem neuern Buch," MGH Schriften, 33.2, *Fälschungen im Mittelalter* (Hannover, 1988); Idem, "'Salvo debito honore et reverentia.' Der Königsparagraph von 1059," *Zeitschrift der Savigny*

*Panvinius*

In 1555 when Panvinius wrote *De origine Cardinalium* he seems to have known only of version A, but in 1563 when he wrote *De varia Romani pontificis creatione* he knew of both versions and concluded that version A was the forgery.[24] He transmits version B a second time in the *Liber Beraldi*, which he extracted from a book of *res gestae* of the monastery of Farfa (in the Sabina) written over four hundred years ago.[25] The *Liber Beraldi* was almost certainly written by Gregory of Catino, a monk at Farfa who was born about 1060 and whose last known date is 1130.[26]

Describing the Easter Council of 1059 Panvinius reports that among the many measures brought forth for confirmation was a canon for papal elections drafted to avoid future schisms like that created by Benedict X.[27] He states that he has excerpted a true and non-corrupted text of the decree from an extremely ancient book written more than five hundred years ago in almost majuscule Lombard letters.[28] Although seemingly not the *Chronicon*, he associates this book with the abbey of Farfa. Ostensibly repeating himself, he says that he possesses an example of the decree *ex antiquissimo libro et huius forte concilii tempore scripto*.[29] The use of the word "*forte*" makes it ambiguous whether the decree he possessed was written at the time of the council, and what paleographic skills he possessed are unknown.[30]

But Panvinius vouched for his source, arguing that it was consistent with the history of the time. He contends that this was especially so in

---

*Stiftung für Rechtsgeschichte* KA 54 (1968), 1–56 at 40; Stroll, *The Medieval Abbey of Farfa*, pp. 206–207 & n. 42.

[24] Onophrius Panvinius, *De origine Cardinalium*, ed. Angelo Mai, *Spicilegium Romanum* 9, pp. 495–504; *De varia Romani pontificis creatione*, Clm 147–152; 148, fols. 98v–99r; Hermann Grauert, "Das Dekret Nikolaus II. von 1059," *Historisches Jahrbuch* 1 (1880), 502–602.

[25] Panvinius, F. Bernardi Monachi et Abbatis Monasterii Farfensis Liber, Clm 148, fols. 186r–196v; version B fols. 191v–193r; Grauert, "Das Dekret Nikolaus II," p. 507; Jasper, *Das Papstwahldekret*, p. 94; Stroll, *The Medieval Abbey of Farfa*, pp. 11, 163, & ns. 32, 33.

[26] Stroll, *The Medieval Abbey of Farfa*, p. 7.

[27] Clm 148, fol. 99v: "ubi inter reliqua multa quae ad bonum ecclesiae statum confirmandum spectabant, ut schismatibus, quae forte oriri in posterum possent obviam iretur canonem, sive novam regulam de electione Romani pontificis eddit, occasione accepta a schismate Benedicti X..."

[28] Ibid.

[29] Ibid.

[30] Stroll, *The Medieval Abbey of Farfa*, pp. 157–159.

its clause attributing authority of electing the pontiff of the Romans to the emperor, at that time King Henry, or rather to his father. He added that, as one can see, the decree also included certain stipulations for avoiding a schism.[31] In arguing that the text that he now possessed was the original, Panvinius said that Nicholas handed over the authority of electing the pope to Henry IV, but that his authority differed from his father's in one respect. The authority of electing was transmitted to the cardinals.[32]

Panvinius seems to have meant that the emperor had the authority to assure the election of a worthy candidate (*salvo debito honore et reverentia dilectissimi filii nostri Henrici*), but that the cardinals carried out the election. It was not under Nicholas II that synods deprived the emperor of the authority of electing the pope, Panvinius asserted, but under Gregory VII. It was accordingly not at the time of Nicholas II, but at that of Gregory VII or Victor III that the corrupted version of the decree was created.[33]

As outside evidence of the authenticity of version B Panvinius adduces a debate between Desiderius, abbot of Montecassino, and Oddo, cardinal bishop of Ostia and the future Urban II (1088–1099), reported in the *Chronicon* of Montecassino.[34] At that time Desiderius was also cardinal priest of Santa Cecilia, and a legate to Henry IV. The debate was held in the presence of Henry IV with imperial ministers and other bishops.[35] Panvinius reports that those supporting Gregory VII stated that the emperor lost his right to participate in

---

[31] Clm 148, fol. 99v: "…verum et Germanum est, historiaeque et rerum narrationibus maxime consentaneum in quo auctoritatem eligendi Romanorum pontificum Imperatori tunc Regi Henrico tribuit vel potius patri suo tributam confirmat, quibusdam additis ad praecavenda schismata, circumstantiis, ut in ipso videri potest."

[32] Ibid., fols. 99v–100r: "Nicolaus enim in suo auctoritatem eligendi papam tradit Henrico IV., ut pater suus habuerat Henricus III., in illo vero Henrico IV. ablata traditur auctoritas eligendi cardinalibus."

[33] Ibid.

[34] Ibid., fol. 100r; *Chron. Mont.*, 3.50, pp. 432–433; Stürner, "Das Papstwahldekret von 1059," pp. 416–419; Idem, "'Salvo debito honore et reverentia'" pp. 54–55; Stroll, *The Medieval Abbey of Farfa*, pp. 160–161 & ns. 25–27.

[35] *Chron. Mont.*, 3.50, p. 433: "Super hec interim quandiu ibi permansit Desiderius, cotidie ac sepe cum episcopis, qui cum imperatore erant. De honore apostolice sedis contendit et precipue etiam cum episcopo Ostiensi [Oddo, the future Urban II], qui etiam pape Gregorio favere videbatur; cum ille et privilegium Nycolae pape, quod cum Hildebrando archidiacono et centum viginti quinque episcopis fecerate, ostendisset, ut numquam papa in Romana ecclesia absque consensu imperatoris fieret, quod si fieret, sciret se non pro papa abendum esse atque anathematizandum."

papal elections because it was contrary to the canons and writings of the Holy Fathers.

The bishop of Ostia responded with arguments that Panvinius believed exposed Gregory's duplicity. Oddo asserted that it was decreed in the council summoned by Nicholas that a Roman pontiff could not be created without the authority of the emperor, and that if he were, he would be anathematized.[36] Panvinius stressed that along with 125 bishops archdeacon Hildebrand had signed the decree. Here some of the alleged facts are inaccurate because by most accounts there were only 113 members of the council, and in version B Hildebrand is identified as subdeacon, not archdeacon. In the *Chronicon* Henry IV is also consistently referred to as "emperor" even though he had not been crowned.[37]

Panvinius stressed that Desiderius never denied Oddo's allegations, but took a different tack. He asserted that neither Nicholas II nor any other pope could promulgate decrees detracting from the liberties of the church, and that if he did so, he did so unjustly. He declared that one should not assent to such a decree, and emphasized that a Roman pope should not be ordained at the will of the German king.[38]

In spite of the acquaintance of Panvinius with the manuscripts, and his broad understanding of the issues, most scholars are not impressed by his evidence, and are convinced by the exhaustive study of Detlev Jasper. But there are quibbles with Jasper's analysis as well, as even those who agree with him that version A is genuine attest. The arguments that Panvinius raises should be taken seriously.

---

[36] CLM 148, fol. 100r: "…in concilio…a Nicolao II. celebratum, statutum fuerat per suum imperatori concessum privilegium, ut non sine imperatoris auctoritate Romanus pontifex creatur, quod si fieri contigisset, sciret se huiusmodi non pro papa habendum sed anathematisandum, cui decreto etiam Hildebrandus archidiaconus post papa Gregorius VII. tunc in minoribus constitutus cum episcopis CXXV subscripserat, quod de illo decreto quod est in registris minime dici potest, sed bene de isto quod ego nunc attuli."

[37] In 1137 Petrus Diaconus revised and extended the *Chronicon*, and he could have been responsible for some of the mistakes. Krause, *Papstwahldekret von 1059*, pp. 232–233; Stürner, "Salvo debito," pp. 54–55; Cowdrey, *The Age of Abbot Desiderius*, p. 241.

[38] Clm 148, vols. 100r–100v: "Quam rem Desiderius numquam negavit sed respondebat, neque Nicholaum II. neque alium Romanum pontificem suis decretis praeiudicium aliquod ecclesiasticae libertati facere potuisse…." Grauert, "Das Dekret Nicholaus II.," pp. 592–594.

## Cardinal Bishops and the King

A critical difference between the two versions was the primary role of cardinal bishops in version A. Since the cardinal bishops had rejected Benedict X and voted for Nicholas, it made sense that he would favor them. Already in 1057 Petrus Damiani had written to the cardinal bishops making a case for their political as well as their liturgical role in the universal church. This responsibility entailed that they had the right to elect a new pope, not simply to consecrate him.[39] After Nicholas' election, but before the promulgation of the decree, Petrus again spoke of the constitutive role of the cardinal bishops in the election of a pope.[40] These letters suggest that the version of the decree emphasizing their role was genuine.

But Ovidio Capitani regards the text that Petrus used in the *Disceptatio Synodalis* to be closer to version B than to version A. It states that he should be pope whom the cardinal bishops unanimously call, whom the clergy elects, and whom the people welcome.[41] Also, more than twenty years after the promulgation of the decree Deusdedit still saw the Holy Roman Church as a corporation represented by the cardinal priests and deacons together with the pope whom they had elected. Omitting any reference to cardinal bishops in summarizing the papal electoral decree of 1059, he refers only to cardinals.[42]

---

[39] Petrus Damiani, *Briefe*, nr. 48, 2:52–61; tr., Blum, 2:263–271; Cushing, *Reform and the Papacy in the Eleventh Century*, p. 70.

[40] Ibid., nr. 58, 2:191–192; tr. Blum, 2:390–391.

[41] Ibid., nr. 89, 2:568: defender of the church: "Quis ergo istorum iusto videbitur examine preferendus, utrum is, quem elegit unus vir perpetuae maledictionis anathemate condempnatus [Cadalus], an ille [Alexander II] potius, quem cardinales episcopi unanimiter vocaverunt, quem clerus elegit, quem populus expetivit, non in extremitate terrarum, sed intra moenia Romanorum et in ipsius sedis apostolicae gremio?" tr. Blum nr. 89, 3:363–364; Ovidio Capitani, *Tradizione ed Interpretazione: Dialettiche Ecclesiologiche del Secolo XI* (Rome, 1990), ch. 2, "*Problematica della 'Disceptatio Synodalis*," first pub. *Studi Gregoriani* 10 (1957), 143–174, p. 169 of 1990 ed.; Stroll, *The Medieval Abbey of Farfa*, pp. 176–177 & n. 41.

[42] *Kannonessamlung*, ed. Glanvell, Lib. I, ch. 168, p. 107: "Ex concilio eiusdem [Nicholas II] cum CXIII; Si qui apostolicae sedi sine concordi et canonica electione cardinalium eiusdem ad deinde sequentium clericorum religiosorum intronizatur, non papa uel apostolicus sed apostaticus habeatur..." Blumenthal, "Fälschungen bei Kanonisten," pp. 250–251; Cushing, *Papacy and Law in the Gregorian Revolution*, pp. 100–101; Robert Benson, *The bishop-Elect: A Study in Medieval Ecclesiastical Office* (Princeton, 1968), pp. 42–43; Stroll, *Medieval Abbey of Farfa*, p. 175.

The prerogatives of the king in either version were vague, but they made little difference at the time because the problem was not the king but the nobles. Later, criticizing the election of Gregory VII, Guido of Ferrara said that the decree was needed because when a pope died, individual Roman counts, driven by avarice, elected individual popes, sometimes as many as four or five.[43] Then, bringing up a factor that was seldom mentioned, Guido said that this situation produced innumerable conflicts, resulting in the dissipation of the treasure of the Roman see. Whoever distributed the most money, he said, became pope.[44]

In this context Guido said that the delegates to the council called by Nicholas sanctioned and ordained that henceforth whosoever defied the apostolic spirit, and assented to the election of any pope without the consent of the emperor and his successors, should receive the sentence of perpetual anathema.[45] The so called king's paragraph became the focus of the decree as hostility between the papacy and the empire intensified, but at the time of Nicholas, the emperor was thought to play a positive role. Not only did he confirm the suitability of a candidate, but he seemingly forestalled the dissipation of the papal treasury.

Although the king's right as *patricius* was not mentioned, Harald Zimmermann concludes that it did not seem to be called into question. He argues that since the approval of the German court had been sought in 1058, the regency believed that it would continue to be sought in the future. For this reason it immediately gave its approval to the decree.[46]

---

[43] Wido of Ferrara, *De scismate Hildebrandi,* MGH LdL 1:529–567 at 551: "Id autem ea necessitate decretum est, quod omnes Romani comites, sicut semper fuit avaricia Romanorum, decedente Romanae sedis episcopo, singuli, prout ferebat animus singulorum, singulos apostolicos eligebant, ut interdum quatuor et quinque episcopos Romana sedes haberet."

[44] Ibid.: "Hinc contentiones innumerae, caedes et bella, turbationes et iurgia exoriri. Fretus quisque multitudine militum et suffragio propinquorum, quicquid Romanae ecclesiae poterat rapiebat. Distrahebatur praedium Romanae sedis in partes innumeras, et is novissime omnium probatissimus et melior apostolicus habebatur, qui maiorem Romani pecuniam contulisset."

[45] Ibid.: "...[the council] mira necessitate compulsus communiter sancxerit et salubriter ordinaverit, ut quiccumque deinceps ad apostolatum animum interdisset, vel electioni cuiuslibet apostolici prebuisset assensum et operam inpendisset absque consensus et opera christiani principis, Heinrici scilicet imperatoris et successorum eis, perpetui anathematis sentenciam excepisset."

[46] Zimmermann, *Papstabsetzungen,* p. 147.

*Questions Continue*

Manuscripts of version B were broadly disseminated in Italy and Germany, and those of version A in France, where, from its perspective of the universal church, there was widespread criticism of local control by the cardinal priests and deacons.[47] By emphasizing the role of the cardinal bishops, the election would be removed from local control.[48] Some of these cardinal bishops like Humbert of Silva Candida were beginning to come from France, and they could have been responsible for composing or forging version A.

Cowdrey believes that the "genuine" decree was mainly the work of the cardinal bishops supported by Petrus Damiani and Humbert.[49] But he maintains that not only did Hildebrand not subscribe it, but also that it cannot be presumed that he was involved in its creation, or even that he wholly approved of it and had any brief for the prerogatives of cardinal bishops in papal elections. Given his contacts with the German court, Cowdrey reasons that the awkwardly inserted clause in version A about the role of the German king in papal elections is at least as likely to have understated as to have overstated what Hildebrand was prepared to countenance. It was the Roman aristocracy, Cowdrey emphasizes, rather than the German monarchy which was the object of Hildebrand's recent hostility.

Cowdrey is right that Hildebrand was not hostile toward the German monarchy, but since Hildebrand had been so instrumental in the election of Nicholas and in the events thereafter, it defies credulity that he would not vigorously have participated in the drafting of the decree that legitimized Nicholas' election and purported to chart future papal elections.[50] Moreover, he is known to have been active in the council. He cared about bringing papal elections under the aegis of the cardinals to strengthen the church and the papacy, and to neutralize the power to the Roman aristocracy.

---

[47] Krause, "Die Bedeutung der neuentdeckten handschriftlichen Überlieferungen," n. 124, p. 126.

[48] Wilhelm Bernhardi, "Das Dekret Nikolaus II. über die Papstwahl," *Forschung zur deutsche Geschichte* 17 (1877), 397–408 at 408; Stroll, *The Medieval Abbey of Farfa*, p. 208.

[49] Cowdrey, *Gregory VII*, pp. 44–45.

[50] Gresser. *Konziliengeschichte*, pp. 44–45; he was active in rejecting the Aachen Rule for the more rigorous Benedictine Rule.

If, as Cowdrey posits, Hildebrand had no particular brief for the cardinal bishops in papal elections, then version B rather than version A with its emphasis on the cardinal bishops would better reflect his vision. Since he had just sought the blessing of the king to validate the election of Nicholas II, it makes sense that he would have found the king's prerogatives in version B to be acceptable. But he had also just observed the weakness of the regency, and had focused on the Normans to be the papacy's allies and defenders. The time was opportune for reducing the authority of the emperor in papal elections, and asserting ecclesiastical control. Which version of the decree was the original has yet to be substantiated, but it is suggestive that the reformers did not leap into complying with the provisions of either version, and that it was frequently the opponents of the reformers who objected when the decree was not observed.

CHAPTER EIGHT

# NICHOLAS II: THE NORMANS AND THE COLLAPSE OF IMPERIAL AMITY

## The New Norman Policy

After Godfrey left Rome following the enthronement, Nicholas lost almost all of his military support against Benedict, and had to call upon Richard of Aversa for support. Benedict had fled to the protection of the count of Galeria, and according to the *Annales Romani*, Hildebrand met Richard at Capua and worked out an agreement whereby Richard provided the military support that eventually defeated Benedict, and swore fealty to the pope.[1] The agreement implied that as his vassal, the pope recognized Richard's right to the land that he had conquered. It is estimated that these arrangements took place in May or June of 1059.

Historians generally concede that it was the diplomatically skilled Hildebrand who took this initiative, but some speculate that it was Desiderius who played the major role in creating the new Norman policy.[2] Stephen IX had designated Desiderius as abbot of Montecassino, but it was Nicholas II who confirmed him in this dignity a few days after he had been ordained as cardinal priest of Santa Cecilia on March 6, 1059 at Osimo in the March of Ancona.[3] During the summer of 1059 Nicholas traveled to Montecassino, and accompanied by Desiderius, he traveled on to Melfi, the old capital of Apulia that lay in the midst of the lands that Robert Guiscard had captured at the expense of the Byzantines.

On August 21 or 23 Nicholas opened a council in the presence of about 100 Latin bishops of the area.[4] The council introduced reforming decrees, and provided the occasion for the pope to meet Richard of Aversa and Robert Guiscard. This meeting resulted in a dramatic shift

[1] *Annales Romani, Lib. Pont.* 2:335; Hägermann, *Das Papsttum*, pp. 89–93.
[2] Hägermann, *Das Papsttum*, p. 91; Gresser, *Konziliengeschichte*, p. 49.
[3] Ibid.; Hüls, *Kardinäle*, pp. 154–157.
[4] JL, pp. 560–561; Mansi 19:919; IP, nr. 13, 8:11; Gresser, *Konziliengeschichte*, pp. 48–51; Hägermann, *Das Papsttum*, pp. 154–160.

in policy both for the papacy and for the Normans. Robert swore fidelity to the Roman Church and to the pope, and obligated himself to retrieve the *regalia* and the possessions of St. Peter.[5] The feudal bond aimed in part at restoring the great wealth that the Roman church had lost to the Byzantines during the Iconoclastic dispute in the early eighth century.[6] Robert Guiscard facilitated the expansion of papal influence in both the political and religious spheres by extinguishing Byzantine and Muslim political power.[7]

Robert also promised to protect the papacy, and to place the churches on Norman property under its jurisdiction. At the same time as the papacy granted the Normans their conquered lands as fiefs, the Normans took a carefully formulated oath to support the candidate of "the more sound cardinals" in case of a disputed papal election.[8] The "more sound cardinals" would be the cardinal bishops who supported the reform candidates. Although the oath heightened the prospect that the papal electoral decree would be applied to subsequent elections, this was not the outcome.

For his part, Nicholas agreed to recognize the usurpation of church lands by both Normans in return for an annual census. He created Robert Guiscard Duke of Apulia, Calabria, and of Sicily once it had been conquered, and confirmed Richard as prince of Capua.[9] For the Normans the result was the legitimization of the conquests of Richard and Robert, and papal sanction of their superiority over other Norman leaders.

---

[5] *Chron. Mont.*, 3.15, p. 377, Aug. 1059: "Hisdem quoque diebus et Richardo principatum Capuanum et Robberto ducatum Apulie et Calabrie atque Sicilie confirmavit, sacramento ac fidelitate Romane ecclesie ab eis primo recepta nec non et investitione census totius terre ipsorum, singulis videlicet annis per singula bonum paria denarios duodecim...." Hägermann, *Das Papsttum*, pp. 156–157 says that Richard's presence is still open to doubt.

[6] Robinson, "Reform and the Church," pp. 286, 321.

[7] Goez, *Kirchen Reform und Investiturstreit*, pp. 123–124.

[8] Ibid., 107.

[9] *Chron. Mont.*, 3.15, pp. 400–401; Loud, *Church and Society in the Norman Principality of Capua*, pp. 38–65; idem, *Conquerors and Churchmen in Norman Italy*, Variorum Collected Studies Series (Aldershot, etc., 1984), nr. IV, "Betrachtungen über die normannische Eroberung Süditaliens;" idem, *The Age of Robert Guiscard: Southern Italy and the Norman Conquest* (Harlow, Pearson Education Limited, 2000); idem, *The Latin Church in Norman Italy* (Cambridge, 2007); idem, "The Papacy and the Rulers of Southern Italy, 1058–1198," pp. 151–184 of Graham Loud & Alex Metcalfe, eds. *The Society of Norman Italy* (Leiden, 2002); Valerie Ramseyer, *The Transformation of a Religious Landscape: Medieval Southern Italy 850–1150* (Ithaca & London, 2007), p. 124.

Bonizo rejoiced that the Normans liberated Rome from the domination of the *capitanei*, but pointed out that Benevento was not included in the pacts with the papacy.[10] However, Nicholas had already held a small synod with the archbishops of Benevento, Amalfi, Salerno, and Naples, and some of their suffragans, and on his way to Melfi, he met with some Normans.[11] Also, a synod attended by many cardinals and bishops at Benevento in August 1059 laid down the provisions for the patrimony of the Roman church in the Beneventano. Many other agreements cemented the authority of the Roman church in the South, and increased the power of Montecassino.

Since the German monarchy claimed sovereignty over the area south of the Apennines, it objected to the papacy's recognition of Norman occupation, asking how the papacy could invest Normans with lands to which it had no title. Like Leo IX, Nicholas II could have appealed to the Donation of Constantine, but essentially the recognition of Norman occupation was robbery from a weak empire, and no one objected. Agnes did call for a synod at Worms during the Christmas season of 1059, but it never was held because an outbreak of a pestilence prevented the bishops from attending.[12] The Normans not only profoundly affected the relations between the empire and the papacy, but they also eliminated the Roman nobility's ability to control the papacy. Their power was likewise successful east of the Tiber, where they wiped out the powerful nobles of Tusculum, Palestrina and Nomentana, and devastated their lands.[13]

## The North

In the North Nicholas tightened his bonds with the French monarchy, and pressed by the *patarini* he sent Petrus Damiani and Anselm of Lucca to Milan in the winter of 1059. Their negotiations with Archbishop Guido were stunningly successful in dealing with the problems of simony and clerical marriage. Even more, the Milanese clergy promised to make amends for their past behavior and to fight against ecclesiastical corruption. Most importantly for the papacy,

---

[10]  Bonizo, *Ad Amicum*, p. 593.
[11]  Mansi 19:921, IP nr. 17, 8:12.
[12]  Lampert, *Annalen*, 1060, p. 77; Gresser, *Konziliengeschichte*, p. 51.
[13]  Cartellieri, *Der Aufstieg*, pp. 49–50.

Milan agreed to recognize the superiority of the Roman church. Archbishop Guido attended the Roman synod in April 1060, and made a good impression.[14]

Strict measures against simony were taken at the council, but the *patarini* were not satisfied, and disorders continued. Anselm of Lucca was there to report on his visit to the German court.[15] At the end of 1059 Nicholas had dispatched him to Germany to inform the regency about his activities, and to smooth over irritations, especially those arising from the papal policy toward the Normans.[16] The presence at the council of Guibert, Henry IV's Italian chancellor, suggests that there were still normal relations with the German court, but they were about to deteriorate dramatically very soon.

Nicholas never relinquished his office as archbishop of Florence, and spent large blocks of time there, much of it with Beatrice and Godfrey along with Humbert of Silva Candida and Hildebrand.[17] It was a great advantage to Beatrice and Godfrey as well as to the reformers that, knowing the local situation, Nicholas elevated three clerics to the important episcopal sees of Perugia, Aquino, and Todi. Appointments such as these generated broad scale support for the reformers in Tuscany, and political advantage for Beatrice and Godfrey.

### Cardinal Stephen of S. Grisogono Rejected at the Imperial Court

Stephen, a Burgundian who had accompanied Leo IX to Rome, followed Frederick as cardinal priest of S. Grisogono when Frederick was elected pope as Stephen IX on August 2, 1057.[18] Taxed with some of the most sensitive commissions of the papacy, in 1057 he was sent by Hildebrand on an assignment to visit the *pataria* in Milan, and in 1058 he was tapped to be a legate to Constantinople, a project cancelled by Stephen IX's death.[19] Petrus Damiani describes him as one of his best friends, and in 1058 he perhaps jestingly requested that Stephen rescue him from the hands of Hildebrand at whose command Herod's prison opened to the great Peter.[20] In 1060 Nicholas sent him and Hugh, abbot

---

[14] Gresser, *Konziliengeschichte*, pp. 51–53.
[15] Marianus Scottus, *Chronik zu 1062*, MGH SS 5:558: "Papa etiam tunc Nicolai legato Alexandro, qui non longe postea papa effectus est, hoc idem in curte regia annuente."
[16] Gresser, *Konziliengeschichte*, p. 52; JL 4431a & pp. 562–563.
[17] Elke Goez, *Beatrix von Canossa*, pp. 155–157.
[18] Hüls, *Kardinäle*, pp. 169–170.
[19] Meyer von Knonau, *Jahrbücher*, 1:180–181; Appendix VIII, 684–687.
[20] Petrus Damiani, *Briefe*, nr. 57, June-December, 1058, 2:190; tr. Blum, 2:389.

of Cluny, to France to reinforce the reform decrees of the Roman council of 1059, and to strengthen the administration of the patrimony of
the church.

Between mid 1060 and the beginning of 1061 Nicholas dispatched
him on a mission to the German court with a personal letter.[21] The
papal council of April 1060, seemed to indicate that even with its tilt
toward the Normans, Rome still enjoyed relatively normal relations
with the regency, but in the short interval between the council and the
legation their relationship had turned sour. Sometime before Stephen's
arrival, the German court and episcopate had met in a council that
denied obedience to the pope, declared all of his measures to be invalid, pronounced him to be excommunicate and deposed, and forbade
the use of the papal name in the mass.

Petrus Damiani describes the entire series of incidents in the debate
between the defender of the church and the imperial advocate in his
*Disceptatio Synodalis*, written between April 14-October 1, 1062. Of
the German council the defender said: "For the officials of the royal
court, together with certain holy bishops of the kingdom of Germany,
conspiring, I might say, against the Roman Church, assembled a council in which you condemned the pope in some sort of synodal decree,
and with absolutely incredible audacity, presumed to quash all the
decrees that he had passed."[22]

The defender called attention to the privilege that the pope had
granted to the emperor that was terminated by the sentence: "Certainly,
in this—I will not call it a judgment, but a preconceived sentence—you
nullified, if I may so to speak, that very privilege the precious pope had
granted to the emperor. And, since what he had ordained was destroyed
by your intervening sentence, it follows also that what had been conceded by him to the emperor was terminated."[23] Although there is
some disagreement about what privilege it was, most scholars believe

---

[21] Hägermann, *Das Papsttum*, pp. 213–217; Hüls, *Kardinäle*, n. 5, p. 170.

[22] Petrus Damiani, *Briefe*, nr. 89, 2:559–560: *Defensor Romanae aecclesiae*: "Rectores
enim aulae regiae cum nonnullis Teutonicis regnis sanctis, ut ita loquar, episcopis con-
spirantes contra Romanam aecclesiam concilium collegistis, quo papam quasi per
sinodalem sententiam condempnastis, et omnia, quae ab eo fuerent statuta, cassare
incredibili prorsus audacia presumpsisti. In quo nimirum non dicam iuditio, sed
praeiuditio id ipsum quoque privilegium, quod regi predictus papa contulerat, si dicere liceat, vacuastis." tr. Blum, 3:356.

[23] Ibid., 2:560: "Nam dum, quidquid ille constituit, vestra sententia decernente
destruitur, consequenter etiam id, quod ab eo regi presitum fuerat, aboletur." tr. Blum,
3:356.

that it involved the rights of the *patricius Romanorum*, granted either prior to the papal electoral decree or the understanding of the decree itself.[24]

Petrus follows this description with a report of Stephen's arrival at the German court, and the regency's refusal to see him:[25]

> *Defender*: "And now, let me review the entire history of this unheard-of calamity of ours. Stephen, a cardinal priest of the Apostolic See, a man renowned for his serious and upright character and, as is well known, outstanding by reason of his many virtues, was sent to the royal court bearing letters from the pope, but failed to be received by the royal officials. He was forced to wait outside the court for almost five days, an action that was an affront to blessed Peter and to the Apostolic See. As a man of dignity and patience, he calmly bore this insult, but as a result was unable to carry out the mission entrusted to him. He brought back the confidential instructions signed by the principals unopened; he was the bearer because the blameworthy indiscretion of the court did not permit them to be presented to the emperor. Indeed, in this unexpected audacity there is so much room for debate that it might well tax the eloquence of Demosthenes and exceed the vast ability of Cicero. Wherefore, if we should wish to be most precise in pursuing the matter of the injury we suffered, we might rightly allege that you have deprived yourselves of the privilege over the Roman Church, since, as a result of your indiscretion, you have done her harm."

Petrus does not reveal what caused the break between the imperial court and the papacy. It would not have been the king's paragraph in the papal electoral decree or the policy with the Normans, especially since Guibert had attended the papal council of April 1060. Subsequent polemical sources provide only clues, but they home in on Archbishop Anno of Cologne. In 1097 Deusdedit, canonist and cardinal priest of S. Pietro in Vincoli, wrote that the king and his nobles had deposed Nicholas, who had chastised Anno for his excesses, and excised his name from the liturgy. It followed that the papal electoral decree was null because Nicholas was not pope.[26]

---

[24] Hägermann, *Das Papsttum*, n. 2, p. 213; Ryan, *Canonical Sources*, nr. 168, p. 89 says that the date was probably the summer of 1060, and that the privilege was prior to the privilege in the papal electoral decree; ibid., nr. 169, p. 89.

[25] Petrus Damiani, *Briefe*, nr. 89, 2:560–561; tr. Blum, 3:356–357; Zimmermann, *Papstabsetzungen*, p. 147.

[26] Deusdedit, *Libellus contra invasores et symoniacos et reliquos schismaticos*, MGH, LdL 2:300–365 at 309–310: "Quod si admittendum est, ut ratione factum dicatur, obicimus ad hoc confutandum prefatum regem et optimates eius se ea constitutione indignos fecisse: primum, quia postea prefatum Nicholaum Coloniensem

At the time that Deusdedit was writing, Anno had replaced Agnes as regent after he, Duke Otto of Nordheim and Count Ekbert of Braunschweig had kidnapped Henry IV in 1062. Possibly resenting the influence of Bishop Henry of Augsburg on Agnes, Anno and the other nobility hoped that through the kidnapping of the child they could regain their influence over imperial affairs. While involved in these machinations, Anno might have done something that Nicholas and his advisors found to be intolerable. Evidence for this theory is that the defender of the church in the *Disceptatio Synodalis* distinguished between the royal court and the king. The defender claimed that by rejecting Stephen the royal court had violated a pact of friendship, but that the Roman church wished to maintain good relations with the king instead of exaggerating what it had endured.[27]

According to Benzo, the papacy excommunicated Anno. Alleging that Nicholas did nothing without Hildebrand's orders, Benzo charged that he struck down men of distinction through the means of excommunication.[28] He said that among those attacked was Anno, archbishop of Cologne, who defended himself and others by revealing that Nicholas had been born out of wedlock. On the advice of what he termed the orthodox, Benzo said that Anno sent Nicholas a letter of excommunication. After reading it, grieving and groaning Nicholas died (July 27, 1061).[29] In a different context Benzo accused Gregory VII of poisoning four of his predecessors, and Cardinal Beno of SS. Martino e Silvestro, specifically alleged that Nicholas was poisoned.[30]

---

archiepiscopum pro suis excessibut corripuisse graviter tulerunt eumque huius rei gratia, quantum in se erat, a papatu deposuerant, nomenque eiusdem in canone consecrationis nominari vetuerunt; ideoque decretum eiusdem iure irritum esse debebit...." Hägermann, *Das Papsttum*, p. 215.

[27] Petrus Damiani, *Briefe*, nr. 89, 2:561: "Verumtamen Romana aecclesia non vult exaggerare quod pertulit, sed persevere cupit in munere, quod regio culmini liberaliter prerogavit." tr. Blum, 3:357.

[28] Benzo, *Ad Heinricum*, Lib.7.2, pp. 596–598 & n. 96; p. 596: "De cetero pascebat suum Nicholaum Prandellus in Lateranensi palacio quasi asinum in stabulo." tr. Robinson, *The Papal Reform of the Eleventh Century*, p. 373 & ns.79–82; Jenal, *Anno II.*, p. 168.

[29] Ibid. 596–598: "Pudet dicere, quot et quales viros pulsavit Prandelli insania per excommunicatricem linguam sui preconis profluentis insania. Ad vindicandam suam aliorumque iniuriam erexit se Anno Coloniensis exquisitis adulterae nativitatis figmentis. Communi ergo consensu orthodoxorum direxit illi excommunicationis epistolam, qua visa dolens et gemens presentem deseruit vitam." tr. Robinson, *The Papal Reform of the Eleventh Century*, p. 373.

[30] Beno, *Contra Gregorium*, MGH LdL 2:379–380: "Et post paucos dies ipse Nicolaus defunctus est, veneno, ut dicitur, suffocatus." Zimmermann, *Papstabsetzungen*, p. 148.

Petrus Damiani reinforces Benzo's assertion of indiscriminate use of the sentence of excommunication, a tool that will be used widely by the reform popes, especially by Gregory VII. In a letter written to Nicholas in 1059 he pleads the cause of the people of Ancona, excommunicated by Nicholas because of the obstinacy of a few leaders. He decries the use of a spiritual weapon that indiscriminately destroys the souls of the innocent. "Yet, venerable lord, I deeply grieve over the people of Ancona, who are dying each day, and am gravely shaken by the confused and indiscriminate danger befalling the innocent and the sinner alike. God forbid, I say, that while wishing to please one person [almost certainly Duke Godfrey, the prefect of Ancona], such a great number of those should perish, for whom Christ's blood was shed.... Use moderation in the way that the Apostolic See normally passes sentence, and restrain the application of ecclesiastical punishment, so that those whom spiteful cruelty seeks to disperse, may be embraced by priestly mercy."[31]

Nicholas was known for his harshness toward the German episcopate, and the regency was none too happy with him because of his tilt towards the Normans.[32] There was clearly a general feeling of dissatisfaction if not hostility toward Nicholas and his administration, which came to a head in the council of the king and the episcopate. Their solution was to get rid of him and all of his decrees, a decision they made clear when Stephen tried to present letters from the pope. Essentially his reign had crashed, and his death soon thereafter could well have resulted from the recognition by someone around him that he had become a liability.

### A Critical Reign

The reign of Nicholas II took a quantum leap toward identifying the papacy with the emperor. As the first pope to celebrate a coronation, he was crowned with a crown bearing both religious and imperial inscriptions.

He and his inner circle drafted the first decree against lay investiture, and crafted a decree on papal elections placing predominant authority

---

[31] Petrus Damiani, *Briefe*, nr. 60 to Nicholas II, 1059, 2:203–204; tr. Blum, 2:404–406.
[32] Hägermann, *Das Papsttum*, pp. 215–216 documents his harshness toward the German episcopate.

in the hands of the cardinals. Canon law began to reflect and substantiate claims to papal superiority in both the secular and ecclesiastical
spheres.

From his record there is little to suggest that Nicholas himself would
have initiated such bold moves, but there is substantial reason to sus-
pect that Hildebrand would have. He was already distancing the papacy
from the weak regency by replacing the emperor as its chief defender
with alliances with the Normans and the house of Lotharingia/Canossa.
As Gregory VII he will challenge imperial authority over the church,
and in the *Dictatus papae* he will delineate papal prerogatives that
would make the pope the virtual monarch over Christendom.
Ironically, this all began in the reign of Nicholas, whose election had
been dependent upon royal approval.

But there was a downside. By the end of his short reign the good
relations established with the German monarchy and episcopate had
turned to dross. Not content with mere grumbling, they ousted him
from the papacy, nullified his decrees, and refused to have anything
further to do with him.[33] Even though his reign is seen as a successful
transition along the path to ecclesiastical reform and the strengthening
of the papacy, seeds of conflict between papacy and the empire had
been sown that would dominate the rest of the Middle Ages.

---

[33] Michele Maccarrone, "La teologia del primato romano del secolo XI," pp. 56–57
of *Le istituzioni ecclesiastiche della <Societas Christiana> dei secoli XI–XII. Papato,
Cardinalato ed episcopato* (Milan, 1974); Ambrosioni, "Niccolò II," p. 177.

## CHAPTER NINE

## THE ELECTION OF ALEXANDER II (1061–1073)

The death of Nicholas II produced a startling reversal of roles. While the Romans had moved swiftly to elect Benedict X after the death of Stephen IX, the reformers sought the sanction of the regency before they elected Nicholas II. This time the reformers, now allied with the Normans, did not wait for the imprimatur of the regency, and beat the Romans with the election of their candidate, Bishop Anselm of Lucca, as Alexander II. Given the regency's total rejection of Nicholas II, they likely would not have received its confirmation anyway.

Besides the regency's renunciation of Nicholas II, and the humiliation of his legate, Cardinal Stephen, the other main difference between this election and its predecessors was the existence of the papal electoral decree. The Romans believed that the decree did not change the emperor's status as *patricius*, and brought the symbols of the patriciate to Henry IV to select a candidate. The regency and the Romans agreed upon Bishop Cadalus of Parma, but in a reversal of the outcome of the previous election, the operative factor would be which pope was elected first. It was Anselm of Lucca as Alexander II.

### Anselm as Bishop

Unlike his recent predecessors, Anselm was not from a German or a Lotharingian family, but was born in Baggio near Milan.[1] His family was not anti-imperial, and, indeed, he was present at the German court during 1048–1050. Milan was the metropolitan of all Lombardy, and in the time of Roman emperors, the see was called "*augustalis*." Many eminent bishops, including St. Ambrose, flourished there, but according to Bonizo the church had become decadent.

---

[1] *Lib. Pont.* 2:281; Cinzio Violante, "Allesandro II," *Enciclopedia dei Papi*, 2:178–185.

In reaction a reform movement called the paterines evolved, which, Bonizo asserted, was also devoted to placing honest men in Rome. They supported Stephen [IX], and along with him religious bishops, who would rebuild the church from its foundations. Bonizo said that Stephen was delighted with the activities of the patarines, and immediately sent bishops *a latere*, and with them Archdeacon Hildebrand.[2]

It is probable that Anselm was in Milan between 1053 and 1055 when the nobility was drawing closer to Henry III, who was creating the city as one of the nodal points of his Italian policies. In 1056 Anselm and Archbishop Guido of Milan were with the emperor, probably at Goslar on the occasion of Henry III's grand reception of Pope Victor II. On that occasion or soon thereafter Henry III nominated Anselm for bishop of the diocese of Lucca, the most important diocese of the Duchy of Tuscany at that time. Early in the eleventh century even before the reform papacy there was reform fervor in Tuscany that found expression in the founding of such monastic foundations as Vallombrosa and Camaldoli.[3]

Anselm's appointment signified his loyalty to Henry III, who saw him as the perfect mediator given his connections to the papal curia and to the imperial court. It is also quite probable that he was chosen to establish an equilibrium between the empire and the Duchy under the control of Godfrey and Beatrice.[4] Their domains spread from the valley of the Po southward across the Apennines into the valley of the Arno and beyond to the border of the Pontifical States of which they became a virtual extension, and a challenge to imperial authority.[5] The couple also held fiefs of bishoprics, abbeys and freehold property acquired by purchase, exchange, or usurpation, and were recognized as being fabulously rich.

---

[2] Bonizo, *Ad Amicum*, pp. 591–592; 592: "Crescebat cottidie gloriosum genus Paterinorum in tantum, ut destinarent mittere honestos viros Romam, qui Stephanum papam rogarent, ut secum mitteret religiosos episcopos, qui illorum ecclesiam a fundamentis reedificarent....Quod ut audivit papa, gavisus est et confestim misit a latere suos episcopos et cum eis Deo amabilem Ildebrandum archidiaconem."

[3] Althoff, *Heinrich IV.*, pp. 296–297.

[4] Cinzio Violante, "L'età della riforma della chiesa in Italia (1002–1122)," *Storia d'Italia*, vol. 1 *Il Medioevo* (Turin, 1959), pp. 55–234, at 126; Elke Goez is skeptical; *Beatrix von Canossa*, pp. 20, 158.

[5] Demetrius B. Zema, "The Houses of Tuscany and of the Pierleone in the Crisis of Rome in the Eleventh Century," *Traditio* 2 (1944), 155–175 at 157.

## Patarines

Anselm is accused of secretly helping to organize the patarines, but the source, Landulph the Elder, is questionable.[6] Cinzio Violante suspects that at the time about which Landulf was speaking, Christmas 1056, Anselm was still in Germany following the death of Henry III at Goslar. Anselm seems to have been present at Henry's death, and it is generally believed that along with other dignitaries he took an oath to the regency at that time. After having attended Henry's burial at Speyer on October 28, 1056, he returned to Italy with Victor II about February 12, 1057.[7] On March 24, 1057, he is mentioned as bishop of Lucca, where he dealt with a plethora of moral, religious, and economic problems, and undertook an aggressive building program, including a new cathedral.[8] He showed himself to be a *Reichsbischof*, and during the first two years as bishop he was seldom in his see, which he continued to hold after his election as pope.

Although not a creator or an organizer of the patarines, he twice returned to Milan to encourage the movement, and to deal with the excesses and abuses of the clergy. The first time was with Hildebrand at the end of 1057, and the second during winter of 1059–1060 with Petrus Damiani.[9] Conditions in Milan at that time were untenable because of a patarine uprising, and unable to cope with the situation, Archbishop Guido, a weak, uncultured man in spite of his high nobility, asked Rome for help.

The papal legations had at first elicited hostility, not just among the Patarines, but also among the upper classes. The Milanese church was proud and independent, basing itself on St. Ambrose rather than on the papacy.[10] The legation of Anselm and Petrus Damiani was able to calm the waters by working out a compromise. Guido and representatives of the high clergy were judged to be guilty of breaking their oath not to tolerate simoniacal consecrations and

---

[6] Landulf, *Historia Mediolanensis* MGH SS 8:76–77 for evidence that Anselm was one of the agitators in the strife in the church of Milan.

[7] Hansmartin Schwartzmeier, *Lucca und das Reich bis zum Ende des 11. Jahrhunderts* (Tübingen, 1972), pp. 136–137.

[8] Ghirardini, *L'antipapa Cadalo*, pp. 247–248; Zema, "The Houses of Tuscany," p. 140.

[9] Petrus Damiani, *Briefe*, nr. 65, 2:228–247 to the archdeacon Hildebrand, December 1059; tr. Blum, 3:24–39.

[10] Goez, *Kirchenreform und Investiturstreit*, pp. 112–114.

married priests, and the patarines were admonished henceforth to live in peace.

In the words of Petrus himself: "Because of the two heresies, namely, simony and that of the Nicolaitans, rather violent fighting broke out, involving the clergy and the people....[describes immorality of unchaste priests] I was received with due regard for the Apostolic See. Three days after I had announced the purpose that had brought me there, a rebellious cry sponsored by the clerical faction arose among the people. They claimed that the Church of St. Ambrose should not be subjected to Roman laws, and that the Roman pontiff had no right to judge or act in matters pertaining to that see....[riots and shouting] I was accused of placing the most reverend archbishop of Milan to my left, and Anselm the bishop of Lucca, a man known for his holiness and sanctity, at my right."[11]

Petrus spoke to the crowd, and received a positive response to his arguments for supremacy of the Roman Church. It was the middle way, but regarded as a great victory in Rome because the pope had exercised his authority over Milan. The optimates were dissatisfied because the patarines were not punished, and the lower classes were unhappy because the decision over clerics and upper classes was too mild, and did not deal with basic social and ecclesiastical problems. Nicholas II gave Guido the pallium representing the subjection of Milan to Rome. It was a transforming point in the evolution of papal authority because thereafter all metropolitans were required to take an oath, and to come to Rome to receive the pallium.

Perhaps under the influence of Hildebrand, Anselm as Alexander II moved slowly towards more open support of the patarines. In Milan Henry IV supported the old oligarchy, backing its candidate, Godfrey, as archbishop even though he had been rejected by the Milanese people and excommunicated by Alexander. Alexander excommunicated five of Henry's counselors for this sin in the closing months of his pontificate, and Henry's association with them meant that he too was subject to excommunication.[12] Thus, even though Anselm as bishop had been a moderate on the patarines, as pope he embraced them when competition with the emperor began to intensify.

---

[11]  Petrus Damiani, *Briefe*, nr. 65, 2:231–232; tr. Blum, 3:26.
[12]  Reuter, "Contextualizing Canossa," p. 150.

*Anselm, Nicholas II and the Regency*

Since he issued no documents in the first half of 1059, Anselm may have been present at the election of Nicholas II, and accompanied him to Rome. He attended the Easter synod of 1059 and signed the papal electoral decree, thus knowing what a canonical election should be. The time that Nicholas II spent in Tuscany created a combination of power and religious zeal that generated an almost perfect background for Anselm when he became pope as Alexander II.

In 1060 Anselm traveled to the court of Henry IV, where in his presence on January 6 Siegfried of Fulda was invested as archbishop of Mainz.[13] It has been suggested that the initiative for his visit came from Hildebrand, who wanted to keep any discord between the papacy and the regency from hardening.[14] If that were the case, Hildebrand failed, for we have only to remember the condemnation of Nicholas II and the aborted legation of Cardinal Stephen. Anselm was last witnessed as bishop in Lucca on July 5, 1061. A few days later Nicholas II died, and Hildebrand came to fetch him and bring him to Rome, where because of fierce fighting, he was not elected until September 30, and consecrated on October 1 as Alexander II.[15]

He appeared to be the perfect choice for both the reformers and the regency, for while empathetic to the values of the reform, he recognized the importance of lay lords to a program of religious renewal. He espoused the customary reform positions, but developed no new theological or political positions.[16] Although he supported the patarines, he was not an impassioned leader, and both as a bishop and as pope he was more of a mediator.[17] He had a pre-Gregorian view of the right order in the world, but showed himself amenable to looking at things in a new way.[18] His Achilles heal with the regency was that he was a product of the same forces that had elected Nicholas II.

As pope he acknowledged his imperial appointment as bishop, which Hildebrand clearly did not regard as an impediment to his

---

[13]  Schmidt, *Alexander II.*, p. 65 & n. 172.
[14]  Ibid., 82.
[15]  Schwartzmeier, *Lucca und das Reich*, p.140.
[16]  Ibid., 139.
[17]  Ibid.
[18]  Schmidt, *Alexander II*, p. 67.

election, but Benzo did.[19] He regarded him as a traitor for violating his oath first to Henry III, and after Henry's death, to Henry IV. Benzo asked how he could relinquish the church of Lucca granted to him by the imperial hand, and invade the Roman Church, the mother of all churches.[20]

The origin of Anselm out of a non Roman bishopric was a reproach to the old tradition, but not in the new thinking, which transcended Rome to a universal Roman Church. In Germany archbishops Adalbert of Bremen and Gerard of Salzburg recognized him, but according to Donizo writing fifty years later, Henry, then only eleven, admired neither Nicholas nor Alexander.[21] Alexander's election through what many saw as nefarious means left him open to criticism.[22]

## The Role of Hildebrand

Most probably after rejecting other candidates such as Petrus Damiani, Desiderius, and cardinals Boniface of Albano and Stephen of S. Grisogono, Hildebrand tagged Anselm to succeed Nicholas II after he died in Florence in July, 1061.[23] Hildebrand knew Anselm well from interacting with him as a legate to Germany, and from attending the Easter Council of 1059 in Rome, and Anselm clearly possessed the qualities that he was seeking.[24] Beatrice and Godfrey were also behind him, although Godfrey was in Germany at the time.[25]

While reversing the order of the elections, and referring to Anselm as the archbishop of Milan, the *Annales Romani* are typical of the

---

[19] Benzo, *Ad Heinricum*, 2.2, p. 200: "At ille "Scio" inquit, "et recolo, quia de manu imperatoris HEINRICI accepi presulatus dignitatem et propter conservandam fidelitatis curam suscepi Romanam prelaturam."

[20] Ibid., 196: "Si quicquam sensus habes, o Anselme, puto, recolis, quod dominus meus imperator HEINRICUS prefecit te Lucensi aecclesiae et, sicut mos est, de omni suo honore fecisti sibi atque filio eius iusiurandum et presertim ad conservandum imperium Romanum. Post decessum vero patris augusti domino meo HEINRICO, filio eius, qui nunc est rex, iurasti hanc eandem fidelitatem."

[21] Ghirardini, *L'antipapa Cadalo*, p. 47.

[22] *Annales Augustani, anno 1061*, MGH SS 3:127: "Quidam Lucanus episcopus a quibusdam Romanis et Normannis electus et ordinatus, a nostratibus respuitur." Cartellieri, *Der Aufstieg des Papstuums*, p. 54; Zimmermann, *Papstabsetzungen*, p. 149.

[23] Schmidt, *Alexander II.*, pp. 80–82; Goez, *Kirchenreform und Investiturstreit*, p. 107; the date was July 27, 1061, according to one estimate, and July 19 or 20 according to others.

[24] JL, pp. 558–559; Schmidt, *Alexander II*, p. 63.

[25] Elke Goez, *Beatrix von Canossa*, p. 158.

sources that uniformly identify Hildebrand as the architect of Alexander's election.[26] Representing a different area and orientation the *Chronicle of Montecassino* also singles out Hildebrand, aided by the counsel of the cardinals and noble Romans, as Anselm's chief sponsor.[27] Benzo, who frequently criticized monastic direction of the reform movement, asked rhetorically whether a monk [Hildebrand] ought to be able to create a pope.[28]

The *Annales Camaldulenses* conjecture that the spark that ignited Hildebrand's decision to select Anselm was the royal court's rejection of Cardinal Stephen.[29] Hildebrand perceived the regency's treatment of Stephen and Nicholas as arrogance of authority, and because of the regency's weakness, he could ignore the king's rights in papal elections with impunity. After hearing Stephen's report, the *Annales* state that he proposed Anselm to succeed Nicholas in an assembly of clergy and laity. He then traveled to Lucca to discuss the offer with Anselm, and no doubt to sound out Beatrice.

While a Roman contingent was en route to Germany with the symbols of the patriciate to elect Bishop Cadalus of Parma, the reformers elected Anselm as Alexander II.[30] Because of fierce opposition

---

[26] *Annales Romani, Lib. Pont.* 2:336: "Hoc audito Hildebrandus qui tunc archidiaconus erat illico perrexit Mediolanum et duxit Anselmum, qui tunc archiepiscopus erat dicte civitatis, [mistake, he was bishop of Lucca] cui posuerunt nomen Alexander." Schmidt, *Alexander II.* p. 82; pp. 80–82 for description of the leading reformers; Meyer von Knonau, *Jahrbücher,* 1:215, & n. 29; 218 & n. 35; Cowdrey, *Gregory VII,* p. 49.

[27] *Chron. Mont.,* 3.19, p. 385: "Hildebrandus archidiaconus cum cardinalibus nobilibusque Romanis consilio habit, ne dissentio convalesceret, Anselmum eligunt eumque Alexandrum vocari decernunt nostro Desiderio simul cum principe Romam proficiescente eique in omnibus suffragante."

[28] Benzo, *Ad Heinricum,* 7.2, p. 600: "Utrum aliquis monachus possit creare quemlibet papam, aut spurium, vel simoniacum, sive hereticum?"

[29] *Annales Camaldulenses,* 2:246: "Electus fuerat, ut vidimus, curante potissimum Hildebrando cardinale, prima die octobris anni elapsi in Romanum antistitem Anselmus episcopus Lucensis; [great opposition to his election described by Petrus Damiani; Stephen, cardinal priest, sent to royal court; not admitted, either by decision of administrators or by Agnes herself;] ...sed per quinque fere dies ad beati Petri & apostolicae sedis injuriam prae foribus mansit exclusus. [returns to Italy] Haec animo suo versans Hildebrandus, ulterius immorandum non esse ratus, Anselmum episcopum Lucensem eligendum in Romanum pontificem proposuit, quem etiam ceteris cardinalibus annuentibus, Nicolao II. in supremum ecclesiae episcopatum successorem dedit."

[30] Ibid., 2:238–239: "Mortem interea oppetierat Romanus pontifex Nicolaus II. Florentiae die 22. julii, & Damianus pro papae novi electione ex eremo fuerat revocatus; Hildebrandus autem post tres menses Anselmum episcopum Lucensem in Romanum pontificem creaverat die prima octobris....[p. 241] scilicet Hildebrandus pro sua prudentia & zelo omnia moderabatur, & Alexandri II. Pontificis, urbisque

it took them more than two months to carry out the election. The
enemies of the reformers reacted swiftly, barring the way from the
Lateran to San Pietro in Vincoli, where the elect was to be enthroned
because the way to St. Peter's was blocked. A coalition of reformers
and Normans responded just as swiftly, according to Benzo having
been paid, and defeated the Romans.[31] Even thereafter the fighting
remained so intense that Alexander could not be consecrated at
S. Pietro in Vincoli until the following day, October 1. He appears to
have chosen his own name, which at least some people identified
as imperial.[32] Once Cadalus had been elected on October 28 as
Honorius II in Germany, he and Alexander would fight the equivalent
of a holy war.

### How the Election was Carried Out

It took over two months for Richard of Capua and the new Roman
aristocracy—Leo, the son of Benedictus Christianus, John Brachiuti,
and Cencius Frangipani—to quell the opposition in Rome. Among
other reasons that these new aristocrats were critical to Hildebrand
and the reformers was that the papacy was in deep financial distress. It
had lost revenue from Southern Italy that had fallen into the hands of
invaders, and the Roman barons had appropriated much of the wealth
within the papal state. The papacy had to seek out new sources of revenue, and the family that would become the Pierleoni and the house of
Lotharingia/Canossa (Tuscany) would save them.[33]

Bonizo reported simply that according to the decree of the *maiorum*
Alexander was elected by the Roman clergy and people.[34] He does not
mention the cardinal bishops, but since they had been selected by the

---

Romanae erat pene dominus…" JL, p. 567; Watterich, 1:235–290; for an analysis of the
situation at the time of the elections see Schmidt, *Alexander II.*, pp. 80–88; Meyer von
Knonau, *Jahrbücher*, 1:80–88; Giovanni Battista Borino, "Cencio del prefetto Stefano,
l'attentore di Gregorio VII," *Studi Gregoriani* 4 (1952), 373–440.

[31] Benzo, *Ad Heinricum*, 7.2, p. 598: "Accepta peccunia conatus est Richardus
Lucensem hereticum deducere ad vincula sancti Petri…"

[32] Schwarzmeier, *Lucca und das Reich*, p. 142.

[33] Zema, "The Houses of Tuscany and of the Pierleone," p. 156.

[34] Bonizo, *Ad Amicum*, p. 594: 1061, "Post cuius obitum secundum maiorum decreta clerus et populus Romanus elegit sibi Anshelmum Lucensem episcopum,
Mediolanensem genere, nobili prosapia ortum, virum utraque scientia pollentem;
quem pro nomine vocaverunt Alexandrum."

reformers to be the replacement of the nobles surrounding Rome, who had previously determined the elections, it was almost preordained that they would take a leading role.

Speaking in the mouth of the defender of the church in the *Disceptatio Synodalis* Petrus Damiani asks whether he ought to be preferred who has been chosen under the curse of perpetual excommunication, or he whom the cardinal bishops unanimously called, whom the clergy elected, and whom the people acclaimed, not in far off lands, but within the walls of Rome, and in the bosom of the Apostolic See itself.[35]

The royal advocate responded that since the king had already confirmed Cadalus, it would be an insult to his authority to change his decision. The defender replied that if even God could say that he regretted his action, why should a man be ashamed to change his opinion for something better.[36] The defender had previously pointed out that the German court had nullified the decrees of Nicholas II, which would have nullified the implied imperial right of confirmation of papal elections.[37]

Benzo charged that the artful Prandellus (Hildebrand) sought out Richard of Capua, and for 1000 pounds brought him to Rome. Richard took the money and strove to bring the heretic from Lucca to San Pietro in Vincoli. The Romans resisted him with weapons, and in the dead of night, after great slaughter and with bloody hands Richard enthroned him in San Pietro in Vincoli and then brought him to the Lateran palace.[38] What an ascent to the see of Peter, Benzo laments. You, he accuses Alexander, did not ascend to the cathedra of Peter with a procession of clerics, but with murders and the effusion of blood. Not the senate, not the people, not the order of clerics, but the satellites of demons carried you. This is not to ascend, but to descend. Both you and Hildebrand deserve to lose that which you have

---

[35] Petrus Damiani, *Briefe* nr. 89, 2:568; Defender: "...an ille [Alexander II] potius [than Cadalus], quem cardinales episcopi unanimiter vocaverunt, quem clerus elegit, quem populus expetivit, non in extremitate terrarium, sed intra moenia Romanorum et in ipsius sedis apostolicae gremio?" tr. Blum, 3:363–364; Meyer von Knonau is less certain that it was held within the walls because of the threatening civil war. *Jahrbücher*, 1:219 & ns. 37 & 38; 220 & n. 40.

[36] Ibid.; tr. Blum, 3:364.

[37] Ibid., 559–560; tr. Blum 3:356.

[38] Benzo, *Ad Heinricum*, 7.2, p. 598; tr. Robinson, *The Papal Reform of the Eleventh Century*, pp. 373–374.

relinquished by despising, and that which you have usurped just as an adulterer.[39]

Benzo made a great point of describing the crown and the coronation of Nicholas II, but he did not mention a coronation of Alexander II, perhaps because he was not present. However, a letter of Archbishop Siegfried of Mainz to Alexander written in 1066/1067 implies that there was such a ceremony. Siegfried said that the crown of the kingdom and the diadem of the Roman Empire is in your hand through the hand of Peter.[40]

One expects Benzo's invective, but when the author of the less partisan *Annales Altahenses* declares that Alexander named himself pope, and was enthroned like a thief in the night, one takes notice.[41] He said that although Anselm was accepted by certain Romans, he did not have the support of the majority, and he attributed the subsequent wars in Rome to Alexander.[42] He was scathing in his description of how Alexander stole the election, and lamented that the king was too young and his mother too weak to do anything about it. The others in the palace demanded money for their cooperation, and without money one could not receive justice. Thus, right and wrong

---

[39] Ibid., 2.2, pp.196–198: "Et hoc cum Normannis, latronibus et tyrannis, et hoc mediante peccunia: Nam Prandellus sarabaita, filius Symonis tuusque trepezita, fuit interventor huius mercati; inde apud deum et homines tu et ille estis ambo dampnati. Tu non ascendisti ad cathedram Petri cum clericorum processione, sed cum homicidiis, cum sanguinis effusione. Nam Richardus [of Capua] sanguineo ense accinctus ea ipsa manu, qua tres ex nobilibus Romanis morti destinavit, hac eadem super cathedram te collocavit, et hoc totum factum est in nocte, non in die, ex qua re cognoscunt omnes, quoniam *filius perditionis* es atque *vas irae*. O qualis ascensio ad sedem Petri, ad quam te asportaverunt satellites demonum, non senatus, non populus, non ordo cleri. Certe hoc non es ascendere, sed descendere. Merito ergo debes utramque perdere; et illam, quam despiciendo reliquisti, et hanc, quam sicut adulter usurpare voluisti." Benzo accuses the Normans in other places of having received gold for their services; e.g. lib. 2, ch. 4, p. 206.

[40] *Codex Udalrici*, nr. 32, ed. Jaffé, *Bibliotheca*, 5: 91: "Corona regni et diadema Romani imperii in manu vestra est per manum Petri…" Blumenthal, *Gregor VII.*, p. 91; B. Sirch, *Der Ursprung der bischöflichen Mitra und päpstlichen Tiara* (Kirchengeschichtliche Quellen und Studien 8), (Erzabtei St. Ottilien, 1975), p. 135.

[41] *Annales Altahenses*, p. 58 "…sola Romana ecclesia bellis intestinis quassatur per Alexandrum, qui se papam nominat, quod tamen non est nec unquam erit, siquidem de eo iuste iudicatum fuerit. Non enim ex consensu regis, utpote patricii nostri, ut pastore in ovile intravit, sed data pecunia Nordmannis, inimicis videlicet vestris, ut fur et latro aliunde ascendit."

[42] Ibid., 55–56, 1060: "Hoc igitur anno obiit papa Nicolaus, pro quo episcopus Luccensis a quibusdam Romanorum in sede apostolica est constitutus, qui statim consecratus Alexander nomen accepit, quamvis communi eorum voluntate electus non fuerit, ut in sequentibus apparebit."

were confused.[43] Like Benzo he alleges that Hildebrand paid the Normans for their efforts, leaving Alexander open to the charge of simony.

The author of the *Annales Altahenses* tells the story of a member of a delegation of Romans who journeyed to Augsburg in 1061 to attend a general council held in the presence of the king to discuss the violence that had erupted after the elections of Anselm and Cadalus. There, he says, the delegate, who had participated in Alexander's consecration, implored the princes to come to the aid of the apostolic see, inflamed in wars. The delegate blamed the wars on Alexander, whom he accused of unjustly naming himself as pope. Alexander had not gained his office from the consent of the king as our *patricius*, he charged, but from money given by the Normans. For these reasons he repented having participated in his consecration.[44]

Many other writers at least mentioned Alexander's election, and some were also less than positive or even critical. In the unrevised version of his chronicle Berthold of Reichenau said that in the meantime (while Cadalus was being elected at Basel) Anselm, bishop of Lucca, with certain Romans' favoring, seized the apostolic see for himself (*usurpavit*).[45] In his second less negative version he changed "*usurparvit*" to "*ordinatus*." He said that twenty seven days before Cadalus was promoted, Bishop Anselm of Lucca was ordained Roman pope by the Normans and by certain Romans, and named as Alexander; he sat for twelve years.[46] Bernold also used the word "*ordinatus*", and mentioned the participation of the Normans and certain

---

[43] Ibid., 56: "Quoniam autem, ut iam diximus, Alexander communi Romanorum voto electus non fuerat, quidam eorum, furto surripientes, crucem auream, quae ante papam portari solebat, et alia quaedam pontificalia ornamenta ad istum detulerunt. Quibus ille mox indutus publice procedebat, et honorem apostolicum sibi ab omnibus exhiberi exigebat, quosdam etiam potentiores data pecunia ad hoc inliciebat. Inicia dolorum haec. Rex enim puer erat, mater vero utpote femina his et illis consiliantibus facile cedebat, reliqui vero palatio praesidentes omnino avariciae inhiabant, et sine pecunia ibi de causis suis nemo iusticiam inveniebat, et ideo fas nefasque confusum erat."

[44] Ibid., 58: "'Ecce adsum ego ipse, qui eum conscravi, sed Deum testor, quia vim patiens et coactus hoc feci. Quapropter, iustissimi iudices, quaeso, huic pesti, dum tempus est, obviate, ne capite mobido putrescente etiam reliqua membra citius incipiant languescere.'"

[45] Berthold, *Chronicon*, p. 190: "Interim dum haec aguntur, Anshelmus episcopus de Luca, quibusdam Romanis faventibus, apostolicam sedem sibi usurpavit."

[46] Ibid., 191: "Sed XXVII. Die ante istius promotionem Lucensis episcopus nomine Anshelmus, a Nordmannis et quibusdam Romanis papa CLVII. ordinatus et Alexander vocatus, sedit annos XII."

Romans.[47] In both cases the Normans are mentioned first, and the Romans are qualified by "certain."

In his usual animus toward Hildebrand, Cardinal Beno alleged that knowing the ambition of Hildebrand, the cardinals implored the emperor to help them elect Bishop Cadalus of Parma. He said that this action struck the heart of Hildebrand, manifestly an enemy of the emperor. Beno accused Hildebrand of breaking all bonds of fidelity, and of forming a conspiracy with the enemies of the emperor and with the Normans. This alliance enabled certain Romans to elect Bishop Anselm of Lucca as Alexander. When Alexander learned of this deceit, he preached a sermon in which he told the people that he was unwilling to occupy the apostolic see without the license and the grace of the emperor.[48]

Beno said that when Hildebrand heard Alexander declare during the mass that he had sent a letter to this effect to the emperor, he could hardly contain himself. As soon as the mass was over he had a military unit abduct Alexander from the altar and take him to an adjoining room. There his garments were removed and he was beaten until he would reveal what grace he had sought from the emperor. Hildebrand stated that from that day Alexander would not be given more than five solidi of Luccan money. Henceforth, Beno contended that Hildebrand would retain all of the income of the Roman church, and that he gathered an immense amount of money.

Beno was writing long after the fact, and his story may be largely a caricature. Yet, it reflects a pattern of reports by Hildebrand's critics that characterize him as imposing a servile relationship on both Nicholas and Alexander.

## Conclusion

However much the sources admired or scorned Hildebrand, they nevertheless agree that he was clearly in charge. Ecclesiastical reform and

---

[47] Bernold, *Chronicon*, p. 391: "Sed XXVII dies ante eius [Cadalus] promotionem Lucensis episcopus nominee Anshelmus, a Nordmannis et quibusdam Romanis papa CLVIII[us] ordinatus, Alexander vocatus…"

[48] Beno, *Contra Gregorium*, Pt. II, Letter from Beno to his beloved fathers and brothers; LdL 2:380.: "Igitur ubi Alexander intellexit se dolis et arte ab Hildebrando et inimicis imperatoris electum et intronizatum, die quadam, cum intra missarum sollempnia sermonem haberet ad populum, praedicavit se nolle sedere in sede apostolica absque licentia et gratia imperatoris."

the thrust toward papal independence and increased authority were in motion, but lay investiture was as yet not the issue. Geopolitics was. Anselm was chosen for strategic reasons, not just because he was a reformer. As a *Reichsbischof*, who had extensive experience at the imperial court, and who had probably sworn fidelity to the regency, he was in a good position to reestablish relations with the regency. Since the papal electoral decree had been nullified, the reformers could ignore any imperial rights over the election, but it was to their advantage to have positive relations with the regency and the German episcopate.

Even though much of the Roman population opposed Alexander's election, and he had almost no military, he enjoyed the advantages of alliances with the Normans and the house of Lotharingia/Canossa. Electing a pope from Lucca almost guaranteed the support of Godfrey and Beatrice, whose uneasy relationship with the regency made an alliance with the papacy an attractive prospect. Bordered by allies on both sides, the papacy viewed the empire as a faint and distant power, but one that it could not ignore. Flexing their muscles, the ambitious reformers would soon find the weak regency to be potential prey.

Anselm's birth in the vicinity of Milan was also advantageous to the reformers, since they wanted to bring the see of St. Ambrose more strictly under Roman jurisdiction. His sympathy with the indigenous lay movement of the patarines, who wanted to weaken the control of the church hierarchy, enhanced the opportunity for the papacy to increase their influence. This sometimes fanatical group of reformers was especially congenial to Hildebrand, who, more than Alexander, found it expedient to combine forces with revolutionary movements.

The number of generally reliable sources critical of Alexander's election is striking. The swift action to elect a successor to Nicholas II without adhering to the letter of the law because of the gathering storm in Rome did not forestall the storm. Ultimately it was Petrus Damiani who would bypass Hildebrand and promote a settlement in a council held at Mantua under the aegis of the king. Seemingly Petrus, and according to one source, Alexander II himself, were not satisfied that canonical decrees could be ignored, and tried to rectify the transgressions already done. The fact that Alexander cooperated with the king demonstrates that his original proclivities as a *Reichsbischof* were not dead, and contributed to the king's jettisoning of his own candidate.

According to Deusdedit, Alexander was not the only contender to have violated the decree. He says that even though the decree stated that the Roman pontiff was to be elected by the Roman clergy and people, and that thereafter the king should be notified, this decree was violated both in the case of Cadalus and Guibert.[49]

---

[49] Deusdedit, *Libellus contra invasores et Symoniacos*, MGH LdL 2:11:310: "Deinde quia, cum in eodem decreto cautum esset, ut Romani pontificis electio a Romano clero et populo ageretur et postea regi notificaretur, ipsi prefatum violantes decretum elegerunt, quo eis non licebat, prius Cadalaum Parmensem, postea Guibertum Ravenatem, induentes eos apostolicis insignibus;"

CHAPTER TEN

## THE ELECTION OF CADALUS, HONORIUS II

The rejection of Nicholas II by the imperial court and the German episcopate presented the Roman and suburban nobility opposed to the reformers with an opportunity of regaining power. Facing the powerful force of the Normans on their doorstep, these local powers could redeem the bond with the monarchy that they squandered when they did not request confirmation of their candidate, Benedict X.

A coalition led by Count Gerard of Galleria and the abbot of SS. Andrea and Gregorio in Clivo Scauro sprang into action. Benzo said that wanting to rectify the mistakes they had made regarding the young king, the Romans sent the symbols of the *patricius*—the cape, miter, ring and crown—with a delegation of bishops, cardinals, senators and representatives of the more distinguished people. Immediately the court convoked prestigious men from all of the kingdoms, because they felt that they must not receive gifts from the Capitolium without their presence.[1] It is not known whether the regency was aware that Count Gerard no longer belonged to the faithful of Christ because he recently had been excommunicated for attacking an English legation to the papacy, but in the *Disceptatio Synodalis* the defender of the church insists that the matter be taken up at the Council of Augsburg.[2]

On October 28, 1061, at the council of Basel Bishop Cadalus of Parma was elected as Honorius II.[3] German sources made it clear that

---

[1] Benzo, *Ad Heinricum*, 7.2, p. 598: "Enimvero Romani in melius recordati convenientes in unum promittunt emendare, quicquid peccaverunt in regem puerum. Itaque mittunt in clamidem, mitram anulum et patricialem circulum per episcopos, per cardinales atque per senatores et per eos, qui in populo videbantur prestantiores. Statim autem ut curiae presentantur, de tota Italia caeterisque regnis procures convocantur. Visum est enim domnae imperatrici suisque silentiariis non esse recipienda Capitolii dona nisi cum regnorum primariis." tr. Robinson, *The Papal Reform*, p. 373.

[2] Petrus Damiani, *Briefe*, nr. 89, 2:566–567; tr. Blum, 3:362–364.

[3] Ibid. Royal advocate: "Non ergo, ut asseris, ignorante Roma, sed praesente atque petente Romani pontificis electio facta est." tr. Blum, 3:362; *Annales Romani, Lib. Pont.* 2:336: "Post mortem vero dicti Nykolay miserunt Romani legatos ad H. regem, qui tunc puer erat, ut pium rectorem sancte Romane ecclesie tribueret."

the lines of division were drawn anew with the empire and many, if not most, of the Romans on one side, and the reformers and the Normans on the other.[4]

## Cadalus as Bishop

The similarities between Cadalus and Anselm were striking. They both were born in Lombardy, they both were invested in their bishoprics by the emperor, they both interacted with the royal court, and they both were reformers. Their differences were in their alliances. While Anselm was promoted by Hildebrand and his allies and supported by the Normans and the house of Lotharingia/Canossa, Cadalus was championed by the Romans and the Lombards.[5] Born about 1010, his noble family almost surely stemmed from Germany.

Parma was especially important to the empire as a pillar of power, and as a center of learning and culture. Since it controlled the county of Parma and permitted access to Rome, it was requisite that its episcopal see be occupied by loyal followers.[6] Supported by Henry, the imperial chancellor of Italy, and later bishop of Augsburg, Cadalus was invested as bishop by Henry III, by May 24, 1045.[7] As vicedominus and legate he probably also functioned as an imperial judge.[8] By the time of his election his parents and siblings had died, leaving him vast territories in the Vicentino and Verona. He used part of this wealth to found S. Giorgio in Braida, the Benedictine monastery in Verona that became his most noted monument.

---

[4] E. g.: *Annales Augustani*, anno 1061, MGH SS 3:127: "Quidam Lucanus episcopus a quibusdam Romanis et Normannis electus et ordinatus, a nostratibus respuitur." *Annales Altahenses*, p. 56; critical of Alexander; of Cadalus they say: "Episcopus autem Parmensis, Kadalo nomine, audita, unius morte, alterius autem electionem simulans se nescire, sumpta secum, ut ferebatur, pecunia inmensa, curtem adiit, regem Augustae reperit, ibique cum matre regis et episcopo Augustensi, qui adhuc palatio praesidebat, res suas agere non quievit, donec se ad sedem apostolicam a rege conlaudari et, ut mos est, infula pontificali investiri impetravit."

[5] Herberhold, "Die Beziehungen," pp. 84–104; Simonetta Cerrini, "Honorio II, antipapa," *Enciclopedia dei Papi*, 2:185–188; Baix, "Cadalus," 53–99; Ghiardini, *L'antipapa Cadalo*; Stoller, "Eight Anti-Gregorian Councils," pp. 254–263; Paravicini Bagliani, "L'Église romaine," pp. 254–263.

[6] Herberhold, "Die Beziehungen, p. 87; April, 1047: Henry confirmed the county of Parma to the church of Parma "cui Cadelous praeest."

[7] Ibid.: Confirmation made "interventu et peitione Heinrici nostri cancellari."

[8] Baix, "Cadalus," p. 55.

Evidence other than commentary suggests that he was humane and supported the main tenants of the reform. For example, in the Roman Council of April 1049 held by Leo IX he signed privileges to the bishops of Treves and Porto. Three diplomas from 1046 indicate that he was very generous to S. Paolo at Parma, and after fires in Parma in 1038 and 1055 he magnificently reconstructed the cathedral and the bishop's palace.

His relations with Henry III were excellent. He was present at the synod of Pavia on Oct. 25, 1046, where Henry solemnly rejected simony, and on May 1, 1047, Henry recognized the countal rights to the bishop of Parma.[9] Chancellor Henry of Italy granted imperial protection to S. Giorgio in Braida, and on July 13, 1052, Cadalus was present at a diet, probably held in Zurich, which treated Italian affairs.[10] On his second trip to Italy in 1055 Henry III took the canons of Parma under his protection, and on June 15 Cadalus was among those with the emperor in the area of Lucca.

### After the Death of Nicholas II

Much of the cause of violence in Rome after the death of Nicholas II was resentment and even hate of Hildebrand and his party of reformers. His opponents viewed him as a monk who functioned as archdeacon, and who created popes at will. The Romans also greatly resented the Normans, who had destroyed their candidate, Benedict X. While Leo, son of Benedictus Christianus, the Frangipani, and Johannes Brachiuto fervently supported Hildebrand and his candidate, the old guard of Gerard, count of Galeria, the abbot of SS. Andrea e Gregorio a Clivo Scauro, and probably Cencius, the prefect, championed Cadalus.[11]

The timing of the two elections is not entirely clear. The *Annales Romani* report that after the death of Nicholas the Romans sent legates to the young king Henry in order that he might grant a head of the

---

[9] Ibid., 56–58; MGH DD H III 5:249, nr. 197; May 1, 1047 Henry III recognizes to the bishop of Parma the countal right over the city "cui Cadelous episcopus preest [and its surroundings:] corroboramus…comitatum tam intra urbem quam extra totum per circuitum secondum priscos fines et discretionis terminus…cum omni districtu ad eundem comitatum pertinente."

[10] MGH DD H III, nr. 298, 5:406.

[11] Borino, "Cencio del prefetto Stefano," pp. 376–378.

Roman church. Having heard this, the *Annales* report that Hildebrand traveled to Milan [Lucca] where he fetched Anselm, who was then archbishop [bishop].[12] This sequence implies that the Romans were already on their way to Germany with the symbols of the *patricius* before Hildebrand moved to elect Anselm of Lucca. The *Annales Altahenses*, on the contrary, seem to imply that it was the election of Alexander that impelled the Romans to approach the royal court.[13] In the *Chronicle of Montecassino* Leo of Ostia reports that when members of the German court heard that Alexander had already been elected, they were highly indignant because the election had been transacted without their authority or any consultation.[14]

In the *Liber Pontificalis* Boso makes the point that under the leadership of Guibert of Parma the Lombards wanted to elect someone from the Paradise of Italy [Lombardy], and chose Cadalus.[15] Bonizo, on whom Boso relied, says that the Lombard bishops met together with Guibert, the imperial chancellor for Italy and that they decided that the new pope could only come from "the paradise of Italy," meaning Lombardy. They then crossed over the mountains to meet with the empress to tell her of their decision, and to affirm that according to the decree of Nicholas no one can be elected pope without the consent of the king.[16]

---

[12] *Lib. Pont.* 2:336: "Post mortem vero dicti Nykolay miserunt Romani legatos ad H. regem, qui tunc puer erat, ut pium rectorem sancte Romane ecclesie tribueret. Hoc audito Hildibrandus, qui tunc archidiaconus erat, illico perrexit Mediolanum, et duxit Anselmum, qui tunc archiepiscopus erat [bishop of Lucca] dictae civitatis."

[13] *Annales Altahenses*, p. 56: "Quoniam autem, ut iam diximus, Alexander communi Romanorum voto electus non fuerat, quidam eorum, furto surripientes, crucem auream, quae ante papam portari solebat, et alia quaedam pontificalia ornamenta ad istum [the king] detulerunt."

[14] *Chron. Mont.*, 3.19, p. 385: "Quod cum ad aures Regis eiusque matris venisset, indignatione nimia conducti, quod haec sine illorum consilio et auctoritate gesta fuissent." Meyer von Knonau, *Jahrbücher* 1:224–231; Baix, "Cadalus," p. 59.

[15] *Lib. Pont.*, 2:338–339.

[16] Bonizo, *Liber ad Amicum*, pp. 594–595: "Interea Longobardi episcopi, nacti se tempus invenisse oportunum, insimul conveniunt auctore Guiberto, quem superius diximus cancellarium, et concilium celebrant malignantium, in quo deliberant non aliunde se habere papam nisi ex paradiso Italiae talemque, qui sciat compati infirmitatibus eorum. Dehinc ultra montes pergunt animumque imperatricis utpote femineum alliciunt, figmenta quedam componentes quasi veri similia. Nam dicebant eorum dominum ut heredem regni ita heredem fore patriciatus et beatum Nicolaum decreto firmasse, ut nullus in pontificum numero deinceps haberetur, qui non ex consensu regis eligeretur."

But it has been suggested that Bonizo was promoting his point of view of twenty five years later during the schism of Gregory VII/ Clement III, and that the synod was apocryphal.[17] Writing in the early seventeenth century, however, Cardinal Baronius, believed that the Lombard synod was more central to the choice of Cadalus than the Council of Basel.[18] It may be indicative that the more contemporary sources, such as Bernold do not mention such a synod, but there is no doubt that the Lombard bishops supported Cadalus, and that given its ambitions in Lombardy, the regency took the initiative.

Representing Lombard interests, and opposed to the *pataria*, Bishops Gregory of Vercelli and Dionysius of Piacenza reputedly selected Cadalus.[19] Cadalus stood out from other bishops of Lombardy because of his connections with Guibert, and because the good relations that he had enjoyed with Henry III continued with Agnes. While remaining faithful to the emperor, he may have wanted to wed the papacy to Lombard aspirations.[20] With the exception of Henry of Augsburg, most of the imperial bishops were ambivalent or uninvolved.[21]

### The Council of Basel

As we have noted, on October 28, 1061, Agnes and the regency called a general council at Basel including Italian bishops and Cardinal Hugo Candidus, purportedly representing the other cardinals. The council was not well-attended, and Bishop Henry of Augsburg, who was roundly disliked, but relied upon by Agnes, exercised decisive influence.[22] In the unedited version of his chronicle, Berthold reports that wearing the crown transported by the Romans, the eleven-year old Henry functioned as *patritius Romanorum*. With unanimous consent

---

[17] Stoller, *Schism in the Reform Papacy*; the council of Basel, pp. 164–185; p. 169 & n. 14.

[18] Baronius, *Annales Ecclesiastici*, 11:361: "Non enim in synodo facta est [election of Cadalus], sed seorsum...Porro isti fuisse noscuntur episcopi, qui Basileam ex Italia convenisse dicuntur."

[19] Stoller, *Schism in the Reform Papacy*, pp. 184–185; Stoller disputes this allegation made by Petrus Damiani.

[20] Baix, "Cadalus," p. 60.

[21] *Annales Augustani*, MGH SS 3:137: "archiepiscopis et ceteris episcopis non consentientibus;" Herberhold, "Die Beziehungen," p. 92.

[22] Baix, "Cadalus," pp. 58–63; Cartellieri, *Der Aufstieg des Papstuum*, p. 55.

Bishop Cadalus of Parma was elected pontiff of the Roman Church.[23] In his version written after he had been influenced by Gregory VII Berthold states that Cadalus was elected simoniacally as Honorius, but that he never occupied the papacy. Alexander, by contrast, elected 27 days before him, held the office for twelve years.[24]

In a similar vein Bernold states that upon the death of Nicholas, Romans came to Henry IV bringing the crown and other gifts, and spoke to him about the election of the highest pontiff. The king called a general council at Basel, where he wore the crown and was called the *patricius Romanorum*. With the common consent of all, Bishop Cadalus of Parma was elected as Honorius, but he never became pope. Rather, the bishop of Lucca was elected 27 days before he was, and was called Alexander.[25]

The author of the *Annales Altahenses* exculpates Cadalus from accepting the papacy after Alexander had been elected. He states that upon hearing of the death of Nicholas II, and not knowing that Anselm had been elected, Cadalus traveled to Germany with an immense amount of money. At Augsburg he encountered the king, his mother and the bishop [Henry] of Augsburg, who presided over the palace. He successfully insisted that he be made pope and invested with the

[23] Berthold, ed. Robinson, version 1, p. 190: "Romae Nicolao papa defuncto, Romani coronam et alia munera Henrico regi transmiserunt eumque pro eligendo summo pontifice interpellaverunt. Qui, ad se convocatis omnibus Italiae episcopis, generalique conventu Basileae habito, eadem imposita corona, patritius Romanorum appellatus est. Deinde cum communi consilio omnium Parmensem episcopum summum Romanae ecclesiae elegit pontificem."

[24] Ibid., 191: "Rome Nicolao papa defuncto VI. Kal. Augusti, Romani regi Heinrico coronam et alia munera mittentes, eumque de summi pontificis electione interpellaverunt. Qui, generali concilio Basilee habito, imposita corona a Romanis transmissa, patricius Romanorum est appellatus. Deinde communi omnium consilio Romanorumque legatis eligentibus Chadalous Parmensis episcopus VIII. Kal. Novembris papa, multis premiis quibusdam ut aiunt datis, symoniace eligitur et Honorius appellatur, papatum numquam possessurus. Sed XXVII. die ante istius promotionem Lucensis episcopus nomine Anshelmus, a Nordmannis et quibusdam Romanis papa CLVII. ordinatus et Alexander vocatus sedit annos XII."

[25] Bernold, *Chronicon*, ed. Robinson, p. 390: "Romae Nicolao papa defuncto VI Kal. Augusti [July 20, 1061], Romani Heinrico regi, eiusdem nominis quarto, coronam et alia munera mittentes, de summi pontificis electione regem interpellaverunt. Qui generali concilio Basilea habito, imposita corona a Romanis transmissa, patricius Romanorum est appellatus. Deinde communi omnium consilio, Romanorumque legatis eligentibus Chadelo Parmensis episcopus VII Kal. Novembris papa eligitur et Honorius appellatur, papam tum nunquam possessurus. [391] Sed XXVII die ante eius promotionem Lucensis episcopus nomine Anshelmus, a Nordmannis et quibusdam Romanis papa CLVIII<sup>us</sup> ordinatus, Alexander vocatus..."

pontifical symbols, and then left for Italy where he discovered that another had already been elected.[26]

As a partisan Benzo states uncharacteristically simply that after the death of pope Victor (he ignores Stephen IX and Nicholas II because they were not initiated by the king) Cadalus, bishop of Parma, was ordained through the hand of the king with the lauds of the three orders of primates of the city of Rome, and also of bishops and optimates from diverse provinces.[27] Returning to form in his summation in Liber VII of *Ad Heinricum* he says that while the king with his bishops ordained their pope justly and legally, Prandellus with the Normans elected their pope simoniacally.[28]

Predictably hostile, Bonizo concentrates on Hugo Candidus, a pivotal figure who supported one side or the other depending upon the circumstances. He notes that Hugo had been ordained cardinal by Leo IX, but was now cut off from the Roman church. Just as his eyes were turned or twisted, so were his deeds.[29] The empress, whom Bonizo stresses was female and had been deceived, gave her consent to the nefarious election. He emphasizes that no Roman clerics or laymen were present when Cadalus, opulent in riches, but lacking in virtues, was elected by fornicators and simoniacs. After his election Cadalus accepted the papal insignia—the cross and the eagle—from the hands of the king and the empress.[30]

---

[26] *Annales Altahenses*, 1060, p. 56: "Episcopus autem Parmensis, Kadalo nomine, audita unius morte, alterius autem electionem simulans se nescire, sumpta secum, ut ferebatur, pecunia inmensa, curtem adiit, regem Augustae reperit, ibique cum matre regis et episcopo Augustensi, qui adhuc palatio praesidebat, res suas agere non quievit, donec se ad sedem apostolicam a rege conlaudari et, ut mos est, infula pontificali investiri impetravit. Qui mox in Italiam regrediens et illum iam consecratum apostolicae sedi publice praesidentem reperiens..."

[27] Benzo, *Ad Heinricum*, 2.1, p. 190–193: "Post Decessum igitur papae Victoris ordinatus est Kadalus, Parmensis episcopus, per manum regis HEINRICI filii item HEINRICI imperatoris, conlaudantibus tripertiti ordinis Romanae urbis primatibus, astipulantibus quoque diversarum provinciarum episcopis et optimatibus. Ex precepto denique pueri regis atque matris reginae acceperunt Italiae proceres ducatum huius viae."

[28] Ibid., 7.2, p. 598: "dum rex cum episcopis ordinat suum papam iuste et legaliter, Prandellus cum Normannis e contrario suum symonialiter." tr. Robinson, *The Papal Reform*, p. 374.

[29] Bonizo, *Liber ad Amicum*, p. 594: Hugo Candidus, ordained cardinal by Leo IX, but now "a Romanae ecclesiae recessit societate; de cuius morum perversitate melius est silere quam pauca dicere. Sed ut brevius cuncta perstringam: qualis fit oculis, talis fuit factis; ut enim habuit retortos oculos, ita eius retorta fuerunt acta.

[30] Ibid., 595: "His et talibus machinationibus decepta, imperatrix feminea licentia assensum dedit operi nefario, quale non fuit a die, qua gentes esse ceperunt, ut, ubi

## Hugo Candidus

Most sources indicating that the Romans brought Henry the symbols of the patriciate do not emerge before the late 1070s during the controversy between Henry IV and Gregory VII when Henry adduced his status as *patricius* as authority for judging Gregory's election.[31] If the allegation that the Romans brought them was created after 1061, then they have problematic significance in the Council of Basel. The evidence that Guibert and Benzo were there is circumstantial, and the contention that Hugo Candidus was present as the only cardinal is also open to question.[32]

Hugo Candidus was a shifting, but key figure from the time of Leo IX through the reign of Gregory VII, whose election he allegedly orchestrated. Bonizo, the chief source for what we know about him, is unreliable because he detested him, and in 1089 dedicated a polemic, since lost, to the despised Hugo.[33] Before accompanying Leo IX to Rome, Hugo had been abbot of Remiremont, the house cloisters of the dukes of Lotharingia in the diocese of Toul, where Leo (Bruno) had been bishop. Possibly Hugo had some contact with the family of Duke Godfrey, husband of Beatrice. Leo created him cardinal priest of St. Clemente, but Hugo did not always support the reform popes.[34]

When the imperial court went over to Alexander II in 1064 Hugo had little alternative but to do likewise, and became active as a papal legate. But according to Bonizo, because of his activities in Southern France a delegation of Cluniac monks came to the Lenten synod in Rome, and raised complaints of simony against him.[35] Still, Hildebrand maintained his trust in him because he was actively promoting papal supremacy, and Hugo purportedly orchestrated Hildebrand's

---

nullus clericorum Romanorum vel laicorum interfuit papae electioni, ibi pontifex elegeretur a consimilibus fornicatoribus et symoniacis, quive accipiens per manus regis et reginae crucem et papalia insignia, ab aquilone veniret Romam, unde secundum Ieremiam pandetur malum super universos habitatores terre; quic plura? Eligunt sibi Parmensem Cadolum, virum divitiis locupletem, virtutibus egenum;"

[31] Stoller, *Schism in the Reform Papacy*, p. 179 & ns. 36, 37.

[32] Ibid., 173–174 & n. 25; 176 & ns. 29, 30; Hüls, *Kardinäle*, pp. 158–160; Hüls accepts the evidence that he was there, while Stoller mounts a careful analysis that the evidence has been misread.

[33] Bonizo, *Ad Amicum*, p. 588: "Ugo Candidus, qui postea apostata est effectu..." Franz Lerner, "Kardinal Hugo Candidus," Beiheft 22, *Historische Zeitschrift* (1931), 4–59; also idem, *Kardinal Hugo Candidus* (Munich and Berlin, 1931).

[34] Hüls, *Kardinäle*, pp. 158–160.

[35] Bonizo, *Ad Amicum*, p. 600.

decidedly unorthodox election as pope. He was active in Gregory VII's reign, but because of his relationship with Gregory's opponents in Northern Italy, he was excommunicated three times. As in the council of Basel, he participated as the only cardinal in the council of Brixen in 1080 where Guibert of Ravenna was elected pope as Clement III.

One hypothesis to explain Hugo's many metamorphoses is that he was particularly in tune with the nobles of upper Italy, who represented the national unification of Italy under the leadership of the Lombards.[36] For this reason the Lombards opposed the centralization of the reform curia and the *pataria*, and wanted a pope who was Italian, not German. Hugo learned about the aspirations of the Lombards from the repeated visits of Guibert to Rome, and conditioned by Leo IX's closeness to the emperor, he opposed the policies of the reform curia. When the political position of the Lombards improved after the condemnation of Nicholas II by the German court in 1060, Hugo broke with the curia, and in all probability participated in the Council of Basel.[37]

## Empress Agnes

How much Agnes personally participated in the selection of Cadalus is uncertain, but it is probably indicative that, as Berthold of Reichenau reports, by the end of the year she relinquished the regency and took the veil. In the second version of his *Annales* Berthold adds some details, but no substantive embellishments that might indicate what motives informed her decision.[38] She hardly consulted her bishops, and her counselors, especially Henry of Augsburg, may have pushed her to support the appointment of Cadalus.[39] She personally knew both Hildebrand and Alexander as Bishop Anselm of Lucca, and it may have pained her to have opposed them.

Bonizo said that in the first place it was audacious to place a woman in the position as regent—Victor II may have been responsible—and that she put the affairs of the empire into the hands of Guibert.[40] Always

---

[36] Lerner, "Kardinal Hugo Candidus," pp. 15–16.

[37] *Vita Anselmi episcopi Lucensis*, MGH SS 12:19.

[38] Berthold, *Annales*, ed. Robinson, Version 1, p. 193, [Nov. 1061]: "Et Agna imperatrix, depositis regalibus vestimentis, sacro velamine circundata." Version 2, p.193: "His temporibus Agna imperatrix, depositis regalibus vestimentis, velamine sacro sese Christo dedicavit, in opidum Fructerciam se contumlit."

[39] Meyer von Knonau, *Jahrbücher*, 1:231.

[40] Bonizo, *Ad Amicum*, p. 593: "Dum hec ita gererentur, Heinrici imperatoris coniunx cum filio parvulo...regni tenebat gubernacula. Que multa contra ius feminea

emphasizing her weakness as a woman, he says that she was deceived by machinations at the imperial court, and gave her assent to the nefarious election.[41] Bonizo, however, was writing twenty five years later when Guibert was functioning as Clement III in opposition to Gregory VII, and he may have been intent upon impugning Guibert, who in 1061 had relatively few German contacts.[42]

Who was the enigmatic Agnes? As the daughter of Duke William the Great of Aquitaine, who founded Cluny in 910, her marriage to Henry III formed a bond between the empire and Cluny.[43] After the death of her young, and much admired husband, she tried to follow in his steps. Not only did she promote bishops from the court chapel, but she also invested them with ring and staff. Relying on Bishop Henry of Augsburg seemed to promote continuity, but it also created many enemies.

The minority of Henry IV fell during a time when the inner contradictions of the empire/church policies became overt, and the tension between *regnum* and *sacerdotium* reached an acute stage. Even though Agnes had a will of her own, she appeared to lack strength, and was too easily influenced by advisors. More responding than commanding, she arrived at timid decisions based upon previous political solutions, and made concessions to local powers without possessing a counter weight.[44]

Even though she visited all parts of the empire yearly, she could not deal with strivings for independence. The Saxons rebelled against the Swabians, the Lower Rhine, Frisia and Liège eluded her control, and she could not subdue Bela, the Hungarian king. Imperial rule disintegrated, and power shifted to the east. She had nothing to do with a decisive shift in papal Italian policy when Hildebrand and Nicholas II invested Normans with imperial lands, and used them as military allies. Thus, imperial rights in South Italy were sacrificed, and from that time the German court held less leverage over the papacy.[45]

---

faciebat audacia. Haec in primordio regni sui omnes eiusdem Italici regni curas cuidam Guiberto commisit Parmensi, nobili orto genere, eumque cancellarium appellavit."

[41] Ibid., 595: "His et talibus machinationibus decepta, imperatrix feminea licentia assensum dedit operi nefario..."

[42] Stoller, *Schism in the Reform Papacy*, n. 14, p. 169.

[43] Jäschke, *Notwendige Gefärtinnen*, esp. pp. 95–137.

[44] Ibid., 125.

[45] Ibid., 126–127.

A conspiracy to undermine her led by Archbishop Anno of Cologne began to materialize.

### Petrus Damiani

As a reformer and a bitter opponent of Cadalus, Petrus Damiani was nevertheless able to understand and analyze the position of both sides. A bevy of letters indicates his extreme distress with the schism, but also his esteem for the emperor, whose authority he deemed to be integral to a Christian society. Early in 1062 he wrote to Bishop Oldericus of Fermo reflecting on the evil days brought about by the schismatic crisis caused by Cadalus.[46] Whereas the *imperium* had once defended the *sacerdotium*, he saw that they now recoiled from one another. To the prejudice of almighty God, he lamented, now that one pope is seated on the apostolic throne, another is considered to have been elected by the lands of the north. In tears, he wrote:

> Alas, the Apostolic See once gloried in hegemony,
> But scoffing men now note with glee your forge transformed to simony.
> Hammers on the anvil pound and hellish coins now abound;
> By God's judgment this is so, that at your hand weal turns to woe...[47]

These bad times stimulated Petrus to contemplate that the corrupt world was nearing its end. But even with the current depredation of ecclesiastical property, he held that bishops and abbots should not take up arms in defense of their temporalities. To him it was absurd that priests of the Lord should attempt to carry out the very thing that they forbade their people to do. What, he asked, is more contrary to Christian law than repaying injury with injury?[48] "Now," he said, "if someone should object to my arguments by stating that Pope Leo [IX] often became involved in acts of war [with Robert Guiscard], even though he was holy, I will tell you what I think." Citing scripture and ecclesiastical precedents, he advocated that secular law or episcopal councils should decide ecclesiastical cases rather than trial by battle.[49] Here, he and Hildebrand frequently were not on the same page.

---

[46] Petrus Damiani, *Briefe*, nr. 87 to Oldericus, bishop of Fermo, early 1062, 2:504–515; tr. Blum, 3:299–308.
[47] Ibid., 2:509; tr. Blum, 3:302.
[48] Ibid., tr. 3:303.
[49] Ibid., 2:511; tr. Blum, 3:307.

In a letter written between March and April 14, 1062, before major violence erupted, he asked Cadalus how, since his episcopal tenure was held in such ill repute, he could dare to presume to be elected bishop of Rome without the knowledge of the Roman Church. He implied that the "subsidiary cardinals" and the lower orders of the clergy and the people should have had a role in the election while acknowledging that the cardinal bishops had the major privilege.[50] The rights of the cardinal bishops surpass not only those of all other bishops, he asserted, but also those of patriarchs and metropolitans.[51]

In response to the allegation that Romans had participated in the irregular election, Petrus prescribed what the procedures should have been. "...this election should in the first instance have been the decision of the cardinal bishops; in the second place, the clergy should by right have given its assent; in the third place, popular approval should have raised its voice in applause; and then the election should have been suspended until the authority of his royal highness had been consulted, unless, as recently happened, some imminent danger should occur which compelled the election to be expedited as soon as possible."[52]

In the *Disceptatio Synodalis* incorporated into the fiercely critical letter to Cadalus written after bitter fighting had broken out in Rome, the defender of the church claimed that had the pontiff [Alexander II] not been inducted immediately, the Romans would have suffered incredible slaughter:

....To this may be added that occasionally, because of the changing times, the order of events must often be altered. For on the day the Roman Church appointed her pontiff [Alexander II] such fiery hostility and seditious action broke out among the inhabitants of the city, such ill will and hatred aroused the feelings of the tumultuous crowd, that it was impossible for us to await a decision from our gracious emperor, who was so far away. For, unless the pope were immediately inducted, the

[50] Ibid., nr. 88 to Cadalus, March-April 1062, pp. 515–531 at 2:517: "...quo pacto praesumpsisti, vel, ut mitius loquar, acquiescere potuisti, ignorante Romana aecclesia Romanum et episcopum eligi? Taceamus interim de senatu, de inferioris ordinis clero, de populo., tr. Blum, 3:311.
[51] Ibid.: "Quid tibi de cardinalibus videtur episcopis, qui videlicet et Romanum pontificem principaliter eligunt, et quibusdam [518] aliis praerogativis, non modo quorumlibet episcoporum, sed et patriarcharum atque primatum iura transcendunt?" tr. Blum, 3:311.
[52] Ibid., 2:526; tr. Blum, 3:318–319.

people would have savagely wounded one another with their swords, and no small slaughter of Roman citizens would have occurred.[53]

The imperial advocate was not mollified. Give any excuse that you wish, and argue as long as you like, he responded, so long as it remains clear that in no way can we alter what the pope granted, what he established by his decree, and what he confirmed in writing.[54] The defender equivocated, asking why we need wonder that the statutes of men should be changed, when even almighty God also changes things that he himself had established? At times he alters a thing that he has promised, at times he diminishes something or even totally withdraws it, and at times he threatens evil and then does not inflict it.[55]

It was not the intention of the electors to inflict injury on our glorious emperor, the defender later insisted; it was not spoliation, but necessity. "It was the imminent danger of civil war that prompted us, unwilling as we were, to take this course, and not a malicious desire to harm or diminish his power."[56] The imperial advocate responded scornfully. "You propose civil war and allege imminent danger in your defense; you might as well say that the heavens would come crashing down and the earth be torn to pieces....All of this concerns me not at all, so long as it is certain that, whatever happens, you will not be allowed to contravene the decision of his holiness, the pope, and in no way be permitted to violate the sacredness of the synodal [papal electoral] decree."[57]

The defender offered no rejoinder, and later the imperial advocate broadened his attack, rejecting the defender's argument that since the reformers were constrained by necessity and the pressure of time, they were not able to wait for his royal majesty's consent. He scoffed at this frivolous objection, emphasizing that about three months had passed between the death of Pope Nicholas and the succession of [Alexander] on the first of October. Over such a long period of time, he asked rhetorically, could not a copy of the confirming document from the royal court have reached you?[58]

---

[53]  Ibid., nr. 89, 2:549; tr. Blum, 3:343.
[54]  Ibid., tr. Blum, 3:344.
[55]  Ibid., 549–550; tr. Blum 3:344.
[56]  Ibid., 552; tr. Blum, 3:346–347.
[57]  Ibid.; tr. Blum, 3:347.
[58]  Ibid., 559; tr. Blum, 3:355.

At this point the defender broke his silence about the royal court's condemnation of Nicholas with the connivance of certain German bishops. Out of reverence for the imperial court he said that he had been reluctant to divulge this information, but now he felt that it was crucial to reveal that the royal court had nullified the privilege that the pope had granted to the emperor. Some scholars interpret this privilege to be the patricianship granted to Henry III, or an early papal grant, but the papal electoral decree makes more sense.[59] The rights over papal elections came from the pope, while the symbols of the *patricius* came from the Roman people.

Since what the pope had ordained was destroyed by the court's intervening sentence, he continued, it followed that what he had conceded to the emperor was terminated. Not wishing to condemn the emperor, however, he declared: "But far be it from us that because of any man's arrogance, the emperor, who was not involved, should on our account lose any of his rights. And he whom, God willing, we thoroughly hope to see promoted to the imperial office, we will not permit, because of another's fault, to suffer damage to his royal dignity." The defender then reviewed the whole history of the attempt of Cardinal Stephen to present letters from the pope to the royal court, and concludes that the Church wishes that what it had liberally granted to his royal highness [the papal electoral decree] should continue to function."[60]

The second Anselm, elected bishop of Lucca in 1073, and author of a collection of canons that strongly advocated papal rights, reinforced the defender's view. He said that there are some who object that Nicholas II constituted a decree in a synod stating that after the death of a pope, a successor was to be elected, and then the king was to be

---

[59] Ibid., 560–561; tr. Blum, 3:356–357, n. 107; the editor believes that the defender was referring to the patricianship; J. Joseph Ryan, *Saint Peter Damian and his Canonical sources. A Preliminary Study in the Antecedents of the Gregorian Reform*; Pontifical Institute of Mediaeval Studies and Texts 2 (Toronto, 1956), nr. 169; Ryan presumes that the privilege in question is that which Nicholas II had granted to Henry IV before the papal electoral decree. Borino, "Cencio del prefetto Stefano," n. 23, p. 380 says that the rupture and condemnation inflicted on Nicholas II had nothing to do with the papal electoral decree because the regency had cooperated as witnessed by the presence of Guibert, the chancellor. Borino says that we don't have enough information to know; what we do know is that the rupture took place at the very end of the administration of Nicholas II. I think that the only decree that makes sense in the context is the electoral decree.

[60] Ibid., 561; tr. Blum, 3:357.

notified. Thereafter the pope could be consecrated. But Anselm maintained that this decree was no longer valid because after Nicholas had excommunicated the archbishop of Cologne, the German court deposed him and prohibited his name from being used in the canon of consecration. Therefore, Anselm said, his decree was null.[61]

The defender admitted that omitting the election of the pope without the consent of the emperor violated the letter of the law, but he gave many examples illustrating why not conforming to the law could be good. In the present case he stated: "Because we elected the pope without the consent of the emperor, you are not at once to judge the external act, but you must rather carefully note the spirit and the intention with which it was done."[62] Disdainful of this argument, the imperial advocate retorted: "We may often sin in performing an evil deed but, because it is secret, we can take refuge in the purity of our intentions."[63] The defender shot back: "Do you think that a question must always be decided on the appearance of things and the literal meaning of words?"[64]

The defender then presented clinching evidence that the church had gone out of its way to choose someone acceptable to the emperor. It could have chosen one of the many holy and learned men from its own clerical family, he pointed out, but instead it chose one who was almost a member of the emperor's household.[65] The imperial advocate appeared to capitulate to this logic, conceding that what he had called damaging to the king was so sharply refuted that it was manifestly proven that in electing the Roman pontiff the Roman people were of tremendous service to his royal majesty. The action did not deprive

---

[61] Ex Anselmi Libro contra eos qui dicunt regali Potestati Christi Ecclesiam subiacere, MGH SS 23:1–35 at 7: "Sunt item qui obiiciunt, Nicolaum iuniorem decreto synodi constituisse, ut obeunte apostolico pontifice successor eligeretur, et electio eius regi notificaretur, facta vero electione et, ut praedictum est, regi notificata, ita demum pontifex consecraretur. Quod si [8] admittendum est, ut ratione factum dicatur, obiicimus ad hoc confutandum, praefaturm regem et optimates eius se ea constitutione indignos fecisse, primum quia postea praefatum Nicolaum Coloniensem archiepiscopum pro sui excessibus corripuisse graviter tulerunt, eumque huius gratia quantum in se erat a papatu deposuerunt, et nomen eiusdem in canone consecrationis nominari vetuerunt, ideoque decretum eius de iure irritum esse debebit, quia cum a toto orbe papa haberetur iuxta eorundem sententiam eisdem papa non fuit, quasi non ex Dei sed eorum tantum penderet voluntate quempiam quemlibet esse vel non esse;"

[62] Petrus Damiani, Briefe, nr. 89, 2:563; tr. Blum, 3:358–359.

[63] Ibid.; tr. Blum, 3:359.

[64] Ibid., tr. Blum, 3:359.

[65] Ibid., 570; tr. Blum, 3:366.

him of his privilege, the advocate emphasized, but rather strengthened it, since it promoted to the Apostolic See a bishop who had belonged not to the Roman Church but to the royal court.[66]

At this point Petrus presents his own view of the relationship between *regnum* and *sacerdotium*. Speaking to counselors of the royal court and servants of the papacy, he said: "...let us conspire to work together that the highest seat of the priesthood and the Roman Empire may be joined in harmony, so that the human race, which under both aspects of its nature is ruled by these two powers, should never again, God forbid, be torn apart, as was recently achieved by Cadalus. Thus, let the summits of government in the world come together in a union of everlasting love, that the lesser orders may not be repelled by their dissension. Thus, as these two, the empire and the priesthood, by divine dispensation are united in the one mediator between God and men, so may these two exalted persons be joined together in such harmony that, by a certain bond of mutual love, we may behold the emperor, reserving to the pope, however, the dignity no other may possess."[67]

He should be able to use civil law, and the emperor with his bishops to adjudicate matters where the welfare of souls is involved, but under the authority of the sacred canons. The pope should always enjoy paramount dignity by reason of his paternal rights, and the emperor as his unique and special son should rest securely in his loving embrace.[68] Elsewhere in the same letter the defender asserted that the Roman Church is the mother of the emperor in a more profound sense than his natural mother, and in that capacity it had acted as a tutor to the young boy in the election.[69]

The main points that Petrus stresses are his condemnation of Cadalus, his respect for the emperor, his recognition that for the empire Anselm was a suitable candidate, that it was at least questionable if not improbable that the papal electoral decree was in force at the time of the election, and that although he advocated that the emperor and pope work in harmony, the pope was superior to the emperor. All of the reformers would have agreed on the pope's superiority, and some were beginning to whittle away at the emperor's authority.

---

[66] Ibid., 570–571; tr. Blum, 3:366.
[67] Ibid., 571–572; tr. Blum, 3:367.
[68] Ibid., 572; tr. Blum, 3:367.
[69] Ibid., 549; tr. Blum, 3:342–343.

## Papal Authority and the Lombards

As the defender emphasized, Anselm should have been a congenial candidate to the emperor, and was probably nominated in part for that reason. But by moving against Nicholas, the regency had raised the ire of the reformers. Previously Hildebrand had cooperated with the empire, but now he was determined to wrest papal elections from imperial control, and to ensure that the pope would have the requisite authority and power as the head of the universal church.

It is indicative of the nature of the two reformers that while Hildebrand focused on the authority of the papacy, Petrus Damiani regarded Hildebrand's "urgent request" to seek out texts to validate its authority to be of little importance. In a letter to Hildebrand in December 1059 Petrus wrote: "...you frequently asked me, with the charity that overcomes all things, that as I read through the decrees and statutes of the Roman pontiffs, I should from here and there thoughtfully excerpt whatever specifically was seen to belong to the authority of the Apostolic See, and put it altogether in some small volume as a new collection. As I neglected this urgent request, thinking it to be of little importance, and considering it superfluous rather than necessary, it happened providentially, I think, that I was commissioned to travel to Milan as the legate of blessed Pope Nicholas".[70]

Inspired by the zeal for reform, the papacy, strengthened and reorganized by Hildebrand, felt itself impelled to contest the power of the emperor over the church, and in the last analysis, over the world.[71] Since the organization of the church rested on the bishops, the right of choosing them represented a basic power over the church, and the majority of the Italian bishops supported the emperor. Indeed, the "hard-necked bulls of Lombardy," as the upper Italian bishops were once entitled by an ecclesiastical writer, offered the stiffest resistance against the pope. Already before the great fight between Gregory VII and Henry IV, it was drawn to a head by the election of Cadalus.

The noble bishops of Lombardy lived in the feudal ambiance of their class and their time. Some of their documents refer to the king or emperor as their lord, and their bishoprics as fiefs. They felt a sense of

---

[70] Ibid., 229–230, nr. 65; tr. Blum, 3:25.
[71] Gerhard Schwartz, *Die Besetzung der Bistümer Reichsitaliens unter den Sächsischen und Salischen Kaisern*, pts. 1,2, abschnitt A (Leipzig, Berlin, 1913), pp. 6–9.

personal fidelity to the king that they did not feel toward the pope. Rather, they tried to elude the grasp for power of the Roman Church. Not all reformers had the same objectives as Hildebrand and the popes he promoted. For example, the monks of Camaldoli and Fonte Avellana, whose views Petrus Damiani represented, at first only aimed to improve the morality of the clergy. They had no quarrel with the emperor, even after the death of their exemplar, Henry III. Their problem was not with imperial rights over the church, but with what they later perceived as abuses under Henry IV. Their goal was the moral improvement, not the independence of the church.

The monks of Vallombrosa in Tuscia or Tuscany took a more political, anti-imperial direction. In their circle simony became more and more associated with lay investiture. The movement took on such a character that bishops would have found it difficult to dissociate themselves from it, and the movement against the emperor in this area was deeply embedded in the episcopate. The situation differed in Lombardy where bishops had a more princely character, they were more secular, and their resistance to the *pataria* was intense. Seeing their position threatened from below and above, the Lombard bishops became even more hostile to the aggressive moves of the papacy when the papacy allied itself with the *pataria*. The raising of Cadalus to the papal throne was a foretaste of the great fight about to come, and when it broke out the empire found its most passionate supporters in Lombardy.

CHAPTER ELEVEN

CONFLICT IN ROME AND THE ABDUCTION OF HENRY IV

The two sides in the schism were quite evenly split. Each charted its first moves to gain recognition and the rejection of the other. Alexander's enthronement, his residence in Rome, and his close proximity to the Normans were huge advantages, but Cadalus had the support of the regency, the Lombards, and a large percentage of Romans. Since in the beginning neither side was able to demonstrate its religious and legal superiority, they each resorted to force. Godfrey would be the arbiter, and in the end recognition would be decided in a council, not on the battlefield.

After the council of Basel Cadalus seems to have returned to Parma to prepare for his trip to Rome.[1] Probably at the command of the regency, in November 1061 he started out for Rome accompanied by Italian nobles, but the expedition collapsed due to horrendous rain and the obstruction of Beatrice.[2] Godfrey was north of the Alps. When the regency learned about these misfortunes and that the Romans were beginning to waver in their support, it sent the chamberlain, Azolinus, with a caravan of mules loaded with gifts and precious furs to Alba with a message to Benzo to go to Rome to prepare the way for Cadalus.[3] Dionysius of Piacenza, who had a personal relationship with Benzo, may have recommended him as a suitable person for this arduous task.

---

[1] Cerrini, "Onorio II. antipapa," p. 187; Herberhold, "Die Angriffe," p. 480; Borino, "Cencio del prefetto Stefano," pp. 373–440; Ghiardini, *Cadalo, l'Antipapa*, pp. 67–84.

[2] Bonizo, *Ad Amicum*, p. 595: "Secundum euangelicum verbum omnis exultatio istorum unius mulieris contradictione terrae prostrata est, tantusque superborum potentatus sola Beatrice interdicente velut fumus evanuit." Elke Goez, *Beatrix von Canossa*, pp. 158–159.

[3] Benzo, *Ad Heinricum*, 2.1, p. 192: "Ex precepto denique pueri regis atque matris reginae acceperunt Italiae proceres ducatum huius viae. Sed denegata est eundi facultas pluviis diluvialiter irruntibus, Gotefredo cum uxore, quoad poterant, impedientibus. Romani vero cognoscentes neoterici papae tarditates, sicut sunt *cerei in vicium flecti*, ceperunt se dividere per diversas voluntates. Quo cognito rex genetrixque eius per Azolinum cubicularium direxit clitellarios honustos preciosarum pellium donis, iussu quoque ad promissione magnae remunerationis mandavit, ut fierem auctor huius legationis. Frater vero BENZO in primis aliquantulum stupidus, eo quod domi remanebat pinguium taurorum cuneus, muniens se signo crucus erexit cor sursum videlicet ad deum et dixit: *In manus tuas, domine, commendo spiritum meum*."

As the lone eyewitness, Benzo relates his version of events in Rome before the arrival of Cadalus. He presents a dramatic picture of what happened and where, and describes the attitudes and feelings of the main protagonists. If his report is anywhere near to being accurate, the charges against Alexander were substantive and substantial, and he was much less sure of himself than his supporters subsequently maintained. According to Benzo, he was even willing to concede the election to Cadalus.

## Benzo in Rome

Benzo set off for Rome soon after receiving the message from Azolinus, probably in December, 1061.[4] Distributing costly gifts throughout Tuscia, he won over many nobles, and having gathered a large militia, he arrived at the Porta San Pancrazio in Rome.[5] There he met a large group of armed men, and passing over the Tiber, he was met by a joyous crowd singing canticles, who brought him in procession to the palace of Octavian on the Capitoline. For several days he presented the case of the boy king, his lord, to the populace, and they all pledged their loyalty. Alexander and Hildebrand did not show their faces.[6]

While Benzo was talking to the citizens, wise men were meeting throughout the city. Deciding that Benzo needed a forum where he could convey the royal message, they chose a hippodrome, which was probably the half-ruined Circus Maximus.[7] As always speaking of Alexander and Hildebrand in the most scathing terms, Benzo mentioned that the appearance of that heretic from Lucca produced grumbling from the people. Quieting the protesting so that the audience

---

[4] Herberhold, "Die Angriffe," p. 481.

[5] Benzo, *Ad Heinricum*, 2.1, p. 192: "Pergens namque per mediam Tusciam honoravi simulque honeravi comites amirandis muneribus, quos feci consortes meis itineribus. Ipsi vero cum multis catervis bellantium deduxerunt me usque ad sanctum Pancratium."

[6] Ibid., 194: Ibi fuit obvia Romanorum maxima multitudo, nullus eorum sine scuto. Ivimus per mediam Transtiberim usque ad pontem et ecce turba magna sicut laetantium suscipiunt me processionaliter cantantes *novum canticum*. Hii omnes ut papam me salutaverunt et cum diversis melodiis ad palacium Octaviani assportaverunt. Ubi per singulos dies septimanae peroravi causam pueri regis, domini mei, et pene totam urbem ad fidelitatem eius sub sacramento collegi. Asinandrellus autem atque Prandellus, inter glandaricios glandaricii, non audebant apparere involuti spinoso tegimine sicut hericii.

[7] Ibid., 2.2, p.194.

could hear his words, Benzo spoke directly to Alexander whom he addressed as Anselm.

He reminded him that he had sworn to the emperor, Henry [III], to preserve the Roman Empire, and that after the emperor's death, he had sworn the same fidelity to his son, Henry [IV]. He asked him why he had broken his word and relinquished the church of Lucca granted to him by the imperial hand, and had invaded the Roman Church, the mother of all churches.[8] And this, he added, with the help of the Norman thieves and tyrants, with Prandellus, the sarabaita (monks who declined regular discipline), and your trepezita (money lenders, especially the Pierleoni).[9]

He accused Hildebrand and his banker of innovating this market, asserting that among God and men they were both damned. You did not ascend the cathedra of Peter with a procession of clerics, he charged Alexander, but with murders and the spilling of blood. Richard [of Capua] killed three noble Romans with his bloody sword, and placed you on the cathedra. Satellites and demons seated you, not the people, not the order of clerics. You merit losing everything.[10] Having broken your oath to my lord and to yours, you must leave Rome without delay and return to Lucca. After one month you must travel to the king and purge yourself; otherwise you shall be subject to penance or canonical sentence. Certainly, Benzo concluded, it is better for you to subject yourself to canonical judgment on earth than to suffer eternal punishment with the devil.[11]

---

[8] Ibid., 196: "....Cur transgressor factus prorupisti in hanc temeritatem, ut imperiali manu tibi commissam relinqueres aecclesiam Lucanam et invasor factus arriperes omnium aecclesiarum matrem Romanam? Et hoc cum Normannis, latronibus et tyrannis, et hoc mediante pecunia."

[9] Ibid., 198: "Nam Prandellus sarabaita, filius Symonis tuusque trepezita, fuit interventor huius mercati; inde apud deum et homines tu et ille estis ambo dampnati."

[10] Ibid.: "Tu non ascendisti ad cathedram Petri cum clericorum processione, sed cum homicidiis, cum sanguinis effusione. Nam Richardus [of Capua] sanguineo ense accinctus ea ipsa manu, qua tres ex nobilibus Romanis morti destinavit, hac eadem super cathedram te collocavit, et hoc totum factum est in nocte, non in die, ex qua re cognoscunt omnes, quoniam *filius perditionis* es atque *vas irae*. O qualis ascensio ad sedem Petri, ad quam te asportaverunt satellites demonum, non senatus, non populus, non ordo cleri. Certe hoc non est ascendere, sed descendere. Merito ergo debes utramque perdere; et illam, quam despiciendo reliquisti, et hanc, quam sicut adulter usurpare voluisti."

[11] Ibid., 2.2, p. 200: "Nunc autem ex contraditione iuris iurandi, quod iurasti dominis meis, scilicet patri et filio contradico tibi Lateranensis palatii stationem simulque Romanae cathedrae sessionem et omnino tocius Romuleae urbis habitationem. Precipioque tibi ex parte domini mei atque similiter domini tui, quo sine dilatione

Following his words, Benzo reported that there was a great clamor. After the crowd was silenced Alexander stated that he recognized that he had received the dignity of his episcopal office from the emperor, Henry, and that on account of preserving the *cura fidelitatis* he had accepted the Roman prelature. Upon receiving counsel, he said that he would direct a legate to them to express the state of his will.[12] When he had finished his remarks, he departed to the shouts and taunts of the people.[13]

In the morning a meeting of the Roman Senate was held at the palace of Octavian. Naming the main participants individually, Benzo asked them as the royal legate what they wanted to do about all of the troubles in the republic. He said that many at the royal court wanted to calm all of the commotion, but that the king did not want to put anyone ahead of those who held the scales of justice in their hand. He asked them to act so that the empire might not be bewitched by fantasies.[14]

Then, wearing a snow white miter, Nicholas, the magister of the palace, stood up and spoke. He thanked the senators, God and the king for allowing them to participate in the public welfare. Not wanting to deviate from the right path, he said that we sent legates from the clergy, the senate, and the people to the king in order that he, along with them, would select a pope according to the will of God, and that this was done. To the praises of bishops and nobles of Italy, Germany and Burgundy, the magister said that Bishop Cadalus of Parma was

---

atque remota occasione a Roma exeas et ad Lucam redeas. Ibique datis induciis per unum mensem postea ad dominum meum regem pergens ex his, quae predicta sunt, te expurga, si poteris. Alioquin aut penitentiae aut canonicae sententiae subiacebis. Certe melius est tibi per canonicam medicinam in hoc seculo animae tuae subvenire, quam cum diabolo, qui te ad hanc transgressionem traxit, aeternaliter perire."

[12] Ibid.: "His dictis confestim clamor omnium tollitur ad aethera perhibentium, quod testibus coelo et terra commissa sunt ab eo hec omnia scelera. Post hec omnes conticuere iterumque facto silentio facultatem respondendi ei dedere. At ille "Scio" inquit, "et recolo, quia de manu imperatoris HEINRICI accepi presulatus dignitatem et propter conservandam fidelitatis curam suscepi Romanam prelaturam. Accepto consilio dirigam sibi meum legatum, qui nuntiabit meae voluntatis statum."

[13] Ibid., "Haec dicens retorsit frenum et popellus eius secutus est eum. Tunc universus populus universaliter cepit clamare: 'Vade, leprose; exi, bavose; discede, perose. Deus omnipotens, contra cuius dispositionem agis, percutiat te Egyptiacis plagis.' Triumphantes denique remeavimus ad palatium Octaviani, ubi erat meum ospicium, diluculo reversuri ad incipiendum de futuris concilium." Meyer von Knonau, *Jahrbücher* 1:248; Herberhold, "Die Angriffe," p. 482.

[14] Ibid., 2.3, p. 202.

elected.[15] When Hildebrand (Prandellus), whom Benzo denounced as the new antichrist, heard this, he took counsel with Leo, who had converted from Judaism (it was Leo's father), Cencius Frangipani, and Johannus Brachiuto.[16]

Benzo then turned to the Normans, reporting that having been given money, Richard of Capua came to Rome, where, during the night he created a pope against all Christianity and the Roman Empire. It was unheard of, he lamented, that the pope would be in the hands of monks, much less Normans. In a long diatribe against the monks and even their garments he focused on those who wander around instead of enclosing themselves in a monastery; those who are supposed to be as though dead are instead placed over the living.

The earth is moved by four men, he declared: Leo Iudeus, Anselm Phariseus, and the false monk [Hildebrand]. The fourth is the Norman, a tyrant from the people. If this root of evil is not extirpated, all of the world will be thrown into the greatest perturbation. Because of this desperate situation, Benzo said that the eminent men from the senate appealed to him as the royal legate to arrange for the one who was designated and elected by God [Cadalus/Honorius] to come as soon as possible, and a delegation was dispatched.[17]

Benzo then brought up a critical geopolitical factor: the Eastern Empire. He reported that he had received a letter from a rich businessman from Amalfi named Pantaleus, who entitled himself as *patricius*, and who acted as political mediator between Constantinople and Italy. To Pantaleus things looked so auspicious for Cadalus that he proposed

---

[15] Ibid., 2.4, p. 204: "Tunc magister palacii Nicholaus candissima redimitus mitra exorsus est ita: 'Gracias agamus, patres conscripti, deo et regi, qui nos dignatur conparticipes in gerenda cura publicae rei. Facit enim, quod se decet, dum unicuique suam iustitiam prebet. Nos autem nolumus oberrare a recta via, sed in omnibus sibi obedientes gradiemur post sua vestigia. Nam satis et *supra* docet nos liber pontificalis, quomodo fieri debeat ordinatio talis. Ideoque ex clero et senatu ac populo legatos misimus ad eum, ut cum his eligeret, quem vellet papam secudum deum. Quod et factum est. Conlaudantibus igitur Italiae, Alemanniae, Burgundiae catholicis episcopis regnorumque optimatibus electus est Parmensis presul venerabilis Kadalus.'"

[16] Ibid., p. 204–206 "'Quo audito Prandellus, diaboli membrum, novus antichristellus, habuit consilium cum Leone, originaliter procedenti de Judaica congregatione, simlque cum Cencio Fraiapane atque cum Brachiuto Iohanne [from Trastevere].'"

[17] Ibid., 208: "'De tribus est unus Leo Iudeus, alter Anselmus Phariseus, tercius falsa cuculla [Hildebrand] Dohech Idumeus. Quartum Normannus, factus de plebe tyrannus. Si non fuerit hec radix peccati penitus extirpata, omnia mundi climata erunt in maxima pertubatione fietque novissimus error peior priore. Ergo si placet domno Albensi episcopo, qui est regius legatus, properent veredarii ex parte senatus, ut quantocius veniat, qui est a deo electus et designatus.'"

that Benzo intervene to renew the alliance of the two emperors, banishing the Norman usurpers, and establishing Cadalus on the papal see.[18] Benzo enthusiastically greeted the proposal that carried such promise for Cadalus and the western empire.

Returning to Hildebrand, Benzo charged him with not putting his faith in God, but in a multitude of rich men. Without our knowledge, he said, Hildebrand bought a hostile force that he intended to use against "our pope" when he arrived. Instead of prevailing by the certainty of canons, Benzo said that Hildebrand intended to conquer by an effusion of blood, and pleaded with Jesus Christ to exercise his judgment against him.[19] He had made the best possible case for the traditional world that he represented.

### The Arrival of Cadalus

Benzo reports that while these things were going on in Rome, Cadalus began to move with an army raised from the whole nobility of Parma. Traveling through Etruria he picked up others, amongst whom was Pepo, a very noble count who was indubitably faithful to the king and to the pope.[20] From a Lombard family, Pepo became one of the most important allies of Cadalus, and probably supported him against Countess Beatrice in Tuscany on his way to Sutri. Cadalus secretly headed to Bologna, which opened its gates to him and his large army while Beatrice had to stand aside.

On March 25, 1062 Cadalus arrived in Sutri where Benzo and a group of Roman senators and their allies met him. Benzo conveyed to him all of the good things that he had seen and heard in Rome, but nothing of the guile and deceit of Prandellus, which he claims not to

---

[18] Ibid., 2.7., p. 214; letter to Benzo from a noble from Amalfi, Malphitanus Pantaleus: "'Sit ergo Romani regis legatus [Benzo] studiosus in hoc opera et incitet koropalates pueri domini sui ad expulsionem ignobilium. Nam et ego hyschyron basileum Constantinum Doclitium [Constantine X Dukas, 1059–1067] continuis allegationibus fatigabo, ut impiger occurrat dilectissimo fratri HEINRICO in ultionem servilis turpitudinis. Domnus Kadalus, dei omnipotentis preco et beati Petri vicarius, secundum consuetudinem precessorum fiat tuba ad convocationem amborum atque liberationem patriae.'"

[19] Ibid., 2.8, pp. 214–216.

[20] Ibid., 2.9, p. 216; *Annales Romani, Lib. Pont.* 2:336: "Rex misit Cadolum episcopum Parmensem cum manu valida." Elke Goez, *Beatrix von Canossa*, p. 159; Herberhold, "Die Angriffe," pp. 481–483.

have known.[21] Together they entered Rome, where Benzo claims that Alexander tried to retreat, but that his supporters, amongst whom were Leo Iudeus and Hildebrand, leapt into action.

Benzo reports that trying to forestall a schism, Alexander spoke to the crowd, informing them that the bishop of Alba had enlightened him about the will of the king. Let the elect of Parma wait on *Monte gaudii* [Monte Mario], Alexander declared, while his [the king's] chancellor [Guibert], whose will must be obeyed according to law, may descend to the porta of the Crescentii [Porta S. Petri] along with the bishop of Alba. There we can communally gather together, and whatever he [the chancellor] prescribes, we shall announce to the clergy, to the senate and to all of the public. The next day Alexander said would be similar, but on the third day he stated that we would receive the lord elect in procession according to our custom.[22]

Benzo claimed that Prandellus/Hildebrand brought this reconciliation to a standstill by provoking us to war. A battle was fought on the *prati Neronis* at the foot of the Vatican, and seeing our eagles, the great multitude [of Hildebrand's forces] turned their backs, and at nightfall returned to their camp. For five days there was an impasse while Hildebrand reinforced his forces on the other side of the Tiber, and Cadalus was unable to cross.[23]

Other sources now begin to transmit reports. The *Annales Romani* relate that the king sent Cadalus with a powerful militia, and that when they arrived Alexander began to fight with the militia, with Pepo, with other counts accompanying Cadalus, and with Romans faithful to the king.[24] They state that in 1062 the Normans were of no help to Alexander, and that later in 1063 counts outside of Rome such as Rapizone of Todi, came to the aid of Cadalus.

Bonizo notes that Beatrice was the only one to stand in the way of the expedition of Cadalus to Rome, but that furtively he was able to get

---

[21] Ibid., 216–218: "Octavo denique kalendas Aprilis ingressus est Sutrium homo dei non tepidus sed virilis, ubi occurrit ei frater Benzo cum senatoribus Romanis associatis sibi principibus Galerianis [sons of count Girard] Omnia valde bona annuntiavi ei, quae audierant aures et viderant oculi mei. De dolis vero Prandelli nichil ei dixi, quia hec omnia ignota erant mihi."

[22] Ibid., 218–220.

[23] Ibid., 220–222.

[24] *Lib. Pont.* 2:336: "Rex misit Cadolum episcopum Parmensem cum manu valida. Tunc illi qui erant ex parte Alexandri coeperunt pugnare cum manu valida cum comite Pepo et aliis comitibus qui erant cum dicto Cadolo et cum Romanis qui erant fideles dictis regis."

to Bologna where he picked up his militia. Carrying a huge amount of gold and silver, he arrived in Rome, where there were large numbers of the avaricious. Amongst them were the *capitanei*, who wished to oppress the city, and to return it to their power from ancient times.[25] Bonizo says that Cadalus seemed to be the victor, but that then Duke Godfrey showed up.

The *Annales Altahenses* report that having collected a large band of Lombards, Cadalus traveled beyond Sutri to a campus where he set up camp to rest his militia while hoping that the Romans would either be terrified by his arrival and disassociate themselves from Alexander, or would join him. His supporters held the tower of the Crescentii (Castel S. Angelo) and Ponte Milvio. When Alexander's supporters demonstrated that they were going to defend themselves, Cadalus broke camp, and attacked Rome. Angry and indignant that hostile forces would take over Rome, Alexander's supporters, including many from the people, took up arms.[26]

In his letter written just after the bloody battle of April 14, 1062, Petrus Damiani reveals how much the reformers despised Cadalus, and how much they feared his power.[27]

"Before your attack on Rome with the aid of the followers of Satan, I recently wrote to you, enjoining and earnestly admonishing you to refrain from such a bloody undertaking, to hold yourself in restraint with every means at your disposal, and not to excite God's fury against you, nor provoke the world into disastrous war against the

---

[25] Bonizo, *Ad Amicum*, 595: "Secundum euangelicum verbum omnis exultatio istorum unius mulieris contradictione terrae prostrata est, tantusque superborum potentatus sola Beatrice interdicente velut fumus evanuit. Sed non longo post tempore prefatus Cadolus furtim Bononiam venit, in qua suos expectavit milites. Quibus receptis Romam tendit, portans secum ingentia auri et argenti pondera. Set tunc non defuere [April] viri pestilentes, amantes semetipsos, avari et cupidi, qui ei se coniunxere; inter quos et Romani capitanei, volentes Romanam urbem opprimere et sub potestate sua ut antiquitus redigere."

[26] *Annales Altahenses*, Anno 1062, p. 60: "Insuper et hoc illum animabat, quod fautores sui intra Urbem turrim Crescentii tenebant, insuper et aliam firmissimam turrim, quae est in ripa Tiberis iuxta pontem Olivi [ponte Milvio]. Alexander autem fautores sui iam dudum adventum istorum praescierant, ideoque et ipsi armis se defendere parabant. Quo cognito, episcopus Parmensis statim elevatis militaribus signis castra movit, sicque instructa acie Romam tendit. Econtra igitur, fautores Alexandri, et ipsi armis instructi, processere, quibus etiam multi ex plaebe se miscuerunt cum propter animi mobilitatem, tum etiam propter iram et indignationem, quoniam ipsis videbatur grande dedecus fore, quod quisquam hostiliter armata manu praesumeret Romam propius accedere."

[27] Petrus Damiani, *Briefe*, nr. 89, 2:533; tr. Blum, 3:327.

Church. But belching hellish flames like Vesuvius, you never remain quiet; you scatter, so to speak, the fiery embers of money among the people and, by heating up their cupidity, corrupt the hearts of miserable men. You ruin your own diocese for the sake of obtaining another. In some quarters gold and silver are put on the scale; in others bargaining, tax assessments, and loans to forward; church buildings are mortgaged, and thus the property of a collapsing church is dissipated. You have fortified towns behind you, armed with gold rather than with steel, and thus money pours forth from your purses like swords drawn from their scabbards. Clearly, it is not the blare of trumpets, horns, or other brass that arouses the ranks that follow your banners, but the source of glittering metal that allures them...."

The passionate views of Petrus were the counterpart to those of Benzo. Petrus tells Cadalus that he wishes that he had never been born, or that he would immediately have died. Would that you had not grown to maturity to destroy the Catholic Church, not just figuratively, but in fact. It was your furious lust for power that propelled you.[28]

For three weeks the army of Cadalus lay inactive between Sutri and Rome while Hildebrand and Alexander mobilized in Rome with the help of Leo (Judeus), son of Benedict. No help was expected from Duke Godfrey or from Richard of Capua. Cadalus also had formidable supporters in Rome, some of whom Benzo and the *Annales Romani* mention.[29] Among them were Cencius, the son of the prefect, Stephen, and his brother. Cencius controlled the Castel S. Angelo, and the strategic bridge of St. Peter's. He later became notorious for violently attacking Gregory VII when he was saying mass at Santa Maria Maggiore on Christmas Eve, 1075.[30]

On April 14, 1062, the forces of Cadalus met those of Hildebrand with allegedly about 1000 men on the campus of Nero on the west side of the Tiber. Friend and foe alike reported that the forces of Hildebrand were soundly beaten.[31] Without opposition, Cadalus occupied the

---

[28] Ibid., 537; tr. Blum, 3:330–331.

[29] *Annales Romani, Lib. Pont.* 2:336: "Cencius Stephani prefecti cum suis germanis, nec non et Cencio et Romano germani, Baruncii filii hac Belizzon Titonis Decaro et Cencio Crescentii Denitta erant cum dicto Cadulo, eo quod erant fildeles imperatoris."

[30] Cowdrey, *Gregory VII*, pp. 326–327.

[31] E. g. *Annales Altahenses*, p. 60: "Nec mora, statim primo congressu victi, Romani terga vertunt, sicque versus Urbem fugientes, multi caesi et vulnerati caecidere. Quidam vero, ad Tyberim festinantes, navem intravere, sed istis subsequentibus et uno tantum lanceam iaculante, cum unusquisque timeret sibi, in unam partem ratis constipantur cuncti, et nave reversata pene omnes suffocati sunt in aqua"; see also *Annales Romani, Lib. Pont.* 2:336; Herberhold, "Die Angriffe," p. 487 & n. 72.

Leonine City, and entered St. Peter's. Since Alexander and Hildebrand had been beaten, there was nothing to hinder his consecration except the folly that his supporters wanted him to be consecrated in S. Pietro in Vincoli where Alexander had been consecrated.[32]

## Only an Electus

In spite of his military victories, without consecration and enthrone-ment Cadalus was only an electus, while Alexander could claim the full title of pope. Adding to the rashness of rejecting consecration in St. Peter's, the forces of Cadalus did not feel themselves strong enough to remain in the city, and under cover of darkness withdrew into their camp on the west side of the Tiber.[33] They had passed up an unprece-dented opportunity, for during the night Hildebrand and Alexander strengthened their forces. The next day it was impossible to cross over to the east side of the Tiber, and to be enthroned in S. Pietro in Vincoli.[34]

Bloody encounters continued, but Cadalus was unable to gain a foothold on the other side of the Tiber.[35] After five days of languishing in the campus of Nero, on the advice of the Roman senate the army moved by way of Fiano to Tusculum, where it camped on the meadows below the castle.[36] Again an eyewitness, Benzo reports that the elders

---

[32] *Annales Romani, Lib. Pont.* 2:336: "Set quia nox erat, mansit ibi nocte illa. Potuerunt eum consecrare pontificem, nisi fuisset eorum insipientia, quia primitus eum consecrare voluerunt in ecclesia beati Petri ad Vincula."

[33] Benzo, *Ad Heinricum*, 2.9, p. 220: "Imminente vero nox coegit nostros revisere castra. Incolumis denique rediit exercitus totus exceptis de minoribus solis duobus." Herberhold, "Die Angriffe," n.78, p. 488 thinks that the *Annales Romani* were wrong in saying: "Set quia nox erat, mansit ibi nocte illa."

[34] *Annales Romani, Lib. Pont.* 2:336–337: "Tunc Ildibrandus cum Leo data pecunia per urbem tota nocte illa; mane autem facto non potuerunt ad dictam basilicam pergere, unde *infra* civitatem multe pugne et homicidia orte fuerunt."

[35] Benzo, *Ad Heinricum*, 2.9, pp. 220–222; Petrus Damiani, *Briefe*, nr. 87 to Bishop Oldericus of Fermo, early 1062, 2:504–515; tr. Blum, 3:299–308.

[36] Ibid., 2.10, p. 222: "HIS ITA gestis ex consulto senatus Romani transivimus Tyberim ad portum Flaiani. [Fiano; protected by castle in control of counts of Galeria] Ibi fuerunt nobis obvii filii Burelli [count of Sangro], viri martifices ad pugnam novelli; sequaces eorum numero mille audacia pares Cornelio Sylle. [Cornelius Sulla] Post hec direximus iter ad Tusculanum et nostro cetui sociavimus iuvenculum nepotem Alberici, olim princeps eiusdem municipii. Deinceps universi comites circum circa subiciunt se regendos domni Kadali apostolica virga. Sub arce vero prenonimata erant ingentia prata, ubi residentes in papilonibus delectabamur herbarum et florum suavis-simis hodoribus. Cotidie autem coram domno electo disputabant seniores, quomodo possent cuculati demonis allidere tergiversationes."

of the neighborhood gathered to recognize Cadalus and to discuss how to deal with the subterfuge of the demonical Hildebrand. Members of the senate brought them what turned out to be false rumors of Alexander's imminent death.[37]

On the same day that this false rumor was transmitted, emissaries of Emperor Constantine Dukas arrived from Constantinople with a letter offering Cadalus the role of mediator between the two emperors.[38] This initiative strengthened Cadalus by demonstrating that he was thought to have the stature to carry out such a role.[39] He appeared to hold the upper hand, but he and the counts around him may have been running out of money, as the *Annales Romani* attest, and he was not in Rome.[40]

At this point around the middle of May, Duke Godfrey appeared with an army at the Ponte Milvio with the request that both candidates return to their episcopal sees so that the emperor might make a decision about resolving the schism.[41] On first consideration, it would

---

[37] Ibid., 2.11, p. 224: "QUADEM vero die venerunt ad nos Iohannes Berardi et Petrus de Via dicentes Asilelmum [Alexander II] esse in agonia et loqui aliena quasi ebrium atque morti propinquare frequenti molestia febrium."

[38] Ibid., 2.12, p. 224: "HAC eadem die allate sunt ex Bizancio regales litterae. Portitores vero litterarum fuerunt tres missi purpura induti cum candore byssi....De quibus nulla fuit dubitatio, quominus forent de basilei palacio" Herberhold, "Die Angriffe," pp. 489–492.

[39] Ibid., 2.12, pp. 226–228: "Romano patriarche, regia consitutione super universali aecclesia sublimato, Constantinus Doclitius, Constantinopolis basileus salutem....[the wisdom of the Romans, derived from their Greek heritage, flourished under the Ottonians; but it has sunk low with the arrival of the Normans] Iam enim sibi usurpant imperialia officia ut in presumptione Lucani pseudopapae. Ad hec corrigenda per manum fidei tuae volo firmare aeternalis amiciciae pactum cum puero HEINRICO, rege Romano....[says that he is also a Roman, and thus they are united; he vows to give his son, born to the purple, as a hostage, and all of his treasure], ut ex faciat, quod voluerit, ad suos usus suorumque militum, quatenus te previo sit nobis facultas ire usque ad sepulchrum domini, et expurgata spurcicia Normannorm sive paganorum refloreat christiana libertas vel in fine seculorum. Tu autem, vir dei, heres beati Petri, claude sermones istos in pectore tuo et *operare operu dei*."

[40] *Annales Romani, Lib. Pont.* 2:337 : "Postea vero pecunia deficiente comites reversi sunt ad propria, Cadolus vero reversus est in Parma."

[41] *Annales Altahenses*, pp. 60–61: "His militiae gestis episcopus Parmensis cum suis iam clari habebatur, et timor eorum per universam Romam cottidie augebatur. Attamen, priusquam urbem intrarent, supervenit huic perturbationi dux Gottefridus, qui dudum post mortem imperatoris in Italiam fuerat reversus et, connubio iunctus viduae Bonfacii, maximus habeatur in illis partibus regni. Hic ergo nunc minis nunc consilio cum ambolus non cessavit agere, donec utrumque persuasit ad sedem pontificatus ire, ut is postmodum sedem apostolicam sine controversia teneret, quem rex et regni principes iudicarent. Huic diffinitioni ambo facile consentiebant, quoniam uterque de regiam venissent et causa haec in curia agitari coepta fuisset, omnibus placuit, ut is, qui consecratus foret, rursus ad apostolicam sedem reverteretur, donec canonico et sinodali iudicio auditus aut eidem sedi iuste praeferretur aut damnatus iuste

seem to have been a poor prospect for Alexander to leave the decision in the hands of the king, but he and his followers appeared to understand that Godfrey's proclivities were with him. Moreover, Godfrey was close to Archbishop Anno of Cologne, and Alexander's episcopal city was Godfrey's favorite residence.

Benzo accuses Godfrey of duplicity.[42] Describing him as an enemy of the child king, and indeed, disloyal to the king's father, he said that Godfrey fashioned a clever and deceptive plan that seemed to come to our aid. Benzo said that from his camp at Ponte Milvio Godfrey accompanied a legation to Cadalus where he himself addressed Cadalus and his followers. He told them that the only way that they could get the man from Lucca [Alexander] to withdraw was by using the sophistry (*cavillatio*) that both candidates withdraw their claims so that the king could make a judgment.[43] He reassured Cadalus that the king and his mother would not change their mind, and he swore that by his (Godfrey's) taking the initiative, you will attain the papacy.[44] Benzo said that Godfrey left immediately, and escorted the man of perdition [Alexander] back to Lucca. Believing that they had won, Cadalus and his supporters returned to Parma.

### Kaiserswerth

Godfrey was using sophistry, but it was against Cadalus, not Alexander. Archbishop Anno of Cologne and other German nobles had kidnapped Henry IV at Kaiserswerth just after Easter that fell on March 31, 1062, and Anno had replaced Agnes as regent. Godfrey undoubtedly knew about all of this when Benzo said that he assured Cadalus that the king and his mother would not change their mind, a moot

---

deponeretur." Bonizo, *Ad Amicum*, p. 595; Elke Goez, *Beatrix von Canossa*, p. 159; Schmidt, *Alexander II.*, pp. 117–121; Herberhold, "Die Angriffe," pp. 491–492.

[42] Benzo, *Ad Heinricum*, 2.13:228–230.

[43] Ibid., 228–230: "Non possumus revocare Lucensem illum a sua intentione, nisi usi fuerimus convenienti cavillatione, scilicet ut uterque vestrum tamdiu se abstineat ab huius prelationis potentia, donec interrogetur deliberativa regis sententia."

[44] Ibid., 330: "'Scitis enim omnes a minimo usque ad maiorem, quia dominus meus rex cum matre totaque curia non mutabit huius rei tenorem. Et sic sopietur iurgium atque uterque nostrum recuperabit ius suum, ego viae ducatum, et vos me ducente pertingetis ad apostolatum. Quod ut verius credatis, iure iurando firmabo certitudinem credulitatis.'"

point since Agnes had acceded to the fait accompli. The whole configuration between the new regency and both papal contenders had shifted to the advantage of Alexander.

The reasons prompting the coup involved both personal ambition and political principle. Many German lay and ecclesiastical nobles were alienated by the powerful sway that Bishop Henry of Augsburg held over Agnes, and their own lack of power.[45] According to Lampert of Hersfeld, the best source for the unfolding drama, the princes were worried about the situation for the kingdom since Agnes had incorporated almost all authority in herself. He mentions rumors that the bishop and the empress were even having an illicit relationship.[46] Bonizo, among others, emphasized the weakness entailed by her gender, and said that in the beginning of her administration she relied upon Guibert of Parma.[47]

Adam of Bremen, reflecting the view of Archbishop Adalbert, described the dire situation of both the Church and the Empire, which he saw as a calamity.[48] Bishop Gunther of Bamberg, who at first had supported Agnes, took umbrage over a decision that she made regarding the nunnery of Bergen. He said that she had not allowed him to justify himself, and that the neighboring lords sided with her,

---

[45] Robinson, *Henry IV*, pp. 43–44; Schmidt, *Alexander II.*, p. 132; Meyer von Knonau, *Jahrbücher* 1:274–279; Herberhold, "Die Angriffe," pp. 492–493.

[46] Lampert, *Annales*, p. 79: "Imperatrix nutriens adhuc filium suum, regni negocia per se ipsam curabat, utebaturque plurimum consilio Heinrici Augustensis episcopi. [suspicion of incestuous love] Ea res principes graviter offendebat, videntes scilicet, quod propter unius privatum amorem sua, quae potissimum in re publica valere debuerat, auctoritas pene oblitterata fuisset."

[47] *Ad Amicum*, p. 593: "Dum hec ita gererentur, Heinrici imperatoris coniunx cum filio parvulo…regni tenebat gubernacula. Que multa contra ius feminea faciebat audacia. Haec in primordio regni sui omnes eiusdem Italici regni curas cuidam Guiberto commisit Parmensi, nobili orto genere, eumque cancellarium appellavit." When referring to the election of Cadalus, Bonizo, p. 595, says: "His et talibus machinationibus decepta, imperatrix feminea licentia assensum dedit operi nefario." Jäschke, *Notwendige Gefährtinnen*, p. 131.

[48] Adam of Bremen, *Gesta Hammaburgensis ecclesiae pontificum*, MGH SRG 16.2:176: "Itaque ex illo tempore [death of Henry III] nostrum ecclesiam omnes calamitates oppresserunt, nostro pastore tantum curiae intento negotiis. Ad gubernacula regni mulier cum puero successit, magno imperii detrimento. Indignanates enim principes aut muliebri potestate constringi aut infantili ditione regi primo quidem communiter vindicarunt se in pristinam libertatem, ut non servirent; dein contentionem moverunt inter se, quis eorum videretur esse maior; postremo armis audacter sumptis dominum et regem suum deponere moliti sunt. Et haec omnia oculis pocius videri possunt, quam calamo scribi."

forcing him to reconcile with her. Not mollified, however, Gunther criticized her age, her family, her nature, and her nationality after she had been removed from power.[49] Public opinion began to turn against her, and seeing the removal of her son as the solution, some of the disaffected nobles formed a conspiracy against her in the spring of 1062.[50]

Archbishop Anno of Cologne was their intrepid leader. Invested by Henry III, he reputedly had raised the ire of Nicholas II, leading to the confrontation between the regency and the papacy, and the regency's condemnation of Nicholas. Prior to the abduction of Henry IV in April 1062, he was seldom present at the court or involved with imperial affairs. He appeared to have had a good relationship with Agnes, as the appointment of his nephew, Burchard, to the bishopric of Halberstadt in 1059 seems to attest.[51] Because Agnes would not have been alert to any duplicity, Anno was the perfect person to lead the conspiracy. He could count on the support of the disgruntled Bishop Gunther of Bamberg, Archbishop Siegfried of Mainz, Duke Godfrey, Duke Otto of Bavaria, Dedi II of Wettin, margrave of the Ostmark, and Count Ekbert I of Braunschweig, all of whom craved neutralizing the reviled Bishop Henry of Augsburg.[52]

---

[49] Giesebrecht, *Geschichte der deutschen Kaiserzeit* 3:1255–1256; In the late summer after Henry's kidnapping in May, Gunther will write to Anno: "....Quod vestra dignatio de fidei devotionisque nostrae constantia tam sincero praesumit iudicio, id vero et debita me afficit gratulatione et multa in futuris onerat sollicitudine, ut tam bonam de me persuasionem perpetuam vobis commendem....Et nostro et totius regni nomine gratulor vobis, quod perditis emulorum consiliis tam mature vos occurrisse, tam prudenter ea dissipasse ex literis vestris cognovi. Verumtamen, dum singula mecum etiam atque etiam retracto, solidum sincerumque gaudium vix audio concipere....De mea cum domna imperatrice disceptatione id solum volo ad praesens rogare, ut, ubi occasio aliqua dederit, solitam ecclesiae nostrae opem et tutelam praetendere non gravemini." Cartellieri, *Der Aufstieg des Papsttums*, p. 57; Meyer von Knonau, *Jahrbücher*, 1:308.
[50] Lampert *Annales*, pp.79–80: "Itaque indignitatem rei non ferentes, crebra conventicula facere, circa publicas functiones remissus agere, adversus imperatricem popularium animos sollicitare, postremo omnibus modis niti, ut a matre puerum distraherent et regni administrationem in se transferrent." *Annales Altahenses*, p. 59: "Rex igitur iam adolescere incipiebat, palatio autem praesidentes sibimet ipsis tantum consulebant, nec regem quisquam, quod bonum iustumque esset, edocebat, ideoque in regno multa inordinate fiebant. Quapropter Anno archiepiscopus Coloniensis, duces et optimates regni crebra conventicula faciebant, quid de hoc agendum foret anxie nimis ad invicem conquirebant."
[51] Jenal, *Anno II.*, 1:171–174; sources 179–180.
[52] Cartellieri, *Der Aufstieg des Papsttums*, pp. 57–58.

## The Kidnapping

Besides Anno, the chief participants in the abduction were Otto of Bavaria and Ekbert of Braunschweig.[53] Lampert reports that having taken council with Otto and Ekbert, Anno sailed down the Rhine to St. Switbert's island, where the king and his escorts were staying at the royal palace of Kaiserswerth after having celebrated Easter in Utrecht. Following a banquet, Anno invited the happy, twelve-year old king to inspect a ship that had been fitted out with special workmanship for this purpose. The minute that Henry stepped on board, the oarsmen swiftly moved the ship into the middle of the river. The frightened child leapt overboard, and had Count Ekbert not dived in after him, he would have drowned. The conspirators then sailed to Cologne with their captive.[54] When they landed a crowd followed them complaining that the captors had infringed the royal dignity, and robbed the king of his freedom.

According to Lampert the empress neither followed her son nor attempted to expose his injuries by means of the law of the people (*ius gentium*). Rather, she capitulated and retreated into her private world. But Anno was sensitive to the charge that he and his cohorts were guilty of *lèse-majesté*, and to make it appear that he had interfered for the common good rather than out of private ambition, he decreed that when the king visited a particular diocese, the bishop of that diocese should ensure that the republic suffer no harm.[55] In cases referred to the king, he said that the bishop should take special responsibility.[56]

---

[53] *Annales Augustani*, 1062, MGH SS 3:123–136 at 127; Robinson, *Henry IV*, pp. 43–45.

[54] Lampert, *Annales*, p. 80: "Ad ultimum Coloniensis episcopus, communicatis cum Ecberto comite, et cum Ottone duce Bawariorum consiliis, navigo per Renum ad locum qui dicitur Sancti Suitberti insula venit. [Kaiserwerth] Ibi tum rex erat. Qui dum quadam die post solemnes epulas factus fuisset hilarior, hortari eum episcopus coepit, ut navim quandam suam, quam ad hoc ipsum miro opere instruxerat, spectatum procederet. Facile hoc persuasit puero simplici et nihil minus quam insidias suspicanti."

[55] Jenal, *Anno II.*, p. 193. Of twenty sources, three were positive, and seventeen were negative, viewing the abduction as a grab for power.

[56] Lampert, *Annales*, pp. 80–81: "Caetera multitudo per terram subsequitur, criminantibus plurimis, quod regia maiestas violata suique impos facta foret. Episcopus, ut invidiam facti mitigaret, ne videlicet privatae gloriae pocius quam communis commodi ratione haec admisse videretur, statuit, ut episcopus quilibet, in cuius diocesi rex dum temporis moraretur, ne quid detrimenti res publica pateretur, provideret et causis, quae ad regem delatae fuissent, potissimum responderet. Imperatrix nec filium

There is no evidence, however, that Anno placed such a broad-based reform into effect, and his objective seems to have been that he and a small group of colleagues would control the government.[57]

The *Annales Altahenses* add that the conspirators stole the royal symbols from the chapel, and that with no one's objecting, they departed for Cologne with the king. Contrary to Lampert, the *Annales* report that the child's mother was sad, but that when it was explained to her how grave the situation was in the Empire, making a virtue of necessity, she donned the veil (actually, 1061), relinquished all of her governing authority, and devoted herself to God.[58] Berthold of Reichenau also mentions that with certain other princes Anno snatched the king by force from his mother along with the lance and other imperial insignia, and took him to Cologne.[59]

A letter that Agnes wrote to Abbot Albert of Fruttuaria (Turin) reveals her humility in the face of the revolt.[60] Placing herself more and more into the hands of Cadalus's fierce critic, Petrus Damiani, as her confessor, she as well as the regency totally abandoned Cadalus. But she did not abandon her son, and Benzo emphasizes her acute distress.[61]

---

sequi nec iniurias suas iure gentium expostulare voluit sed in propria recedens, privata deinceps aetatem agere proposuit." Robinson, *Henry IV*, p. 45; Meyer von Knonau, *Jahrbücher* 1:279; Jäschke, *Notwendige Gefährtinnen*, p. 131.

[57] Robinson, *Henry IV*, p. 45.

[58] *Annales Altahenses*, p. 59: "Tandem ergo firmato consilio, cum rex esset iuxta Rhenum in loco, qui Werida dicitur, cum grandi multitudine ex improviso curtem adeunt, crucem et regiam lanceam ex capella auferunt, regem ipsum navi imponunt nulloque obsistente ad Coloniam usque deducunt. Mater ergo regis tristis discessit inde, sed cum recordaretur, quam grave est regni negocia tractare, faciens ex necessitate virtutem, sacrum sibi velamen postulavit imponi."

[59] Berthold, *Chronicon*, ed. Robinson, version 1:194: "Henricus rex apud Traiectum Frisiae urbem, diem paschae, cum matre imperatrice egit. Hiis diebus Hanno Agrippinae Coloniae archiepiscopus, adnitentibus quibusdam regni principibus, Henricum regem cum lancea et aliis imperii insignibus a matre imperatrice vi arripuit secumque Coloniam adduxit."

[60] Giesebrecht, *Geschichte der deutschen Kaiserzeit*, 3:1255: Agnes to the abbots and monks of Frutturia, 1062: "A[gnes] imperatrix et peccatrix A[lberto] patri bono et fratribus in Fructuaria congregatis in nomine Domini servitutem ancillae, cuius oculi in manibus dominae suae sunt. Conscientia mea terret me peius omni larva omnique imagine. Ideo fugio per sanctorum loca, quaerens latibulum a facie timoris huius, nec minimum desiderium est mihi veniendi ad vos, de quibus comperi, quia vestra intercessio certa salus est. Sed nostrae profectiones in manu Dei sunt, et non in nostra voluntate. Interim vero mente adoro ad pedes vestros, rogans ut Gregoriana pietate in Traianum petatis mihi veniam a Domino;"

[61] Benzo, *Ad Heinricum*, 2.15:236: "Ancxius non cessans adicere peccata peccatis cum predicto Anna rapuit puerum regem de gremio matris. Flens et eiulans remansit sicut umbra declinans mater augusta, excussa quemadmodum in deserto locusta."

When Henry was presented with the sword to celebrate his coming of age on March 29, 1065, it was said that she had to keep the young king from using it against Anno.[62] He hated Anno because when the archbishop seized the right to govern from his mother, he had also put himself in the greatest danger.[63] By this time Anno was losing influence and power to Adalbert of Bremen, and was susceptible to the king's animus that had been seething since the archbishop's cruelty and deceit at Kaiserswerth.

As far as the schism was concerned, it was a new world. With the abduction at Kaiserswerth Cadalus had lost the support of the Empire and had become vulnerable to the duplicitous Godfrey. The *coup de grâce* would be the Council of Mantua in 1064 where both the Empire and the Church would recognize Alexander as pope. It is not obvious what all of these moves had to do with ecclesiastical reform.

---

[62] *Annales Camadulenses*, p. 293: 1065, "Agnes olim imperatrix, postea Romae sanctimonialis in Germaniam hoc anno profecta fuerat, ut auctoritate sua modum imponeret ejus regni turbis & juniorem adhuc Henricum regem filium suum plura molientem compesceret, qui indignatus arma praesertim hoc anno moverat contra Annonem [294] archiepiscopum Coloniensem. Rex cessit ex voto, & Agnes Regis filii animum ad pacem, & ad archiepiscopum recipiendum, honoreque habendum allexit." Jäschke, *Notwendige Gefährtinnen*, p. 132.

[63] Robinson, *Henry IV*, p. 52.

## CHAPTER TWELVE

FROM KAISERSWERTH TO MANTUA

The departure of Cadalus and whatever militia accompanied him started his long slide to desuetude. Although he was briefly able to return to Rome, and his flame again flickered, the forces against him were too great, and his campaign proved to be futile. He still harbored pretensions of being acknowledged as pope until both the reformers and the regency united to recognize Alexander at the Council of Mantua in 1064. In the intervening two years all of the main participants jockeyed for power and for victory in achieving their ideals and goals.

*The Effects of the Abduction on the Schism*

The abduction of the king at Kaiserswerth is usually relegated to one more move in the deadly game of politics played out among various Germanic factions, but Alexander greatly benefitted from it, and some scholars question whether he might have had something to do with it.[1] The psychological impact on both Henry and his mother was obviously searing, and influenced their behavior from that time forward. Agnes appears to have yielded to the forces that destroyed her as a political entity, while Henry's hate simmered, and bubbled up in his encounters with Anno and the other German nobles who had raped him of his legacy. The child had lost his father at age six, and was kidnapped and taken away from his mother six years later. The trauma inflicted on him must acutely have affected his attitudes towards the church and the pope whom his tormentors supported.

Anno may not have tipped his hand immediately, but in a letter that he wrote to Alexander in 1065 he protested that he had never favored Cadalus.[2] He informed Alexander that he had always worked for him

---

[1] Carl Adolf Fetzer, *Voruntersuchungen zu einer Geschichte des Pontificats Alexander II.* (Strassburg, 1887), p. 54 for references.

[2] Giesebrecht, *Geschichte der deutsche Kaiserzeit*, 3:1257–1258: "An non ego plus omnibus atque revera solus usque in hunc diem in vestram gratiam atque statum

even when others began to murmur, more out of thoughtlessness than for the sake of justice, and elected Cadalus at Basel. Anno acknowledged that he was present at the council, but claims that he did not consent. He reiterated three times that Alexander was reinstated in his see [1064] by the word of the king, and the approval of the princes, bishops, dukes, and marchesi.[3] By the "word of the king," he meant essentially himself, since he was speaking for the fourteen-year old king when Alexander was recognized as pope at the Council of Mantua in 1064.

The elephant in the room after the abduction was Godfrey, who became the prime mover in subsequent events. He was the most powerful prince in Germany, and although he had made peace with the king, he was always seen as devious and involved in intrigue. He was also the most powerful noble in Central Italy, and was opposed to the ambitions of the Lombard nobility.[4] Chroniclers mention his intelligence, his strong will, his eloquence, his bravery and his incomparable military prowess, all thought to be talents of a great man.

He had already established ties with the papacy through his brother, Stephen IX, and while he protected the papacy, the papacy secured his position in Italy. This ideal arrangement was put to the test when Hildebrand threw in the papacy's lot with the Normans, whom Godfrey detested. The new situation could have threatened Godfrey's position in central Italy, and probably was the impetus for his energetic response to the schism, demonstrating that the papacy still needed him. His intervention reinforced his position in Italy, and heightened it in the Empire.[5]

Having established an accord with Anno before Kaiserswerth, he traveled to Rome as *missus imperialis*, where he cajoled Cadalus and Alexander into withdrawing to their bishoprics. Bonizo saw him as a

honoris omni laboravi studio....Spero nulla vos necessitate compelli supplicam in vestris rebus quicquam agere, quippe cum testimonium habeatis satis amplum prima de investitura sedis apostolicae. Sed et postea, cum de ingressu vestro, ut fieri solet, certe magis ex levitate sua quam ex zelo iustitiae, mussare coepissent, nonne manifestum est Ecclesiae bis atque tertio iam vos in sedem vestram ex verbo regis, ut dignum erat, esse reductum, principibus, episcopis, ducibus, marchionibus in hoc obsequie vos comitantibus?"

³ Borino, "Cencio del prefetto Stefano," p. 393.
⁴ Baix, "Cadalus," pp. 74–75.
⁵ Cartellieri, *Der Aufstieg des Papstuums*, pp. 49–50.

divine benediction.[6] Alexander was happy to be in the good graces of the king under the control of the princes, but Godfrey and Anno still harbored reservations about Alexander's alliance with the Normans. Anno's lack of sympathy with the overture of Nicholas II to the Normans likely had contributed to the papacy's displeasure with him, and the regency's retaliation against Nicholas.

## The Council of Augsburg

We have seen that after Godfrey had set up camp at Ponte Milvio he approached the two candidates with the request that they return to their bishoprics to await a decision by the king and the princes over which one of them should be recognized as pope.[7] He affected to remain neutral in the schism, but by this maneuver he kept Cadalus out of Rome.[8] Since Godfrey had sworn on the apostles, Cadalus appeared to believe him, and accepted his mediation. Even though by this time he must have known about the kidnapping at Kaiserswerth, he may not have realized that the new regency under Anno had radically altered its positions.[9] The *Annales Altahenses* said that both he and Alexander were convinced that the king and the princes would choose himself as pope.[10]

After Godfrey had escorted Alexander back to Lucca, Alexander issued documents from June to December 1062, and amidst the grumbling of his followers, Cadalus abandoned his successes in Rome, and departed for Parma.[11] Convinced of the superiority of the spiritual power, Alexander awaited the progress of events calculated to resolve

---

[6] Bonizo, *Ad Amicum,* p. 595: "...Qui [Cadalus] victor extitit, antequam mensis esset transactus, veniente duce Gotefrido Romam, multis precibus et magnificis donis eidem duci collatis vix, ut victus discederet, impetravit..."

[7] Zimmermann, *Papstabsetzungen,* pp. 148–149.

[8] Baix, "Cadalus," p. 73.

[9] Ghirardini, *L'antipapa Cadalo,* pp. 94–95.

[10] *Annales Altahenses,* p. 61: "Hic ergo nunc minis nunc consilio cum ambobus non cessavit agere, donec utrumque persuasit ad sedem pontificatus ire, ut is postmodum sedem apostolicam sine controversia teneret, quem rex et regni principes iudicarent. Huic diffinitioni ambo facile consentiebant, quoniam uterque de regiam venissent et causa haec in curia agitari coepta fuisset, omnibus placuit, ut is, qui consecratus foret, rursus ad apostolicam sedem reverteretur, donec canonico et sinodali iudicio auditus aut eidem sedi iuste praeferretur aut damnatus iuste deponeretur."

[11] JL, pp. 569, 593; Herberhold, "Die Angriffe," p. 492 & n. 103; Schwarzmeier, *Lucca,* p. 143.

the schism, especially at the council of Augsburg called by Anno from October 24–29, 1062.[12] It was the council for which Petrus Damiani had constructed the theoretical arguments for each side in the *Disceptatio Synodalis*.[13]

Accompanied by Anno, and most probably by Godfrey, the king arrived along with representatives from Rome and the churches of Lombardy and Germany. Guibert and Siegfried of Mainz were among them.[14] Anno opened the proceedings by telling the participants that the Holy Roman Church was suffering grave difficulties because of the altercation between the two contestants. He called upon those present to come to the aid of the church, and to decide which man should be pope.[15] Augsburg had previously rejected Alexander, probably because at the time of the election Bishop Henry was a confidant of Agnes.[16]

Even if the outcome of the council may have been predetermined, the side of Cadalus did receive a hearing. According to the *Annales Altahenses* objections against Alexander were raised, including those raised by the bishop who had held Alexander's hand during his enthronement. In a startling conversion, he complained that Alexander had not received the favor of Henry IV, and that he had been raised to the Holy See as a robber and a thief through the money paid to the Normans.[17] Benzo reports that when the Italian bishops objected that one should not arrive at a definitive judgment without the presence of the archbishops of Milan and Ravenna, Anno responded that the

---

[12] Gresser, *Konziliengeschichte*, pp. 60–63; Ghirardini, *L'antipapa Cadalo*, p. 96; Meyer von Knonau, *Jahrbücher* 1:296–301.

[13] Zimmermann, *Papstabsetzungen*, p. 147.

[14] MGH DD HIV: 93–94.

[15] Benzo, *Ad Heincirum*, 3.25, pp. 336–338: "Interim decursis per longa intervalla multis diebus adgreditur perficere Annas [Anno], quod testibus evangelio et cruce spopondit regi suisque fidelibus. Itaque convocatis undecumque episcopis disponit celebrare sub specie synodi conventiculum, quasi suae voluntatis indiculum. Interfuerunt autem quidam de partibus Liguriae appelllati tamquam ex iussione curiae....[Anno's address]: 'Videtis, fratres karissimi, quia sancta Romana aecclesia grave patitur preiudicium. Propter duorum enim altercationem ducuntur filii eius ad occasionem.'" Schmidt, *Alexander II.*, pp. 119–121.

[16] *Annales Augustani*, anno 1061, MGH SS 3:127.

[17] *Annales Altaheneses*, p. 58: "Ob hanc igitur causam legati Romanorum Augustam venere, cum rex ibi adsumptionem Deiparae Virgiinis ageret et generale conloquium haberet. Ex his vero idem episcopus unus erat, qui Alexandrum consecraverat. Is ergo accepto dicendi loco tali perorabat modo: 'Succurrite, potentissimi principes, ecclesiarum matri, succurrite apostolicae sedi. Ecce enim, cum omnes per vos in pace agant, sola Romana ecclesia bellis intestinis quassatur per Alexandrum, qui se papam nominat, quod tamen non est nec unquam erit, siquidem de eo iuste iudicatum fuerit.'"

decisions reached at this council would be provisory, and made permanent in a second council.[18]

Benzo concludes his account with a conversation between Anno and Bishop Romuald of Constance in which Romuald criticized Alexander as he had done frequently before. Anno said that if Alexander had attained his office just as I have, then he will preside over the next council. Romuald responded that canon law did not prohibit your entry [into your office] because you were legally ordained and consecrated, but that this was not true for Alexander, who was enthroned in the night by the Normans after they had received money. The Romans resisted, he continued, and therefore Alexander's enthronement was not achieved without the shedding of blood.[19] Anno replied that what he had said, he had said, and that Alexander should sit until the next synod. He hoped for an end of the situation through the mercy of God.[20]

On Alexander's side, many of the delegates believed that disciples could not judge their master, meaning Alexander himself. After much deliberation it was decided to send Anno's nephew, Bishop Burchard of Halberstadt, to Rome with letters from the king and certain prelates. He was authorized to present the allegations to both sides, and then to make a judgment.

Surely the report of Petrus Damiani that Cadalus was condemned and deposed by all of the German and Italian bishops as well as by the metropolitans was exaggerated.[21] Reflecting his conclusion, the *Annales Camaldulenses* state simply that Cadalus was condemned with the assent of the German clergy, and that Alexander's election was

---

[18] Benzo, *Ad Heincirum*, 3.25, pp. 338–340: "Ad hec Italici episcopi responderunt: 'Non est aequa super hac re diffinitivam sententiam dare sine Ambrosio et Appollinare.' Et ille [Anno] 'Aliqua reservemus et aliqua dicamus, ne incassum convenisse videamur. Nostri vero conventus sententia erit suspensiva, in altera diffinitiva.'" Jenal, *Anno II.*, p. 235.

[19] Benzo, 3.25, pp. 340.

[20] Ibid.: "'Non ergo ita intravit iste, sicut vos intrastis.'" At ille: 'Quod dixi, dixi. Si ita intravit, sicut ego intravi, dico Alexandrum sedere usque ad proximam synodum.'... Fiducialiter quidem expectabamus finem rei sperantes in misericordia salvatoris nostri dei."

[21] Petrus Damiani, *Briefe*, nr. 112 to bishop Kunibert of Turin, 1064, 3:286–287: "Kadalous siquidem ipso festivitatis die sanctorum apostolorum Symonis et Iudae quasi in papam Deo reprobante ac repellente fuit electus, eodemque vertente anno in praedictorum apostolorum vigiliis ab omnibus Teutonicis et Italicis episcopis ac metropolitanis, qui cum rege tunc aderant, damnatus est depositus."

confirmed as legitimate.[22] The account in the *Chronicle of Montecassino* expresses the same assessment, but includes the Italian bishops.[23]

## *Dissension within the German Church*

It is not known when Burchard left Augsburg, and little is known about his activities.[24] The *Gesta* of the bishops of Halberstadt describes him as the faithful and suitable mediator between the pope and the king.[25] He is known to have met Alexander in Burgo S. Quirici on the south Tuscan coast in January after Alexander had celebrated a small synod in Lucca on December 12, 1062. Burchard reputedly asked Alexander why he had accepted the papacy without the consent of the king, and when he was satisfied with his answer, he allegedly recognized him as the legitimate pope.[26] While there, on January 13, 1063, Alexander acknowledged his contributions by granting him the pallium and other insignia of an archbishop.[27] Thereafter Burchard came to Rome, where the *Annales Altahenses* report that after his inquiries he decided in favor of Alexander.[28]

Escorted by Godfrey, Alexander is known to have been in Sutri on January 25–26, 1063, and probably to have arrived in Rome the same

---

[22] *Annales Camaldulenses* 2:251–251: "Synodus revera Germanica hoc eodem anno celebrate fuit, in qua die vigesima-octava octobris, quae anniversaria nimirum erat electionis Cadaloi antipapae, damnatus ipse fuit communi consensu Germanorum antistitum, atque confirmata ut legitima electio Alexandri papa."

[23] *Chron. Mont.*, p. 385: "Quippe qui [Cadalus] eodem anno [Oct. 27, 1062], idest in predictorum apostolorum vigiliis, ab omnibus Teutonicis et Italicis episcopis, qui cum rege tunc aderant [in Augsburg] iusto Dei iudicio dampnatus est ac depositus."

[24] Meyer von Knonau, *Jahrbücher* 1:306–310; Herberhold, "Die Angriffe," pp. 492–494.

[25] *Gesta Episcoporum Halberstadensium*, MGH SS 23:97–98: "...tam fidelis quam ydoneus inter papam et regem mediator."

[26] Gresser, *Konziliengeschichte*, p. 62 & n. 52; Ghirardini, *L'antipapa Cadalo*, p. 97.

[27] JL 4498. "Burchardo, episcopo Halberstadensi pallium salva tamen auctoritate Moguntinae ecclesiae, mitramque concedit, et ecclesiae eius privilegia ac possessiones confirmat, haec prefatus: opus ministerii tui...ad iussionem dilectissimi nostri filii Henrici IV. regis, scilicet ut ecclesiasticae pacis inquietudinem regius advocatus propulsares, cum omni gaudio susecpisti, atque post susceptum legationis obsequium semper sincera affectione pro nobis ad Romana ecclesia nobiscum sollicitus fuistis." Elke Goez, *Beatrix von Canossa*, pp. 159–160.

[28] *Annales Altaheneses*, p. 59: "Is ergo Romam veniens et singula, prout gesta erant, perdiscens, quibusdam comprobantibus, quibusdam etiam adhuc contradicentibus, etiam ipse Alexandri electionem ratam esse firmavit, sicque ad propria remeavit." Meyer von Knonau, *Jahrbücher* 1:301, n. 126 for sources.

month.[29] It was more than two months after the decisions at Augsburg before Rome was finally calm enough for him to take up residence. He renewed the appointment of Anno as archchancellor of the Roman see, and it is probable that at this time he sent the pallium to Anno's friend, Bishop Gunther of Bamberg.[30] In these ways Alexander immediately rewarded Anno and his followers for their support. The sending of the pallium instead of receiving it in person in Rome was beginning to become a special privilege, which had been denied to Archbishop Siegfried of Mainz.[31] Although Anno had calmed his ire, Siegfried was already furious that his authority had been ignored in the granting of the pallium to Burchard, and that Alexander had granted Burchard the pallium while denying it to him.[32]

Harboring nothing but contempt for Burchard, in 1064 Siegfried again petitioned Alexander to deny him the use of the pallium, and the use of the cross while riding in procession. He accused Burchard not only of usurping his office, but also of rejecting the superhumerale and the rationale worn while saying the sacred mass, and of glorying in using the pallium. He utilizes the cross, not for praying, Siegfried complained, but lifts it up for bragging (*iactandum*) between lances or swords while in procession.[33] If in secular things the proper order must be observed, how much more important that there be no confusion in ecclesiastical matters, he asks. It is not proper to sow discord among the priests of Christ, where peace and concord ought to reign. In ecclesiastical matters *equitas* is more valid than power. Because of all of this Siegfried requested that Alexander remove this impediment to the

---

[29] Benzo, *Ad Heinricum*, 2.15, p. 238: "Postquam autem conspirationem, quam mente conceperant, foras efferunt et verbis et rebus ad Italiam se contulit Gotefredus. Quasi ex iussione regis ad regiam urbem Asinelmum reportavit." Gresser, *Konziliengeschichte*, p. 64; Herberhold, "Die Angriffe," p. 493; Elke Goez, *Beatrix von Canossa*, p. 160.

[30] JL, p. 567; JL 4499, March 23, 1063; see also JL 4630, May 10, 1067 where Anno is mentioned as archchancellor; Gresser, *Konziliengeschichte*, p. 63 & n. 54.

[31] Meyer von Knonau, *Jahrbücher* 1:308, n. 5.

[32] JL 4498, Jan. 13, 1063; Jaffé, *Bibliotheca*, 5:46–48; Codex Udalrici, nr. 23, letter of Gunther to Anno complaining about the disturbances of Siegfried among others; Jenal, *Anno II.*, p. 238; Meyer von Knonau, *Jahrbücher* 1:327–328 & n. 42.

[33] Letter of Siegfried to Alexander, 1064; Jaffé, *Bibliotheca* 5:54–56; nr. 28, p. 55: "Qui, non contentus honore praedecessorum suorum, illustrium utique virorum, novum sibi usurpavit papatum; abietoque super humerali et rationali, quo illi inter sacra missarum sollempnia utebantur, novo in ecclesia pallio stupentibus parietibus gloriatur, nova cruce non ad orandum sed ad iactandum inter erubescentes lanceas vel gladio in eqitatu suo extollitur;"

church, a move that he claimed was shared by the unanimity of the brothers.[34]

But having cast his lot in with Anno and his nephew, Alexander did not respond to the suggestion. As the indisputably dominant figure in the regency Anno collaborated with other figures such as Adalbert of Bremen, and Duke Otto of Bavaria, but he was clearly causing dissension within the German church. Giovanni Batista Borino and Ian Robinson have collected a number of opinions analyzing Kaiserswerth and its repercussions for the schism.[35] One writer said that [Anno] "seized King Henry from his mother and set himself over him, as his master."[36] Another said that "with rash daring he did not hesitate to transfer the right of dominion to himself."[37] Besides reservations about Agnes and whatever other reasons the princes might have had for usurping the regency, Anno clearly was very ambitious for power.

Between 1062–1064 he had four objectives: enriching his church, advancing his family, educating (conditioning) the king, and reversing the regency's commitment to Cadalus.[38] Adam of Bremen, one of his chief critics, acknowledged that the empress's rule was a disaster, and that the princes moved to stop the decline, but he said that although Adalbert of Bremen and Anno feigned to restore peace, their hearts fought in mortal hate.[39] Adalbert backed off and swore fidelity to the king, Adam asserted, but Anno, of dreadful character, was always in

---

[34] Ibid.: "Quapropter apostolatus vestri auctoritate hoc novitatis scandalum de ecclesia auferatur; et unanimitas fratrum, que hoc usurpativo tumore pocius quam honore graviter concussa est, ad suam pacem revocetur. Non enim haec causa mea est, sed generaliter fratrum."

[35] Borino, "Cencio del prefetto Stefano," n. 81, p. 392; Robinson, *Henry IV*, pp. 46–47.

[36] *Annales Weissenburgenses*, 1062 in Lampert, *Opera*, p. 51.

[37] *Triumphus sancti Remacli Stabulensis de coenobio Malmundariensi*, MGH SS 11:433–461 at 438.

[38] Robinson, *Henry IV*, pp. 46–47.

[39] Adam of Bremen, *Gesta Hammaburgensis ecclesiae Pontificum*, MGH SRG 2, III. 34–35, pp.175–178; 34, p. 175: "Indignantes enim principes aut muliebri potestate constringe aut infantili ditione regi primo quidem communiter vindicarunt se in pristinam libertatem, ut non servirent; dein contentionem moverunt inter se, qui eorum videretur esse maior; postremo armis audacter sumptis dominum et regem suum deponere moliti sunt." pp. 176–177: "...et quamvis lingua utriusque pacem sonare videretur, cor tamen odio mortali pugnabat in invicem."

the middle of the conspiracies.[40] Known for his avarice, he corrupted his church, and exalted his kinsmen and friends.[41]

Critics noted a deterioration in political appointments after Agnes was driven from power and Anno took over.[42] In 1063 Anno obliged Henry to overrule the election of the cathedral chapter and to appoint his brother, Werner, a mild, dim-witted man, as archbishop of Magdeburg. A twelfth-century historian of the church of Magdeburg deplored the harm inflicted on his church by Werner's appointment. Free elections had been violated, he lamented, and Werner was not up to the task.[43]

In the same vein, with the sole purpose of consolidating his influence in the Kingdom of Germany, Anno secured the investiture of his nephew, Conrad, as archbishop of Trier against the will of the clergy and the people. Conrad was murdered, and the clergy and people elected a canon of their cathedral, whom Anno denounced to the pope to no avail. His attempt to exploit the royal right of investiture resulted in the victory of free election, and again, he was on the wrong side of the reform.

On September 24, 1063, Anno replaced Guibert, Cadalus's main backer, as chancellor of Italy with Bishop Gregory of Vercelli, who was partial to Alexander.[44] His efforts to promote his church and his family elicited biting criticism, and by 1064 his influence had begun to wane. His staunch support for Alexander did not signify a commitment to ecclesiastical reform by either of them.

---

[40] Ibid., 177: "Et Bremensis quidem presul eo iustiorem induit causam, quoniam pronior fuit ad misericordiam, regique domino suo fidem docuit servandam esse usque ad mortem. At vero Coloniensis, vir atrocis ingenii, etiam violatae fidei arguebatur in regem; preterea per omnes, quae suo tempore factae sunt, conspirationes semper erat medioximus."

[41] Ibid, 35, pp. 177–178: "Coloniensis enim, quem avaritiae notabant, omnia, quae [vel] domi vel in curia potuit corrodere, in ornamentum suae posuit ecclesiae. Quam, cum prius magna esset, ita maximam fecit, ut iam comparationem evaserit omnium, quae in regno sunt, ecclesiarum. Exaltavit etiam parentes suos et amicos et capellanos, primis honorum dignitatibus omnes cumulans, ut illi altris succurrernt infirmioribus. [names them including Eberhard of Parma, elected in 1072] et alii, quos enumerare longum [178] est, studio et favore Annonis elevate sunt, qui et fautori suo in temptationibus auxilio decorique fuisse certarunt. Multa igitur ab illo viro in divinis et humanis egregie facta comperimus."

[42] Robinson, *Henry IV*, p. 116.

[43] *Gesta archiepiscoporum Magdeburgensium*, MGH SS 14:376–416 at 400; Robinson, *Henry IV*, n. 98, p. 47.

[44] Meyer von Knonau, *Jahrbücher* 1:323 & n. 35 for sources.

*The Easter Council of 1063 and the Renewal of Violence*

After returning to Rome Alexander's primary objective was to deal with the challenge of Cadalus, since he had not been condemned in the Council of Augsburg. For that purpose, and for promulgating the platform of the reformers, he called his first synod in Rome at the Lateran on April 20, 1063, just after Easter. Although there are doubts about the number of delegates, it was reported that more than 100 bishops and abbots attended.[45]

Focusing on Cadalus, they charged that he had tried to gain the papacy through the heresy of simony. Failing in this attempt, they said that he attacked Rome, where his forces murdered countless people. For all of these crimes, and because he had not attended the council nor sent a representative, the delegates condemned him and imposed the sentence of excommunication.[46] In addition, the council repeated the decrees of the council of Nicholas II of 1059, emphasizing the regulations for the lives of priests.[47] Alexander may have been signaling that he stood solidly in the tradition of the reformers, and it may have been at this time that an inscription celebrating his victory over Cadalus was placed in the Lateran Palace.[48]

---

[45] JL 4500 to bishops, clerics and judges of Italy telling them about the council; JL 4501 to all catholic bishops, and all clergy and people describing the council; JL p. 570; Mansi, 19:966; Gresser, *Konziliengeschichte*, pp. 64–70; p. 65 & n. 68 for doubts about the number of delegates; Meyer von Knonau, *Jahrbücher* 1:309.

[46] *Annales Camaldulenses*, 2:250: 1062: "Alludit nimirum ad synodum, quae post expulsionem anti-papae ex Romana urbe celebrata fuit mens majo in ecclesia Lateranensi ab Alexandro, in qua synodo anathema dictum fuit contra refratarium & schismaticum, perduellionisque reum insensissimum Cadaloum, ad quam vocatus est & Damianus, qui etiam interfuit, ut mox videbimus." *Annales Altahenses*, 1063, p. 61: "Alexander ergo papa, ut iam diximus, Romam reversus erat et, ut mos est Romanae ecclesiae, post pasca sinodum episoporum et abbatum convenire fecit. In hac igitur sinodo de episcopo Parmensi mota est questio, quod datis pecuniis, per heresim scilicet simoniacam, sedem obtinere tentasset apostolicam et, cum hoc non proveniret ad votum suum, bellum et armatuas manus intulerit Romae, [p. 62] matri ecclesiarum, sicque eo praesidente et consiliante homicidia et membrorum obtruncationes ibi multae forent factae. Haec igitur eius crimina cum cunctis essent manifesta, et ad negandum vel satisfaciendum pro his nec ipse venieret nec quemquam transmitteret, iudicatus ab omnibus, anathematis iaculo est percussus."

[47] It is almost certain that the canons that Alexander promulgated in a synod in the Constantiniana (Lateran) thought to be 1063 recorded in the Codex Udalrici were those of this council; Gresser, *Konziliengeschichte*, p. 65; Jaffé, *Bibliotheca*, nr. 24, 5:48–50; JL 4501; Mansi, 19:1023–1024; PL 146:1289.

[48] Gresser, *Konziliengeschichte*, p. 65.

But disdainfully rejecting these acts as a *fait accompli*, Cadalus gathered his own bishops and clerics at Parma, and condemned Alexander's election. He said that he was the pope because he was canonically elected by the king acting for the Roman people as *patricius*. Alexander, by contrast was not canonically elected by the Roman priests or people, but by the Normans, who were enemies of the Empire.[49] Since he was present, Benzo adds details.

Deeming that victory comes from heaven, he said that Cadalus summoned a synod and asked for support. He avowed that he was elected not by his own efforts, but by the ineffable piety of omnipotent God, to whom he offered obedience. After he had spoken, those present rose up, and with flowing tears, sang the sacred litanies. At the end Benzo prayed that God would interfere with the duplicitous plan of the arch devil [Godfrey], and the conspiracy of Annas and Kaiphas [Anno and Alexander], and extend the virtue of his arm over his elect. The synod ended with hymns of Augustine and Ambrose.[50]

## Cadalus Returns to Rome

In Rome the excommunication of Cadalus had heightened the passions of his partisans, who, Benzo says, asked him to take up arms and to return to Rome. His allies still controlled the Leonine side of the Tiber with St. Peters's and the Castel S. Angelo, and the area around S. Paolo fuori le mura even though S. Paolo was administered by Hildebrand. Cadalus must have had strong support, for Godfrey had to call in the Normans—not his natural allies—to pacify the hostile

---

[49] Ibid., 71; *Annales Althahenses*, 1063, p. 62: "Ille [Cadalus] vero, ut haec audivit, episcopos et clericos, quos potuit, apud Parmam colegit et ipsum Alexandrum similiter damnavit, dicens, se pastorem dominici gregis iure habendum, utpute a rege, Romano scilicet patritio, electum se constitutum, illum vero ab omnibus fore detestandum et insequendum, qui non a sacerdotibus vel a Romano populo canonicc esset electus, sed a Normannis, Romani imperii inimicis, lupina fraude et furtim et subdole fuerat introductus. Hoc igitur modo se invicem isti invidiose mordentes accusabant et defendebant."

[50] Benzo, *Ad Heinricum*, 2.13, pp. 232–234: "….de itinere domini mei futuri imperatoris, quos proiciunt Normanni impulsione Gotefredi ad dedecus regis atque totius imperii. Quis ego sum, quem disignarunt ad apiem summum? Non meis meritis ad hanc electionem veni, sed ineffabili pietate omnipotentis dei, qui de animalibus infirmis Pharaonem edomuit et *infima mundi, ut confundat fortia eligere* voluit…. [offers obedience to God] His dictis surrexerunt et sacras laetanias effusis lacrimis cantaverunt." Benzo offers a prayer, and the council ends with hymns of Augustine and Ambrose.

populace. Having collected funds, Cadalus started out in May or June, but met resistance from Godfrey in the mountains and in the forests. Godfrey, again outwardly belligerent toward Henry IV, incited the enemies of the king throughout Italy, and invaded Spoleto and Camerino as well as several counties along the Tyrrhenian See. He also persuaded the Normans to attack the fortifications of S. Paolo.[51]

While Godfrey and Beatrice were able to delay the return of Cadalus for some time, the Normans were gaining strength. During this time Benzo claims that Agnes sent him a letter praising him for supporting the cause of the king and resisting his adversaries. She urged him to persevere in his support of Cadalus, who was threatened by Godfrey, and asserted that she knew that by contrast with others, he would act in defense of her son.[52] Most historians believe that she had totally succumbed to the agenda of the reformers, and that the letter was a forgery. Some suggest that Benzo fabricated the letter based upon what he imagined to be her reaction to the abduction of her son, the removal of her intimate advisor, Henry of Augsburg, and the excommunication of her candidate for the papacy.[53]

Benzo, however, alleged that her words were greeted with great joy, and that thereafter he happily accompanied Cadalus to Rome. Like the entry of Jesus into Jerusalem, they entered Rome in May or June 1063 and prayed at St Peter's.[54] Less charitably, Bonizo says that having collected a great deal of money, the tainted group supporting Cadalus

---

[51] Ibid., 2.15, p. 238: [Godfrey] "Normannos Romam venire faciens socios et amicos rei publicae appellavit, Camerinam et Spoletum invasit, plures comitatus iuxta mare tyrannice usurpavit. Quid plura? Per totam Italiam, quos valuit, ad regis inimicicias incitavit. Normannis quoque persuasit inrumpere sancti Pauli munitionem ad nostrorum civium contritionem."

[52] Ibid., 2.16, p. 244: "'Agnes, dei gracia imperatrix, Benzoni, Albensi episcopo, salutem et omne bonum.... [praises him for supporting the cause of the king, and resisting his adversaries; since things are not yet finished, urges him to persevere in supporting Kadalus, who is threatened by Godfrey;] Scio enim, quoniam ultra vires tuae possibilitatis sunt ista, quae precipio; tu tamen constanter age, eo quod merces multae retributionis erit tibi a me et ab eo, pro quo dimicas, filio.'"

[53] E. g. Meyer von Knonau, *Jahrbücher* 1:311 & n. 14; von Knonau thinks that it is preposterous to conclude that the letter is genuine.

[54] Benzo, *Ad Heinricum* II, 2.16, pp. 244–246: "Intravit Romam fortis et mansuetas [reference to Jesus' entry into Jerusalem]; oravit in loco, ubi requiescit beatus Petrus, dehinc ascendens in poliandrum Adriani [burial place of Hadrian, the Castel San Angelo], ubi conveniunt per singulos gradus maiores Romani. Quos salutavit paterno osculo, stanti deorsum benedixit populo." *Annales Romani, Lib. Pont.* 2:337; the *Annales* add dryly that it profited him nothing, and that he returned to Parma and died; Meyer von Knonau, *Jahrbücher* 1:310–318.

entered the Leonine city at night, and invaded St. Peter's.[55] Both Bonizo and Benzo report that Cadalus then sought safety in the Castel S. Angelo as the guest of Cencius, son of the prefect, Stephen. Benzo adds the embellishment that after saluting the major figures of the city with a fatherly kiss, Cadalus blessed the people standing down below.

Proclaiming a call to war, Cadalus moralized that no one knows how long he will live, but that while living, one must do the will of God. He ventured that if it were not pleasing to God, his return to Rome would not have been possible. Therefore, he declared, for the reconciliation of the Catholic faith and for the defense of the Roman Empire, with the favor of God I have returned to St. Peter and to you. The Roman Empire, of course, was in the hands of Anno and his allies, but Cadalus was declaring his loyalty to the institution, and distinguishing himself from Alexander and the reformers, who sought the protection of the Normans.

Then indicating which part of Rome his enemies held, he called for the people to stand before those within the walls, and God willing, to triumph over them. He declared that with the prayers of the apostles, they knew that the audacity of Simon (Hildebrand) shall come to nothing. Similarly he urged them to purge the city from the stench of the Normans and to show themselves as princes and patrons of the Romans.[56]

As if through one mouth, Benzo said that they all responded: "Blessed are you and the sermon of your mouth, through which are built the walls of the new Jerusalem." They declared that God speaks through you, and they promised to do everything that he ordered. They prayed that he would continue to offer his wise counsel in the future, and promised to fight against Simon (Hildebrand), the recent adversary of Peter and Paul. They called on mighty Rome to fight

---

[55] Bonizo, *Ad Amicum*, lib. 6, p. 595.

[56] Benzo, *Ad Heinricum* 2.16, p. 246: "Quibus dixit: '[no one knows how long they will live; must do the will of God while living] Quid de nobis fieri debeat, ab aeterno predestinavit, nam et omnes potestates, quae fuerunt, sunt et erunt, per intervalla temporum ordinavit. Itaque in eo ponamus spem nostram, quia si ei non placuisset, non esset reditus meus ad Romam. Pro reconciliatione igitur catholicae fidei, pro defensione Romani imperii deo propitio ad sanctum Petrum et ad vos redii. Ergo simul stemus, quia intra muros hostes habemus. De quibus deo volente facile triumphabimus, eo quod victricia signa nostri certaminis portabunt nostri apostoli sacris manibus. Scitis enim, quia orantibus apostolis ad nichilum devenit audatia Symonis [Hildebrand]. Simili modo expurgabunt hanc urbem ex fetore Normanorum et monstrabunt se principes et fautores Romanorum.'"

not just a civil war, but a war of good against evil, and beseeched omnipotent God, the true judge, to decide between each side in the controversy.[57]

Benzo then reports that his nemesis, Hildebrand, enclosed himself in his *proseuca* (a little Jewish place of prayer), and refused to see anyone.[58] People whispered that he was sacrificing to demons or performing magic. At length he appeared, and Benzo concurred that his pallor revealed that he had been in the presence of demons. Petrus Crassus in his *Defensio Heinrici IV Regis*, and Beno in the *Gesta Romanae Ecclesia contra Gregorium* similarly accuse Hildebrand of engaging in necromancy and demonology.[59] Such accusations by hostile writers should be appropriately discounted, but the fact that they were not isolated, and that they were even noted in the decrees of the council of Brixen suggests they may have been prevalent in common parlance.[60]

When Hildebrand emerged from the prayer hut, Benzo said that he rallied the Normans with a call to war. He proclaimed them to be unbeatable on land and sea, and complemented them for being with us at the palace of Constantine (Lateran palace). With the reward that they might be exalted over all of Lazio, he incited them to expel Cadalus. After the Parmensians had vanished by sword or by flight, he exhorted the Normans to raise the diadem on him whom they, with the praise of the Romans, had elected [Alexander].

---

[57] Ibid., 246–248: "Tunc omnes quasi ex uno ore dixerunt: "Benedictus tu et sermo oris tui, per quem aedificabuntur novae Hierusalem muri. Credimus enim, quia per hos tuum loquitur deus; ideoque in cunctis quae iusseris, tibi oboediemus. Denique ad multiplicandas vires nostrae fidei facta est nutu dei regressio Albensis episcopi, per cuius saluberrimum consilium speramus nobis adfuturum divinae pietatis auxilium. Quin enim celestia disponit et humana, septiformi gracia suae mentis replet archana. Tali igitur suffragante consiliario fiducialiter possumus pugnare cum recenti Symone [Hildebrand], Petri et Pauli adversario."

O potens Roma, cuius caput olim tangebat paralella, nunc infimi omnium parant tibi *plus quam civilia bella*, ex una parte Trinkynot et Tancredus, ex altera Annas et Cornefredus, in medio sarabaita cinedus. Iudicet inter utramque controversiam verus iudex, omnipotens deus".

[58] Ibid., 2.17, p. 248.

[59] *Petri Crassi Defensio Henrici IV. Regis* IV. MGH LdL 1:432–453 at 451; Beno, *Contra Gregorium*, p. 373: "Die quadam cum de Albano Romam veniret, oblitus est secum afferre familiarem sibi librum nigromanticae artis, sine quo nusquam aut raro incedebat. Quod cum in itinere ei ad memoriam redisset, in introitu portae Lateranensis festinanter vocavit duos de familiaribus suis, assuetos et fidos ministros scelerum suorum, et ut eundem librum citissime sibi afferent, precepit et terribiliter interminatus est, ne librum in via aperire presumerent nec ulla curiositate secreta libri investigarent. Sed quanto amplius inhibuit, tanto vehementius eorum curiositatem ad investiganda eiusdem libri archana accendit...."

[60] MGH Const. 1:52, line 20.

Benzo said that Hildebrand boasted that he understood men, and could recruit them to whichever side he liked with a piece of gold. Further, Hildebrand claimed that the majority of Germans, who were separated from mother and son (Agnes and Henry IV), communicated their wishes and their counsel to his side. Because of this, Hildebrand exhorted the Normans to "raise your heart on high, and with your hunting spears, pursue not men, but bear."[61] However dramatized Benzo's account of Hildebrand's harangue of the Romans and Normans might have been, there is no doubt that Hildebrand sought alliances with some Roman factions, the Normans, and elements in the German Church. Benzo was probably wide off the mark in seeing Agnes as a supporter of Cadalus after Kaiserswerth.

*War*

Continuing, Benzo narrated that as though drunk from false promises, the Normans ran through the piazzas screaming, "war, war." Inflamed by anger the forces of Cadalus put the Normans to flight, fighting fiercely all the way to the top of the Coelian hill just south of the Lateran. Benzo claimed that their side suffered more casualties than his, and that the Normans were forced to flee. Gathering at St. Peter's, the supporters of Cadalus sang hymns and gave thanks.[62] But knowing that the fortunes of war change, Hildebrand (Prandellus) persisted in encouraging the Normans, and after a month, hostilities recommenced. Cadalus sought help from the suburban counts, who responded enthusiastically, and essentially fought the battles.[63]

---

[61] Benzo, *Ad Heinricum*, 2.17, pp. 250–252: "Sive gladiis seu fuga evanescentibus Parmenianis, quem de grege elegeritis, sublimabo diademate conlaudantibus Romanis. Novi enim homines; in quam partem quippe voluero, possum detorquere singulos singulari hobolo. Maior vero pars Teutonicorum segregata a matre et filio [Agnes and H IV] communicant nobiscum voluntate atque consilio. Propterea erigite cor sursum et venabulis persequimini non hominem, sed ursum."

[62] Ibid., 2.18, p. 254.

[63] Ibid., 256; cf. *Chron. Mont.*, p. 546; Desiderius, abbot of Montecassino, *Dialogi* Victoris III Papae, lib. III, PL 149:1010: "Illustris vir Maximus, Romanae urbis civis, nuper retulis mihi de eodem venerabili praesule quae narro. Bernardus quidam pessimae mentis miles exstitit, qui apostolicae sedi contrarium se in omnibus, quibus potuit modis exhibeat. Sed in bello quod a vicinis circa Urbem manentibus, conjurantibus cum Cadaloo (sic) Parmensi episcopo qui tunc apostolicam sedem evadere tentabat, cum militibus qui Romanam Ecclesiam defendebant commissum est, justo Dei judicio confossus interiit." Meyer von Knonau, *Jahrbücher*, 1:306–317; Borino, "Cencio del prefetto Stefano," p. 386.

Benzo described the fighting in predictably partisan detail, mocking Hildebrand, who, sly as ever, collected many supporters. His forces fought those of Parma to a stand off, and then it was man against man. Parma's forces attacked with the cry of "*supra, supra*," and the frightened Normans replied, "ferrite, ferrite." After terrible slaughter Benzo said that the Normans asked for peace and under oath, promised to leave our land. What Benzo called the Romans spared the Romans who had fought with the Normans, and hostages were exchanged.[64]

Thinking that they had won, the allies triumphantly returned to Cadalus, elevating their spoils and their banners, and singing the kyrie eleison. All of Rome broke out into song and praise to God, and with lord [Cadalus] elected, they proceeded to the basilica of Saint Peter. At the entrance the cathedra was prepared, and there Cadalus sat as pope on the designated day. The people and the militia stood on the steps, and a papal official (numenculatorus) read from the gospel of Matthew (20.8): "[…the lord of the vineyard said unto his steward] call the laborers and give them their hire, beginning from the last to the first." These, he said, we rightly ought to call friends of the republic."[65] Benzo paints a scene of triumph, but it is indicative that the basilica where Cadalus sat as pope was not S. Pietro in Vincoli, where Alexander was enthroned, but St. Peter's.

Benzo gave thanks that danger and death had been averted by divine protection, and declared that soldiers should not just gain fame, but also tangible rewards as examples to posterity. He said that they were richly rewarded with horses, mules, clothes, armor, golden coins, and more. The whole city applauded for so much happiness. After this revelry it was decreed by *senatus consultum* that the city would be defended by citizens in the contiguous comitatus. Benzo asserted that this would have been the end of hostilities were it not that Godfrey was able to ignite the feeble spirit of the sarabaite [Hildebrand].[66]

### Change of Fortunes and the Appeal to the King

Benzo said that Prandellus was very upset with these developments, and requested that his forces remain for at least a month. They, in turn,

---

[64] Benzo, *Ad Heinricum* 2.18, pp. 258–260; Herberhold, "Die Angriffe," pp. 498–501.

[65] Ibid., 260.

[66] Ibid., 262: "Esset procul dubio litigandi finis, ni instigasset languidum animum sarabaitae legataria Gotefredi infernalis Herinis."

asked why they should fight when the conflict had concluded in an abyss. They acknowledged that they had failed in their struggle, and that the hand of the Lord was with their saints, not with the supporters of your (Hildebrand's) cause. "It is hard, therefore, to kick against a stake (*stimulus*)," they protested. Observe what you are doing, and why we are no longer able to stand with you. "We shall go, we shall go," they exclaimed, "for it is certain, if we stand with you, we shall perish."[67]

But fortunes changed with the arrival of Godfrey along with the Normans, who had been waiting outside of the city keeping the Romans unsettled. War raged again, and the assurance of victory by the forces of Cadalus was shattered. The scornful Romans supporting Cadalus asked Benzo to write to the king and to the whole college of pontiffs and other princes to tell them what shame and sadness raged in their chests.[68] Benzo complied, writing to the king and his senate.[69] After citing precedents, he called attention to royal authority over Calabria and Apulia, and said that whatever riches Liguria had, it gave without stinting. Clearly, he wanted to incite the king to defend his sovereignty in the face of the Norman threat.

He accused the Normans, who might better be called Nullimanni, the most stinking dung of the world, of scheming to control the fortress of S. Paolo. They aspire to subject other parts of the empire, and then quickly to take over the Capitoline, he charged. Already they are besieging the Porta Appia. He made an emotional appeal to the Germans, defenders of the Romans, to come to our aid, pleading with them to expurgate this rotten ferment through the hand of Pope Cadalus.[70] This was the first of a bevy of letters, which might not be accurate word for word, but which express the feeling of pressure felt within the camp of Cadalus. The general theme was to request the young king to come to Italy to defend his rights and to receive the imperial crown.

---

[67] Ibid.: "'*Durum est itaque contra stimulum calcitrare*; videte, quid agatis, non possumus vobiscum amplius stare. Ibimus, ibimus; certum est, si vobiscum stamus, quoniam peribimus.'"

[68] Ibid., 264: "'Quomodo possumus tanta ferre regio solamine desolati? Et quia communis est honor, communis et dolor, communiter rogamus domnum Albensem episcopum, ut scribat hec regi atque universo collegio pontificum ceterorumque principum, quatenus de communi dedecore seviat communis dolor in eorum communiter pectore. Et si amant preesse, studeant et prodesse.'"

[69] Ibid., 3.1, pp. 266–272.

[70] Ibid., 272: "Igitur, o gemme Romani palacii, o gloria imperantis Lacii, expurgate per manus papae Kadali hoc putribile fermentum, quia sic potestis illum fere nostrum basileum Doclitium adducere ad communem conventum."

Benzo wrote letters 2–4 to Anno's rival, Archbishop Adalbert of Bremen, who seemed to be leaning toward Cadalus, but who had not committed himself. Benzo asked who was opposing the Normans, and where were the bishops who had supported the king, who is only a boy, and who is being injured by the imposition of the Normans. Seeing the Church in a state of almost death-like throes, he implored that you alone must act, O Father, because the world is tumbling down and the church is endangered before the end of time. Come to the aid of the universal church and the king, he pleaded; support his men that he may counteract the audacity of the Normans.[71]

In a subsequent letter to Adalbert Benzo cited a letter from the emperor Constantinus Doclitius delivered through the hand of the *patricius* of Amalfi [Pantaleus] to Cadalus and himself.[72] The emperor asked them as protectors of the boy king to act with other Germans and Italians to ensure that the king might come with a militia into Apulia and Calabria, and settle all of the problems.[73] Benzo implored Adalbert to respond, and in another letter to Adalbert and others, he pleaded with them to free us from evil.[74] Writing to King Henry himself, Benzo inquired when he was coming to Italy or whether they should expect another. In still another letter he speaks of eating the bread of sadness, and advises the king to cultivate the arts of the *triumphatore*.[75]

A legate delivered these letters to Adalbert and Henry in Germany toward the end of September or early October 1063.[76] He returned with a brief message to Cadalus from the king and his magnates calling Cadalus the bridegroom of the Holy Roman Church, and asking him to persevere from his good beginning all the way to the end. We hold

---

[71] Ibid., 3.2, p. 276: "Cernis, o pater, quia ruit mundus, periclitatur aecclesia, ante tempus finiuntur secula. *Qui succurrere perituro potest, dum non succurrit occidit.* Succurre ergo pereunti mundo. Succurre universali aecclesiae sub ultimo gementi discrimine. Succurre domino nostro regi, suggere vires ei ut conterat audaciam Normannorum, quo Romana aecclesia resummat flatum vel in fine seculorum." Herberhold, "Die Angriffe," p. 500; Meyer von Knonau, *Jahrbücher* 1:315–316 & n. 20.

[72] Ibid., 3.3, pp. 276–278; 276: "Per manum enim Malfitani patricii direxit [Constantinus Doclitius] domno Kadalo et michi rescriptum pytacii in hec verba:"

[73] Ibid., 278.

[74] Ibid., 3.4, pp. 280–282.

[75] Ibid., 3.6, p. 284.

[76] Ibid., 3.7, pp. 286–288; 286: "Harum portitor litterarum, noster legatus presentavit se Bremensi archiepiscopo, et sicut a nobis acceperat, apperuit illi quare venerat. Archiepiscopus autem convocatis paucis de procerum grege introduxit Romanum legaturm coram domino nostro rege."

you in our hearts, the king said affectionately, and citing the prophets, asked him to be patient; a little here, a little there. In the end what your heart desires, you shall see in truth.[77]

After Benzo delivered a long speech to bolster the [Roman] "senate" in its convictions, a wise man responded that Benzo was truly a man of God, and promised that they would continue to fight. He appealed to God that his will be done on earth just as it is in heaven."[78] Commenting on the ambiguity of Henry's letter, the senators suggested that Cadalus deliberate with the counts from all cities.

Rapizo, count of Todi, responded that the Normans were a threat to the Roman Empire, and that the cohorts of the fighters must be increased. Everyone agreed, and divided themselves into groups that then dwelled in the city like inhabitants, but with no lack of weapons. This activity threw the *falsa cuculla*, (Hildebrand), who had been used to treating Nicholas like a donkey in a stable, and collecting money into a very large sack (*centenario sacculo*), off his stride. For the Romans, it was a time of great troubles [79]

Turning to the south, Benzo mentions that the more distinguished people of Apulia and Calabria, who had been living under the yoke of Godfrey, were overjoyed to join Pantaleus, *patricius* of Amalfi and an agent of the basileus of Constantinople, in boarding a ship for Rome. They arrived at the Castel S. Angelo, where they greeted the lord elect on bended knee as a hero because Godfrey, whom they saw as a second Judas to the king, had disappeared from their midst.

Pantaleus declared that he was now prepared to grant what the basileus had promised in his letter, and he asked Cadalus and his senators, and similarly the king and his curia to carry out their promises. He affirmed that those who were with him held the keys and possessed the power in Bari and other cities. Whenever and however you wish to enter, he concluded, you shall enter if the faith we hold in you, you will make to us. Cadalus responded: "These things must be announced to our lord king, who is the chariot of the church, and the charioteer of

---

[77] Ibid., 288: "Ergo vos, qui cum Petro habitatis, paciencer expectate, quoniam, quod cor vestrum desiderat, videbitis in veritate." Herberhold, "Die Angriffe," pp. 500, 502.

[78] Ibid., 3.9, p. 296: "Igitur postquam finem loquendi fecit episcopus B., regis legatus, tale dedit responsum sapiens senatus: 'Vere *vir dei es, vere verbum domini in hore tuo verum est*; tacebimus, expectabimus, pugnavimus et pugnabimus. Sive sit pax sive sit vvera, *fiat voluntas tua, rex aeterne, domine, sicut in caelo et in terra*.'"

[79] Ibid., 3.10, pp. 296–300.

the empire."[80] Thus, at this late date the Byzantines still saw their salvation in a partnership with Cadalus and the king, and must have wagered that they could successfully counter the alliance of the reformers and the Normans.

After the southern contingent had departed, Cadalus addressed the senate, asking them to select a legate, who would be pleasing to the king. Upon hearing some murmuring he responded that it was obvious from the legation that we have just received that the mercy of God was looking down from heaven. For in his mercy is contained a respite in our labors and a hindrance and crumbling of our enemies, he added optimistically. After further admonitions Benzo was chosen as legate to the king because he could speak German, and speaking for himself, he said that he loved the king so much that he was willing to go to prison or to die for him. He then spoke, and the others responded positively.[81] His account is the only report that he was dispatched to the royal court where he would arrive early in 1065.

### Conclusion

The challenge of Cadalus to be recognized as pope was not a trivial blip in the reformers' march to power. At one point he and his allies had Alexander and Hildebrand on the point of defeat, and major prelates supported his legal position and criticized the weakness in Alexander's. He was also an intricate part of the web of profound geopolitical changes, and his stature was such that the Byzantines in Southern Italy sought him out as an ally against the alliance of the reformers and the Normans. Had it not been for Anno's coup, it is possible if not probable that the Church would have recognized him as pope.

It is simplistic to see him primarily as an imperial minion set up by the regency to thwart the reformers, who were trying to free the Church from imperial control. The German episcopate was divided, and without this conflict the regency would have remained a much more viable force, defending traditional imperial rights that they believed had been acknowledged in the papal electoral decree of 1059. After his visit to the imperial court Benzo may have expected Henry's arrival in Italy,

---

[80] Ibid., 3.11, pp. 300–302; 302: "Ad hec domnus Kadalus: 'Nuncianda sunt hec domino nostro regi, qui es currus aecclesie et auriga imperii....'"

[81] Ibid., 3.12, pp. 302–306.

but Henry was not a free agent, and the strangely silent Anno may have been acting behind the scenes. With Kaiserswerth and Agnes's withdrawal, Cadalus was left dangling with support mainly from the Lombards and the Roman and suburban nobility.

Godfrey, who was ambivalent about the king, but not about the Normans, whom he hated, became the decisive arbiter. Pursuing his own advantage, he bit his tongue, and threw in his lot with the reformers backed by the Normans. Cadalus had no choice but to flee Rome, and to return to Parma. These events had little to do with ecclesiastical reform, and indeed, Alexander's strongest supporters including Anno committed many of the abuses that the reformers vowed to eradicate.

But the schism was not over. Dissatisfaction with Alexander's election remained, and Petrus Damiani took it upon himself to allow each side to air its position in a council summoned under the patronage of the king. That council would decide which candidate should be recognized as pope.

CHAPTER THIRTEEN

## THE COUNCIL OF MANTUA

The appeals for Henry IV to come to Italy were predictably of no avail. He still had not reached his majority, and was under the control of those who did not want him to come. The longer that Cadalus waited for help and money in the Castel S. Angelo, the more the Romans drifted away.[1] Even his supporters from Parma departed in August 1063 because of the heat and the accompanying fevers.[2] The city leaders met with the counts of the surrounding cities to plant some militia from the outlying areas in the city, but Cadalus suffered one misfortune after another, and soon he was more of a captive than a guest of Cencius in the Castel S. Angelo.[3]

What actually happened is not precisely known. In dire financial straits Cadalus waited six months for the regency to come to his aid, while Alexander fared little better with the Normans. In the end it was Godfrey who determined the outcome.[4] Facing grim reality, Cadalus paid Cencius a generous sum, and left the city in utter humiliation with a single retainer and a mule, probably at the beginning of 1064.[5] The city was now in the hands of Hildebrand, and Alexander, who had found increasing acceptance after the Council of Augsburg. But they were not home free. Anno would respond to Petrus Damiani's request that the regency summon a council to adjudicate the schism, but his loyalties were mixed. While siding with the reformers, his conscience

---

[1] Meyer von Knonau, *Jarhbücher* 1:316–317; Herberhold, "Die Angriffe," pp. 500–501; Baix, "Cadalus," p. 83.
[2] Donizo, *Vita Matildis*, Lib. 1, v. 1187, MGH SS 12:348–409 at 375: "Ob terrae febres Parmenses mox rediere, pontificem solum linquunt proprium Cadaloum."
[3] Benzo, *Ad Heinricum*, 3.10, pp. 296–298.
[4] Schmidt, *Alexander II.*, pp. 121–123.
[5] Bonizo, *Ad Amicum*, p. 595: "Qui consilio Cencii, cuiusdam pestiferi Romani, castrum Sancti Angeli intravit ibique se tutatus est. Quo in eodem castro per duos annos obsesso [1064], post multas et varias calamitates, quas inibi passus est, non ante datum est ei inde exire, quam ab eodem Cencio trecentis libris argenti se comparavit; unoque clientulo contentus, unius iumenti adiumento inter oratores Bercetum egre pervenit." Benzo, 3.26, pp. 342–344: "Denique tanta velocitate regressus est Parmae, ut videretur sibi, quod angelus domini, qui asportavit Abacuc super lacum Babyloniae, trantulisset eum in locum Parmensis coloniae."

was tormented for having betrayed Henry III, who had made him what he was, and he had incurred the wrath of the court.

### Petrus Damiani Calls for a Council

Already in 1063 Alexander and Hildebrand had directed their focus toward France, to which they sent a legation under the guidance of Petrus Damiani. Alexander commanded Gervais of Reims and three other archbishops to obey Petrus, who demanded total obedience to Rome.[6] At the end of the year Alexander wrote to Gervais announcing the fall of Cadalus.[7] Perhaps this statement was intended to counter any notion that Cadalus might still be a viable candidate, for Petrus had opened up the whole issue in an earthshaking letter to Anno in June 1063.

Writing from France, he emphasized that while the priesthood is protected by the defenses of the realm, the realm is supported by the sanctity of the priestly office.[8] He praised Anno for saving the boy [Henry IV] left in his care, for having brought order to the kingdom, and for having guaranteed to his ward the imperial rights of his father. Getting to the subject at hand, he complimented Anno for having reached out to the priesthood by laboring:

> to sever the scaly neck of the "beast of Parma" with the sword of evan-gelical rigor and to reinstate the bishop of the Apostolic See on the throne of his dignity. But once the work has begun, unless you give it the finish-ing touch and use the opportunities that still remain, the holy edifice to which you have set your hand is in danger of collapsing. For the infa-mous Cadalus, the disturber of Holy Church, the subverter of apostolic discipline, the enemy of man's salvation; he, I say, who is the root of sin, the herald of the devil, the apostle of Antichrist, the arrow drawn from the quiver of Satan, the rod of Assyria, son of Belial, the son of perdition who claims to be so much greater than all that men call 'god,' so much

---

[6] JL 4516, May 15? 1063; Alexander to Gervais and other archbishops; Alexander commended Petrus Damiani as his legate; "qui et noster est oculus, et apostolicae sedis immobile firmamentum."

[7] JL 4527; PL 146:1298: "Annuntiamus tibi…Cadaloi, praesumptionem extollentem se adversus apostolicam sedem, tanto amplius ad maiorem sui ignominiam devenisse quanto ipse speraverat altioris superbiae culmen ascendisse…Ad reparandam pecu-niam, in periculum capitis sui, a fautoribus suis distributam, cuiusdam turris praesidio gemebundus servitor." Baix, "Cadalus," p. 85.

[8] Petrus Damiani, *Briefe*, nr. 99, to Archbishop Anno of Cologne, June 1063, 3:97–100; tr. Blum, 5:103–106.

greater than anything that is worshipped, still breathes fire like some hideous dragon, with the filth of his poisoned money causes a stench in the nostrils of men, and by the wind of his perfidy like a new chief of heretics disturbs the faltering faith of many.[9]

Petrus admonished Anno that in order that the Christian people may not be placed permanently in error, it was necessary to call a general council as soon as possible to settle the schism once and for all. He volunteered to come to Anno to discuss the situation, but not expecting to be granted such a favor, he suggested that Anno use his good judgment to wipe out the pestiferous Cadalus so that the Christian religion could return to a peaceful existence. He hoped that through Anno both the Church and the Empire could enjoy the peace that we all desire, and he prayed that "he who is the Author of both authorities may grant you the reward of eternal peace that you deserve. "But," he concluded, "since my horse is ready, and my companions have all set out, I now turn away from my letter and set my feet to the stirrup."[10]

Petrus may not have anticipated Hildebrand's hostile reaction to his letter, but from Hildebrand's perspective the schism had already been resolved at Augsburg, and Cadalus had lost. Now Petrus was approaching the regency, and opening up the whole controversy to an uncertain outcome. After the excommunication of Nicholas and the nullification of his decrees, the regency's disdainful treatment of Cardinal Stephen, and now its election of Cadalus, he saw the Empire both as antagonistic and as weakened. He knew that the regency had become much more supportive under Anno, but Anno did not stand alone.

Petrus reveals Hildebrand's fury in a letter that he wrote to Alexander and Hildebrand during Lent, 1064.[11] It is indicative of how close he saw the relationship between Alexander and Hildebrand that he addressed them as Father and Son, the pope and the archdeacon. In reply to their request for a copy of the letter that he had sent to Anno the previous summer, he spoke humbly to Alexander, but sardonically to Hildebrand.

Petrus told Hildebrand that he was sending him the letter [to Anno] because you have beaten me black and blue, and you can see and verify what it contained and what I did to oppose you. He swore that he had not sent a letter to anyone else in the area, and that not one iota was changed in the letter [to Anno] that he was forwarding. As for the rest,

---

[9] Ibid., 99; tr. Blum, 5:104–105.
[10] Ibid., 100; tr. Blum, 5:105–106.
[11] Ibid., nr. 107, 185–189; tr. Blum 5:192–194.

he humbly begged "my holy Satan" not to act so cruelly toward me, nor allow your impressive pride to beat me with such frequent blows. Having had its fill, "it should show pity for its servant."[12]

Petrus pleaded old age as the reason that he would not be able to come to Rome as Alexander had requested, but he promised to come to Mantua, a promise that in the end he did not fulfill. Addressing himself to the differences between Alexander and Hildebrand, he said: "In sending me this holy message, however, each of you seems to have taken a different approach. One, it appears to me, is charming and friendly with a fatherly interest, while the other threatens terror and hostile attack. One of you, like the sun, bathes me in the warmth of his brilliant splendor, but the other, like the blustery north wind, blows up a violent storm."[13] He devoted the rest of his letter to complaints about the violence and cruelty of Hildebrand.

The *Annales Camaldulenses*, closely tied with Petrus Damiani, contain an account of the interchange between Petrus and Hildebrand and Alexander.[14] The author notes that the letter that Petrus sent to Anno offended both Alexander and Hildebrand, and suggests that they may have seen it as an attack or as an act of disloyalty.[15] The author surmises that they twisted his words, but whatever the problem was, he is certain that Petrus wrote the letter to placate them. He said that Petrus swore that he had meant no wrong, and called upon Jesus and the angels as his witness. He implored Hildebrand, his holy Satan, no longer to rage against him.[16] Both of them ordered him to come to Rome in haste, and then to accompany them to Mantua, the author continued, but Petrus did not respond to either command. The author gives short shrift to Mantua, mentioning only briefly that Anno was present, and that Cadalus and his supporters were condemned.

---

[12]  Ibid., 186; tr. Blum, 5:192–193.

[13]  Ibid., 187; tr. Blum, 5:193.

[14]  *Annales Camaldulenses*, 2:319.

[15]  Ibid.: "Epistolam scripserat Damianus anno 1063 ut diximus, Annoni archiepiescopo Coloniensi, vel etiam aliam posteriorem, qua Alexandri summi pontificis & Hildebrandi cardinalis animos offenderat, perinde ac in illa aliquid contra eos scribendo attentasset."

[16]  Ibid.: "Quidquid sit, ut Romanaum pontificem & Hildebrandum iratos placaret, epistolam ipsam ad utrumque mittit Damianus, imprecans sibi mala, Jesumque & angelos ejus in testimonium vocans, se nil prorsus adversus ipsos scripsisse, atque humiliter obsecrat Hildebrandum, quem vocat *sanctum* suum *Satanan, ne contra se desaevire* ulterius pergeret."

Three themes stand out in these letters. The first is that Petrus called for peace between *regnum* and *sacerdotium*, which he treated as equals. The second is that he did not believe that it had been established that Alexander was the legitimately elected pope. He acknowledged past accomplishments (allusions to Augsburg and the mission of Burchard), but said that they could come undone unless further steps were taken. He did not appeal to the papal electoral decree of 1059, but called upon Anno acting for the king to adjudicate the dispute. The third is Hildebrand's character. When Benzo or Cardinal Beno unleashed their venom against Hildebrand, their remarks could be discounted, but if Petrus lamented his violent and harsh behavior, one pays attention. Clearly Hildebrand had a fiery temperament, and lashed out at those who stood in his way. He did not want the legitimacy of his pope to be settled at a council called under the auspices of the royal court.

Anno responded to Petrus's plea to organize a council, consulting with some of the magnates of the realm including Duke Godfrey at Kaiserswerth at the end of April, 1064.[17] According to Wenzel, the abbot of Altaich (Altahenses), legates from Rome visited the king at Cologne to discuss the schism, and it was decided to call a council at Mantua, a city controlled by Godfrey, and convenient both to Germany and to Italy, where each side could present its case. Both contenders freely assented, for each of them thought that his cause was just, and a date was set for May 31, 1064.[18] Probably Cadalus had been informed about the discussions by an emissary from Germany in February when he was still in Rome, and since in spite of Henry's promises, no help arrived from Germany, he may have calculated that the council constituted his only hope.

---

[17] MGH DD HIV: 128.

[18] *Annales* Altahenses, 1064, p. 64: "Dominicam incarnationem rex peregit apud Wangionem [Cologne]. His diebus rursus legati Romanorum venerunt conquesti, singulis episcopiis singulos praesules sufficere, de sola apostolica sede duos simul contendere. Hac illorum quottidiana querela rex et principes permoti, statuerunt apud Mantuam sinodum fieri, ubi possent concurrere ambo papae, si fas est dicere, pontifices Teutoni, Romani et Longobardi. Huic decreto ambo simul, Alexander et Kadalo, libenter assentiebantur, quoniam, ut diximus, uterque de causa sua praesumebat. Synodus autem ista in die sancti penthecostes denunciatur futura." Jenal, *Anno II.*, pp. 243–274; Zimmermann, *Papstabsetzungen*, pp. 155–158.

## *The Council of Mantua (May 31-June 3, 1064)*

Since both Wenzel of Altaich and Benzo were present, we have two eye witness accounts.[19] Wenzel mainly reported the events, and Benzo his version of the background drama. Benzo said that Anno came to Mantua with a militia of three hundred, and that they were ceremoniously received by Countess Beatrice.[20] Wenzel reports that Anno and a sizeable number of bishops and princes arrived in Mantua from Germany, and that with a huge number of men Cadalus camped near by in Aqua Nigra, an area outside of the control of Beatrice and Godfrey.[21] From there he sent legates to Anno demanding that he be appointed president of the council. Anno's legates were unreceptive, stating that it would be unjust if he, who was already pope [Alexander], even though absent and unheard, would be deposed.[22]

Cadalus may not fully have appreciated that the abduction of Henry IV had transformed the regency, and that it would not treat him as its candidate. As Wenzel reports, he was reduced to sending observers every day to inform him about what was happening. In the meantime Alexander, anxious to obey the rules to the letter, arrived at the synod. Many bishops, abbots and princes also came from Italy, but Hildebrand was not among them. Each participant felt strongly about the candidate that he was supporting, and expressed differing points of view.[23]

Wenzel reports that on the first day everyone congregated in the church, and after the invocation of the Holy Spirit, Alexander spoke of

---

[19] Gresser, *Konziliengeschichte*, pp. 71–77; pp. 73–74 & ns. 121–127 for sources other than Wenzo and Benzo; Hefele & Leclercq, *Histoire des conciles*, 4:859–871; Jenal, *Anno II.*, pp. 243–272; Meyer von Knonau, *Jahrbücher* 1:377–384.

[20] Benzo, *Ad Heinricum*, 3.26, p. 342.

[21] *Annales Altahenses*, p. 64: "Episcopus autem Parmensis cum ingenti multitudine ad locum, qui Aqua nigra dicitur, accessit." It is disputed whether Godfrey accompanied Anno. Gresser affirms that he did, and Elke Goez that no sources confirm that he was there, and that it was improbable that he was. Gresser, *Konziliengeschichte*, p. 72; Elke Goez, *Beatrix von Canossa*, p. 16 & n. 171.

[22] Ibid.: "Exinde legatos ad archiepiscopum Coloniensem misit, mandans huic, huic concilio se nolle interesse, nisi sibi permitteretur synodum tenere et in loco iudicantis papae praesidere."

[23] Ibid.: "Sed cum caesareis nunciis indecens ac iniustum hoc videretur, ut Alexander, qui iam papa erat, absens et inauditus deponeretur, ipse quidem in loco, quo diximus, substitit, exploratores tamen inde cottidie Mantuam misit, per quos sciret, quaeque illic dicta vel gesta fuissent. Alexander autem ad synodum promptus occurrit, quoniam regulis ecclesiasticis in omnibus semper obedire studuit. Ex Italia autem pontifices et abbates aliique principes innumeri undique confluent, et propter studia partium, quae inter illos magna erant, diversi diversis favebant."

peace and concord, and ordered what ought to be said. Anno began by transmitting formal complaints from the king and the princes against Alexander: that he had attained his office through the heresy of simony; that he had curried the support and friendship of the Normans, enemies of the Empire, and that by their help, and against ecclesiastical regulations and the will of the king, he retained this power. Anno asserted that he was authorized by the king to determine what was true.[24]

Alexander responded that if his accusers wanted to be believable, they must be present. But even if they were present, he could not be forced to respond, since students cannot accuse their *magister*. Wishing to purify his election from any objection, however, he swore that he was free from simony, and emphasized that under protest he was raised to the papacy under the old Roman custom by those who had the right to elect and consecrate the pope. To the charge that he had accepted help from the Normans, he said that he could say nothing, but that when the king, my son, comes to Rome for receiving the imperial crown and the benediction, he himself will learn what is true.[25]

The implication of Alexander's statements is enormously revealing. Because he had been consecrated and enthroned, he identified himself as pope, and everything followed from there. He could absolve himself from any charges by taking an oath, and he was not obligated to defend himself from collaboration with the Normans. Perhaps, most

---

[24] Ibid., 64–65: "Igitur feria secunda sancti penthecostes cunctis in ecclesiam congregatis, post invocationem sancti Spiritus omnibus secundum morem positis subselliis, primum Alexander sermonem fecit de pace et concordia, postmodum proferre iussit, is qua essent dicenda. Tunc archiepiscopus Coloniensis: 'Rex,' inquit, 'et regni principes audierunt de te multorum, qui haec vera adfirmant, relatione, quod per heresim symoniacam perveneris ad sedem apostolicam, cumque tibi conscius fores criminis tanti, Northmannos, Romani imperii hostes, socios et amicos tibi adscivisti, ut eorum auxilio contra regulas ecclesiasticas, etiam rege invito potestatem hanc retineas: quapropter nos a rege directi sumus, ut, quid inde verum sit cognoscamus.'" Zimmerman makes the point that instead of Anno, Alexander took over the presidency of the council. *Papstabsetzungen*, p. 156.

[25] Ibid., 65: "'Attamen nunc, ne sancta Dei ecclesia scandalum habeat super me, testor et iuro per hunc, quem colimus, adventum Spiritus sancti, quia conscientiam meam nunquam symoniaca heresi conmaculavi, sed me reclamantem et renitentem traxerunt et in sede apostolica invitum statuentes consecraverunt. Et hoc illi fecere, qui secundum antiquum Romanorum usum eligendi et consecrandi pontificis curam et potestatem noscuntur habere. Quod autem mihi obicis Northomannorum societatem et amiciciam, nihil est, quod de hoc modo respondeam, sed si quando filius meus rex ipse venerit Romam ad suscipiendam imperialem benedictionem et coronam, ipse tunc praesens comprobabit, quid ex his verum sit.'"

importantly, he made no attempt to demonstrate that his election was legal because it followed the norms of the papal electoral decree of 1059.[26] Blithely ignoring the rights of the cardinals and the king, he justified his election by affirming that it conformed to ancient custom.

Wenzel said that the council accepted Alexander's moves and confirmed his election. Alexander then raised complaints against Cadalus, calling him a heretic. Since there was no representative to speak for Cadalus, Alexander condemned him again with the loud support of the Germans and Italians. Thus ended the first day. On the second day Anno was not present, and no doubt feeling that their candidate had not been treated fairly, the supporters of Cadalus broke up the meeting. Calling Alexander a heretic, they threatened him with the sword, but while almost everyone else fled, Alexander stayed. Wenzel came to his aid, and Beatrice entered with her people and restored order. On the third and fourth days there were peaceful discussions, after which Alexander returned to Rome and all of the others to their respective homes.[27]

Writing after the death of his model, Gregory VII, and when he was severely wounded, Bonizo was a fount of misinformation. Before the council he said that Anno had come to Rome because he thought that that was the best course of action to unite *regnum* and *sacerdotium*.[28] When he asked *the pope* why he dared to accept the office of Roman pontiff without the king's command, *Hildebrand* responded that according to the decrees of the holy Fathers, the king had no role in the election of Roman pontiffs. When Anno replied that this authority was granted him by virtue of his office as *patricius*, Hildebrand countered with a decree from the synod of Symmachus that stated that no layman may hold any power over the church.[29]

---

[26]  Gresser, *Konziliengeschichte*, n. 131, p. 74.

[27]  *Annales Altahenses*, pp. 65–66; p. 65: "Tandem silentio facto Alexander papa de Parmensi episcopo quaestionem movebat, quem tamen ipse non episcopum, sed hereticum nominabat....Sequenti vero die archiepiscopus Coloniensis non intererat, et ecce fautores Parmensis episcopi ecclesiam cum magno strepitu irrumpebant, Alexandrum papam hereticum vociferabantur, quidam etiam evanginatis gladiis mortem ei minabantur." Jenal, *Anno II.*, pp. 249–250.

[28]  *Ad Amicum*, p. 596: "Prefatus vero Anno nil melius cogitans quam ut regnum sacerdotiio uniretur, Italiam veniens, Romam tendit papamque convenit, cur absque iussu regis ausus sit Romanum accipere pontificatum."

[29]  Ibid.: "Cui cum Deo amabilis Ildebrandus dixisset [1064] in electione Romanorum pontificum secundum decretum sanctorum patrum nil regibus esse concessum, et ille

Anno reminded him of the [papal electoral] decree of Nicholas, but Hildebrand shot back with another decree by the same pope. Anno then requested that the pope call a council to give an accounting of himself, and Alexander promised to do so even though it was beneath the dignity of a pope. He immediately summoned the synod of Mantua, where he could meet Cadalus and the Lombard bishops.[30] Bonizo said that Cadalus feared to come, but that the venerable pope did come, and giving a favorable accounting of himself, he turned his enemies into friends. A staunch paterine and hardly neutral on the subject, Bonizo adds that the bishops from the province of Milan turned away from Cadalus, throwing themselves down at Alexander's feet to obtain his pardon.[31] With *regnum* and *sacerdotium* united, the pope returned to Rome with honor.[32]

However inaccurate, Bonizo's account reveals a wealth of information. Like Petrus Damiani, Anno regarded it as a good thing that *regnum* and *sacerdotium* be united, and did not emphasize any competition between the two major institutions. The same was not true for Hildebrand, who answered when Anno asked Alexander a question about the king's prerogative in papal elections. In Bonizo's account Hildebrand did not feel bound by the papal electoral decree of 1059, and denied the king any authority in papal elections. He appeared to regard the decree as a mere expediency for the time.

### Benzo's Purported Exposé

Garbed in his usual dramatic hyperbole, Benzo reported that on the first day of the proceedings, Alexander, stuttering, gave a speech admonishing his followers to perform the service of God. Since no one could understand him, Anno advised him to stop and to try again the

---

respondisset ex patriciatus hoc licere sibi dignitate, mox venerabilis archidiaconus has sinodale obiecit propositiones: [....cites decisions of church fathers in ancient synods prohibiting participation of laymen;]"

[30] Ibid.: "Quod ut ille audivit, licet a Romanorum pontificum hoc esset alienum dignitate, tamen, quia necessitas urguebat, facere promisit; moxque apud Mantuam synodum evocavere, in qua Cadolus cum Longobardorum episcopis posset convenire."

[31] Ibid., 597: "Nam mox omnes Langobardi episcopi, pedibus suis advoluti, reos se esse confessi veniam petiere et impetravere.

[32] Ibid.: "Sicque regno et sacerdotio unito papa cum honore Romam remeavit."

next day.[33] After the synod ended at mid day, Alexander went to his lodgings accompanied by members of the *pataria*. With tears in his eyes, Anno ascended to the altar in the sanctuary, and began to pray. Beatrice approached him and said that it was time to eat. Anno said that he could not because of a head ache, and when Beatrice asked him again, he remained firm. At length, he asked her to invite the others to eat, and then went with her alone to the inner church. After entrusting a secret to her, he said that he would eat if he were able.[34]

Then, suddenly, he made a movement to fall at her feet. Bracing her arms against him, she told him that he should not do that. Both broke into tears, and then sniffling, Anno dried his tears and began to speak. Before the altar he confessed the sadness of his heart. He said that she knew of his origin and that of his parents, and that Henry III had raised him out of dung (*stercore*), and had wanted to place him over all princes, and make him second in the empire. More he (Henry III) could not have done, but I, a sinner turned into a rapacious wolf, snatched his son from his mother when I should have opposed such cruelty.[35]

Continuing, Anno said that since he had approved the promotion of Alexander, whom the Normans placed on the cathedra of St. Peter, he had alienated the whole court. They call me an unfaithful betrayer, a Judas, and unless I correct this, I will be alienated from them like a leper.[36] This is my death, if falling into the inferno I relinquish heaven (*galaxea*). Responding to his plea for advice, Beatrice, pale faced and

---

[33] Benzo, *Ad Heinricum*, 3.26, p. 344: "Baburrus [dumbhead] Alexander in cathedra collocatur, et prout valebat, baburrando eos de servitio dei ammonebat. Et cum diu multumque frendens blaterando verba perstreperet nulllusque balbutationem eius intelligeret, Annas ammonuit esse cessandum atque in crastinum reservandum." Jenal, *Anno II.*, pp. 261–275.

[34] Ibid., 3.27, p. 344: " 'Est secretum, o domina, quod tibi volo confiteri; post cuius confessionem tecum cenabo, si forte aliquid hodie manducabo.' " Elke Goez, *Beatrix von Canossa*, pp. 160–161.

[35] Ibid. 344–346; 346: "Luce clarius est, quod sanctus imperator, secundus HEINRICUS, me *erigens de stercore* super altitudines ceterorum procerum preesse voluit meque se alterum in imperio constituens nil plus facere potuit. Et ego miser et peccator factus lupus rapax rapui filium eius de sinu matris, cum debuissem me opponere presumptori huisce crudelitatis." Lampert of Hersfeld was among the many contemporaries who were critical of Anno for his abduction of Henry; Sagulo, *Ideologia imperiale e analisi politica in Benzone*, p. 134 & n. 165.

[36] Ibid., 346: "Et quoniam approbavi promotionem istius Alexandri, quem in cathedra beati Petri statuerunt Normanni—inde inimicatur michi tota curia domini mei regis, inde appellor Iudas et desertor et infidelis, et nisi ista correxero, tamquam leprosus elongabor ab eis."

with her whole body trembling, advised him to do what he thought was good for this cause, and promised never to reveal his sadness, and to help where she could. Taking three or four breaths, Anno committed himself to her and to God, and asked her to speak to no one about what he was about to say.[37]

What he said was that he wanted to bring Alexander to the royal court, and that he would swear to him that he would bear him no injury. If friendship between Alexander and the king should endure, Alexander should remain in Cologne and rule over the whole archbishopric, and that he would function as his chaplain. A jubilant Anno praised Beatrice when she agreed to his plan.[38]

Benzo reported that on the second day of the synod Anno was unwilling to sit with Alexander because he found all of his blather to be tedious. On the third day the Parmensian army appeared in Mantua, ready to follow the orders of *Anno*, who had permitted them to remain outside of the city. No other writer makes the astonishing connection between Anno and the forces of Parma, which branched out throughout the piazzas of the city, spreading fear and horror by screaming out taunts and threats, and blowing from their horns. Hearing all of this, Benzo said that Alexander refused to come to the synod, and that Beatrice was so frightened that she fell on her bed as if dead. Anno ran to her side, and when he saw her he fell on the ground also as if he were dead. The whole city was in turmoil, and fortunes changed as the men of Parma attacked.[39]

After an hour Anno gathered himself together, and in a tearful voice, told the people to get out. He pleaded with Beatrice to open her eyes, and to save them. When she revived, with night falling, she commanded all but a few women to go to their quarters, while men and animals ate and slept a little together. After she had slept for about an hour she called Anno and told him that if you carry out what you told

---

[37] Ibid., 346–348.

[38] Ibid., 348: "O domina, deo et tibi committo. Vide, ne me interficias. Vide, ne hoc alicui dicas: Volo istum Alexandrum ducere ad curiam et iurabo illi, quod nullam pacietur iniuriam; et si de pacto amiciciae inter istum et regem fuerit fortasse aliquod intervallum, morabitur Coloniae et imperabit super totum archiepiscopatum, me autem habebit sicut capellanum."

[39] Ibid., ch. 28, pp. 348–350; 348: "Tercii vero diei diluculo adest Parmensis exercitus maxima multitudo promptissima perficere iussionem Coloniensis Agrippae, discurrens per plateas Mantuanae urbis;"

me—presumably his plan to make Alexander archbishop of Cologne—
you will have killed me, you, and the king.[40]

We would be branded with the name and deeds of Judas, and be
judged as the sons of perdition, she said. This is not your right, but that
of the emperor, and it should be done in a synod with bishops, who
could examine the case with witnesses. She said that it is better to avoid
the anger of the king than to be absorbed into the abyss of infamy. She
advocated that he choose the lesser of two evils to avoid bloodshed,
and pointed out that if Herod had followed that maxim, he would not
have been guilty of homicide. Act not through guilt, she warned, lest
other men of God be seen by the people as betrayers.[41]

Anno followed the advice of the [new] Eve, Benzo lamented, leaving
everything and returning to the royal court with his head shaved.
When he learned how indignant the king and the court were towards
him for the injury that he had caused to all, like a demon he began to
conspire against him who was anointed by the Lord [Cadalus], a pur-
suit that persists until this day, Benzo declared.[42]

Alexander returned to the Lateran, glorying in the fact that he had
won in accordance with the law.[43] Everyone came to him and formed
alliances, while Benzo alone tried to convince people of their false
thinking, and to lead them to the right belief. He wrote a series of
poems to them individually and collectively, urging them to maintain
their fidelity to the emperor, Henry.[44] Lampert, a fierce opponent of
Cadalus, said that while Alexander attained the favor of princes,
Cadalus continued to think of himself as pope, and to celebrate masses,
perform ordinations and issue decrees until the end.[45]

---

[40] Ibid., 350: "'O domine, si hoc vis perficere, quod michi dixisti, me et te et regem occidisti."

[41] Ibid., 352: "'Age ergo, o pater, ne tua culpa ceteri sacerdotes per popularia conventicula vocitentur traditores.'"

[42] Ibid.: "Quod ut cognovit rex eiusque curia, indignanatur sibi pro communi
omnium iniuria. Annas autem habens similitudinem Apopompei cepit conspirare
adversus christum domini. Quod malum adhuc perdurat;"

[43] Ibid.

[44] Ibid., 352–354.

[45] Lampert, *Annales*, pp. 91–92; 1064; "Anshelmus tamen, qui et Alexander, et vir-
tute militum et favore principum sedem optinuit. Alter vero, etsi per contumeliam
repulsus, tamen quo advixit ab iure suo non cedebat; huic semper derogans, hunc
adulterum ecclesiae Dei, hunc pseudoapostolum appellans; missas quoque seorsum
celebrans, ordinationes facere et sua per aecclesias decreta et epistolas more sedis
apostolicae destinare non desistebat. Verum nullus attendebat, criminanatibus universis, quod in ultionem privatae contumeliae sedem quoque apostolicam homicidio
maculasset."

*Analysis of Mantua*

Benzo's melodramatic account of the council of Mantua could hardly differ more from Wenzel's sober report.[46] Unquestionably Wenzel's description is accurate as far as it goes, but even though Benzo was not an eyewitness to the personal encounters between Anno and Beatrice, he could nevertheless have heard rumors. He also could have been creating a fantasy to explain the motivations of his two enemies. He indicates that Anno and Beatrice enjoyed a close rapport, but that while Anno suffered from guilt for his betrayal of both Henry III and Henry IV, Beatrice as the Eve figure urged him to rationalize his rejection Cadalus.

Even though many scholars follow Wilhelm Giesebrecht in viewing Mantua as a confrontation between *regnum* and *sacerdotium*, almost everyone at the council was on the same side.[47] Henry IV had no viable representative since Anno, torn though he was, sided with Alexander, and Cadalus was not a participant. Anno's proclivities were to support the reformers as opposed to his rivals at the German court, especially Archbishop Adalbert of Bremen, who may already have replaced him in the king's favor.

Godfrey was not present at the council, but it was held on the borderline of lands that he and Beatrice controlled. He may have been somewhat of an embarrassment to the reformers, for contemporaries describe him as rude, brutal and destructive, and his chaplains defended simony and clerical marriage. He probably had his own reservations about Hildebrand, who had thrown the papacy into the hands of the Normans, whom he detested.[48] This alliance appeared to threaten Godfrey's predominant position in Central Italy, but his energetic defense of Alexander demonstrated that he was still needed by the reformers.

The summoning of the council exposed basic disagreements between Hildebrand, who was satisfied that the Council of Augsburg had settled the legality of Alexander's election, and Petrus Damiani, who still harbored reservations. Petrus could have suggested calling a Church council at the Lateran to resolve the complaints, but he took

---

[46] Sagulo, *Ideologia imperiale e analisi politica in Benzone*, pp.136–140 for an analysis.
[47] Jenal, *Anno II.*, p. 273.
[48] Baix, "Cadalus," pp. 74–75.

the more contentious route of contacting Anno as the head of the regency, tacitly acknowledging the imperial right to intervene in papal schisms.

As Petrus most probably foresaw, Anno allowed Alexander to be the head of the council, but even though Alexander had received a qualified endorsement at Augsburg, the justification for his presidency of the council was weak. It was assumed that both candidates had been consecrated, but Alexander had been enthroned, and presumably Cadalus had not. Benzo mentions that a cathedra had been set at the doors of St. Peter's, but even if his report is accurate, it would not comprise an enthronement, and Cadalus, always spoke of himself as an *electus*. It remains a mystery why with many opportunities to be enthroned in St. Peter's he insisted on the ceremony's taking place in S. Pietro in Vincoli, where Alexander had been enthroned under very dubious circumstances.

The purification oath that Alexander swore at Mantua had precedents, but it presumed that Alexander was pope, and was hardly a validation of his election. Although the council was dedicated to determining the legality of the elections, the papal electoral decree of 1059 played virtually no role, and Alexander could fluff off the emperor's rights. The Council of Mantua encapsulated the new balance of power.[49]

---

[49] Krause, "Das Papstwahldecret von 1059," p. 158.

CHAPTER FOURTEEN

INSTABILITY FOLLOWING MANTUA

*Adalbert of Bremen and Anno*

It might seem as though the Council of Mantua would have ended the schism, and that Cadalus would have faded away into obscurity. Not quite. Cadalus retreated to Parma, but he was still a significant symbol to those like Archbishop Adalbert of Bremen, who supported him as the candidate of the regency.[1] It was said that seizing the opportunity of Anno's absence at Mantua, Adalbert replaced him as the most powerful man at court. Since June 27, 1064, Henry had named him his *patronus* and *fidelis*, and Anno as his *magister*.

Adalbert was not just an ordinary archbishop, but the archbishop of the whole North, a province that Leo IX had created to preclude the Danish king's creation of an archbishopric. Adalbert had grandiose ambitions of establishing a northern Patriarchate, and even though he did not obtain approval from Rome, he exercised the position without the title.[2] As we have seen, Adam of Bremen, regarded as a good reporter, spoke of the rivalry between the two ambitious archbishops, and lauded Adalbert while calling attention to Anno's failings.[3] He emphasized Adalbert's loyalty to the king, and his inclination toward mercy, while noting Anno's corruption in promoting his friends and family.[4]

While Anno, Henry's kidnapper and guardian, would be brushed aside even before Henry received his majority, Benzo was in his good graces. Probably his reaction to Mantua and his determination to continue the fight for Cadalus inspired Benzo to write his acerbic account

---

[1] Jenal, *Anno II.*, pp. 309–310; Bayer, *Spaltung der Christenheit*, pp. 130–131; D. Lück, "Die Kölner Erzbishchöfe Hermann II. und Anno II. als Erzkanzler der Römischen Kirche," *Archiv für Diplomatik* 16 (1970), 1–50, 21–25.

[2] Cartellieri, *Der Aufsteig des Papsttums*, p. 61.

[3] See ch. 12, pp. 176–177.

[4] Adam of Bremen, *Gesta Hammaburgensis ecclesiae pontificum*, MGH SRG 2, 34:177; "Coloniensis enim, quem avaritiae notabant, omnia, quae [vel] domi vel in curia potuit corrodere, in ornamentum suae posuit ecclesiae." See n. 41, ch. 12 above.

*Ad Heinricum*, and to satirize Anno amongst others whom he considered to be villains.

Benzo carried on negotiations at the king's court, especially with Adalbert, whom he had known since 1055, and the *pataria* stepped back, for the king's expedition to Rome had already been announced. Whether Henry's intention was to be crowned by Alexander, as Alexander stated during the council of Mantua, was not made explicit, but Cadalus still entertained the hope that he would be recognized as pope.

For Anno this situation carried great political consequences, for he held the office of archchancellor of the Roman Church. In the first years of his reign Alexander only sporadically referred to Anno by this title, but after Anno's nephew, Burchard of Halberstadt had come to Italy following the Council of Augsburg, and had recognized Alexander as the lawful pope, Anno again appeared as archchancellor in Alexander's documents.[5] This honorific title was a great advantage in his competition with Trier for ecclesiastical primacy in Lotharingia. Since the papacy was the principal patron of the church of Cologne, Anno had a motive for avoiding controversy between the papacy and the imperial church. It is speculated that this concern more than a commitment to the ideals of the reform governed his conduct.

When Henry received his majority the year following Mantua, he was able to impose his own will, and however faintly, Cadalus' star flickered yet again. Although he made no attempt to take over the papacy in Rome, in Parma he still signed documents, dispatched decrees and privileges as the elected pope, and performed mass with papal pomp. Petrus Damiani and other supporters of the reform still did not feel that the church was stable, and that until the emperor came to Rome and was crowned by Alexander, they feared a bifurcation between *regnum* and *sacerdotium*. Petrus urged that like his illustrious father, Henry should fight for the church.

## Quedlinburg

Early in 1065 Benzo met Henry at Quedlinburg in Saxony, where Adalbert and others loyal to the king were present.[6] This meeting took

---

[5] Zimmermann, *Papstabsetzungen*, p. 239; Meyer von Knonau, *Jahrbücher* 1:397–399.

[6] Meyer von Knonau, *Jahrbücher* 1:396–400.

place prior to the ceremony marking Henry's majority, and may indicate that Adalbert was already Henry's key advisor before that time. Benzo said that when he arrived he told Henry that he was the balance in the causes of St. Peter, but that the king, showing concern for his fatigue from the trip, recommended that he spend eight days resting [before conveying information from Rome]. Thereafter he would be informed where an audience revealing his mercy would be held.[7]

After the eight day hiatus had elapsed, the king asked Benzo to speak about the situation in Rome. Like Alexander and Petrus Damiani, Benzo wanted Henry to continue on the path of his great predecessors, and not to hesitate in coming to Italy. The reasons, however, differed. Alexander and Petrus wanted Alexander to crown Henry, while Benzo urged him to come for the sake of the Italians, the Romans, and at the request of the emperor of Constantinople.

Standing before the princes as though he were speaking through the mouth of the apostle Peter, Benzo told the young king not to fear, for he was, is, and would be with him. He affirmed that he sought victory for him daily in his prayers, and that Rome defended his heredity by counsel and by arms. Turning to the South, he declared that Apulia and Calabria awaited him with open gates in order that he might punish those who range over the Roman countryside like wild beasts of burden.[8] These two kingdoms will replenish your treasury, he affirmed, but first Badaculus (Godfrey) and Prandellus (Hildebrand), who are the cause of the evil, must be eradicated, and thereafter the Normans, sons of filth.[9]

He told the senior Germans that their arrival would make the beetles flee, because heaven and earth conspire against them. Godfrey was a problem, he acknowledged, but concerning you, Rome has no bad feelings.[10] But he said that there was one thing that he feared. He feared the whispering of Prandellus (Hildebrand) in his frequent clandestine legations, and he warned them against Anno, noting that there is no

---

[7] *Ad Heinricum*, 3.12, pp. 302–306; ch. 13, pp. 306–308; 308: Henry responds: "'Mi frater, quia fatigatus es ex itinere, volo te per hos octo dies in requie consistere. Postea dabitur tibi locus audientae ante conspectum nostrae clementiae.'"

[8] Ibid., 3.14, pp. 308–314.

[9] Ibid., 3.15, pp. 314–316: "Praeterea ex his duabus procinciis Apuliae scilicet atque Calabriae replentur condicionaliter imperatorum kamereae....hec duo regna ministrant vobis. Sed prius eradicentur Badaculus et Prandellus, qui sunt causa malicie, deinde Normanni, filii spurciciae."

[10] Ibid., 316.

more effective evil than an enemy in your own house.[11] He said that
Rome prayed that they would hold firm in their hearts. He complimented Adalbert as a force for good, describing him as the highest
column of the empire firmly fixed in the world.[12]

Responding to Benzo's description in Rome, where daily the Romans
had to fight for you (the Germans) against the Normans, the king
asked Adalbert, from whom he hid nothing, to reply. Adalbert said
that the Roman legation was not to be treated lightly, but should be
combined into one with bishops and dukes, and that along with the
royal court, the king wants you—Benzo—to scrutinize the dark depth
of this legation. For you brother [Benzo], are the legate of my lord, sent
to Rome for the salvation of the republic and for destroying the heresy
of Arius and Manicheus [Alexander and Hildebrand]. He complimented Benzo for knowing both the inside and the outside, and advocated that his counsel be followed. Appreciating that Benzo understood
both the Greeks and the Romans, Adalbert said that it was not necessary to seek further advice regarding Apulia and Calabria.[13]

After Benzo and the prelates responded, the session ended with a
plea to resist the two-headed antichrist [Alexander and Hildebrand].[14]
When he returned to Rome, Benzo was delegated to announce to
Cadalus and various dignitaries that within a short time the king would
be arriving with power and in majesty.[15] Loaded down with gifts from
the king, he departed from the royal court.[16]

Seeing himself as a faithful interpreter between the king and the
Roman people, Benzo believed that God led him back to the Vatican.[17]
There he conveyed the ringing words from the king and the princes to
the Romans that they were created as the head of all peoples because of

---

[11] Ibid.: "De solo uno dubitat, qui clamdestinis legationibus cum Prandello sepis-
sime musitat. Exquirite inter vos, utrum *corde et corde loquatur* super hac re Annas
Agripinus, et cavete, quoniam nulla *pestis es efficatior ad nocendum quam familiaris
inimicus.*"

[12] Ibid., 3.16, p. 316: "Imperii summa defixus in orbe columpna,"

[13] Ibid., 3.18, p. 320: " 'Romana legatio non est cursim pertractanda, sed morose
atque diutius coadunatis in unum episcopis et ducibus. Qua propter imperat dominus
noster rex, ut perscruteris nobiscum huius legationis tenebrosam habyssum....' "

[14] Ibid., 322: "Prestante domino nostro Iesu Christo, cui placet, ut resistamus
bicipiti antichristo."

[15] Ibid., 3.19, p. 324: "...rogans, [Adalbert] ut affirmarem cunctis in ea quae Christus
est, veritate, quoniam citissime *videbunt regem venientem cum potestate magna et
majestate et omnes tribus terrae* cum eo. Tunc cantabimus simul *Gloria in excelsis deo.*"

[16] Ibid., 3.21, p. 328.

[17] Ibid., 328–330.

their bravery and loyalty to the emperors, and concluded with an encomium to the emperor.[18] His declaration that when the king arrived, Apulia and Calabria would soon be freed, was greeted with great joy throughout Italy, and messengers conveyed the welcome news to Cadalus.

### Ceremony of Henry's Coming of Age

At the age of fifteen a German king reached his maturity and took over the rule of the Empire. The festivities celebrating Henry's coming of age began on Easter Sunday 1065 at Worms with a sermon preached by Adalbert during mass. On March 29 two days later the pageantry began. Since Archbishop Siegfried of Mainz was on a pilgrimage to Jerusalem, Archbishop Eberhard of Trier gave the blessing, while Adlabert girded Henry with the sword, and Godfrey acted as shield bearer.[19] This role signified Godfrey's position as chief vassal of the realm, an honor that he probably assumed he had received through Anno. The two were allies, but by this time Anno had been superseded by Adalbert.

Agnes was present at the ceremony, and allegedly had to muster whatever maternal influence she possessed to keep her son from using his sword against Anno. Lampert indicated that there was no mistaking the object of Henry's ire: Henry "would immediately have made his first trial of the arms which he had received against the archbishop of Cologne and would have hastened to pursue him with fire and sword, had not the empress calmed the storm by her timely counsel. He hated [Anno] in particular because some years before, when the latter wished to seize from the empress the right and the power to govern, he had placed the king himself in the greatest danger."[20]

---

[18] Ibid., ch. 23, p. 330: "Roma, o Romani, ideo super omnes gentes preposuit vos creator generis humani, quia non timuistis subire periculum pro patriis honoribus atque inflexibili fide domi militieque semper adhesistis imperatoribus." p. 334: "Hiis auditis tollitur clamor in coelum 'Vivat rex in aeternum et de rege factus imperator regnet in sempiternum.'"

[19] *Annales Weissemburgenses*, Lampert, *Annales*, p. 53: "Heinricus quartus in tertia feria paschae gladium cinxit Wormaciae, Heberardo archiepiscopo Treverensi benedicente." Lampert emphasizes that the sword symbolized the use of force, p. 93: "Ibi per concessionem eiusdem archiepiscopi primum se rex arma bellica succinxit." Meyer von Knonau, *Jahrbücher* 1:400–401, n. 11 for sources.

[20] Lampert, *Annales* 1065, p. 93: "...statimque primam susceptae armaturae experientiam in archispiscopum Coloniensem dedisset et ad persequendum eum ferro et

Lampert, who supported Anno and reviled Adalbert, reported that "when Henry had reached maturity, he abandoned [Anno] and lived according to his own will...Anno renounced the court to the extent of going into retirement. Archbishop Adalbert of Breman replaced him in his office, although not in his diligence."[21]

Adam of Bremen tells a different story. He says that there was great fear that with the weak regency of Agnes after the death of Henry III, the empire could fall apart. Both Adalbert and Anno were named consuls, and henceforth decisions depended upon their advice. He said that they both seemed to desire peace, but that with a heart filled by hate, one of them [Anno] fought instead. Adalbert had the more just cause, Adam said, since he was more prone to mercy, and vowed to serve the king until death. Filled with innate brutality, Anno proved himself to be unfaithful to the king, and was involved in all of the conspiracies of the time.[22]

In early 1065 about the same time that Adalbert had authorized Benzo in the name of the king to go to Rome to deal with Alexander and with Hildebrand, Alexander sent Cardinal Mainhard of Silva Candida to the king to arrange for his coronation in Rome just as he had promised at Mantua. Mainhard arrived at Eastertide during the assembly of princes at Worms to celebrate Henry's coming of age, and in spite of Alexander's alliance with the Normans, Henry accepted the invitation.[23] The expedition was scheduled for the forthcoming May, a critical period for the Empire, for Henry was just beginning to establish himself as ruler, and what appear to have been conflicting policies

---

igni preceps abisset, nisi res turbatas imperatrix tempestivo valde, consilio composuisset." *Annales Camadulenses*, p. 293: 1065, "Agnes olim imperatrix, postea Romae sanctimonialis in Germaniam hoc anno profecta fuerat, ut auctoritate sua modum imponeret ejus regni turbis & juniorem adhuc Henricum regem filium suus plura molientem compesceret, qui indignatus arma praesertim hoc anno moverat contra Annonem [294] archiepiscopum Coloniensem." Robinson, *Henry IV*, p. 52; Jäschke, *Notwendige Gefährtinnen*, p. 132.

[21] Lampert, *Libellus de institutione Herveldensis ecclesiae, Lamperti Opera* II, p. 353: "Heinricus, cum ad maturam venisset aetatem, relicto episcopo, secundum propriam vixit voluntatem...." Robinson, *Henry IV*, p. 52; Robinson's translation.

[22] Adam of Bremen, *Gesta Hammaburgensis ecclesiae pontificum*, MGH SRG 2:176–177: "...inclinatis Adalbertus et Anno archieipscopi consules declarati sunt, et in eorum consilio deinceps summa rerum pendebat. Sed cum ambo essent viri prudentes et strennui in procuratione rei publicae, tamen alter alterum felicitate aut industria sua longe precurrisse videtur." See ns. 39–41, ch. 12 above; Meyer von Knonau, *Jahrbücher*, 1:406.

[23] JL 4544; *Vita Anselmi Lucensis*, MGH SS 12:14; Jenal, *Anno II.*, p. 282; Robinson, *Henry IV*, p. 54; Hüls, *Kardinäle*, p. 135 & n. 18.

may be explained by that transition. On the one hand he seemed to be supporting Benzo's attempt to instate Cadalus as Honorius II, and on the other to be acceding to Alexander's wish to crown him as emperor in Rome.

## Anno's Letters

However confident Alexander may have appeared, Anno's subsequent letters reveal his underlying insecurity, and, indeed, his own, for he perceived what had happened to him at Mantua as a disaster. In a letter to Alexander on May 15, 1065, he defended himself against the rumors that he was disloyal, and that while Alexander still reigned, he wished to occupy the apostolic see.[24] Anno speculated that Alexander would suffer more than he if he lent credence to these lies, and he submitted his record to demonstrate how faithful he had been. Anno asked Alexander how he could imagine that after all that he had done that he would ever oppose those very things, and he asked rhetorically if he appeared to be a Judas.[25] He warned Alexander not to be persuaded of anything of the sort, and he stated that he wished to help him with Roman matters.

He said that he had been involved in the consultations leading to the consensus that he and Godfrey would lead an army to Rome to help the papacy.[26] He added that he did not know what had happened to the remains of the army that was prepared to set out for Italy, but that it had been disbanded without his having been consulted.[27] Five days before they were to depart a messenger of the king arrived in great haste from Augsburg stating that the expedition had been postponed

---

[24] Giesebrecht, *Geschichte der deutschen Kaiserzeit* 3:1257–1258 at 1257; doc. 4, summer 1065: "Inter alia tam sancte Dei ecclesie quam imperii titubantis pericula ad exaggerationem doloris mei me apud vos audio insimilari, quasi vivente atque sedente Romano pontifice sacram hanc sedem apostolicam ego affectaverim."

[25] Ibid.: "Ne dicam per memetipsum, etiam si per alium aliquem econtra niti voluissem, nonne quovis Iuda infelicior apparerem? Tantum enim abest, ut etiam si id fieri potuisset, Rome manere cogitem, ut vel ad horam oratum venire durum estimem. "Nemo...vestre paternitati persuadeat de me quicquam huiusmodi." Meyer von Knonau, *Jahrbücher* 1:424.

[26] Ibid.: "Definitum erat ad presens exercitum in Italiam ducere: iis ego interfui consiliis."

[27] Ibid.,: "Qualiter remanserit [exercitus], nec plane scio nec nescio; unum scio, quia quod dissipatum est, me factum est inconsulto." Meyer von Knonau, *Jahrbücher* 1:427, n. 64.

until the fall.[28] He described in great detail the plans that he and
Godfrey had worked out to take their army to Italy through France and
Burgundy because the valley to Trento was too narrow to secure the
care for men and animals. They planned to unite with the royal army
in Verona.

Anno admitted that he was aware that the papacy would interpret
this series of events negatively, but he swore that he was doing nothing
other than what he had expressed openly to Alexander.[29] In addition to
his loyalty to Alexander, he professed loyalty to the king, and said that
when the king left for Italy, he and Godfrey would accompany him.[30]
He also urged Alexander to remain in the royal way through all of the
tribulations.[31]

While acknowledging the criticism leveled at Alexander, he
reminded him that he had been able to return to his see two or three
times on the word of the king, supported by the most important ecclesiastical and lay figures. Obviously trying to bolster Alexander's confidence, he promised that as long as he and the duke [Godfrey] lived,
they would be there for him.[32] In the end he said that even if we do not
come to Italy, we shall provide for both *sacerdotium* and *imperium*, and
assure that neither of them be treated with contempt or violated by
those who think that they have them in their hands, but to whom they
do not pertain.[33]

In sum, Anno described the circumstances at the German court and
the postponement of the expedition to Italy. He declared his loyalty to

---

[28] Ibid.: "Et ecce, cum instaret profiscendi articulus, cum magna festinatione de
Augusta domni nostri regis, ad nos venit nuntius ante nostrum exitum die quinta
prius. Is nobis indicavit ex parte omni nostri regis, ipsum, quod institutum erat, in
autumnum transtulisse proximum."

[29] Ibid.: "Et fortassis, ut de papatu, male nobis haec omnia interpretature inimicus.
At ego vobis per Deum iuro, nihil aliud nos molitos in occulto, quam quod fecimus in
publico."

[30] Ibid., 1258: "...quandocunque ierit, ut etiam veniamus cum illo, insuper ei gratias
agentes ad beneficium singulare, scilicet pro gratis indulta nobis requie, invitis et coac-
tis, ut in hostem irent, aliis; erimusque tanto studiosiores in eius servitio, quanto
remissius apud nos factum est ex eius gratuito beneficio." Jenal, *Anno II.*, pp.
284–285.

[31] Ibid.: "Ut salvis reverentia et gratia vestra commoneri vos liceat, inter has turbationes et collisions rerum omnium validissimas viam vos tenere oportet regiam."

[32] Ibid.: "Quapropter nulla remaneat in animo vobis hesitatio, quonaim, quoad vix-
erimus, ego et dux nullatenus vobis deerimus."

[33] Ibid.: "Et etiam, si nulla nobis esset causa eundi in Italiam, certe sola hec nos ire
compelleret, ut adiuvante Domino et sacerdotio provideamus et imperio, ne vel hoc
vel illud ab illis conculcetur aut violetur hominibus, qui nunc ea sese putant habere in
manibus et revera ad quos minime pertinet, et talibus."

the king and to Alexander, and pledged to protect both *imperium* and *sacerdotium*. He rejected the startling rumor that he had strived after the papacy, a suspicion that might have arisen if he had a secret plan that Alexander would replace him as archbishop of Cologne. Even though according to the plan he would serve as Alexander's chaplain, some could have speculated that he had ambitions to replace Alexander.

The situation changed dramatically with Adalbert's downfall in January 1066. His influence at court had been so great that it had elicited strong opposition, and he was driven from the court. His flight from Tribur was humiliating, and the king had to protect him from a possible revenge attack. Anno and Archbishop Siegfried of Mainz led the opposition, and behind them were Archbishop Gebhard of Salzburg, and dukes Otto of Bavaria, Rudolf of Swabia, Berthold of Carinthia and Godfrey. Even though Anno's influence never returned to its former level, it nevertheless increased at court.

The only source for Tribur is a letter that Anno wrote to Alexander early in 1066.[34] In his letter he states that the king and some of his princes called a council [at Tribur] in which he was present along with the archbishops of Mainz and Salzburg, and some bishops and dukes including Otto of Bavaria. He said that he offered to give advice to the king, first and foremost recommending that he cease doing those things that had vexed the Apostolic See. He counseled the king to make suitable satisfaction for the many injuries that had been inflicted, and to exhibit due honor to the pope.[35] He said that the king promised that he would follow these recommendations, but that there was the question of who would administer them. The king listened to the arguments that he, Anno, be appointed archchancellor for Italy, but Anno said that the king unconditionally refused because he recalled with horror what had happened to him at Mantua.[36]

Sensing Anno's reaction, his friends, Dukes Rudolph and Berthold, secretly took him aside and persuaded him to accept a legation to Italy even though they understood that if all did not go well, the blame

---

[34] Ibid., 1258–1259, doc. 5, early 1066; Jenal, *Anno II.*, pp. 307–308; Robinson, *Henry IV*, pp. 58–61.

[35] Ibid., 1259: "hoc videlicet primum et maximum, ut ipse cessaret ab ea, qui diu iam sedem apostolicam vexavit, calumnia; oportere quoque, ut post multas iniurias cum satisfactione dignum exhiberet honorem summo pontifici."

[36] Ibid.: "At ego memor omnium, quae mihi Mantuam eunti ante et retro in via illa, domi quoque parata fuerant, negotium, quod offerebatur, exhorrui, idque retratione refutavi."

would fall on him rather than on the king.[37] After listening to their counsel Anno returned to the conference, pledging that he would go when he could do so both on account of the peace of the church and the honor of the whole empire.[38] When the king and those around him heard this, Anno said that they were silent and did not speak about it later.[39] The implication was that he would not be nominated again.[40] Alexander saw the danger that Anno was under, but he had his own reservations that were intensified by the delayed expedition to Rome.

There was no break between Alexander and the monarchy, but along with Hildebrand, Alexander seems to have lost his enthusiasm for an imperial coronation. He was now more secure, and did not want to be beholden to Henry, still under the influence of Adalbert, much less to Anno and Godfrey.[41] As for Henry, he showed his ambivalence about coming to Rome to be crowned by Alexander, and appeared to want to uphold the election of Cadalus at Basel.

The postponement of Henry's expedition to Italy was a blow to the Italians, who had prepared for his arrival. Desiderius had anticipated that the king would visit Montecassino, and had traveled to Amalfi to buy silk cloths for gifts for the king in return for what he hoped would be the king's defense of his monastery.[42] But the most profound effect was on Alexander, ambivalent though he may have been. Since the waning threat of Cadalus still had not been scotched, the coronation would incontrovertibly have committed the king to Alexander.[43]

*Letter of Petrus Damiani to Henry*

Petrus Damiani also testifies to the shaky position of the papacy and the Church itself after the Council of Mantua and Henry's coming of age, not by seeing the king as the cause, but as the potential savior.

---

[37] Ibid.: "Intellexerant enim ipsi, certum fuisse regem, me, ut in Italiam irem, sibi contradicturum, talique occasione, si res Italicae remanerent infecte, omne pondus et culpam eum in me transferre."

[38] Ibid.: "Igitur ego eorum audiens consilium, reversus ad conventum constanter spopondi, me iturum, cum propter aecclesiae pacem tum propter imperii tocius honorem."

[39] Ibid.: Eo audito rex et omnes, qui cum eo aderant, siluerunt, nec unquam michi postea inde verbum fecerunt."

[40] Jenal, *Anno II*, pp. 307–308.

[41] Giesebrecht, *Geschichte der deutschen Kaiserzeit* 3:118–120.

[42] Meyer von Knonau, *Jahrbücher* 1:430, & n. 69.

[43] Robinson, *Henry IV*, p. 54.

Petrus saw the two powers as bound together in mutually supportive synchrony. In a letter written to Henry between 1065 and 1066 he responded to Alexander's worsening position with a pressing appeal to the young king.[44] He reminded Henry that he must give an account to the Creator, and that a situation so serious had arisen that it exceeded almost every evil that the world had ever seen.

Painting the circumstances in apocalyptic terms, he asserted that the Apostolic See was torn asunder by the prince of heretics of the church of Parma, that the Christian religion was in a state of disarray, that the work of the apostles was overturned, and that the splendor of the universal Church was eclipsed by the lusting darkness of one schismatic. Petrus challenged Henry as the defender of the church not to make excuses, but to do something about it. He asked the king as one who can hardly wait to go to war over an earthly city, if he was not aroused to defend the liberty of the universal Church.[45]

He informed Henry that an ugly rumor was being spread around that certain of his counselors, specifically some of the administrators at his court [Adalbert of Bremen?], were overjoyed at the persecution of the Church of Rome.[46] Petrus charged that while supporting and flattering both sides, they first assert with fawning adulation that they are loyal to the venerable pope, and then assure the firstborn of Satan of the pleasure of imaginary success. Petrus exclaimed that it was shocking that this should be true of some of the holy men in your service, and admonished Henry that he must beware lest it be said that in your time the Church was divided. "Be careful, I repeat, O king, lest while allowing the *sacerdotium* to be divided, your empire too, which God forbid, should be divided."[47]

Petrus exonerated Henry, but warned that unless his subjects corrected their ways that after his reign his kingdom could be given to foreigners. Again, Petrus pleaded with Henry to turn a deaf ear to the

---

[44] Petrus Damiani, *Briefe*, nr. 120, 1065–1066, 3:384–392; tr. Blum, 5:387–396.

[45] Ibid., 385: "Apostolica nimirum sedes per heresiarcham Parmensis aecclesiae scinditur, religio christiana confunditur, apostolorum labor evertitur, et universalis splendor aecclesiae per tenebrosam unius scismatici hominis concupiscenciam obscuratur. Quid ad haec dices, qui aecclesiasticae defensionis officio fungeris, qui in paterni vel aviti sceptri iura succedis? An plenae forte robur aetatis adhuc tibi deesse conquereris?" p. 388: "Tu quaeso, gloriose rex, a pravis consiliariis tamquam a venenatis serpencium sibilis aures optura, in virile te robur per ardorem spiritus excita. Collapsae matri tuae Romanae aecclesiae manum porrige..."

[46] Ibid., 386; tr. Blum, 5:389.

[47] Ibid., 386–387; tr. Blum, 5:390.

advice of his wicked counselors, and to reach out his hand to his fallen
mother, the Roman Church. He emphasized that the royal and the sacerdotal dignities are joined to one another in Christ by a unique mystery, and that they are united in the Christian people by a kind of
mutual agreement. Since the *sacerdotium* is protected by the defensive
capability of the Empire, and the royal power is supported by the holiness of the priestly office, each needs the other. "The king wears a
sword, that so armed he may confront the enemies of the Church; the
priest engages in watchful prayer, that he may appease God for the
benefit of the king and his people."[48]

Citing Paul on the authority of the king, Petrus states: "He is God's
agent working for your good, but if you are doing wrong, have fear; it
is not for nothing that he has the power of the sword. For he is God's
agent, an avenger punishing the offender in his anger."[49] And so, Petrus
asks Henry, if you are God's agent, why do you not defend God's
Church? Let that ancient dragon, Cadalus, take note: "Let this dis-
turber of the Church, this destroyer of apostolic discipline, this enemy
of man's salvation understand."[50]

Reaching the acme of his tirade against Cadalus, Petrus called him:
"the son of perdition, who rises in his pride against every god, so called,
every object of men's worship, the whirlpool of lust, the shipwreck of
chastity, the disgrace of Christianity, the ignominy of bishops, the
progeny of vipers, the stench of the world, the filth of the ages, the
shame of the universe." And since "the fool says in his heart: there is
not God," let him come to learn of the devotion to the Christian faith
that resides in the king's heart as he valiantly fights on the side of the
army of God.[51]

In conclusion Petrus asks Henry to think of him as a man who faithfully counsels you, not as one who impudently reproaches you. "But if,
like another Constantine in the case of Arius, you quickly destroy
Cadalus and strive to restore peace to the Church for which Christ
died, may God shortly cause you to progress from kingship to the sub-
limity of empire, and gain a singular victory over all your enemies.
But if you should still compromise, if you should refuse to abolish the
scandal endangering the world, even though you can...I hold my

---

[48]  Ibid., 389; tr. Blum, 5:392.
[49]  Ibid.; tr. Blum, 5: 393.
[50]  Ibid., 389–390; tr. Blum, 5:393.
[51]  Ibid., 390; tr. Blum, 5:394.

breath, and leave the consequences to the imagination of my readers. Amen."[52]

It was a barely veiled threat. Either you come to the aid of Alexander, or you will never become emperor. Implicit in Petrus' letter was that Cadalus was still a vital presence, that the position of Alexander was insecure, and that the Church was in a perilous state. In his eyes the king was not a villain, but the person who could restore the right balance between *regnum* and *sacerdotium*.

In sum, after Mantua Alexander's position was still precarious, and even though his tenure became more secure, as long as Henry was at best ambivalent, the threat to his recognition remained. Henry was disinclined to provide that recognition by coming to Rome and being crowned, and there the situation rested.

---

[52] Ibid., 392: "Porro si Kadaloum cito velut alter Constantinus Arrium destruis, et aecclesiae pro qua Christus mortuus est pacem reformare contendis, faciat te Deus in proximo de regno imperiale fastigium scandere, et a cunctis hostibus tuis insignis gloriae titulos reportare." tr. Blum, 5:396.

## CHAPTER FIFTEEN

## AMBIVALENCE AND SELF INTEREST

In 1066 Cadalus acted as pope in Parma and the surrounding area, but was not recognized by the Church. Alexander reigned in Rome, but precariously, since Henry had not solidified his recognition by assenting to an imperial coronation. The king was still angry at Anno for his betrayal at Mantua, and was reluctant to follow his advice to come to Rome to be crowned by Alexander.

Alexander faced one challenge after another even from his erstwhile allies. Godfrey and the Normans always put their own interests first, and Anno was in an anomalous position from the start. Some lesser known figures illustrate a tenuous commitment to either side. Cardinal Hugo Candidus, who claimed to represent the cardinals at the Council of Basel, and Cencius Stephani, who had provided Cadalus with security in the Castel San Angelo, were both active in the election of Hildebrand as Gregory VII. The frequency with which they were courted or rejected, and accordingly shifted from side to side shows how fluid the situation was, and how weak the dedication to ecclesiastical principle.

The most influential reformers also differed among themselves, as is exemplified in the conflict between Bishop Petrus Mezzabarba of Florence and the Vallombrosan monks, where Alexander took one side and Hildebrand the other. Councils repeated the main tenants of the reform, and excommunication was the penalty for non conformance, but the political reality was far more complex.

### Expedition of Godfrey to Rome

After the cosmic menace of Cadalus and his supporters had abated, Alexander faced a local threat from Richard of Capua, his Norman vassal, who had pushed his way through the Campagna to the doorstep of Rome.[1] Since Alexander saw his only viable option as seeking help

---

[1] Althoff, *Heinrich IV*, pp. 69–71; Robinson, *Henry IV*, p. 108.

from the North, the empress, Agnes, was dispatched to the royal court to urge her son to mount an expedition to Italy on behalf of the Holy See. In return he was to receive the imperial crown.[2]

Agnes made the perilous journey during the winter of 1066 with the reluctant blessing of Petrus Damiani, who later in Rome changed his mind, and begged her to return. "I can hardly tell you how distressed I am, as in dreadful suspense I daily await the joy of your return. What a fool I was, and why in my stupidity and lack of wit did I ever agree to your journey?"[3]

He strongly implied that she would be more effective in Rome as a beacon for the reform than she would be at the German court. He clearly feared that she might not return, for he said that he hoped that the regal splendor of the imperial court would cause her disgust, and that only the fisherman's boat would pleasantly satisfy her sense of smell. Along with Petronilla, the legendary daughter of St. Peter, he said that he hoped that she would find her burial place in Rome.[4]

Henry IV was ready to protect the pope, and in February 1067 he went to Augsburg, the traditional staging ground for expeditions to Italy, albeit not so early in the year.[5] Although he received his mother's entreaties with open ears, a month before the princes had forced him to dismiss his closest counselor, Adalbert of Bremen, and he was now surrounded by princes with their own agendas. When he heard the unwelcome news that Hildebrand had called Godfrey to Italy, he told the princes that Godfrey had betrayed him, and canceled the expedition.

According to Bonizo, because of Godfrey's interests in Italy, and having been summoned by Hildebrand, he set off for Italy with Matilda to defend the papacy. There he congregated an army with the help of Matilda and Beatrice. Since he had not informed Henry of his plans, the king vented his displeasure to the princes, postponed his own

---

[2] *Chron. Mont.*, 23, p. 389: "Interea [1066] cum supradictus princeps Richardus victoriis ac prosperitatibus multis elatus subiugata Campania ad Romam iam se viciniam porrexisset ipsiusque iam urbis patriciatum omnibus modis ambiret, Teutonici regis pertinxit ad aures. Qui ut et bona sancti Petri de manibus Normannorum eriperet et imperii coronam de apostolici manu reciperet, magna cum expeditione pervenit Augustam..."

[3] Petrus Damiani, *Briefe*, nr. 144, to Agnes, January 1067, 3:525–527 at 526; tr. Blum, 5:148–149 at 148.

[4] Ibid., 526–527; tr. Blum, 5:148–149.

[5] Robinson, *Henry IV*, p. 108.

expedition to Italy, and headed north. Godfrey, however, succeeded in his objective. Without war, but in a personal encounter he convinced Richard of Capua to concede that the area he occupied was under the authority of the papacy. With that acknowledgement Alexander could resume his friendly relations with the Normans.[6]

The Chronicle of Montecassino presents essentially the same story. It emphasizes that the king was indignant that Godfrey had long preceded him, and reversed himself from Augsburg and his intended expedition. Godfrey collected a large army, and when the Normans heard of it, they were frightened and deserted the Campagna.[7] Berthold reported that the Normans wished to invade Rome, but that they ceased when Godfrey intervened.[8] Alexander had wanted Henry to come to Rome to save the papacy and to receive the imperial crown, but Hildebrand thwarted his wish by urging Godfrey to settle the problem with the Normans.

On July 9, 1067, Hildebrand and Alexander turned south to the Normans. On their return in October they stopped at Melfi and at Capua, where they sealed the modus vivendi with Richard worked out by Godfrey.[9] On October 12 while still in Capua Alexander wrote to Anno about another important matter. In early 1067 Adalbert of Bremen had written Anno a letter dealing with a number of problems about which Anno had consulted him including the monastery of S. Remacli at Malmedy, which Adalbert said that he should return to the abbot of Stablo.[10] Presumably by October Anno still had not

---

[6] Bonizo, *Ad Amicum*, p. 599: "Eodem quoque tempore [1066] Normanni Campaniam invadunt. Quod cernens Deo amabilis Ildebrandus, continuo magnificum ducem Gotefridum in auxilium sancti Petri evocat. Forte enim his diebus prefatus dux venerat Italiam, ducens secum excellentissimam cometissam Matildam, incliti ducis Bonifacii filiam. Is congregans universam exercitus sui multitudinem, cum uxore et nobilissima Matilda Romam veniens, Normannos a Campania absque bello expulit et eam Romanae reddidit dicioni." Althoff, *Heinrich IV*, p. 70 & n. 53; Robinson, *Henry IV*, pp. 107–108; Meyer von Knonau, *Jahrbücher* 1:550 & n. 2.

[7] *Chron. Mont.*, 23, pp. 389–390: "Ibi [Augsburg] prestolans Gotfridum Tuscie ducem ad marchionem, qui regem, quotiens Italiam intrare deberet, cum sua solitus erat preire militia. Sed quoniam Gotfridus idem longe precesserat, rex hoc indigne ferens eandem mox expeditionem remittens in sua reversus est. Dux autem copioso nimis vallatus exercitu Romama accessit…"

[8] Berthold, *Chronicon*, ed. Robinson, p. 206: 1067, "…Nordmanni Romam invadere voluerunt hostiliter, sed a duce Gotifrido eis interminante cessaverunt."

[9] JL, p. 581, synod of Melfi; JL 4635–4636.

[10] JL 4638; Giesebrecht, *Geschichte der deutschen Kaiserzeit*, 3:134–135; nr. 6, 1259–1260; 1260: "Verum quia votis semel cepimus locum, nunc dicendeum esse videtur, quod iam dudum disideraveramus vos petere, quod scilicet causa salutis facti

followed his advice, thus eliciting Alexander's letter indicating his disapproval of Anno's treatment of the monastery. Alexander prohibited Anno from inflicting any further injuries on the monastery, and at the same time authorized its privileges.[11]

The main thrust of Adalbert's letter had been to respond to Anno's complaint that he had not expressed sympathy over the murder of Anno's nephew, Cuno (Conrad). Without any election, Anno had had the king appoint Cuno of Pfullingen, then provost of Cologne, as archbishop of Trier, and had granted him his ring and staff. The citizens—clerics and laymen alike—rebelled, and on June 1, 1066, under the leadership of Count Theodoric at Bitburg (near Trier) they murdered Cuno in a particularly gruesome way. The citizens then elected Udo, the provost of Trier, who lived at the king's court, and enjoyed his special trust.

Adalbert refused to support Anno in his demand for justice, saying that there was wrong on both sides. In 1066 or 1067 Anno wrote to Alexander to ask for his help, and although Archbishop Siegfried of Mainz joined him in demanding that the pope punish the murderers, Alexander did not intercede.[12] Anno was guilty of nepotism in its purest form, and the penalty for his malfeasance was a terrible blow to his authority and self esteem. Since the citizens believed that the king was on the point of going to Rome, they set off with Udo, and knowing the ways of Rome, with a sack of gold.

### Expedition of Anno, Henry of Trent, and Otto of Bavaria to Italy

But the citizens were to be disappointed in Henry, for he had lost any interest in coming to Rome when Godfrey upstaged him by answering Hildebrand's plea to defend the papacy against the Normans. Royal supporters in Italy scathingly accused Godfrey of having acted out of hate for Henry, and it was a sign of the king's irritation that for two years Godfrey had not appeared in his entourage.[13]

---

Malmundariense monasterium suo capiti reformetis, misericorditer postponentes, si qua de abbate illo vobis dicta sunt, que lenitatem vestram merito possint offendere."
[11] JL 4639.
[12] Giesebrecht, *Geschichte der Deutschen Kaiserzeit*, nr. 7, 3:1260: "Poteram enim ab Treverensibus illatas iniurias usque ad publicam vindicasse iusticiam, nisi tuam sententiam prestolaret Dei iudicium."
[13] Benzo, *Ad Heinricum*, pp. 236–238; Althof, *Heinrich IV.*, pp. 70–72; Meyer von Knonau, *Jahrbücher* 1:556–557.

Although Henry himself did not come to Italy, in 1068 the princes convinced him to return to Saxony, and to send three legates in his stead. In the first months of that year he dispatched a delegation consisting of Anno, Duke Otto of Bavaria, and Archbishop Henry of Trent (Italian).[14] While the monarchy and the papacy's disapproval of the affair of S. Remacli, and the appointment of Anno's nephew as archbishop of Trier did not preclude Anno's selection as an envoy, it did affect his reception in Rome.

At Mantua Anno had been the dominant figure, but that was before Henry's coming of age and his assumption of the rule of the Empire. This time Anno was coming not as the head of the regency, but as Henry's legate, a change that may account for his odd itinerary. Possibly carrying out instructions influenced by Adalbert of Bremen, the three emissaries stopped at Ravenna to see Archbishop Henry, the excommunicated supporter of Cadalus, and if that was not insulting enough to Alexander, they met with Cadalus himself.[15] Whatever the intent of their mission, they must have known that these meetings would not garner a warm reception in Rome.

Bad went to worse when Anno discovered that he had been preceded by one of his opponents, Abbot Theoderich of Stablo, who was in Rome to complain about Anno's mistreatment of the monastery of S. Remacli.[16] When Anno finally was admitted to see Alexander at the Easter synod of 1068, he was forced to walk barefoot with Beatrice standing at his side before he could speak with the pope.[17] Abbot

---

[14] *Annales Altahenses*, p. 74: "Mittuntur igitur Anno Coloniensis archiepiscopus, Henricus Tridentinus, Otto dux Baioaricus. Meyer von Knonau, *Jahrbücher* 1:585–591; Jenal, *Anno II.*, pp. 317–328; Robinson, *Henry IV*, pp. 108–109.

[15] Ibid.: "Hi ergo cum Ravennam venissent, civitatis illius pontificis usi sunt confabulatione et convivio, nec etiam devitabant Parmensem episcopum, sese adeuntem alio in loco, quos utrosque Alexander papa ligaverat anathematis vinculo." Gresser, *Konziliengeschichte*, p. 89; Petrus Damiani later asked Alexander II to absolve Henry in order not to destroy the souls of so many innocent people. *Briefe*, nr. 167, 4:237; tr. Blum, 6:234; John Howe, "Did St. Peter Damian Die in 1073? A New Perspective on his Final Days," *Analecta Bollandiana* 128 (2010), 67–86 at 80.

[16] Triumphus S. Remacli, MGH SS 11:448, ch. 22: "sed abbas praeveniens, eisdem quod ante adierat, eandem repetit proclamationem, de qua re sane consultus a domno apostolico."

[17] Ibid.: "pro delicto…nudis pedibus procedit in publicum." *Annales Altahenses*, p. 74: "Ob hanc igitur causam noluit eos videre, cum Romam venissent, videlicet quia excommunicatis, a se communicassent. Sed quia scriptum est: *Corripe sapientem et diliget te*, citius reconciliari meruere humillima satisfactione, tandemque audita eorum legatione post paucos dies dimissis illis, mandat regi, quae voluit." The synod

Theoderich brought complaints against him in the presence of the judges of the Roman Church, and he was found guilty by all of them. Alexander commanded him to return the monastery of S. Remacli.

It was also in this council that Alexander resolved the dispute involving the Archbishop of Trier totally to Anno's disadvantage. Udo and the citizens of Trier had arrived at the council with their sack of money to plead Udo's case, and to receive the pallium. Udo purified himself from the charge of simony with an oath, which Alexander immediately accepted, and granted him the pallium.[18] The Altaich *Annales* emphasize that thereafter Udo was held in great esteem by the pope and the Romans. The whole affair was a rejection of Anno, who was proving to be a liability to both the pope and the emperor.[19]

Otto also was hardly seen as a pillar of virtue. On his way back to Germany he stopped at Piacenza, where he held a court at which Godfrey was present. The Italians rose up against them, insisting that they must desist from their nefarious activities. Otto was suspected of disloyalty to the king, and of tarrying in Italy only in order to win over Godfrey for his dubious plans. Shattering the proceedings, the Italians forced Otto to withdraw. He and Anno were neither able to stabilize the relationship between the monarchy and the papacy, nor to contribute anything to the Italian kingdom.[20]

*Petrus Mezzabarba*

As for Godfrey, late in the summer of 1067 he was in Pisa. Presumably he remained in Tuscany (Tuscia), where a heated quarrel had been raging for some time between Bishop Petrus Mezzabarba of Florence and the monks of Vallombrosa, whose abbot, Johannes Gualberti, happened to be from Florence.[21] Concerned with maintaining public order, Godfrey wanted Mezzabarba to remain in his bishopric in spite of charges of simony that had been raised against him.

---

seemingly took place fifteen days after Easter, which fell on March 23; Gresser, *Konziliengeschichte*, p. 90.

[18] *Annales Altahenses*, p. 74: "Affuit etiam illic Uto, Treviorum praesul venerandus, qui et ipse de eadem heresi est accusatus, sed mox, per iusiurandum se excusans, innocens est iudicatu et post haec in magna veneratione a papa et Romanis est habitus." JL 4646.

[19] Jenal, *Anno II.*, p. 314.

[20] Althof, *Heinrich IV.*, p. 73; Meyer von Knonau, *Jahrbücher* 1:589.

[21] Schmidt, *Alexander II.*, pp. 206–207; Meyer von Knonau, *Jahrbücher* 1:585–587.

The dispute going back to the death of Nicholas II on July 20, 1061, highlights the differences between Alexander and Hildebrand.[22] Hildebrand routinely allied with the more radical or revolutionary movements, while in general Alexander identified with those more temperate. As pope, Nicholas II had retained his episcopal see in Florence, and after his death Petrus Mezzabarba, a scion of a rich family in Pavia, was elected. The fact that he was from Pavia may not have been incidental, for behind his election stood the Lombard bishops, who had been instrumental in electing their partisan, Cadalus, at Basel.[23] This connection could have been a factor in the disputes that followed.

At first there was little reaction against Mezzabarba outside of the almost routine charges of simony. It was not until toward the end of 1062 when Alexander seemed to be gaining recognition over Cadalus that the cathedral chapter and even more forcefully, the monks of Vallombrosa, initiated stiff opposition against the new bishop. In that year a German court summoned him along with a few canons to defend himself against these complaints. Alexander responded to this initiative in a letter to the head of the cathedral chapter, sharply castigating Mezzabarba for submitting himself to this investigation because ecclesiastical affairs did not fall under the authority of the emperor. To Alexander the regency's action showed contempt for the apostolic see.[24]

The cathedral canons immediately took the side of Alexander, who had indicated his favor for them by confirming all of their privileges on November 24, 1062.[25] But Mezzabarba was not without his own advocates, for the following year Godfrey and Gregory of Vercelli, the chancellor for Italy, defended him in military clashes initiated by the monks of Vallombrosa and their house of S. Salvi.[26]

---

[22] Berthold, *Chronicon*, version 2, ed. Robinson, 1067 [fusing 1067 and 1068 into one report], pp. 203–206; tr. I.S. Robinson, *Eleventh-Century Germany*, pp. 120–122; Schmidt, *Alexander II.*, pp. 204–208; pp. 205–206 & n.338 for sources; Gresser, *Konziliengeschichte*, pp. 82–85.

[23] Ibid., 204.

[24] JL 4540; *IP* III, 8, nr. 3, 1063: Alexander wrote "audivisse se, (Petrum) episcopum cum quibusdam canonicis regiam curiam adisse, ut 'ibi introitus et vita eius examinatur;' 'quod,' inquit 'cum nulli regum vel imperatorum ecclesiastica negotia licit tractare, ad apostolicae sedis contemptum videtur factum fuisse.'"

[25] JL 4489.

[26] Robert Davidsohn, *Forschungen zur älteren Geschichte von Florenz*, vol. 1 (Berlin, 1896), p. 225.

Alexander reacted negatively to the increasing agitation of the monks. In a letter to the clergy and the people of Florence on April 4, 1064, he referred to the Council of Chalcedon that prohibited monks from wandering in cities, and commanded the monks in Florence [the Vallombrosans] to return to their monastery and to cease their preaching.[27] Like Hildebrand when Henry III reprimanded him and Humbert of Moyenmoutier as monks for traveling to Germany to engage in diplomacy, and demanded that they pledge not to stand as candidates for the papacy, the Vallombrosans ignored Alexander's command. The monks not only did not return to their monastery, but they stepped up their preaching, accusing Mezzabarba of simony and heresy, and urging the Florentines to reject the ministrations of any priest ordained by him because his sacraments would be invalid.

In 1066 or 1067 Mezzabarba struck a blow against the Vallombrosans by commanding his men to attack and pillage the monks in their house of St. Salvi, and then to burn it down. The attack elicited sympathy for the Vallombrosans and their abbot, Johannes Gualberti, and the charge of simony against Mezzabarba gained widespread attention. Alexander invited both Johannes Gualberti with a delegation of monks and Mezzabarba to the Easter synod of 1067.[28] At the synod the monks vigorously accused Mezzabarba of simony and heresy, while bishops loyal to the Empire such as Rainald of Como fervently defended Mezzabarba, and chastised the monks for raising weapons against their bishop.

According to the anonymous author of the life of Johannes Gualberti, even Petrus Damiani spoke against the monks.[29] In a letter written to the people and monks in Florence dated to Lent 1067, and thus before the synod, Petrus had attempted to arbitrate between Mezzabarba and the monks.[30] But in the Easter synod the anonymous author pointed out that Petrus had compared them to locusts that ate the greenery of the meadows of the Holy Church, and prayed that a storm would arise

---

[27] JL 4552; April 4, 1064; *IP* III, 35, nr. 1; Cushing, *Reform and the Papacy*, pp. 130–131.

[28] Berthold, *Chronicon*, version 2, ed. Robinson, pp. 204–206; tr. Robinson, *Eleventh-Century Germany: The Swabian Chronicles*, second version, pp. 120–121; Gresser, *Konziliengeschichte*, pp. 82–85.

[29] *Vita S. Johannis Gualberti anonyma*, MGH SS 30:1104–1110 at 1107: "Inter omnes autem Rainaldus episcopus Cumanus vehementius restitit nostris."

[30] Petrus Damiani, *Briefe*, nr. 146, 3:531–542; Gresser, *Konziliengeschichte*, pp. 83–84 & n. 180 for the date; Cushing, *Reform and the Papacy*, pp. 130–131.

and toss them onto the Red Sea.[31] By contrast, the author attributed a mediating role to Alexander, who said that the monks should not just be blamed, and attributed good qualities to many of them.[32] Berthold of Reichenau, stated that Alexander wanted to resolve the issue in the Catholic manner, and invited both sides to a council at Rome.[33]

While Petrus Damiani castigated the monks, and Alexander wanted both sides to present their case at a council in Rome, Hildebrand passionately sided with the monks. Rising in the council, illustrious and very imposing like a second Gamaliel, the monk and archdeacon of the Roman church did not temporize, but openly and forcefully defended the monks against the opinion of all.[34] Andreas Strumi, who also wrote a life of Johannes Gualbertus, likewise attested to Hildebrand's partisanship for the monks. By contrast, Andreas characterized Alexander as opposing the Vallombrosans, as unwilling to depose Mezzabarba, and as against the monks' suggestion of settling the dispute by trial by fire.[35]

Berthold of Reichenau also reported that it was decided to resolve the conflict by trial by fire, but Alexander explicitly opposed what he termed this uncanonical means of determining God's will.[36] Hildebrand supported it, and although he did not directly demand the deposition

---

[31] *Vita S. Johannis Gualberti*, MGH SS 30:1106–1107: "Dome pater, isti sunt locustae, quae depascuntur viriditatem sanctae ecclesiae; veniat auster et perferat eas in mare rubrum." Petrus Damiani, *Briefe*, nr. 146, 3:542; Gresser, *Konziliengeschichte*, pp. 83–84.

[32] Ibid., 1107.

[33] Berthold, *Chronicon*, version 2, ed. Robinson, p. 204; tr. *Swabian Chronicles*, p. 121.

[34] *Vita S. Johannis Gualberti*, MGH SS 30:1107: "Interea surrexit in concilio quidam vir egregious et excellentissimus alter Gamaliel, scilicet Ildebrandus monachus et archidiaconus ecclesie Romanae, qui non pedetemptim ratiocinando, sed aperte atque fortissime defendit monachos contra omnium opinionem." Gamaliel had advised his fellow members of the Sanhedrin not to put to death St. Peter and the apostles, who, in spite of the prohibition by Jewish authority, had continued to preach to the people (Acts 5:34–36).

[35] Andreas von Strumi, *Vita S. Johannes Gualtberti* MGH SS 30:1080–1104 at 1095; Schmidt, *Alexander II.*, p. 207 & n. 343.

[36] Berthold, *Chronicon*, version 2, ed. Robinson, pp. 204–206: "Ergo ea illic sententia episcopis expostulantibus diffinita est, ut iudice flamma ignis, veritas sanctae aecclesiae patefacta innotuerit." tr. Robinson, *The Swabian Chronicles*, p. 121; JL 4505, April 20, 1063; in a letter to Raynald of Como Alexander states his position on trial by fire: "Vulgarem denique legem, a nulla canonica sanctione fultam, ferventis scilicet sive frigidae aquae ignitique ferri contactum, aut cuiuslibet popularis inventionis nec ipsum exhibere, nec aliquot modo te volumus postulare, imo apostolica auctoritate prohibemus firmissime." Schmidt, *Alexander II.*, p. 207 & n. 344.

of Mezzarabarba, he advocated that the monks be allowed to return to their house without interference. The ritual was performed in February 1068 at Settimo (most likely), or at Florence according to Berthold. A monk named Petrus volunteered to carry out what almost certainly was an order issued by Johannes Gualberti without authorization of the council.[37] Bernold of S. Blasien described the procedure: [38]

> He was that Peter who proved by means of a trial by fire that Peter of Pavia, the intruder in the bishopric of Florence, was a simoniac and for this reason holy Church afterwards gave him the surname 'fiery'. For he confidently stepped on to a great pyre and passed through it without any injury, so that the flames caused his garments to move to and fro but in no way harmed them, to say nothing of himself. The aforementioned Peter of Pavia was therefore deposed by Pope Alexander, but the other Peter, who was then a monk in a very poor monastery, was elevated to the bishopric of Albano.

Mezzabarba's deposition took place in the Easter synod on March 30, 1068.[39] Berthold said that he acknowledged his guilt, and having been called to Rome by the pope, he was convicted of his heresies and returned his ring and staff. But how can one account for what happened at the trial by fire itself? Was it a matter of mass hypnosis, the mastery of a technique for walking through fire, or clever trickery? Certainly there was a belief in necromancy, but not even Mezzabarba's supporters are known to have suspected necromancy in this case. It would not, however, be a leap into absurdity to imagine that Hildebrand was responsible for the selection of Petrus Igneus as cardinal bishop of Albano.[40]

A complex of conflicting issues characterized this affair. It was not simply a matter of whether Mezzabarba was a simoniac and not a reformer, but what he meant for the stability of Tuscany, and what his dispute with the Vallombrosans implied for the alliances with the

---

[37] Gresser, *Konziliengeschichte*, p. 84.
[38] Bernold of St. Blasien, *Chronicle*, tr., Robinson, *The Swabian Chronicles*, pp. 297–298.
[39] JL p. 583; *Annales Altahenses*, 1068, p. 74: "Florentinus, autem praesul, quia per heresim simoniacam in episcopatum intraverat, accusatus et manifestis indiciis convictus protinus deponitur." Berthold, *Chronicon*, version 2, ed. Robinson, pp. 204–206: "(1067) Petrus [Mezzabarba] vero tandem Romam a domno papa advocatus, et pro heresis praedictae reatu huius iudicii argumento convictus, virgam et annulum episcopalem apostolico confusus reddidit, sicque dignitate, qua iniuste est sublimatus, recessit iuste privatus." tr., Robinson, *The Swabian Chronicles*, p. 121; Gresser, *Konziliengeschichte*, p. 91; Meyer von Knonau, *Jahrbücher* 1:600–601.
[40] Hüls, *Kardinäle*, pp. 90–91.

reformers. Hildebrand sought out the monks against the hierarchical church to institute reforms and chart new courses. Alexander and other reformers such as Petrus Damiani were more tentative, and saw virtue in tradition.

### Beatrice and Godfrey Chastised

A letter written by Petrus Damiani to Godfrey during Lent 1068 reveals that Godfrey marched to his own beat. While acknowledging that Godfrey and Beatrice had been steadfast in opposing Cadalus in the past, Petrus asked how he could possibly have had anything to do with the person whom the whole church had condemned. He cited Old Testament sources declaring that for trafficking with an enemy of God, one automatically becomes an enemy of God, and insisted that Godfrey publicly apologize, and ask God for forgiveness.[41] Alexander took the further step of separating Godfrey from Beatrice, ostensibly because of their too close degree of consanguinity.[42] According to one account, on his deathbed Godfrey revealed that as punishment Alexander had forced him to separate from his wife until he demonstrated his contrition by founding a monastery.[43]

Beatrice was present at the Easter synod of 1068 shortly after Petrus wrote his letter, and Alexander may have used her as a surrogate for the absent Godfrey. As mentioned above, Alexander commanded her to accompany Anno in his performance of penance for stopping to see Archbishop Henry of Ravenna and Cadalus on his way to Italy. As a parallel figure to Godfrey, Anno was guilty of the same malfeasance. Presumably Beatrice supported the decision to depose Mezzabarba, a price almost certainly exacted to restore her in Alexander's good graces.[44]

---

[41] Petrus Damiani, *Briefe*, nr. 154, 4:72–75: "…et quidem adversus antichristum hunc viriliter dimicasti, eiusque conatibus sacrilegis atque perversis cum serenissima atque clarissima uxore tua frequentius obstitisti." Elke Goez, *Beatrix von Canossa*, p. 210; Meyer von Knonau, *Jahrbücher* 1:602–603.

[42] Elke Goez, *Beatrix von Canossa*, p. 162.

[43] *Chronicon sancti Huberti Andaginensis* MGH SS 8:565–630 at 581: "ex edicto Alexandri papae separatum se esse a marchissa Beatrice, et pro eiusdem separationis conditione structurum, se congregationem monachorum de communibus possessionibus utriusque Deo devovisse."

[44] Gresser, *Konziliengeschichte*, pp. 87–92.

It may have been on this occasion that Alexander told Beatrice that she and Godfrey must found a monastery in order to reinstate their marriage, since Beatrice made a donation to construct a monastery in both of their names.[45] Godfrey, however, showed no contrition, and after discussions with Mezzabarba at Lucca, in July, 1068 he took him by the hand and led him to his church in the monastery of Santa Maria of Pomposa. Elke Goez, Beatrice's biographer, conjectures that because of Alexander's reliance on her and Godfrey, he had gone along with their protection of Mezzabarba, but that when Mezzabarba could no longer hold out, he let him fall. At the same time Goez believes that Alexander emancipated himself from the Lotharingia/Canossa party.[46]

Further evidence that Alexander was backing off from Godfrey and Beatrice is that at the council Alexander also deposed Bishop Samuel of Ferrara, a partisan of Cadalus, but who also had enjoyed a good relationship with Beatrice and Godfrey. Alexander consecrated Bishop Gratianus to replace Samuel, and later sent the canons of Ferrara a bull confirming certain goods, some of which had long been in Canossan hands.[47] Godfrey's defiance seems to have gone too far, for the power and prestige of the house of Lotharingia/Canossa was weakening, and major figures in Tuscany were beginning to turn against it. Hildebrand was already aligned with the Vallombrosans and the *pataria*.

Godfrey died in December 1069 at Verdun in the presence of Beatrice, Matilda, and his son, Godfrey, married to Matilda. On her return from Lotharingia Beatrice met Alexander at Siena, where she emphasized her relationship with him in order to stabilize her own rule. In the fall of 1070 she spent much time with him when he was in Lucca. Whatever independent inclinations that Godfrey had pursued were superseded by alliances with Alexander and Gregory VII, with whom Matilda became exceedingly close.

### Hugo Candidus

The Empire and the Church were clearly in a state of flux if not disarray. Henry III, under whom royal sacrality had reached its apogee, had pleased the reformers by saving the papacy from what they perceived

---

[45]  Robinson, *Henry IV*, p. 109.
[46]  Elke Goez, *Beatrix von Canossa*, pp. 161–162.
[47]  JL 4651; Elke Goez, *Beatrix von Canossa*, p. 163.

as the clutches of the Roman—or extra urban—nobility.[48] But his premature death followed by the overthrow of the weak regency provoked
the beginning of a shift in the balance of power from the Empire to the
Church. The alliance of the papacy with the Normans and with the
house of Lotharingia/Canossa further marginalized the Empire.

But when Beatrice and Godfrey and the Normans became unreliable allies, and Hildebrand aspired to create a theocracy, both the papacy
and the Empire became unstable. The gyrations of Cardinal Hugo
Candidus reflect this turmoil. Hugo himself left no writings, and much
of what we know about him comes from Bonizo, who vilified him just
as Petrus Damiani vilified Cadalus.

Leo IX created him cardinal priest of San Clemente, and like Leo
IX, Hugo remained both a reformer and a loyal adherent of the emperor.[49] Perhaps for this reason, claiming to represent the cardinals, he
cooperated with the Roman nobility and Henry IV as *patricius* in the
election of Cadalus at Basel in 1061. Arch chancellor Guibert, a colleague of Cadalus from Parma, and Gregory VII's future challenger as
Clement III, was almost certainly a prime influence.

Guibert was in Rome for the April synod in 1060, and as a cardinal
Hugo almost certainly would have come into contact with him. Both of
them may have been involved in the condemnation of Nicholas II by
the German court in the fall of 1060. The repudiation of Nicholas and
his decrees improved the prospects of the Lombards, who expected
Cadalus as Honorius II to champion their leadership in the Kingdom
of Italy.[50]

Although after the Council of Mantua in 1064 the regency relinquished its recognition of Honorius II and recognized Alexander II, it
is not clear when Hugo did. Bonizo said that after suffering many and
various miseries with Cadalus, Hugo admitted his sins and returned to
Alexander.[51] Other sources indicate that even in 1063 he was carrying
out tasks for Alexander, and it is indicative of Alexander's lack of reservations about his loyalty that he allowed him to continue as cardinal
priest of San Clemente. Still in the lifetime of King Ferdinand of Castile,

---

[48] Nicolangelo D'Acunto, *L'Età dell'obbedienze. Papato, Impero e poteri locali nel
secolo XI*; Nuovo Medioevo 75 (Naples, 2007), p. 272.

[49] Hüls, *Kardinäle*, pp. 158–160.

[50] Lerner, "Kardinal Hugo Candidus," p. 16.

[51] Bonizo, *Ad Amicum*, p. 598: "Eodem tempore Ugo Candidus...post multas et
varias miserias, quas sub Cadolo passus est, tandem ad venerabilem papam veniens,
veniam peciit et impetravit." Lerner, "Hugo Candidus," p. 25.

who died in December, 1065, Alexander appointed him legate to Spain
to spread the authority and doctrine of the reformers. According to
Bonizo whatever he built up, he tore down, and when his disastrous
performance was discovered, he was immediately recalled to Rome.[52]

In 1071 Hugo again was sent as legate to Spain, and according to
most sources he faithfully carried out his duties. They included assign-
ments in Southern France, which are the last account of his activities
during the reign of Alexander II, and which Bonizo reported he badly
mishandled.[53] After reporting the death of Cadalus in 1071 and the
negotiations over the consecration of Guibert of Parma as archbishop
of Ravenna in the Lenten synod of 1073, he added that Cluniac monks
and certain bishops accused Hugo Candidus of simony in his legation
to Spain, and France.[54] Bonizo is the only source for this charge, but
what really was at stake was authority over the Spanish church. Hugo
had diminished Cluny's influence, and had placed it directly under the
papacy.

Hildebrand, no doubt, was behind the initiative to place Cluny
directly under the papacy as well as the confirmation of Guibert as
archbishop, and he defended Hugo from any allegations.[55] One theory
explaining his strategy is that at the same council advisors of Henry IV
were excommunicated for inspiring his ecclesiastical policy, and that
Hildebrand wanted Hugo Candidus and Guibert to replace them as
counselors to the king.[56] If this was his policy, in the short run it worked
out, but in the long run it was a disaster.

Hugo Candidus soon had the opportunity to compensate Hildebrand
for his support. A few weeks after the Lenten synod Alexander died

---

[52] Ibid.: "Cunque ad Hyspaniam legati fungens officio mitteretur, quidquid edifi-
cabat, iterum dissipabat. Nam symoniacos primum quidem validissime persequeba-
tur, postea vero accepta pecunia reconciliabat. Quod dum compertum Romae fuisset,
eum ab Hyspanis statim revocant et Romae habitare precipiunt, hanc in eum humani-
tatem ostendentes precipue reverentia ordinatoris eius, beati scilicet papae Leonis."

[53] Ibid., 600: "Ugo vero Candidus,...Gallicanam a domno papa impetravit lega-
tionem; ubi multa contra ius et fas operatus est, quod suo ordine postea narrabitur."

[54] Ibid.: "Prefatus Guibertus veniens Longobardiam, Ravennam intravit in multitudine gravi et in magno, ut sui moris est, potentatu. Et non multos dies...Romam venit
causa consecrationis [1073], synodo iam celebrata; in qua et Ugo Candidus a
Cluniacensibus monachis et a quibusdam religiosis episcopis publice symonia argui-
tur, et in qua ortatu imperatricis quosdam regis consiliarios, volentes eum ab unitate
ecclesiae separare, publice domnus papa excommunicavit." Lerner, "Hugo Candidus,"
pp. 37–38; Gresser, *Konziliengeschichte*, p. 111.

[55] Gresser, *Konziliengeschichte*, p. 111.

[56] Cinzio Violante, "Alessandro II," *Enciclopedia dei Papi*, 2:178–185 at 184.

(April 21, 1073). Along with a number of clerics and other men and women Hildebrand was participating in the burial of Alexander in the Lateran basilica, when Benzo alleges that they called out, "Hildebrand, bishop." Terrified, Hildebrand ran toward the pulpit to placate the people, but Hugo stopped him and spoke to the throng. He reminded them that since the days of Pope Leo [IX] it was Hildebrand who had exalted the Roman church, and who had liberated that city. Because of this, Hugo declared that there was no better candidate to become the Roman pontiff, and accordingly that we must elect him.[57] Boso, much influenced by Bonizo, also mentions the leading role of Hugo Candidus in the *Liber Pontificalis*.[58]

One of Gregory VII's first acts was to appoint Hugo as legate to Spain. Touting his capabilities, he made the announcement in a letter of April 30, 1073, to Bishop Gerard of Ostia, and Subdeacon Raimbald, legates to France.[59] For almost three years thereafter there is no sure witness of Hugo, but something happened during that time that alienated Gregory.[60]

On the way to his legation to Spain including Southern France, Hugo had the opportunity to speak with his friends in Northern Italy, and to tell them about Gregory's election. Bonizo speaks of a general coalition of opponents to Gregory that was forming that included Cencius, son of the prefect, Stephen, a partisan of Cadalus, and the leader of the Roman resistance against both Alexander and Gregory.[61] Bonizo accuses another Cencius, son of Count Gerard, of enticing Hugo away from Gregory.[62]

---

[57] Bonizo, *Ad Amicum*, p. 601: "Eodem itaque die prefati pontifcis corpore in ecclesia sancti Salvatoris humato, cum circa sepulturam eius venerabilis Ildebrandus esset occupatus, factus est derepente concursus clericorum, virorum et mulierum clamantium: 'Ildebrandus episcopus.' Quo audito venerabilis archidiaconus expavit, et velociter volens populum placare cucurrit ad pulpitum; sed eum Ugo Candidus prevenit et populum sic allocutus est: 'Viri fratres, vos scitis, quia a diebus domni Leonis papae hic est Ildebrandus, qui sanctam Romanam ecclesiam exaltavit et civitatem istam liberavit. Quapropter, quia ad pontificatum Romanum neque meliorem neque tale, qui eligatur, habere possumus, eligimus hunc, in nostra ecclesia ordinatum virum, vobis nobisque notum et per omnia probatum.'"

[58] *Lib. Pont.* 2:361; Cowdrey, *Gregory VII*, pp. 71–74.

[59] JL 4777.

[60] Lerner, "Hugo Candidus," n. 2, p. 47 for speculations by notable scholars.

[61] Bonizo, *Ad Amicum*, p. 602: "Inter quos et Cencium, prefecti Stephani filium, quem *supra* temporibus papae Alexandri cum Cadalo fuisse memoravimus."

[62] Ibid., 604: "Sed eius [Cencius, son of count Gerard] furor non quievit. Nam eiusdem pestiferi consilio Ugo Candidus, de quo *supra* memoravimus, secundo ad apostasiam conversus est." Lerner, "Hugo Candidus," pp. 48–49.

According to Bonizo there was yet another piece to the puzzle that involved the Normans. Count Evulus of Roucy, the leader of the planned undertaking to Spain, was a son in law of Robert Guiscard, with whom Gregory VII was at this time in conflict. At the beginning of his reign Gregory had tried in vain to force Count Evulus to swear a feudal oath to the papacy, and with this situation in mind, Hugo took a fresh look at the friendship between the papacy and the Normans. As a result of his reassessment Bonizo said that Hugo went to Apulia, contacted Guiscard, twice excommunicated by Gregory, and incited him and other Normans against the Roman church.

Hugo allegedly even told Guiscard that his excommunication was not in effect because Gregory had not been elected pope by the Roman church. He vowed that he and his allies would offer Guiscard the royal crown if he would eject Gregory from the papal see.[63] Bonizo said that Guiscard rejected Hugo's entreaties, and stated that Hugo could not persuade him to take up arms against the pope, who had been elected and instated in his office in accordance with all of the canonical procedures.[64] Bonizo concludes that having been repudiated with great scorn, Hugo conducted himself to the presence of Guibert, the patron of his wickedness.[65]

Most scholars conclude that this story was a total fantasy constructed to explain Hugo's alienation from Gregory.[66] As a dedicated follower of Leo IX, who staunchly supported the emperor, it seems improbable that Hugo would have offered the imperial crown to Guiscard. But if Bonizo's account does not explain Hugo's apostasy, what does? Quite probably it was Gregory's increasing confrontation with the Empire.

Almost certainly Hugo was present at the Lenten synod of 1075, and was excommunicated, as Robert Guiscard definitely was.[67] Whether Guibert was present, and what his relations with Gregory were at that

---

[63] Ibid.: "Nam dicebat eos falso excommunicatos et papam non secundum decreta sanctorum patrum pontificem, sed sancte Romanae ecclesiae invasorem, adiciens se cum suis fautoribus Roberto coronam imperialem daturum, si eum militari manu ab ecclesia pelleret."

[64] Ibid.: "'mihi vero suadere non poteris contra Romanum me armari pontificem. Nefas enim est credere per tuas inimicicias vel alicuius posse papam deponi, qui electione cleri et laude populi Romani, cum kathedra pontificalis vacaret, intronizatus, ad altare sancti Petri ab episcopis cardinalibus consecratus est.'"

[65] Ibid.: "Sicque cum magno dedecore repudiatus ad Guibertum, suae nequiciae fautorem, se contulit."

[66] Lerner, "Hugo Candidus," n. 2, p. 49.

[67] Gresser, *Konziliengeschichte*, p. 133 & n. 119.

time is a matter of dispute.[68] Later in the year Hugo backed Guibert in a conflict over the appointment of an archbishop of Milan. Tedald, the imperial candidate, prevailed, and was consecrated by the bishops.[69] Bonizo described the two prelates as Gregory's future opponents, and notes that Hugo had recently been excommunicated.

Between 1076–1080 there was feverish activity between the Empire and the papacy, but no news of Hugo's activities. In 1076 Henry held a council of German bishops at Worms in which he called upon Hildebrand, being guilty of usurpation of power, tyrannical domination of the church, and outrageous assault on the rights of an anointed king, and now not pope, but false monk, to step down from the papal throne. Gregory responded by excommunicating and deposing Henry in the Lenten synod of 1076, and Henry was forced to secure absolution from the pope by appearing as a penitent at Canossa in 1077.[70]

It was against this background that Hugo was excommunicated for a third time in the Lenten synod of 1078.[71] As recorded in his Register, Gregory expressed his great disappointment in his one-time partisan.[72] He declared that he had excommunicated Hugo three times because Hugo was the instigator and the collaborator of the heresy of Bishop Cadalus of Parma. Gregory said that having been installed again as legate of the Holy See, Hugo banded with heretics, simoniacs and others condemned by the Holy See, and for the third time he was declared to be an apostate and a heretical schismatic. Because he attempted to split

---

[68] Ibid., 138–139; Gresser argues that Bonizo was wrong, and that Guibert's relationship with Gregory was still good. He thinks that it is probable that Guibert was at the synod.

[69] Cowdrey, *Gregory VII*, pp. 130–131.

[70] Thomas N. Bisson, *The Crisis of the Twelfth Century: Power, Lordship, and the Origins of European Government* (Princeton, and Oxford, 2009), pp. 204–207 for a sweeping assessment of this period.

[71] Lerner, "Hugo Candidus," 51–53; Bonizo, *Ad Amicum*, p. 606; *Lib. Pont.* 2:284; Lampert, *Annales* p. 253: "...Hugo cognomento Blancus, quem ante paucos dies propter ineptiam eius et mores inconditos papa de statione sua amoverat, deferens secum de vita et institutione papae scenicis figmentis consimilem tragediam:" Gresser, *Konziliengeschichte*, p. 170.

[72] Erich Caspar, ed., *Das Register Gregors VII*. MGH Epistolae. Selectae, 2 vols. (1920–23), V 14a, 2:369: "Ugonem cardinalem tituli sancti Clementis tertio ab apostolica sede damnatum, eo quod aspirator et socius factus heresis Cadoloi (sic) Parmensis episcopi et iterum constitutus legatus apostolice sedis hereticis et symoniacis et ab apostolica sede damnatis se coniunxit et tertio factus apostata et heresiarcha scismata et divisiones atque scissuras in ecclesia Dei temptans eam scindere fecit, ab omni sacerdotali officio privamus et tam ab ingressu et honore predicte ecclesie quam omnium ecclesiarum sub perpetua et inrevocabili sententia submovemus et usque ad satisfactionem anathemate percutimus"

the church of God asunder, Gregory declared that he was irrevocably and perpetually removed from any ecclesiastical office, and was anathematized until he made satisfaction.

In Germany the political situation was at a boiling point. Gregory had excommunicated Henry a second time, and had declared Henry's rival, Rudolf of Swabia, to be a vassal of the Holy See, a status that Rudolf rejected. The Germans were furious with Gregory, and viewed the renewal of Henry's excommunication as persecution. Henry called a council at Brixen, where Gregory was deposed, and Guibert was elected pope as Clement III. Undeterred by his sentence of excommunication, Hugo was present as the only cardinal, and signed the decree of June 25, 1080, in the name of all of the cardinals. It is speculated that it was he who wrote the decree.[73] From then on Hugo was active in the administration of Clement III, and in 1089 was appointed cardinal bishop of Palestrina.[74]

What Hugo reveals for the reform is that major figures, including Hildebrand/Gregory VII himself, could be very pragmatic. Some like Humbert of Silva Candida stood firm on deeply held principles, but others allied themselves with those who could be supportive to their cause. Even though Hugo had represented the cardinals in the election of Cadalus, Hildebrand defended him on charges stemming from his legation to Spain and Southern France because Hugo was helpful in establishing the papacy as universal. Hugo seems to have returned the favor by swaying those at the Lateran to select Hildebrand as pope. Gregory rewarded him with another legation, but for various reasons thereafter they became mortal enemies, and Hugo was instrumental in creating Clement III as a challenger to Gregory.

### Cencius Stephani

Frequently associated with Hugo Candidus was Cencius Stephani, called de praefecto because his father had been prefect of Rome.[75] When Hildebrand entered Rome with Nicholas II through Trastevere, the first thing that he did was to replace the prefect, Petrus, a supporter

---

[73] Lerner, "Hugo Candidus," p. 54 & n. 3.
[74] Hüls, *Kardinäle*, pp. 159, 111.
[75] Borino, "Cencio del prefetto Stefano," pp. 373–440; Cowdrey, *Gregory VII*, pp. 326–327.

of Benedict X, with the Trasteverino, Johannes Tignoso. Sometime before February 25, 1071, Cencius Stephani held this office, but on that date Johannes' son, also named Cencius, took over. That Cencius Stephani, strongly opposed by Cencius Johannis, had been able to gain the office is an example of the slippery maneuvering that characterized this period.

Cencius (Stephani) was an abbreviation of Crescentius, one of the old Roman families that vied with the reformers. Paul of Bernried, Gregory VII's biographer, described how truly awful and ferocious Cencius Stephani was, going so far as to assassinate his godfather. For this heinous act Hildebrand convinced Alexander to excommunicate him, and Cencius in turn threw his support to Cadalus.[76] We have seen that Cencius controlled the imposing tower on the Ponte S. Pietro, and the Castel San Angelo, where he allowed Cadalus to stay while he was challenging Alexander for control of the city. Things ended badly between Cencius and Cadalus, who, before he finally left the Castel San Angelo, was said to have been treated more like a prisoner than like a guest.

Then, if the anti-Gregorian source is correct, showing his diaphanous adhesion to one side or another, Cencius Stephani participated in the tumultuous election of Gregory VII.[77] It seems almost certain that both of Hildebrand's opponents, Cencius and Hugo Candidus helped to elect him as pope, and that he accepted their support.[78] Indeed, after the death of Cadalus, Paul of Bernried reports that Cencius came to an agreement with Gregory VII, and swore an oath of fidelity to him.[79]

In the summer/fall of 1074 Cencius profited from Gregory's illness to falsify the will of another Cencius, the son of Count Gerard of

---

[76] Paul of Bernried, Watterich, chs. 45–46, 1:498: "Qui ad sui destructionem quemdam suum compatrem occidit;....Ad cuius facinus vidicandum vir Dei [Hildebrand] accensus, una cum adhuc vivente Papa Alexandro, maleditionis et anathematis eum vinculis alligavit." tr. Robinson, *The Papal Reform of the Eleventh Century*, p. 293; Cowdrey says that it was reported that Alexander lifted the sentence at Hildebrand's insistence; *Gregory VII*, p. 326.

[77] *Dicta cuiusdam de discordia papae et regis*, MGH LdL 1:459: version 1: "Hildebrannus…per Chinchium, unum de nobilibus Romanis, et partem quam iste et ille fecerat sibi, papa constituitur; version 3: Hildebrandus… per Cinthium, unum ex nobilibus Romanorum, et partem quam ille et iste sibi fecerant, reclamante iustitia, constituitur papa."

[78] Cowdrey, *Gregory VII*, p. 326.

[79] Paul of Bernried, Watterich, chs. 45–46, 1:499: "Sed haeresiarch tandem illo mortuo, confusus iste pactum se cum domino Papa facere et fidelitatem iurare spopondit. Quod et fecit." tr. Robinson, p. 293.

Galeria. As the executor of the will he granted himself a *curtis* and most of the money that had been left to the church. When Gregory recovered he demanded that Cencius (Stephani) provide hostages and return the *curtis* to the Roman church. But Cencius, son of Johannes Tignoso, the prefect of the city, did not drop the issue. He arrested Cencius and sentenced him to death for collecting tolls along the Ponte S. Pietro and plundering those who entered and left the city.[80]

In another strange twist Countess Matilda, who was in Rome for the Lenten synod of February 24–28, 1075, joined Roman nobles in pleading for his freedom. Gregory granted clemency, although not without substantial punishment.[81] After swearing oaths on the tomb of St. Peter to improve his conduct and surrendering hostages, Cencius was forced to relinquish his fortress, which was destroyed by battering rams, engines of war, and finally, by iron hammers.

Cardinal Beno, who characteristically presents the other side, said that it was Gregory who captured Cencius, his former vassal (*prius fidelem suum*), and subjected him to a thousand tortures.[82] Cencius escaped, probably during the night, but the prefect, Cencius di Johannes Tignoso had nine of his supporters hung to death before the porta S. Pietro. Whether or not Gregory had anything to do with the capture of Cencius, in a letter to Hugh of Cluny written on January 22, 1075, he revealed his antipathy for those among whom he lived— Romans, Lombards, and Normans. In certain ways, he complained, they were worse than the Jews and the pagans.[83]

Cencius was not intimidated by Gregory, and in a well planned attack in Santa Maria Maggiore on Christmas Eve, 1075, he wounded

---

[80] Ibid., ch. 47, p. 499; tr. Robinson, p. 294; Borino, "Cencio del prefetto Stefano," p. 413; Cowdrey, *Gregory VII*, pp. 326–327.

[81] Bonizo, *Ad Amicum*, p. 605: "Sed precibus gloriosae Matildis, que ibi aderat illis diebus, et multorum Romanorum civium vix emeruit, ut vivus dimitteretur, datis obsidibus in manu papae et turri per quam ad celum ascendere nitebatur; que funditus destructa est."

[82] Beno, *Contra Gregorium*, p. 372: "Cencium, filium prefecti Stephani, prius fidelem suum, in carcerem misit, et in vase undique aculeis vestito eum diu mille mortibus cruciavit. Qui postquam evasit, ipsum Hildebrandum cepit. De cuius captione antequam evaderet, omnibus, qui captionis illius cooperatores fuerant, hoc debitum publice remisit, quod postea infideliter vindicavit. Cencium, cui omnia remiserat, persequi cepit, et novem de hominibus Cencii in patibulis suspendio interficit ante portam sancti Petri."

[83] JL 4926: "Eos autem inter quos habito, Romanos videlicet, Longobardos et Normanos Iudaeis et paganis quodammodo peiores esse redarguo;"

and captured the pope while he was saying mass. He brought him to his fortified house in Parione, which was in turn attacked by Gregory's supporters. Whatever he intended to do, seeing the possible dire consequences, most sources claim that he humbled himself before Gregory, and pleaded for mercy.[84] Gregory forgave him, but demanded that he make a pilgrimage to Jerusalem, and when he returned, to put himself in the hands of the reformers.

Gregory then signaled to the attackers to desist, and he was freed in time to complete the mass at Santa Maria Maggiore on Christmas Day. Thereafter, crowned, and projecting triumph, Gregory rode in procession to the Lateran, while Cencius reputedly skulked away, probably to Palestrina.[85] His house and towers were trashed, but unbowed, he continued to oppose the reformers, and was excommunicated by Cardinal Bishop Hubert of Palestrina on Gregory's command. With no hope of any further rapprochement he captured Gregory's ally, Bishop Raynald of Como, near St. Peter's at Rome, and tried to deliver him to Henry IV. But not wanting to curry Gregory's animosity, Henry delayed meeting Cencius, and when at last he agreed to do so, Cencius suddenly died of an alleged tumor in his throat.[86]

Most probably he was dispatched in the usual way by one of his opponents. His life charts the downfall of one of Rome's most powerful families, but also displays the ambivalence of both the reformers and their Roman adversaries. Like Hugo Candidus, Cencius and Gregory danced around one another, sometimes supporting, and at others attacking in their quest to fulfill their ambitions and carry out their programs.

### Frayed Loyalties and the Deaths of Cadalus and Alexander II

What is striking about the situation following the Council of Mantua is that all of the major figures established liaisons according to their needs and objectives. There were few clear ideological boundaries, but there were propensities. Alexander, for example, was more temperate

---

[84] For example, Paul of Bernried; Watterich, chs. 50–57, 1:501–505; tr. Robinson, 296–301.

[85] Cowdrey, *Gregory VII*, pp. 327–328; Borino, "Cencio del prefetto Stefano," pp. 431–436.

[86] Bonizo, *Ad Amicum*, pp. 610–611; Cowdrey, *Gregory VII*, n. 294 for other sources.

than Hildebrand. Neither patrons nor supporters, ecclesiastical or secular, could be assumed to be loyal allies as they slithered in and out of bonds. Anno could be the spokesman for the king or for his nemesis. He could support Alexander, but toy with Cadalus. Godfrey could support the king or the king's enemy; he could be a mediator with the Normans or their opponent. Hugo Candidus and Cencius would swing from one side to the other, always with reasons, but motivated by self interest.

A rare constant was that Hildebrand/Gregory VII almost always opted for the more radical cause or solution. He embraced the *pataria*, and backed the Vallombrosans, who were rejected by the church hierarchy, but ultimately won in their struggle with Bishop Petrus Mezzabarba when Mezzabarba was deposed. Hildebrand/Gregory VII always attracted fervent adherents, but by his own admission he had problems with such major powers as the Lombards, the Romans, and the Normans. His relationship with Robert Guiscard was prototypical. At times he regarded him as an enemy, and excommunicated him, but in the end he relied upon him to save him from Henry IV and the wrath of the Romans. There is even evidence that he excommunicated Desiderius, abbot of Montecassino, and his successor as Victor III. Rather than a smooth transition to ecclesiastical reform, there was also chaos and instability.

Caught up in these machinations, Cadalus drifted into his last days. The Archivio capitulare di Parma records a placitum held in 1069 and another in 1071.[87] He died at an indeterminate date in 1071 or 1072, according to Lampert believing until his dying breath that he was pope, and having continued to hold ordinations and to issue decrees that were not observed by anyone outside of Parma.[88]

An epitaph composed by his devoted followers and recorded at the end of the codex of canons of Burchard of Worms depicts him as the pope elected by Rome, who as universal pope would have been able to

---

[87] Archivio capitulare di Parma, Appendix XXIX, pp. 329–333; Affo, p. 89.
[88] Lampert, *Annales* 1064, p. 92: "Alter [Cadalus] vero, etsi per contumeliam repulsus, tamen quo advixit ab iure suo non cedebat; huic semper derogans, hunc adulterum aecclesiae Dei, hunc pseudoapstolum appellans; missas quoque seorsum celebrans, ordinationes facere et sua per aecclesias decreta et epistolas more sedis apostolicae destinare non desistebat." Howe, "Did St. Peter Damian Die in 1073?," pp. 81–83; Lerner, "Hugo Candidus," Affo, p. 89.

restore the Apostolic See to its apex, and to free Apulia and Calabria from the Normans.[89]

> Grieving Parma has laid in a small tomb your Pope Cadalus; Rome, duly appointed you. With whom as shepherd you were able to restore the honors of the world and the pinnacle of the lofty Apostolic See. The Apulian land would be free by putting the Normans to flight, and the Calabrian [would be] free, who lately occupies it as a slave. You are the head of Latium, but would then flourish as head of the world, controlling the uncontrolled, stamping on proud necks…. But too much dared to itself rash Rome of what was kept….With you overcoming fate, it would with you conquer the world for you, if everlasting life were then a companion for you.[90]

Alexander died a few weeks after the Lenten synod on April 21, 1073, according to Benzo at the instigation of Hildebrand: "Truly, those [popes] whom Prandellus planted were grass: they lived as long as he wished and went the way of all flesh, when he wished. Finally, when it pleased him that the man of Lucca, whom he called Alexander should depart, he ordered Archigenes [a famous physician; Juvenal] to come and cut open a vein, so that through loss of blood the souls might be divorced from the body. And this was done."[91]

He strived to do what he thought was right for the Church, but he was faced with strong personalities and events that left a mixed heritage. He would not even be buried before chaos broke out, and the chief proponent of the reform and the international papacy finally became pope himself as Gregory VII.

———————

[89] Affo, p. 91: Papam Roma tuum Cadalum tibi
     Rite statutum
Parma dolens tumulo condidit
     Exiguo
Quo Pastore potens reparare orbis
     Honores,
Culmen & excelsae Sedis Apostolicae.
Libera Normannis foret Apulia
     Terra fugandis,
Et Calaber liber, qui modo servus inest.
Tu Latii sed caput orbis inde vigeres,
Frenans effrenes, colla superba premens.
Sed nimis ausa sibi temeraria Roma retenti
………
Tu superans sortem tecum tibi vinceret orbem,
     Si sibi vita comes tunc diuturna foret.
[90] I should like to thank James Diggle of Cambridge University and Marianne McDonald of UCSD for this translation.
[91] Benzo, *Ad Heinricum*, 7.2, pp. 600–602; Robinson tr., *The Papal Reform*, p. 375.

CONCLUSION

THE STATE OF THE PAPACY AT THE END OF THE SCHISM

Calixtus II (1119–1124) regarded Cadalus as a serious enough opponent to render him as a *scabellum* under the feet of Alexander II in a
series of paintings in the Lateran Palace of enthroned reform popes
demeaning antipopes as footstools.[1] Below the painting an inscription read that Alexander reigned while Cadalus was rejected and
overcome.[2] Such is the ignominious way that Calixtus, the pope who
reached a compromise with Henry V in The Concordat of Worms of
1122, portrayed the antipopes of the reform. But Cadalus was far from
just a foil for Roman or imperial interests, and like Alexander II, he
was a reformer. Their main differences were that Cadalus was more
sympathetic to the traditional relationship between *regnum* and
*sacerdotium*, and Alexander represented those who were trying to
expand the authority of the papacy into the dominant international
institution.

The deaths of Cadalus and Alexander II were followed by the tumultuous reign of Gregory VII, who made radical claims for papal authority, and forcefully challenged Henry IV. Influential though he may
have been, he also provoked hostile opposition, which in turn created
a far more successful rival than Cadalus to Alexander II in Guibert
of Ravenna as Clement III. This time the seemingly indomitable former monk was forced to flee Rome to the safety of the Normans,
and Clement III functioned in his place in Rome with considerable
support.

Even though first as Hildebrand and later as Gregory VII he sparked
fundamental changes in Christian society, many historians now recognize that the baptism of this era as the reform or as the Gregorian
reform was simplistic. It was in fact a tectonic shift with the emergence
of new powers such as the Normans, and the retreat of others such as
the Greek Orthodox Empire and the Muslims. This variegated and

---

[1] Stroll, *Symbols as Power*, pp. 20–21; plate nr. 9.
[2] Ibid.: "Regnat Alexander, Kadolus cadit et superatur" The only word that can be
read on the second line is "nihilatur."

complex period started with Henry III's exercising his undisputed sacral authority by ridding the church of three claimants to the papal throne, and earning praise as the savior of the papacy from the parochialism of the Roman aristocracy. After many perturbations, at least as much political as ecclesiastical, it ended in a shift of power from the Empire to the papacy.

Tension between the reformers and the king/emperor developed only slowly. The ruler as minister of God and *vicarius Christi* reached its apogee under Henry III Dedicated reformers such as Petrus Damiani still acknowledged the king's sacral powers, and saw the world as a unity of *regnum* and *sacerdotium*. Even Hildebrand, the firebrand, who ignited the reformers, was slow to diverge from the concept of the emperor as apostle and as *pontifex maximus*.[3] But by the time he became pope he accentuated papal authority in the *Dictaus Papae*, and excommunicated and deposed Henry IV. Within one generation the concept of the sacral emperor had plunged to its nadir.

The reasons for the change were not that the views of Henry III and Henry IV were distinctively different, but that first the regency and then Henry IV at the beginning of his reign were weak. Many forces took advantage of the boy-king: the Saxons, the German ecclesiastical hierarchy, and the reformers. In the duel with Gregory VII Henry IV ultimately triumphed, forcing his nemesis to seek refuge with the Normans, and seating his own candidate on the papal throne, but it was only one battle in a war. Henry's son, Henry V, neutralized his father, and then compromised with the papacy.

There were other major changes. The Lombards wanted their province, "The Paradise of Italy," to be acknowledged for its importance, and their Ambrosian capital of Milan to maintain its traditions and independence from Rome. On the whole they were able to maintain control of ecclesiastical discipline and administration with the emperor at the top. Hildebrand as advisor to popes and then as Gregory VII liberally used the weapons of excommunication and synodal decrees to impose papal discipline, but without significant success. It is no accident that both Cadalus and Guibert were born in Parma, and that they mutually supported one another. This is not to say that Guibert as imperial chancellor for Italy and as archbishop of Ravenna did not also cooperate with the papacy and attend its councils.

---

[3] Franz-Reiner Erkens, *Herrschersakralität im Mittelalter. Von den Anfängen bis zum Investiturstreit* (Stuttgart, 2006), p. 648.

The establishment of the house of Lotharingia/Canossa in Central Italy was a critical development that had the potential for virtually extending papal rule to the borders of Lombardy. What characterized the formidable figures as heads of this house, first Beatrice and Benedict, then Beatrice and Godfrey the Bearded, and finally Beatrice, Matilda, and for a short time, her discordant husband, Godfrey the hump-backed, was their sporadic commitment to a given power. Godfrey the Bearded could at any time be allied with the king, the papacy or the Normans. He could visit Cadalus or he could lend a hand to Alexander, but he was always working in his own interests. It was only Matilda, who became a reliable devotee of the reform papacy.

Weak alliances reflecting expediency were common if not the norm. Hugo Candidus and Cencius Stephani could gyrate between the papacy and its opponents or between factions within the reformers. The popes would chastise them after some major conflict, but then accept them back into the fold when they could be useful and conditions were appropriate. For example, by helping to establish the authority of the papacy in Spain, Hugo earned the gratitude of Hildebrand, who defended him from charges of simony brought by Cluny. He, in turn, propelled the crowds to proclaim Hildebrand as pope, but then in another twist, helped to seat Guibert of Ravenna as Clement III.

It is tempting to see the actions of Hugo and Cencius as the height of cynicism, but they were probably less opportunistic than responsive to the flow of changes, frequently initiated by the reformers themselves. Little can be said in defense of Anno, however, who, now on one side, and then on the other, ruthlessly pursued his own ambitions.

The papal response to the Normans after they first drifted into Southern Italy and Sicily, and then consolidated their power follows a similar pattern. Leo IX fought them, but his successors were more ambivalent, at times controlling them by subjecting them as their vassals, and at others opposing them. Like every other faction, the Normans pursued their own interests, and since their interests did not always coincide with those of the papacy, they frequently were at odds. Gregory VII excommunicated Robert Guiscard more than once, but had to rely upon him to save him from the wrath of Henry IV and his allies in Rome.

Desiderius of Montecassino, who had reason to hate the Normans, nevertheless realized that it was in his interest to accommodate this powerful force. While he and Gregory VII pretty much supported the same principles, they also had their problems. Given the virtual

anarchy at the end of Gregory's reign, it is understandable that
Desiderius only reluctantly acceded to the wishes of a troubled church
to succeed the most dominant churchman of his time as Victor III.

Unlike the papacy, the Empire was not indecisive about the Normans.
It regarded them as usurpers of their sovereignty, and in this convic-
tion they made common cause with the Greek Orthodox Empire. Both
were trying to hold on to their property and influence in Southern Italy
even though the pope and the patriarch were at dagger points over
theology, and Leo IX had taken the first steps toward schism between
the two churches. This struggle made Cadalus an attractive ally for the
Greeks, because he supported the western emperor against the
Normans, their common enemy. But Cadalus never was able to develop
a stronghold in Southern Italy, and eventually the papacy and the
Normans made common cause in expropriating the authority of the
Greeks over their settlements.

Even Canossa, the quintessential exemplar of the waxing of papal
authority and the waning of royal sacrality, was a trade off. Henry IV
objected that Gregory VII had been chosen pope without reference to
him as *patricius Romanorum*, hence unlawfully. Gregory excommunicated and deposed him, and forced him to agree to appear before a
council to be held in Augsburg. On his way to the council Gregory felt
threatened by some urban elites in Lombardy, and since the escort
promised by the German princes never arrived, he turned south to the
safety of Canossa.

In his famous concession Gregory released Henry from the sentence
of excommunication, but entered into another unheralded, but critical
agreement. As a condition of his absolution Henry agreed to furnish
him with a military escort to Augsburg even though Gregory never
used it.[4] Canossa was a way out of difficulties for both sides, a deal
incorporated into public ritual that marked the weakening of theocratic kingship, but recognition of the value of royal power.[5]

In sum, the elections of Alexander and Cadalus were not the
opening salvoes in the battle between *regnum* and *sacerdotium*, but
skirmishes among the reformers, the old Roman aristocracy, the
regency before and after Anno, the patarines, the Lombards, Godfrey

---

[4] Timothy Reuter, "Contextualising Canossa: excommunication, penance, surrender, reconciliation," pp. 147–166 of *Medieval Polities and Modern Mentalities*; Cowdrey,
*Gregory VII*, pp. 157, 168.
[5] Reuter, "Contextualising Canossa, p. 165.

and Beatrice, and the Normans. The schism did not develop because Alexander represented reform and Cadalus imperial control of the church, and there is no reason to believe that Hildebrand and Alexander would not have welcomed Henry IV's confirmation of Alexander's election had the Romans not intervened by requesting that the young king exercise his rights as *patricius*. The Council of Mantua unleashed new clashes of interest when Anno betrayed the king just coming into his majority, and sharpened the king's defense of imperial rights.

The papacy likewise honed its opposition to the Empire when Hildebrand as Gregory VII finally assumed the papacy that he had more or less controlled for a quarter of a century. In the short run many of his revolutionary pursuits were rejected, but in the long run his struggle for theocracy prevailed. In 1294 the curia tried in vain to restore the sense of piety and spirituality to the Church that at one time Gregory seemed to have encapsulated. It elected an Abruzzese hermit as Celestine V, but it was too late, and his reign was doomed to failure. He was replaced by the lawyer pope, Boniface VIII (1294–1303), but the papacy's spiritual aura had been dimmed.

# BIBLIOGRAPHY

## Manuscript

Onophrius Panvinius, *De Varia Romani pontificis creatione*. Bavarian Staatsbibliotek, Clm 147–152. Munich.

## Sources

Adam of Bremen, *Gesta Hammaburgensis ecclesiae pontificum*. MGH SRG 16.2.
Amatus of Montecassino. *Storia de' Normanni di Amato di Montecassino*, ed. V. de Bartholomeis. *Fonti per la Storia d'Italia*. Rome, 1935.
——. *The History of the Normans*. Tr. Prescott N. Dunbar; revised with introduction and notes by Graham A. Loud. Woodbridge, Eng. & Rochester NY, 2004.
*Annales Altahenses maiores*. MGH SRG 4.
*Annales Augustani*. MGH SS 3:123–136.
*Annales Camaldulenses*. Ed. Johanne-Benedicto Mittarelli & D. Anselmo Costadoni, vol. 2. Venice, 1756.
*Annales Patherbrunnenses*. Ed. Paul Scheffer-Boichorst. Innsbruck, 1870.
*Annales Romani, Liber Pontificalis*, 2:331–350.
*Annales Weissenburgenses. Lamperti Monachis Hersfeldensis Opera*. MGH SRG 38, pp. 8–57.
Arnulf, *Gesta Archiepiscoporum Mediolanensium*. MGH SS 8:1–31.
Baronius, Caesar. *Annales ecclesiastici, 1046–1093*. Rome, 1593–1607, Paris, etc., 1887.
Beno. *Benonis aliorumque cardinalium schismaticorum contra Gregorim VII. et Urbanum II. scripta*. MGH LdL 2:366–422.
Benzo von Alba. *Ad Heinricum IV imperatorem libri VII*. Ed. & tr. Hans Seyffert; *Sieben Bücher an Kaiser Heinrich IV*. MGH. SRG 65.
Berthold of Reichenau and Bernold of Konstanz. *Die Chroniken Bertholds von Reichenau und Bernolds von Konstanz, 1054–1100*. Ed. Ian S. Robinson, MGH SRG Nova Series XIV. Hannover, 2003.
"Bertholds und Bernolds Chroniken" = *Bertholds und Bernolds Chronicon*." Ed. Ian S. Robinson; German tr. Helga Robinson-Hammerstein & Ian S. Robinson. Darmstadt, 2002.
Böhmer, Johannes Friedrich, ed. *Fontes rerum Germanicarum. Geschichtsquellen Deutschlands*. 4 vols., 1983–68; vol. 3, *Die Regesten unter Heinrich IV 1056 [1050] – 1106*, new ed. Tilman Struve. Cologne, Innsbruck, 1984.
Bonizo of Sutri. *Liber ad Amicum*. MGH LdL 1:568–620.
——. *Liber de Vita Christiana*. Ernst Perels, ed. Berlin, 1930.
*Briefsammlungen der Zeit Heinrichs IV*. Ed. Carl Erdmann, Norbert Fickermann; MGH Briefe der deutschen Kaiserzeit 5. Weimar, 1950.
Caspar, Erich, ed. *Das Register Gregors VII*. MGH Epp. sel. 2, 1920–1923; 3rd ed., 1967.
Cenci, P. *Documenti Archivio Storico per le Province Parmensi*, new ser, 23 (1923), 185–223; 24 (1924), 309–344.
*Chronica monasterii Casinensis*; (*Die Chronik von Montecassino*). MGH SS 34.
Cowdrey, H.E.J. *The Register of Pope Gregory VII 1073–1085*; an English translation. Oxford, 2002.

*De Unitate Ecclesiae Conservanda.* MGH LdL 2:173–284.

Deusdedit Presbyteri Cardinalis. *Libellus contra Invasores et Symoniacos et Reliquos Scismaticos.* LdL 2:292–365.

Donizo. *Matilde e Canossa: Il Poema di Donizone.* Ed. with Italian translation, Ugo Bellochi & Giovanni Marzi. Modena, 1970.

——. *Vita der Mathilde von Canossa: Der Text des Codex Vat. Lat. 4922. Vita der Mathilda von Canossa.* Transcription and translation, Carlo Golinelli, Axel Janeck. 2. Introduction and Facsimile of Cod. Vat. Lat. 4922. Zurich, 1984.

——. *Vita Mathildis Celeberrimae Principis Italiae.* Vol. 5.2 of *Raccolta degli Storici Italiani,* ed. L.A. Muratori. Bologna.

Drei, Giovanni. *Le Carte dagli Archivi Parmensi dei secoli X-XI.* Parma, 1928.

Ekkehard of Aura. *Frutolfs und Ekkehards Chroniken und die anonyme Kaiserchronik.* Ed. Franz-Josef Schmale & Irene Schmale-Ott. Darmstadt, 1972.

Erdmann, Carl. *Ausgewählte Briefe aus der Salierzeit* (Texte zur Kulturgeschichte des Mittelalters 7). Rome, Leipzig, 1933.

Falco. *Falcone di Benevento, Chronicon Beneventanum. Città e Feudi nell'Italia dei Normanni.* Ed. Edoardo d'Angelo. Florence, 1998.

*Fontes Historiam Heinrici IV. Imperatoris illustrantes.* Epistolae Heinrici IV.; Carmen de Bello Saxonico; Brunonis Saxonicum Bellum; Vita Heinrici IV. Imperatoris; ed. C. Erdmann, etc.; new ed. Franz-Josef Schmale. Berlin, 1963.

*Gesta Trevorum. Pars III, prior usque ad a. 1101.* MGH SS 8:175–200.

Girgensohn, Dieter, ed. "Miscellanea Italiae pontificiae. Untersuchungen und Urkunden zur mittelalterlichen Kirchengeschichte Italiens, vornehmlich Kalabriens, Siziliens, und Sardiniens," *Nachrichten der Akademie der Wissenschaften in Göttingen. Philologisch-historische Klasse* (1974), 129–196.

Guido of Ferrara. *De scismate Hildebrandi.* MGH LdL 1:529–67; *On Hildebrand's Schism: For and Against Him.* (abridged), : Extracts from Two Anti-Gregorian Tracts. University of Leeds Electronic Text Centre, pp. 9–21.

Hefele, Charles Joseph. *Histoire des Conciles d'après les documents originaux;* tr. H. Leclercq, vols. 4, 5.1. Paris, 1910.

Henry IV. *Epistolae;* pp. 41–142 of *Quellen zur Geschichte Kaiser Heinrichs IV;* Ausgewählte Quellen zur deutschen Geschichte des Mittelalters, vol. 12 ed, Rudolf Buchner; introduction by Franz-Josef Schmale, trans. by Irene Schmale-Ott, pp. 407–467. Berlin, 1963.

——. *The Letters of Henry IV;* pp. 138–200 of *Imperial Lives & Letters of the Eleventh Century,* tr. Theodor E. Mommsen and Karl F. Morrison, intro. Karl F. Morrison. New York, 2000.

Humbert of Silva Candida. *Libri III Adversus Simoniacos.* MGH LdL 1:95–253.

*Imperial Lives & Letters of the Eleventh Century.* Tr. Theodor E. Mommsen & Karl F. Morrison, with an historical introduction by Karl F. Morrison. New York, 2000.

Jaffé, Phillip. *Bibiotheca Rerum Germanicarum,* vol. 5, *Monumenta Bambergensia.* Scientia Verlag Aalen, 1964.

——. *Regesta Pontificum Romanorum,* vol. 1. Graz, 1956.

Kehr, Paul Fridolin, ed. *Italia Pontificia,* vols. 1–10. Berlin, 1905–1974.

Lampert of Hersfeld. *Annales,* pp. 3–304 of *Lamperti monachi Hersfeldensis Opera.* MGH SRG 38.

Landulf senior. *Landulfi historia Mediolanensis usque ad anno 1085.* MGH SS 8:32–99; ed. Muratori, RIS 4.2. Bologna, 1942.

*Liber Censuum de l'église romaine.* Ed. Louis Duchesne and Paul Fabre, vols. 1–3. Paris, 1889–1952.

*Liber de unitate ecclesiae conservanda,* Anonymous monk of Hersfeld, MGH LdL 2:172–284.

*Liber Pontificalis.* Ed. Louis Duchesne, 3 vols. Paris, 1886–1892; 2nd ed. Bibliothèque des Écoles française d'Athènes et de Rome. Paris, 1955–1957.

Mabillon, J. *Annales ordinis S. Benedicti occidentalium monachorum patriarchae* 6 vols. (Lucca, Paris, 1739–1740).

Malaterra, Geoffrey. *De rebus Gestis Rogerii Calabriae et Siciliae Comitis auctore Gaufredo Malaterra*. Ed. E. Pontieri, RIS, 2nd ed. Bologna, 1927–1028.

——. *The Deeds of Count Roger of Calabria and Sicily and of his Brother Duke Robert Guiscard*, tr. Kenneth Baxter Wolf. Ann Arbor, 2005.

Manegold of Lautenbach. *Manegoldi ad Gebehardum Liber*. MGH LdL 1:300–430.

Mansi, Johannes. *Sacrorum Conciliorum Nova et Amplissima Collectio* (Venice, 1776), vol. 19.

Matilda, Countess of Tuscany. *Die Urkunden und Briefe der Markgräfin Mathilde von Tuzien*. MGH Diplomata 5, *Laienfürsten – und Dynasturkunden der Kaiserzeit 2*. Hannover, 1998.

Ménager, Léon-Robert. *Recueil des actes des ducs normands d'Italie (1046–1127)*, 1: *Les premiers ducs (1048–1087)*. Società di Storia Patria per la Puglia. Documenti e monografie, vol. 45. Bari, 1981.

Paul of Bernried. *Vita Gregorii VII papae*. Ed. Johannes Watterich, *Pontificum Romanorum Vitae* 1:474–546.

Petrus Crassus. *Defensio Heinrici IV regis*. MGH LdL 1:432–453; *A Defense of King Henry*. The Age of Gregory VII, 1073–85: Extracts from Two Anti-Gregorian Tracts. University of Leeds Electronic Text Centre, pp. 1–9; Treatise to Henry IV in which he defended his rights against the illegalities of Pope Gregory VII (Ravenna, June 1080).

——. Ed. Julius Ficker, *Urkunden zur Reichs- und Rechtsgeschichte Italiens*. 4: 106–124. Innsbruck, 1874.

Petrus Damiani. *Die Briefe des Petrus Damiani*. Ed. Kurt Reindel. vol 1, 1–40; vol. 2, 41–90; vol. 3, 91–150; vol. 4, 151–180. MGH, *Briefe*, 4, 1983–1993.

Peter Damian. *Letters*, tr. Owen J. Blum; 6 vols.; vol. 2, 31–60; vol. 3, 61–90. Washington D. C., 1989–2004.

*Pontificia commissio ad redigendum codicem iuris canonici orientalis, Fontes*, series III, 4 vols. (1943–1954).

Sigibert of Gembloux. *Chronicon*. MGH SS 6:300–374.

*Die Touler Vita Leos IX*. Ed. & tr. Hans-Georg Krause, with Detlev Jasper & Veronika Lukas; MGH SRG 70. Hannover, 2007.

Tractatus de investitura episcoporum, MGH LdL 2:498–504.

Triumphus S. Remacli. *De Malmundariensi Coenobio*. MGH SS 11:433–461.

*Vita Anselmi episcopi Lucensis*. MGH SS 12:1–35.

*Vita Henrici IV imperatoris. Quellen zur Geschichte Kaiser Heinrichs IV*; Ausgewählte Quellen zur deutschen Geschichte des Mittelalters, vol. 12 ed, Rudolf Buchner; introduction by Franz-Josef Schmale, trans. by Irene Schmale-Ott, pp. 407–467. Berlin, 1963.

Watterich, Johannes. *Pontificum Romanorum qui fuerunt inde ab exeunte saeculo IX usque ad finem saeculi XIII vitae ab aequalibus conscriptae*. Vol. 1 *Johannes XIII – Urbanus II. (872–1099)*. Lepizig, 1862, repr. Aalen, 1966.

Wido Episcopus Ferrariensis. *De Schismate Hildebrandi*. MGH SS 12:148–179.

William of Apulia. *Guillaume de Pouille. La Geste de Robert Guiscard*. Ed. M. Mathieu. Palermo, 1961.

*Literature*

Affo, Ireneo. *Storia della città di Parma*, vol. 2. Parma, 1792.

Althoff, Gerd. *Heinrich IV*. Darmstadt, 2006.

Ambrosioni, Annamaria. "Niccolò II," *Enciclopedia dei Papi*, 2:172–177.

252     BIBLIOGRAPHY

Bagge, Sverre. *Kings, Politics, and the Right Order of the World in German Historiography c. 950–1150.* Leiden, 2002. Lampert of Hersfeld, *Annales,* 231–312; *Vita Heinrici IV,* 313–363.

Baix, F. "Cadalus," *Dictionnaire d'histoire et de géographie ecclésiastique* 11 (1949), 53–99. Ed. Alfred Card. Baudrillart. Paris, 1949.

Bayer, Axel. *Spaltung der Christenheit. Das sogennante Morgenländische Schisma von 1054.* (Beihefte zum Archiv für Kulturgeschichte 53), Cologne, 2004.

Berman, Harold J. *Law and Revolution: The Formation of the Western Legal Tradition.* Cambridge, Massachusetts & London, England, 1983.

Berschin, Walter. *Bonizo von Sutri: Leben und Werk.* Beiträge zur Geschichte und Quellenkunde des Mittelalters, 2. Berlin, 1972.

——. *Bonizone di Sutri. La Vita e le opere* (Centro Italiano di Studi sull'Alto Medioevo. «Medievo-Traduzioni» 1). Spoleto, 1992.

Beumann, Helmut. "Tribur, Rom und Canossa," pp. 33–60 of *Investiturstreit und Reichsverfassung,* ed. Josef Fleckenstein. Sigmaringen, 1973.

Bisson, Thomas N. *The Crisis of the Twelfth Century: Power, Lordship, and the Origins of European Government.* Princeton, and Oxford, 2009.

Black-Veldtrup, Mechthild: "Kaiserin Agnes (1043–1077)," *Quellenkritische Studien* (Münstersche historische Forschungen 7). Cologne, Weimar, Vienna, 1995.

Blumenthal, Uta-Renate. "The Coronation of Pope Nicholas II," in *Life, Law and Letters*; Miscelánea hisórica en honor de Antonio García y García, ed. Peter Linehan (Studia Gratiana 28, 1998).

——. *Gregor VII. Papst zwischen Canossa und Kirchenreform.* Darmstadt, 2001.

——. "The Papacy, 1024–1122," pp. 8–37 of of *The New Cambridge Medieval History* 4.2.

——. *Papal Reform and Canon Law in the 11th and 12th Centuries* (Variorum Collected Studies Series CS 618). Aldershot, 1998.

Borino, Giovanni Battista. "L' archidiaconato di Ildebrando," *Studi Gregoriani* 3 (1948), 463–516.

——. "Cencio del prefetto Stefano, l'attentore di Gregorio VII," *Studi Gregoriani* 4 (1952), 373–440.

——. "La Lettera di Enrico IV al madre Agnese Imperatrice (1074)," *Studi Gregoriani* 6 (1959–1961), 296–310.

——. "Perche Gregorio VII non annunzio la sua elezione ad Enrico IV e non ne richiese il consenso (Relazioni tra Gregorio VII ed Enrico IV dall'aprile 1073-aprile 1074)," *Studi Gregoriani* 5 (1956), 313–343.

Boshof, Egon. *Heinrich IV. Herrscher an einer Zeitenwende (Persönichkeit und Geschichte 108–109).* Göttingen, Zürich, Frankfurt, 1979.

——. *Die Salier.* Stuttgart, Berlin, Cologne, 1995.

Bossi, G. "I Crescenzi di Sabina, Stefaniani et Ottaviani," *Archivio della Società Romana di Storia Patria* 41 (1918).

Brasington, Bruce C. & Cushing, Kathleen G., eds. *Bishops, Texts and the Use of Canon Law around 1100: Essays in Honour of Martin Brett.* Aldershot, Eng. & Burlington Vt., 2008.

Bulst-Thiele, Marie Luise. *Kaiserin Agnes*; Beiträge zur Kulturgeschichte des Mittel Alters und der Renaissance 52. Leipzig, Berlin, 1933; new ed. Hildesheim, 1972.

Büttner, Heinrich. "Die Bischofsstädte von Basel bis Mainz in der Zeit des Investiturstreits," pp. 351–362 of *Investiturstreit und Reichsverfassung,* ed. Josef Fleckenstein. Sigmaringen, 1973.

Cantarella, G.M. "Pier Damiani e lo scismo di Cadalo," *Pier Damiani: l'eremita, il teologio, il riformatore (1007–2007),* ed. M. Tagliaferri (=*Ravennatensia*), 23, pp. 233–267. Bologna, 2009.

Capitani, Ovidio. "Benedetto X antipapa," *Enciclopedia dei Papi,* 2:168–171.

——. *L'Italia Medievale nei Secoli di Trapasso: La Riforma della Chiesa (1012–1122).* Bologna, 1984.

——. "Per un riesame dei 'falsi ravenati,'" *Atti e Memorie della R. Deputazione di Storia Patria per le Province de Romagna*, n. ser. 22 (1977), 21–42.
——. "Politica e cultura a Ravenna tra Papato e Impero dall'XI al XII Secolo," pp. [c. 193] of *Storia di Ravenna*, vol. 3 *Dal Mille all fino della signoria polentana*, ed, A. Valsina. 1993.
——. "Problematica della 'Disceptatio Synodalis,'" *Studi Gregoriani 10* (1975), 141–174.
——. *Tradizione e interpretazione. Dialettiche ecclesiologiche del secolo XI*. Rome, 1990.
——. "Nobiltà romana e nobiltà italiana nel medioevo centrale: parallelismi e contrasti," pp. 15–42 of *La Nobiltà Romana nel Medioevo*, ed. Sandro Carocci. École Française de Rome, 2006.
Cartellieri, Alexander. *Der Aufstieg des Papsttums im Rahmen der Weltgeschichte 1047–1095*. Munich, Berlin, 1936.
Cerrini, Simonetta. "Honorio II, antipapa," *Enciclopedia dei Papi*, 2:185–188.
*La Chiesa Greca in Italia dall'VIII al XVI secolo. Atti del Convegno storico interecclesiale, Bari, 30 April-4 May 1969*. Padua, 1973.
Cilento, Nicola. "La politica 'meridionale' di Gregorio VII nel contesto della riforma della Chiesa," *Rassegna Storica Salernitana*, n.s. 3 (June, 1985), 123–136.
Claussen, Peter Cornelius. *Die Kirchen der Stadt Rom im Mittelalter, 1050–1300: A - F*. Stuttgart, 2002.
Coué, S, "Acht Bischofsviten aus der Salierzeit—neu interpretiert," *Die Salier und das Reich* 3 (1991), 347 ff.
Cowdrey, Herbert Edward John. *The Age of Abbot Desiderius: Montecassino, the Papacy and the Normans in the Eleventh and Early Twelfth Century*. Oxford, 1983.
——. *Pope Gregory VII, 1073–1085*. Oxford, 1998.
——. *Popes and Church Reform in the 11th Century*. Aldershot, Hants., 2000.
——. "The Structure of the Church, 1024–1073," pp. 229–267 of *The New Cambridge Medieval History* 4.1; c. 1024–1198, ed., David E. Luscombe and Jonathan Riley-Smith.
Cushing, Kathleen G. *Papacy and Law in the Gregorian Revolution. The Canonistic Work of Anselm of Lucca*. Oxford, 1998.
——. *Reform and Papacy in the Eleventh Century: Spirituality and Social Change*. Manchester and New York, 2005.
D'Acunto, Nicoangelo. *I Laici nella Chiesa e nella Società secondo Pier Damiani. Ceti dominanti e riforma ecclesiastica nel secolo XI*. Rome, 1999.
*Dizionario dei Concilii*. Ed. P. Palazzini. Rome, 1965.
Dressler, Fridolin. *Petrus Damiani: Leben und Werk*; Studia Anselmiana 34. Rome, 1954.
*Enciclopedia dei Papi. 2: Niccolo I, santo Sisto IV* (Istituto della Enciclopedia Italiana, 2000).
Fenske, Lutz. *Adelsopposition und kirchliche Reformbewegung im östliche Sachsen. Entstehung und Wirkung des sächsischen Widerstandes gegen das salische Königtum während des Investiturstreits*. Göttingen, 1977.
Fetzer, Carl Adolf. *Voruntersuchungen zu einer Geschichte de Pontificats Alexanders II*. Strassberg, 1887.
Fleckenstein, Josef. "Heinrich IV. und der deutsche Episkopat in den Anfängen des Investiturstreits. Ein Beitrag zur Problematik von Worms, Tribur und Canossa," pp. 221–236 of *Adel und Kirche. Gerd Tellenbach zum 65. Geburtstag dargebracht von Freunden und Schülern*, ed. Karl Schmid. Freiburg, Basel, Wien, 1968.
——. "Hofkapelle und Reichsepiskopat under Heinrich VI." pp. 117–140 of *Investiturstreit und Reichsverfassung*, ed. Josef Fleckenstein. Sigmaringen, 1973.
Fliche, Augustin. *La réforme grégorienne et la reconquête chrétienne (1057–1125)*, vol. 6 of *Histoire de l'Église*. Paris, 1946.
Fornasari, Giuseppe. *Medioevo reformato del secolo XI: Pier Damiani e Gregorio VII*. Naples, 1996.

——. "S. Pier Damiani e la storiografia contemporanea: osservazione in margine a recenti studi damianei," *Bullettino dell'Istituto Storico Italiano per il Medioevo e Archivio Muratoriano* 88 (1979).

Fössel, Amalie. *Die Königen im mittelalterlichen Reich: Herrschaftsausübung, Herrschaftsrechte, Handlungsspielräumung.* Stuttgart, 2000.

Fuhrmann, Horst. "Heinrich IV. und die deutsche Friedensbewegung," pp. 175–204 of *Investiturstreit und Reichsverfassung,* ed. Josef Fleckenstein. Sigmaringen, 1973.

——. "Quod catholicus non habeatur, qui non concordat Romanae ecclesiae: Randnotizen zum Dictatus Papae," pp. 263–287 of *Festschrift H. Beumann.* Sigmaringen, 1977.

Galland, Bruno. "La role du royaume de Bourgogne dans la reforme gregorienne," *Francia* 29 (2002), 85–106.

Ghirardini, Lino Lionello. *L'antipapa Cadalo e il tempo del Bene e del Male: Grandezza e Miseria del piu'Famoso Vescovo di Parma (1045–1071).* Centro di Studi Canossiani, 1984.

Giesebrecht, Wilhelm. *Geschichte der deutschen Kaiserzeit,* 4 vols., 3, *Das Kaiserthum im Kampfe mit dem Papsttum.* Leipzig, 1890.

Gilchrist, John. *Canon Law in the Age of Reform, 11th-12th Centuries;* Variorum Collected Studies Series, CS 406. Ashgate, 1993.

——. "The reception of Pope Gregory VII into the canon law (1073–1141)," *Zeitschrift der Savigny Stiftung für Rechtsgeschichte* KA 59 (1973), 35–82.

——. "Was There a Gregorian Reform Movement in the Eleventh Century?," *The Canadian Catholic Historical Association, Study Sessions* 37 (1970), 1–10.

Goez, Elka. *Beatrix von Canossa und Tuszien. Eine Untersuchung zur Geschichte des 11. Jahrhunderts;* Vorträge und Forschungen Sonderband 41. Sigmaringen 1995.

Goez, Werner. *Kirchenreform und Investiturstreit 910—1122.* Stuttgart, 2000.

——. "Rainald von Como: Ein Bischof des 11. Jahrhunderts zwischen Kurie und Krone," pp. 462–494 of Helmut Beumann, ed. *Historische Forschungen für W. Schlesinger.* Cologne, Vienna, 1974.

——. "Riforma ecclesiastica – Riforma gregoriana," *Studi Gregoriani* 13 (1989), 167–178.

——. "Reformpapsttum, Adel und monastische Erneuerung in der Toscana," pp. 205–240 of *Investiturstreit und Reichsverfassung,* ed. Josef Fleckenstein. Sigmaringen, 1973.

——. "Zur Erhebung und ersten Absetzung Papast Gregors VII.," *Römische Quartalschrift* 63 (1968). 117–144.

——. "Zur Persönlichkeit Gregors VII.," *Römische Quartalschrift* 73 (1978), 193–216.

Golinelli, Paolo. *La Pataria: Lotte religiose e sociali nella Milano dell'XI secolo.* Novara-Milano, 1984.

Grauert, Hermann. "Das Dekret Nikolaus II. von 1059," *Historisches Jahrbuch* 1 (1880), 502–602.

Grégoire, Réginald. "Le Mont-Cassin dans la réforme de l'Église de 1049–1122," pp. 21–44 of *Il monachesimo e la riforma ecclesiastica (1049–1122). Atti della quarta Settimana internazionale di studio Mendola, 23–29 agosto 1968;* (Miscellanea del Centro di Studi Medioevali 6). Milan, 1971.

Gresser, Georg. *Clemens II. Der erste deutsche Reformpapst.* Paderborn, etc., 2007.

——. "Sanctorum patrum auctoritate. Zum Wandel der Rolle des Papstes im Kirchenrecht auf den päpstlichen Synoden in der Zeit der Gregorianischen Reform," *Zeitschrift der Savigny Stiftung für Rechstgeschichte* KA 122 (2005), 59–73.

——. *Konziliengeschichte: Die Synoden und Konzilien in der Zeit des Reformpapsttums in Deutschland und Italien von Leo IX. bis Calixt II. 1049–1123.* Paderborn, etc. 2006.

Greulich, O. "Die kirchenpolitische Stellung Bernolds von Konstanz," *Historisches Jahrbuch* 55 (1935), 1–54.

Grosse, Rolf. *L'Église de France et la papauté (X<sup>e</sup> – XIII<sup>e</sup> Siècle). Actes du XXVI<sup>e</sup> Colloque historique franco-allemand* (Studien und Documente zur Gallia Pontificia, 1). Bonn, 1993.

Gussone Nikolas. *Thron und Inthronisation des Papstes von den Anfängen bis zum 12. Jahrhundert.* Bonn, 1978.

Hägermann, Dieter. *Das Papsttum am Vorabend des Investiturstreits: Stephan IX. (1057–1058), Benedikt X. (1058), und Nikolaus II. (1058–1061),* vol. 36 of Päpste und Papsttum. Stuttgart, 2008.

——. "Untersuchungen zum Papstwahldekret von 1059," *Zeitschrift der Savigny Stiftung für Rechtsgeschichte* KA 87 (1970), 157–193.

——. "Zur Vorgeschichte des Pontifikats Nikolaus' II." *Zeitschrift für Kirchengeschichte* (1970), 352–363.

Healy, Patrick. *The Chronicle of Hugh of Flavigny: Reform and the Investiture Contest in the Late Eleventh Century.* Ashgate, 2006.

Hehl, Ernst Dieter. "War and the Christian Order," pp. 185–228 of *The New Cambridge Medieval History* 4.1.

Heinemann, Lothar von. "Das Papstwähldekret Nikolaus II. und die Entstehung des Schismas vom Jahre 1061," *Historische Zeitschrift* NF 29 (1890), 44–72.

Herberhold, Franz. "Die Angriffe des Cadalus von Parma (Gegenpapst Honorius II.) auf Rom in den Jahren 1062 und 1063," *Studi Gregoriani* 2 (1947), 477–503.

——. "Die Beziehungen des Cadalus von Parma zu Deutschland," *Historisches Jahrbuch* 54 (1934), 84–104.

Herbers, Klaus, ed. *Europa an der Wende vom 11. zum 12. Jahrhundert: Beiträge zu Ehren von Werner Goez.* Stuttgart, 2001.

Herde, Peter. "The Papacy and the Greek Church in Southern Italy between the Eleventh and Thirteenth Century," tr. Carine van Rhijn, Inge Lyse Hansen, G.A. Loud, and A. Metcalfe in *The Society of Norman Italy,* ed. G.A. Loud & A. Metcalfe, pp. 213–251. Leiden, 2002; tr. of "Das Papsttum und die griechische Kirche in Süditalien vom 11. bis zum 13. Jahrhundert," *Deutsches Archiv für Erforschung des Mittelalters* 26 (1970), 1–46.

Herklotz, Ingo. "Zur Ikonographie der Papstsiegel im 11. und 12. Jahrhundert," pp. 116–130 of *Für irdischen Ruhm und himmlischen Lohn: Stifter und Auftraggeber in der mittelalterlichen Kunst,* ed. Hans-Rudolf Meier, Carola Jäggi, Philippe Büttner. Berlin, 1995.

Hiestand, Rudolf. "Les légats pontificaux en France du milieu du XI<sup>e</sup> à la fin du XII<sup>e</sup> siècle," pp. 54–80 of *L'Église de France et la papauté (X<sup>e</sup> – XIII<sup>e</sup> siècle). Actes du XXVI<sup>e</sup> Colloque historique franco-allemand* (Studien und Documente zur Gallia Pontificia, 1). Bonn, 1993.

Horn, Michael. "Zur Geschichte des Bischöfe und Bischofskirche von Augsburg," pp. 251–266 of *Die Salier und das Reich,* vol. 2, *Die Reichskirche in der Salierzeit,* ed. Stefan Weinfurter & Frank Martin Siefarth. Sigmaringen, 1991.

Houdin, Hubert. "Die Normannen und das Papsttum," pp. 47–53 of Jarnut, Jörg; Wemhoff, Matthias, eds. *Vom Umbruch zur Erneuerung? Das 11. und beginnende 12. Jahrhundert—Positionen der Forschung,* unter Mitarbeit von Nicola Karthaus (Mittelalter Studien 13). Munich 2006.

Howe, John. *Church Reform and Social Change in Eleventh-Century Italy: Dominic of Sora and His Patrons.* Philadelphia, 1997.

——. "Did St. Peter Damian Die in 1073? A New perspective on his Final Days," *Analecta Bollandiana* 128 (2010), 67–86.

Hüls, Rudolf. *Kardinäle, Klerus und Kirchen Roms 1049–1130.* Tübingen, 1977.

Hülsen, Christian. *Le Chiese di Roma nel Medio Evo. Cataloghi ed Appunti.* Florence, 1926, new ed. Rome, 2000.

*Imperial Lives and Letters of the Eleventh Century.* Tr., Theodor E. Mommsen and Karl F. Morrison, ed. Robert L. Benson. New York, 2000.

Jaffé, Philippus. *Regesta Pontificum Romanorum*. Vol. 1, ed. S. Loewenfeld. Leipzig, 1885.

Jarnut, Jörg; Wemhoff, Matthias, eds. *Vom Umbruch zur Erneuerung? Das 11. und beginnende 12. Jahrhundert—Positionen der Forschung*, unter Mitarbeit von Nicola Karthaus (Mittelalter Studien 13). Munich, 2006.

Jäschke, Kurt-Ulrich. *Notwendige Gefärtinnen. Königinnen der Salierzeit als Herrscherinnen und Ehefrauen im römisch-deutschen Reich des 11. und beginnenden 12. Jahrhunderts* (Historie und Politik 1). Saabrücken-Scheidt, 1991.

Jasper, Detlev. *Das Papstwahldekret von 1059: Überlieferung und Textgestalt*. Sigmaringen, 1986.

Jenal, Georg. *Erzbischof Anno II. von Köln (1056–75) und sein politisches Wirken. Ein Beitrag zur Geschichte der Reichs- und Territorialpolitik im 11. Jahrhundert*. 2 vols. Stuttgart, 1974–1975.

Kamp, Norbert. "The Bishops of Southern Italy in the Norman and Staufen Periods," pp. 185–209 of *The Society of Norman Italy*, ed. G.A. Loud & A. Metcalfe. Leiden, 2002.

Keller, Hagen. "Pataria und Stadtverfassung, Stadtgemeinde und Reform: Mailand im Investiturstreit," pp. 321–350 of *Investiturstreit und Reichsverfassung*, ed. Josef Fleckenstein. Sigmaringen, 1973.

——. *Zwischen regionaler Begrenzung und universalem Horizont. Deutschland im Imperium der Salier und Staufer 1024 bis 1250*. Frankfurt am Main, Berlin, 1990.

Klewitz, Hans-Walter. "Studien über die Wiederherstellung der Römischen Kirche in Süditalien durch das Reformpapsttum," *Quellen und Forschungen aus italienischen Archiven und Bibliotheken* 25 (1934–1935), 105–187; repr. *Refompapsttum und Kardinalkolleg*, pp. 137–205. Darmstadt, 1957.

Kölzer, T. "Das Königtum Minderjäriger im Fränkisch-Deutschen Mittelalter," *Historisches Zeitschrift* 251 (1990), 291–323.

Krause, Hans-Georg. "Das Papstwahldecret von 1059 und seine rolle im Investiturstreit," *Studi Gregoriani* 7 (1960), 1–285.

Ladner, Gerhard. *The Idea of Reform: Its Impact on Christian Thought and Action in the Age of the Fathers*. New York, 1967.

Laudage, Johannes. "'Ein Römer durch und durch': Zu Zwei Neuerscheininugen über Gregor VII," *Francia* 29/1 (2000), 221–228.

Lehmbrübner, H. *Benzo von Alba. Ein Verfechter der kaiserlichen Staatsidee unter Heinrich IV.* (Historische Untersuchungen, Heft 6). Berlin, 1887.

Lerner, Franz. "Kardinal Hugo Candidus," Beiheft 22, *Historische Zeitschrift* (1931).

Liebermann, F. "Lanfranc and the Antipope," *The English Historical Review* 16 (1901), 328–332.

Lindner, Th. "Benzos Panegyrikus auf Heinrich IV. und der Kirchenstreit zwischen Alexander II. und Cadalus von Parma," pp. 495–526 of *Forschungen zur Deutschen Geschichte* 6, 1866.

Loud, Graham. *The Age of Robert Guiscard: Southern Italy and the Norman Conquest*. Harlow, Pearson Education Limited, 2000.

——. *Church and Society in the Norman Principality of Capua*. Oxford, 1984.

——. "Churches and Churchmen in an Age of Conquest: Southern Italy, 1030–1130," *Haskins Society Journal* 4 (1992), pp. 37–53; repr. in *Conquerors and Churchmen in Norman Italy*. Aldershot, 1999.

——. *Conquerors and Churchmen in Norman Italy*. Aldershot, 1999.

——. *Montecassino and Benevento in the Middle Ages*. Aldershot, 2000.

——. *The Latin Church in Norman Italy*. Cambridge, 2007.

——. "The Papacy and the Rulers of Southern Italy, 1058–1198," pp. 151–184 of Graham Loud & Alex Metcalfe, eds. *The Society of Norman Italy* ( Leiden, 2002).

Loud, Graham & Metcalfe, Alex, eds. *The Society of Norman Italy*. Leiden, 2002.

Lück, D. "Die Kölner Erzbischöfe Hermann II. und Anno II. als Erzkanzler der Römischen Kirche," *Archiv für Diplomatik* 16 (1970), 1–50.

Martin, Guido. "Der salischer Herrscher als *Patricius Romanorum*. Zur Einflussname Heinrichs III. und Heinrichs IV. auf die Besetzung der *Cathedra Petri*," *Frühmittelalterlich Studien* 28 (1994), 257–295.

Melve, Leidulf. *Inventing the Public Sphere. The Public Debate during the Investiture Contest (c. 1030–1122)*. Leiden, 2007.

Meneghini, R. *Roma nell'alto Medioevo. Topografia urbanistica della città dal V al X secolo*. Roma Libreria dello Stato, 2004.

Meyer von Knonau, Gerold. *Jahrbücher des deutschen Reiches unter Heinrich IV. und Heinrich V.*, 4 vols., 1 *1056–1069*, 2nd ed. Berlin, 1964.

Miccoli, G. *Chiesa Gregoriana. Ricerche sulla riforma del secolo XI*. Florence, 1966.

Michel, Anton. *Amalfi und Jerusalem im Griechischen Kirchenstreit (1054–1090) Kardinal Humbert, Laycus von Amalfi, Niketas Stethatos, Symeon II. von Jerusalem und Bruno von Segni über die Azymen*; Orientalia Christiana Analecta 121. Rome, 1939.

Miller, Maureen. *The Formation of a Medieval Church: Ecclesiastical Change in Verona, 950–1150*. Ithaca, 1993.

——. *Power and the Holy in the Age of the Investiture Conflict: A Brief History with Documents*. Boston, New York, 2005.

Morghen, G. *Gregorio VII e la riforma della Chiesa nel secolo XI*. Palermo, 1974.

Morris, Colin. *The Papal Monarchy: The Western Church from 1050 to 1250*. Oxford, 1989.

Munier, Charles. *Le Pape Léon IX et la Réforme de l'Église 1002–1054*. Strasbourg, 2002.

Nobili, M. "L'idiologia politica in Donizone," *Studi Matildici*. pp. 263–279 of *Atti e memorie del III Convegno di Studi Mathildici (Reggio E. 7–9 Ottobre, 1977)*. Modena, 1978.

Offergeld, Thilo. *Reges Pueri: Das Königtum Minderjähriger im frühen Mittelalter*. MGH Schriften, 50. Hannover, 2001.

Panvinius, Onophrius. *De origine Cardinalium*. Ed. Angelo Mai, *Spicilegium Romanum* 9:495–504. Rome, 1845, repr. Graz 1974.

——. *Le Vite de'Pontifici di Bartolomeo Plantina Cremonese*. Platina, 1462; reedited by Panvinio and others until 1703, Cologne.

Panzer, Konrad. *Wido von Ferrara: De Scismate Hildebrandi. Ein Beitrag zur Geschichte des Investiturstreits*. Leipzig, 1880.

Paravicini Bagliani, A. "L'Église romaine de 1054 à 1122," pp. 254–263 of *Histoire du christianisme des origins à nos jours*. Ed. J.M. Mayeur et al. Paris, 1993.

Parisse, Michel. "Stefano IX," *Enciclopedia dei Papi*, 2:166–167.

Patschovsky, Alexander. "Heresy and Society: On the Political Function of Heresy in the Medieval World," pp. 23–41 of *Texts and the Repression of Medieval Heresy*, ed. Caterina Bruschi & Peter Biller; York Studies in Medieval Theology 4. York, 2003.

Pennington, Kenneth. "The Eleventh Century and the Reform of the Latin Church," http://faculty.cua.edu/Pennington/Canon%20Law/ShortHistoryCanonLaw.htm#

Radding, Charles M. & Ciarali, Antonio. *The Corpus Iuris Civilis in the Middle Ages*. Leiden, Boston, 2007.

Ragg, Sascha. *Ketzer und Recht: Die weltliche Ketzergesetzgebung des Hochmittelalters unter dem Einfluss des römischen und kanonischen Rechts*. MGH Studien und Texte, 37. Hannover, 2006.

Ramseyer, Valerie. *The Transformation of a Religious Landscape: Medieval Southern Italy 850–1150*. Ithaca & London, 2007.

Reuter, Timothy. "Contextualising Canossa: excommunication, penance, surrender, reconciliation," pp. 147–166 of *Medieval Polities and Modern Mentalities*, ed. Janet L. Nelson. Cambridge, 2006.

——. "The 'imperial church system' of the Ottonian and Salian rulers: a reconsideration," pp. 325–354 of *Medieval Polities and Modern Mentalities*.

Robinson, Ian Stuart. *Authority and Resistance in the Investiture Contest: The Polemical Literature of the Late Eleventh Century.* New York, 1978.
——. *Eleventh-Century Germany: The Swabian Chronicles.* Manchester & New York, 2008.
——. *Henry IV of Germany, 1056–1106.* Cambridge, New York, 1999.
——. *The papal reform of the eleventh century: Lives of Pope Leo IX and Pope Gregory VII.* Manchester, 2004.
——. "Reform and the Church," pp. 268–334 of *The New Cambridge Medieval History* 4.1; c. 1024–1198, ed., David E. Luscombe and Jonathan Riley-Smith.
Rolker Christof. "The *Collection in Seventy-four Titles*: A Monastic Canon Law Collection from Eleventh-Century France," *Readers, Texts and Compilers in the Earlier Middle Ages: Studies in Honour of Linda Fowler-Magerl,* ed. Martin Brett & Kathleen G. Cushing (Bodmin, Cornwall, 2009), pp. 59–72.
Ryan, J. Joseph. *Saint Peter Damian and his Canonical sources. A Preliminary Study in the Antecedents of the Gregorian Reform.* Pontifical Institute of Mediaeval Studies and Texts 2. Toronto, 1956.
Sagulo, Saverio. *Ideologia imperiale e analisi politica in Benzone, vescovo d'Alba.* A cura di Glauco Maria Cantarella. Bologna, 2003.
Scheffer-Boichorst, Paul. *Gesammelte Schriften. Historische Studien,* 1: *Kirchengeschichtliche Forschungen.* pt. 42, Berlin, 1903.
"Hat Nikolaus II. das Wahldekret widerrufen?" pp. 174–183.
"Die Synoden von Sutri und Rom, der Ausbruch des Streits," pp. 196–210.
"Textkritische Bemerkungen zu des Petrus Damiani Disceptio synodalis," pp. 210–220.
"War Gregor VII. Mönch?," pp. 158–173.
Schieffer, Rudolf. *Die Entstehung des päpstlichen Investiturverbots für den deutschen König.* (Schriften der MGH 28). Stuttgart, 1981.
——. "Erzbischöfe und Bischofskirche von Köln," in *Die Salier und das Reich,* vol. 2 *Die Reichskirche in der Salierzeit,* ed. Stefan Weinfurter, Frank Martin Siefarth, pp. 1–29. Sigmaringen, 1991.
——. "Gregor VII.—Ein Versuch über die historische Grösse," *Historisches Jahrbuch* 97/98 (1978), 87–107.
Schieffer, Theodor. *Die deutsche Kaiserzeit.* Deutsche Geschichte. Ereignisse und Probleme, ed. Walther Hubatsch 1 I, Ullstein Buch Nr. 3841. Frankfurt, 1973.
Schlesinger, Walter: *Kirchengeschichte Sachsens im Mittelalter,* 2 vols., Mitteldeutsche Forschungen 27. Graz, 1962.
Schmid, Paul. *Der Begriff der kanonischen Wahl in den Anfängen des Investiturstreit.* Stuttgart, 1926.
Schmid, Karl. "Adel und Reform in Schwaben," pp. 295–320 of *Investiturstreit und Reichsverfassung,* ed. Josef Fleckenstein. Sigmaringen, 1973.
Schmidt, Tilmann. *Alexander II. (1061–1073) und die Römische Reformgruppe seiner Zeit.* Stuttgart, 1977.
——. "Zu Hildebrands Eid vor Kaiser Heinrich III.," *Archivum Historiae Pontificiae* 11 (1973), 378f.
Schneidermüller, Bernd, & Weinfurter, Stefan. *Salisches Kaisertum und neues Europa: Die Zeit Heinrichs IV. und Heinrichs V.* Darmstadt, 2007.
Schnith, Karl Rudolf. "Die Herrscher der Salierzeit," pp. 181–248 of *Mittelalterliche Herrscher in Lebensbildern. Von den Karolingern zu den Staufern,* ed. Karl Rudolf Schnith. Graz, etc. 1990.
Schramm, Percy Ernst. *Die deutschen Kaiser und Könige in Bildern ihrer Zeit, 751–1190.* new ed. Florentine Mütherich with Peter Berghaus & Nikolaus Gussone. Munich, 1983.
Schwartz, Gerhard. *Die Besetzung der Bistümer Reichsitaliens unter den Sächsischen und Salischen Kaisern,* pts. 1,2, abschnitt A. Leipzig, Berlin, 1913.

Schwartzmeier, Hansmartin. *Lucca und das Reich bis zum Ende des 11. Jahrhunderts.* Tübingen, 1972.

Sommerlechner, Andrea. "*Mirabilia, munitiones fragmenta*: Rome's Ancient Monuments in Medieval Historiography," pp. 223–244 of *Pope, Church and City: Essays in Honour of Brenda M. Bolton,* ed. Frances Andrews, Christoph Egger, and Constance M. Rousseau. Leiden, Boston, 2004.

Stoller, Michael Edward. "Eight Anti-Gregorian Councils," *Annuarium Historiae Conciliorum* 17 (1985) 254–263.

——. *Schism in the Reform Papacy: The Documents and Councils of the Antipopes, 1061–1121.* Diss. Columbia University, 1985.

Struve, Tilman. "Kaisertum und Romgedanke in salischer Zeit," *Deutsches Archiv für Erforschung des Mittelalters* 44 (1988), 424–454.

——. "Lambert von Hersfeld. Persönlichkeit und Weltbild eines Geschichtsschreibers am Beginn des Investiturstreits," *Hessisches Jahrbuch für Landesgeschichte* 19 (1969/1970), 19:1–123; 20:32–142.

——. "Die Romreise der Kaiserin Agnes," *Historisches Jahrbuch* 105 (1985), 1–29.

——. "La trasformazioni dell'XI secolo alla luce della storiografia del tempo," pp. 41–72 in *Il secolo X: una svolta?,* ed. Cinzio Violante & Joachim Fried. Bologna, 1993.

——. "Zwei Briefe der Kaiserin Agnes," *Historisches Zeitschrift* 104 (1984), 411–424.

Stürner, Wolfgang. "Der Königsparagraph im Papstwahldekret von 1059," *Studi Gregoriani* 9 (1972), 39–52.

——. "Das Papstwahldekret von 1059 und seine Verfälschung. Gedanken zu einem neuen Buch [Jasper]," pp. 157–190 of *Fälschungen im Mittelalter* 2. Hannover, 1988.

Sybel, Heinrich and Lehmann, Max. "Die Päpstwahl Nikolaus II. und die Entstehung des Schismas vom Jahre 1061," *Historische Zeitschrift* 65, NF 29 (1890), 44–72.

Tabacco, Giovanni. "Autorità pontificiae e impero," pp. 123–152 of *Le Istituzio ecclesiastiche della «societas christiana» dei Secoli X-XII: Papato, Cardinalato ed Episcopato.* Milan, 1974.

Takayama, Hiroshi. "Law and Monarchy in the South," pp. 58–81 of *Italy in the Central Middle Ages,* ed. David Abulafia. Oxford, 2004.

Tellenbach, Gerd. "Der Charakter Kaiser Heinrich IV. Zugleich ein Versuch über die Erkennbarkeit menschlicher Individualität im hohen Mittelalter," pp. 344–367 of *Person und Gemeinschaft im Mittelalter. Karl Schmid zum 65. Geburtstag.* Ed. Gerd Althoff, Dieter Geuenich, Otto Gerhard Oexle, Joachim Wollasch. Sigmaringen, 1988.

——. *Church, State and Christian Society at the Time of the Investiture Contest.* Oxford, 1966.

——. "Die westliche Kirche von 10. bis zum frühen 12. Jahrhundert," *Die Kirche in ihrer Geschichte. Ein Handbuch,* vol. 2, Lieferung F1, ed. Bernd Moeller. Göttingen, 1988.

*The New Cambridge Medieval History.* Vol. 4.1, *1024–1198,* ed. David Luscombe & Jonathan Riley-Smith. Cambridge, 2004.

Thomas, Heinz. "Zur Kritik an der Ehe Heinrichs III. mit Agnes von Poitou," pp. 224–235 of *Festschrift für Helmut Beumann zum 65. Geburtstag,* ed. Kurt-Ulrich Jäschke and Rinhard Wensklus. Sigmaringen, 1977.

Toubert, Pierre. *Les Structure du Latium médiéval: le Latium méridional et la Sabine du IX$^e$ à la fin du XII$^e$ siècle.* Rome, 1973.

Tramontana, Salvatore. *Il Mezzogiorno medievale. Normanni, Suevi Angioni, Arogonesi nei sec. XI-XIII.* Rome, 2000.

Violante, Cinzio. "Alessandro II," *Enciclopedia dei Papi,* 2:178–185.

——. *L'età della Riforma della Chiesa in Italia (1002–1122).* Turin, 1965.

Vogelsang, Thilo. *Die Frau als Herrscherin im hohen Mittelalter. Studien zur 'Concors regni' Formel.* Göttinger Bausteine zur Geschichtewissenschaft 7. Göttingen, 1954.

Vollrath, H. "Kaisertum und Patriziat in den Anfängen des Investiturstreits," *Zeitschrift für Kirchengeschichte* 85 (1974), 11–44.

Weinfurter, Stefan. *Canossa: Die Entzauberung der Welt*. Munich, 2006.

———. *Die Geschichte der Eichstätter Bischöfe des Anonymus Haserensis*. Edition, Übersetzung, Kommentar=Eichstätter Studien NF 24. Regensburg, 1987.

———. *The Salian Century: main currents in an age of transition*. English translation of *Herrschaft und Reich der Salier. Grundlinien einer Umbruchzeit*, trans. by Barbara M. Bowlus. Philadelphia, 1999.

Weisweiler, "Die päpstliche Gewalt in den Schriften Bernolds von St. Blasien aus dem Investiturstreit," *Studi Gregoriani* 4 (1952), 129–147.

Weitlauff, Manfred. "Von der Reichskirche zur 'papstkirche': Säkularisation, Kirchliche Neuorganisation und Durchsetzung der papalistischen Doktrin," *Zeitschrift für Kirchengeschichte* 113 nr. 3, (2002), 355–402.

Welsby, Alison Sarah. "Pope, Bishops and Canon Law: A Study of Gregory VII's Relationship with the Episcopate and the Consequences of Canon Law," http://www.leeds.ac.uk/history/studentlife/e-journal/welsby.pdf.

Werner, Ernst. *Zwischen Canossa und Worms*. Berlin, 1978.

Whalen, Brett. "Rethinking the Schism of 1054: Authority, heresy, and the Latin Rite," *Traditio* 62 (2007), 1–24.

Will, C. *Acta et Scripta quae de controversies Graecae et Latinae saeculo XI conscripta extant*. Leipzig, Marburg, 1861; new ed. Frankfurt, 1963.

Wilmart, André. "Une lettre de S. Pierre Damien à l'impératrice Agnès," *Revue béné- dictine* 44 (1932), 125–146.

Wollasch, Joachim. "Reform und Adel in Burgund," pp. 277–294 of *Investiturstreit und Reichsverfassung*, ed. Josef Fleckenstein. Sigmaringen, 1973.

Wolter, Heinz. *Die Synoden im Reichsgebiet und in Reichsitalien von 916–1056*. Paderborn, 1988.

———. "Die Wahl des Papstes Nickolaus II," pp. 205–220 of *Adel und Kirche: Festschrift G. Tellenbach*. Freiburg, 1968.

Zema, Demetrius B. "The Houses of Tuscany and of the Pierleone in the Crisis of Rome in the Eleventh Century," *Traditio* 2 (1944), 155–175.

Zimmermann, Harald. *Papstabsetzungen des Mittelalters*. Graz, Cologne, Vienna, 1968.

Zöpffel, Richard. *Das Bistum Augsburg und seine Bischöfe im Mittelalter* 1. Munich, Augsburg, 1955.

———. *Die Papstwahlen und die mit ihnen im nächsten Zusammenhange stehenden Ceremonien in ihrer Entwicklung vom 11. bis zum 14. Jahrhundert. Nebst einer Beilage: Die Doppelwahl des Jahres 1130*. Göttingen, 1871.

# INDEX OF SUBJECTS

*Ad Heinricum* (Benzo), 18
Adalbert of Bremen, 167, 176, 186, 205, 206–209, 220, 221–222
Adam of Bremen, 163, 176, 205, 210
Agnes (wife of Henry III) (regent), 21, 209, 219–220
  Anno's displacement of, 162–163
  and Benedict X, 81
  and Cadalus of Parma, 137–139, 141–143, 180
  dons veil, 166
  weakness of, 15
Albert of Fruttuaria, 166
Alexander II (Anselm of Lucca), 7, 16–17, 48, 239–240
  and Anno of Cologne, 169–170, 175, 211–214
  Benzo's accusations, 153
  as bishop, 119–120
  and Cadalus of Parma, 126
  coronation, 88
  and Council of Mantua, 191–204
  criticisms of, 172–173
  death of, 241
  Easter Council of 1063, 178–179
  election of, 126–130
  and Henry IV, 123–124, 214
  and Hildebrand, 124–126
  and Nicholas II, 123–124
  and *patarini*, 121–122
  and regency, 123–124
  reign of, 130–132
  schism with Cadalus of Parma, 133–139, 169–189
  and Vallombrosa monastery, 225–229
  violence and conflict with Cadalus, 179–188
Amalfi, 96
Amatus of Montecassino
  *History of the Normans,* 33
  on Leo IX, 35, 36, 37
  on popes following Stephen IX, 67
  on Stephen IX, 63–64
  on Victor II, 57
Anaclet II (Petrus Pierleoni), 74
*Annales* (Berthold), 141
*Annales Altahenses,* 79, 128–129, 138, 166, 171

*Annales Camaldulenses,* 125, 173, 194
*Annales Romani,* 27, 51–52, 64–65, 71, 86, 124, 135–136, 157
Anno of Cologne
  and Alexander II, 175–177, 211–214, 221–222
  Council of Augsberg, 171–174, 193
  Council of Mantua, 191–204
  decline of, 205–206, 207–208, 209–210
  expedition to Italy, 222–224
  kidnapping of Henry IV and effects, 162–171
  letters of, 211–214
  as regent, 114–115, 143
Anselm of Lucca (Alexander II)
  as bishop, 119–120
  and Henry III, 120
  and Nicholas II, 111
  signs papal electoral decree, 98
  and Stephen IX, 62, 84–85
Apulia, 35, 60, 187, 209
Azezzo, 60
Azolin of Compiegne, 34
Azolinus, 151, 152

Baronius, Caesare, 4, 137
Bayer, Alex, 40–41
Beatrice of Canossa, 24, 55, 56, 58, 59, 63, 84, 112, 124, 151, 157, 200–202, 229–230, 245
Benedict, canon of St. Peter's
  *Liber politicus,* 89
Benedict IX, 23, 29, 30
Benedict X, 7, 12, 15
  described by Bonizo, 79–80
  defeat of, 109
  election of, 69–71
  in German sources, 78–79
  in Leo of Ostia, 77
  in *Liber Pontificalis,* 77–78
  in Panvinius, 80–82
  and Petrus Damiani, 75–76
  reign of, 71–74
Benedictus Christianus (Baruch), 74, 81
Benevento, 35, 36–37, 60, 65, 96, 111
Beno of SS. Martino e Silvestro, 115, 130, 238

Benzo of Alba, 17–19
  and Adalbert of Bremen, 205–206,
    208
  on Alexander II, 123–124,
    127–128
  on Cadalus, 139
  on Clement II, 25–26
  and Henry IV, 205–206
  and Hildebrand, 74, 153, 155, 157
  on imperial relations, 115–116
  on Nicholas II, 87, 88
  and papal electoral decree, 98
  at Quedlinburg, 206–209
  and support of Cadalus, 151–160,
    180–188
  on Victor II, 53–54
Berengar of Tours, 42, 45
Bernold of Constance, 78–79, 91, 93,
    129–130, 137, 138, 228
Berthold of Carinthia, duke, 213
Berthold of Reichenau, 227–228
  Chronicon, 78–79, 129, 137, 141, 221,
    227–228
Blumenthal, Uta Renate, 54, 87, 100
Boniface (margrave), 24, 27, 30, 31,
    55, 84
Boniface IX, 29, 30
Boniface of Albano, 61
  and election of Victor II, 51–54
Boniface VIII, 247
Bonizo of Sutri, 12–15, 18, 111
  on Benedict X, 79–80
  and Cadalus, 139, 180–181
  on Clement II, 25, 27–28
  on Council of Mantua, 198
  on Damasus II, 31
  on election of Alexander II, 136–137
  on Hugo Candidus, 139–140,
    230–236
  on Stephen IX, 66, 120
  on Victor II, 52–53
Borino, Giovanni Batista, 176
Boso
  Liber Pontificalis, 136
Braczutus, 64–65
Bruno of Segni, 34
Bruno of Toul. See Leo IX
Burchard of Halberstadt, 164, 173,
    174, 206
Burchard of Worms, 240–241
  Decretum, 89–90
Byzantine Empire
  and Leo IX, 38–46

Cadalus of Parma (Honorius II), 7, 8, 10,
    16, 17, 19, 48, 56, 119, 125, 128–129.
    See also Honorius II
  and abduction of Henry IV, 169–171
  and Alexander II, 126
  Benzo in Rome, 151–156
  as bishop, 134–135
  and Cencius Stephani, 237
  Council of Augsberg, 171–174, 193
  Council of Basel, 137–139
  Council of Mantua, 191–204
  death of, 240–241
  as electus, 160–162
  and Empress Agnes, 137–139,
    141–143
  entry into Rome, 156–160
  and Hugo Candidus, 140–141
  and kidnapping of Henry IV, 162–167
  and Petrus Damiani, 143–148
  as reformer, 243
  schism created, 133–139
  violence and conflict with Alexander
    II, 179–188
Calabria, 35, 60, 187, 209
Calixtus II, 243
Camoldoli monastery, 92
Canossan family, 54–56, 59, 245. See also
  Beatrice of Canossa
capitanei, 158
Capua, 35, 60, 96
Celestine V, 247
Cencius (son of Gerard), 233
Cencius (son of Johannes Tignoso),
    237, 238
Cencius Frangipani, 126, 135, 155
Cencius Stephani, 236–239, 245
Chronicle of Montecassino, 11, 19, 25, 52,
    59, 65, 77, 125, 136, 174, 221
Cinzio Violante, 121
Civitate, battle of, 38, 57
Clement II, 11, 18, 19, 24–30
Clement III (Guibert of Parma/
    Ravenna), 34, 81, 236, 243
Cluny monastery, 49, 54, 63, 142, 232
Codex Aureus, 21–22
The Collection of 74 Titles, 90–93
Conrad II, 9, 21, 24
Conrad of Trier, 177
Constantine I, 18, 42–43
Constantine IX Monomachus, 39–46
Constantine Doclitus, 186
Corpus Iuris Civilis (Justinian), 6
Council of Augsberg, 171–174, 193

Council of Basel, 137–139
Council of Chalcedon, 226
Council of Florence, 56
Council of Mantua of 1064, 7, 167, 169, 191–204
Cowdrey, H.E.J., 100, 106–107
Crescentii, 62, 66–67
Crescentius *patricius*, 14
Cuno of Pfullingen, 222

Damasus II, 11
and Henry III, 30–31
*De ordinando pontifice*, 29
*De origine Cardinalium* (Panvinius), 101
*De varia Romani pontificis creatione* (Panvinius), 80, 101
Dedi II of Wettin, 164
Desiderius (Victor III), 25, 63, 65, 77, 98, 102–103, 109, 240, 245–246
Deusdedit, 114
*Dictatus Papae* (Gregory VII), 20, 244
Dionysius of Piacenza, 137
*Disceptatio synodalis* (Petrus Damiani), 16–17, 113–114, 133, 144–145, 172
*Diversorum patrum sententiae*, 90–93
Dominikus Marango of Grado, 43, 46–47
Donation of Constantine, 20, 43, 88, 89, 111
Drogo, brother of Robert Guiscard, 36, 37

East-West Schism, 39–46
Easter Council of 1063, 178–179
Eastern church, 39–46, 155–156
Eberhard of Trier, 209
Ekbert I of Braunschweig, 164, 165
Evulus of Roucy, 234
excommunication, 20, 116

Ferdinand of Castile, 231
Fournier, Paul, 91
Fowler-Magerl, Linda, 91
Frangipani, 74
Frederick of Lotharingia (Stephen IX), 60
and Constantinople, 43–44, 47
and Leo IX, 34, 35, 37, 38
and Victor II, 54, 58, 59–60

Gebhard of Eichstätt (Victor II), 22n4, 38
Gebhard of Regensburg, 58

Gebhard of Salzburg, 213
Gerard, bishop of Florence (Nicholas II), 60, 73, 84
Gerard (Girard) of Galleria, 77, 133, 135
Gerard of Ostia, 233
Gervais of Reims, 192
Giesebrecht, Wilhelm, 203
Gilchrist, John, 5–6
Gisela (wife of Conrad II), 21
Gisulf of Salerno, 38
Godfrey the Bearded of Lotharingia
and Alexander II, 124, 189, 211–212
alliance with Victor II, 59
and Anno, 195
and Benzo, 207
and Council of Mantua, 203
marries Beatrice, 55
and Mezzabarba, 224–225, 229–230
and Nicholas II, 112
and Normans, 220–221
opposes Benedict X, 71, 79
opposes Cadalus, 185
power of, 63, 81, 84, 85–86, 116, 170, 245
during schism, 161–162, 164, 170–172, 180
and Stephen IX, 65
Godfrey the Humpbacked, 55–56, 245
Gotebald of Aquileia, 58
Gozelo, Duke, 55
Gratianius, Bishop, 230
Gregorian Reform, 1–8, 243–247
Gregory of Catino (*Liber Beraldi*), 101
Gregory of S. Angelo (Innocent II), 74
Gregory of Tusculum, 15, 77, 79–80
Gregory of Vercelli, 98, 137, 225
Gregory VI, 23–24, 29
Gregory VII (Hildebrand), 1, 4–6, 8, 19, 34, 41, 88. *See also* Hildebrand (Gregory VII)
and Bonizo, 12
and Cencius Stephani, 237–238
*Dictatus Papae*, 20, 93, 244
election, 233
and Henry IV, 236, 243–244, 246
and Hugo Candidus, 141, 232–236
Guaimar of Salerno, Prince, 37–38
Guibert of Parma/Ravenna (Clement III), 85, 243, 244
and Agnes, 141–142, 163
and Anno, 177
and Benedict X, 81
and Cadalus, 136

Council of Augsberg, 172
and Hugo Candidus, 231, 232, 234–235, 236
Guido of Ferrara, 105
Guido of Milan, 17, 120, 121
Guido of Salerno, 37–38
Gunther of Bamberg, 163–164, 175

Halinard of Lyons, 34
Henry of Ravenna, 75
Henry III, 2, 3, 4–5
and Anselm of Lucca, 120
authority over papal elections, 9–20, 21–22, 29–30, 52–53
and Clement II, 24–30
and Damasus II, 30–31
depositions of popes, 22–24
legacy, 244
and Leo IX, 41
and Lotharingia and Canossa houses, 55–56
and Victor II, 51–54
Henry IV, 4, 7, 10
and Alexander II, 210–211, 220
and Cadalus's claim, 186–187
coming of age ceremony, 209–211
excommunicated, 236, 246
and Gregory VII, 243–244
kidnapping of, 162–167, 169–171
and Nicholas II, 70–71, 112
and patarines, 122
and Petrus Damiani, 214–217
at Quedlinburg, 206–209
succession of, 57–59
Henry of Augsburg, 137, 141, 163, 164
Henry of Trent, 222–224
Henry V, 7
Herman of Cologne, 53
Herman the Lame, 78–79
Hildebrand (Gregory VII), 2, 3, 14, 17, 61, 62. See also Gregory VII (Hildebrand)
after death of Nicholas II, 135–136
and Alexander II, 121, 124–132
archdeacon controversy, 99–100
Benzo and, 74, 153, 155, 157, 182–183
and Cluny, 232
and coronation of Nicholas II, 86–89
and election of Nicholas II, 84–85
and election of Victor II, 51–54
and fall of Benedict X, 71–72, 82, 109
and Henry III, 52–53
and imperial authority, 117
and Leo IX, 34, 35

and papal electoral decree, 98–100, 106–107
and Petrus Damiani, 75, 193–194, 203–204
radicalism of, 240
and Vallombrosa monastery, 227–228
and Victor II, 60
History of the Normans (Amatus), 33
Honorius II (Cadalus of Parma), 7, 19, 34. See also Cadalus of Parma
Hubert of Palestrina, 239
Hugh of Besançon, 96
Hugh of Cluny, 112–113
Hugo Candidus of Lotharingia, 7, 34, 140–141, 230–236, 245
Humbert of Moyenmoutier (Silva Candida), 2, 16, 34, 47, 60, 61, 77, 98, 112, 236
and Eastern church, 40, 42, 43–44
and election of Victor II, 51–54

imperial authority and papacy, 4–7, 9–20, 21–22, 29–30, 52–53, 83, 91–92, 113–117
papal electoral decree of Nicholas II, 95–107
Innocent II (Gregory of S. Angelo), 74

Jasper, Detlev, 96, 99
Johannes Gualberti, 224–229
Johannes Tignoso, 237
John Brachiuti, 126, 135, 155
John of Trani, 40, 42, 43
John of Velletri (Benedict X), 61, 69
Justinian
Corpus Iuris Civilis, 6

Kaiserswerth abduction, 162–167, 169–171
Kerularius (Michael I). See Michael I Kerularius

Lampert of Hersfeld, 85, 163, 165, 202
Landulph the Elder, 121
lay investiture, 116–117, 150
Lenten councils, 46
Leo IX (Bruno of Toul), 2, 11, 19, 56, 231
and the Byzantine Empire, 38–46
election of, 33–35
and Hugo Candidus, 140
legacy of, 46–48
Libellus, 42–43
and the Normans, 35–38, 46
reforms of, 35

summary of, 48–49
Leo Judeus, 74, 86, 126, 135, 155
Leo of Ochrid, 40, 42, 47
Leo of Ostia, 52
  on Alexander II, 136
  and Benedict X, 77
*Liber ad Amicum* (Bonizo), 12
*Liber Beraldi* (Gregory of Catino), 101
*Liber de Vita Christiana* (Bonizo), 12
*Liber politicus,* 89
*Liber Pontificalis,* 77–78, 136
Lombardy, 6, 12, 35, 65, 149–150
Lotharingia, house of, 54–56, 59, 63,
  245. *See also* Godfrey the Bearded of
  Lotharingia

Mainard of Silva Candida, 63, 210
Mancius, 99, 100
Mantua, synod of (1053), 56
Matilda (daughter of Beatrice of
  Canossa), 13, 24, 55, 56, 81, 230,
  238, 245
Mezzabarba. *See* Petrus Mezzabarba
Michael I Kerularius
  and Leo IX, 39–46
  and Victor II, 57
Milan, 75, 111–112, 119–120
monasticism and papacy, 1, 92
Monomachus (Constantine IX). *See*
  Constantine IX Monomachus
Montecassino monastery, 60–61

Nicholas II (Gerard), 10, 15, 16, 17, 48,
  60, 225
  and Anno of Cologne, 164
  and Anselm of Lucca, 123–124
  in *The Collection of 74 Titles,* 89–93
  coronation of, 86–89
  election of, 69–71, 84–86
  imperial relations, 113–117
  importance of, 83–84
  and the Normans, 109–111, 116
  papal electoral decree, 83, 95–107
Normans, 221, 234, 245
  and Alexander II, 155
  and Leo IX, 35–38, 46
  and Nicholas II, 109–111, 116
  and schism, 180, 182, 185, 187
  and Stephen IX, 63
  and Victor II, 57

Oddo, cardinal bishop of Ostia (Urban
  II), 102–103
Otker of Perugia, 61

Otto I, 1
Otto II, 14
Otto III, 18
Otto of Bavaria, 164, 165, 176, 213,
  222–224
Otto of Novara, 57

Palestrina, 111
Pantaleus (Pantaleo) of Amalfi, 47–48,
  155, 186, 187
Panvinius, 96, 101–103
  on Benedict X, 80–82
papal electoral decree of 1059, 83,
  95–107, 119, 198, 204
papal curia, establishment of, 46
Paschal II, 7
*patarini,* 83–84, 111, 121–122
patriciate/*patricius Romanorum,* 9,
  10–12, 53, 105, 114
Patrimony of St. Peter, 84
Paul of Bernried, 237
Pepo, 156
Peter of Amalfi, 43–44
Peter of Tusculum, 61, 77
Peter William
  *Liber Pontificalis,* 77–78
Petrus Damiani, 15–17, 20, 28, 45, 56, 92
  and Agnes, 166
  and Alexander II, 121–122, 127,
  131–132
  appointed cardinal bishop of Ostia, 66
  and Benedict X, 75–76
  and Cadalus, 143–148
  and Council of Mantua, 191–204
  *Disceptatio Synodalis,* 16–17, 113–114,
  127, 133, 144–145, 172
  and Hildebrand, 75, 193–194,
  203–204
  imperial relations, 112–114
  letters to Henry IV, 214–217
  and Nicholas II, 76, 84, 88, 111
  and papal electoral decree, 98, 104,
  106
  and Stephen, cardinal of S. Grisogono,
  112–113
  and Vallombrosa monastery, 226–227
Petrus Igneus, 228
Petrus Leonis, 74
Petrus Mezzabarba, 219, 224–229
Pierleoni family, 74
Poppo of Brixen (Damasus II), 30
Prandellus. *See* Hildebrand (Gregory
  VII)
priests

clerical chastity, 1
clerical marriage, 54, 57, 84

Quedlinburg, 206–209

Raimbald, Subdeacon, 233
Rainald of Como, 226, 239
Rapizone of Todi, 157, 187
regency of Henry IV. *See* Agnes (wife of
　Henry III) (regent); Henry IV
*rex et sacerdos,* 9
Richard of Aversa, 109, 110
Richard of Capua, Prince, 36, 71, 126,
　128, 155, 219–220, 221
Richer of Montecassino, 59–60
Robert Guiscard of Apulia, Duke, 36,
　109–110, 234
Robinson, I.S., 13, 176
Rolker, Christof, 91–92
Romuald of Constance, 173
Rudolf of Swabia, 213, 236

S. Remacli, monastery of, 221, 223, 224
Salerno, 6, 35, 60, 65, 96
Salian emperors, 4–5
Santa Maria of Pomposa, 230
Saxons, 142
Sicily, 35
Siegfried of Mainz, 88, 123, 128, 164,
　172, 175, 213
Sigibert of Gembloux, 1–2
Silvester I, pope, 88, 89
simony, 1, 28, 54, 57, 76, 84, 129
Stephen, cardinal of S. Grisogono, 63,
　112–114, 119, 123, 125

Stephen IX (Frederick of Lotharingia),
　12, 16, 34, 38, 112, 120, 170
　election of, 61–63
　and the Normans, 63
　papacy of, 63–65
　significance of, 65–67
Sylvester III, 23
synods, reform, 54

Theodorich, abbot of Stablo, 223–224
Trastevere, 74
Tribur, 213
Tusculani, 14, 30, 62, 66–67, 111

Udo of Toul, 34
Udo of Trier, 222, 224

Vallombrosa monastery, 54, 92, 150,
　224–229
Victor II (Gebhard of Eichstätt), 11, 15,
　22n4, 38
　after Henry III's death, 57–61
　election of, 51–54
　and the Normans, 57
　papacy of, 54–56
Victor III (Desiderius), 25, 246
*Vita Leonis IX,* 33, 42
*Vita of Victor II,* 52

Wazo of Liège, 29
Wenzel of Altaich, 195, 196, 198, 202,
　203
Whalen, Brett, 40, 41
William of Aquitaine, Duke, 142
Wipo, 9, 22